nights

THE POLITICS OF HUNTING

To Rosemary
and to my Father and Uncle
for their help and encouragement.

The Politics of Hunting

RICHARD H. THOMAS

Gower

Published by

Gower Publishing Company Limited,
Gower House, Croft Road,
Aldershot, Hants GU11 3HR, England

British Library Cataloguing in Publication Data

Thomas, Richard H.
The politics of hunting.
1. Hunting—Great Britain—Political aspects
I. Title
799.2941 SK185

ISBN 0 - 566 - 00614 - 6

Made and printed in Great Britain by
Robert Hartnoll Ltd, Bodmin.

Contents

Preface

Throughout this century a number of pressure groups have conducted a campaign to abolish hunting; this book seeks to discover the reasons for their lack of success. Hunting as an activity would appear to be an anomaly in an urban, industrial and progressively more humane society. The question is: why have these pressure groups failed?

In this examination an historical approach has been taken, since the heritage of hunting is part of the argument used by those who wish to argue for its survival, and its longevity by those who wish to argue against it as an anachronism and an irrelevance in modern daily life. The origins of hunting as a sport and its social acceptability in society go back to the Middle Ages, and it is there that the examination begins.

The structure and political culture of British society has radically altered in the last 200 years. New ideas about what constitutes democracy and humane behaviour have spread to an increasingly literate and socially conscious electorate. Both the political decline of the class which formed the hunting community and the rise of the ecology movement have made the demise of hunting more likely, but as this study shows the hunting community has made efforts to adapt itself to the changing environment by becoming less élitist on the one hand and by uniting to protect the sport itself on the other.

The hunting community has sought to establish a new identity for itself by allying itself to modern causes. In its own eyes it has become the leading influence in conservation, its basic issue is freedom of choice, its methods involve the least possible element of cruelty, and its aims are humanitarian. The vocabulary of its literature emphasises the legitimate and democratic nature of its activities.

Those against hunting have suffered from the lack of community that single-minded defence has given to the other side. The abolition of hunting is only a small part of the moral and philosophical question as to whether animals have rights, and to what extent it may be man's duty to voice the rights of those who are silent, oppressed or exploited members of society. For animal rights campaigners animal welfare is no longer a sufficiently precise aim for their activities. The alleviation of suffering, which was the basic purpose behind the early organisation of the animal protection societies, is now seen as a matter for individual acts of conscience. But how wide is the issue? Must all those who are against hunting become vegetarians? Must they be prepared to campaign against factory farming and the use of animals in scientific research as well?

In this book the pressure groups involved in the hunting issue are compared, both as organisations and as political actors, in order to suggest where the secret of success lies – in their internal structures or in their external activities. Since the groups involved not only interact with each other but are also part of the political process, a survey has been carried out of the major arenas in which the debate has taken place: parliament, public opinion and the major political parties.

It is argued that although hunting is not a major 'political' or 'economic' issue, nevertheless social norms and the values of the pro- and anti-hunting activists are important, for if society deems one group or another to be 'extremist', then its views on hunting will be neither credible nor acceptable. Accordingly, an attitude survey has been conducted on groups of Hunt Saboteurs and Masters of Hounds, and their opinions on a range of issues have been compared with each other and with a 'normal' population.

Evidence gathered in this study includes data on the pro- and anti-hunting communities, a comparison of the tactics of the relevant pressure groups, a survey of the main changes in public opinion and the political culture and an analysis of the degree and quality of access granted by the major targets of pressure group activity. From such sources light can be shed on the apparently paradoxical survival of hunting in 20th century Britain. Among the reasons for the survival of hunting which are illustrated and analysed are the deep roots of hunting in rural society, the internal dissension among members of the anti-hunting movement, the effective appropriation of the levers of power at critical moments by the hunting community, the greater social acceptability of the leaders of the pro-hunting community, and the close correspondence between their attitudes and those of the decision makers, the difficulty of forcing anti-hunting legislation through an indifferent parliament against a determined and organised minority, and the ability of some individuals to dominate a pressure group and unduly influence its chances of success or of failure.

This book concludes, however, that despite the effectiveness of the pro-hunting lobby the issue of hunting has become part of the wider and increasingly politicised debate on animal welfare and ecology. Therefore, supporters of hunting, however adaptable, are unlikely in the long run to be able to prevail against their opponents in a society which claims to be increasingly humane and egalitarian if the majority within that society deems hunting to be neither of these things. This will be especially the case at a time when governments are prepared to enforce these values at the expense of the 'freedoms' of minorities. It is these developments within the political culture rather than the activities of pressure groups which will decide the future of hunting. Hence the constant repetition by the hunting community that 'hunting is not a suitable issue for party politics'.

Books of this kind, which attempt to describe and analyse a process which has been continuing for over 150 years, are usually written as the movement draws to a close. However, the fascination of this subject is that it remains the current daily concern of a large number of people who are passionately concerned about the deepest of moral questions. Those on both sides of the hunting issue claim to be working for the improvement of society; both sides identify the relationship between man and his environment as one of the most critical in the 20th century; both sides have a vision of a return to a more natural harmony between man and animal; both are attempting to protect freedoms and to preserve heritages. Because of this I have been given and continue to be given a great deal of help with the research and analysis of the material contained in this book. People of such differing views as Lord Soper, Sir Marcus Kimball, Richard Ryder, General Brockbank, Captain Ronnie Wallace and Dave Whetton have all given me their time, their ideas and their assistance. So too has Richard Course, not least because when I was researching either the HSA, or the LACS, or the RSPCA or GECCAP Richard Course's presence was somewhere to be found in the stories of these organisations.

The fact that the debate continues and in early 1983 seems to be increasing in intensity in time for the election means that finishing a number of chapters has involved many drafts and subsequent redrafts. I hope that as a record of the story so far this book will help those who wish to understand the problem of the hunting issue and will contribute to its solution.

Introduction

Hunting, like many other activities, produces its own ironies and paradoxes. For those who follow the sport the aim of hunting is culling not killing, and the effect of hunting individual animals to death is the preservation of the species. Indeed, it is the unlikely but sincere claim of many fox and stag hunters that they are the true naturalists and conservationists. Opponents of hunting are thought by hunting enthusiasts to be not animal lovers or humanitarians, but part of a political plot. Anti-hunting people are, for the most part, passionately opposed to hunting on the grounds of its cruelty, and yet there are among them many people who advocate methods of control which others, including independent witnesses, consider to be equally cruel. There are those who deny that hunting is a sport, and yet themselves spend days out following the hunt making a 'sport' of hunting the hunters.

These paradoxes can be partially solved by dividing the inhabitants of the animal welfare universe into two main groups, for both of whom ends are more important than means. There are people, such as those who hunt, who believe that animals exist for the service and pleasure of mankind, and there are those who believe that using animals for pleasure is immoral and that animals should be protected as far as possible from those who seek to exploit them. The issue of hunting is therefore a microcosm of that larger philosophical debate between 'other-regarding' and 'self-regarding' people and organisations.

Hunting has the rare distinction among 'causes' in that there are organisations on both sides promoting different and antagonistic points of view. On the pro-hunting side is the British Field Sports Society (BFSS), which acts as an umbrella organisation for all those engaged in hunting, shooting and fishing (which they call 'field' sports). At a more specific level there is the Master of Foxhounds Association (MFHA), the Master of Deerhounds Association (MDHA), and the National Coursing Club (NCC) as well as the Association of Masters of Harriers and Beagles and the Mink and Coypus Hunting Association. On the anti-hunting side there is the League Against Cruel Sports (LACS), the National Society for the Abolition of Cruel Sports (NSACS), and the Hunt Saboteurs Association (HSA).[1] Members of these organisations refer to hunting as 'blood' sports. As with the pro-hunting side membership of these groups is overlapping.

Also involved in the hunting debate is the largest animal welfare society in England, the Royal Society for the Prevention of Cruelty to Animals (RSPCA). It has long tried to separate the hunting issue from the wider issues of animal welfare, and its treatment of this dilemma must be included in any study of the hunting lobby.

The issue of hunting is frequently debated by these organised pressure groups who claim to be doing so, not only in the interests of themselves or of the hunted animals, but also in the public interest. The state, that is government and parliament, is regularly asked to abolish hunting or to refrain from abolishing it. The government is influenced in the response it gives to these demands by its own interpretation of both the public interest and the state of public opinion.

Hunting is defined in this book as the pursuit of otters, hares, mink, stags and foxes by hounds under the control of men who are usually on horseback. Hare-coursing, which is a 'branch of hunting in which dogs pursue game by sight only'[2] is included also. Although undoubtedly a 'field' or 'blood' sport it is only marginally a form of hunting. However public and political opinion as well as pressure groups operating both for and against hunting have decided that it is a branch of hunting, and it is important because both sides believe that it might be the first sport to suffer abolition and that its demise would be the 'thin end of the wedge' for the subsequent abolition of all other forms of hunting.

In general terms, the aims of the various pressure groups are straightforward. On the one hand are the animal welfare groups which wish, by legislation, to abolish hunting. To do this they need to gain the sympathy of the media, public opinion, and the decision-makers. On the other there are those who wish to protect the status quo against

1 These abbreviations will be used throughout.

2 O. Stable and R.M. Stuttard, *A Review of Coursing*, British Field Sports Society, London, 1971, p 5.

legislative interference, and so are equally keen to influence the media, public opinion, and the decision-makers with the validity of their arguments.[1] Groups on either side may have additional goals, such as the abolition of vivisection, or, alternatively, the promotion, rather than just protection, of all field sports, but these are not the central issue.

The politics of hunting is of interest for the following reasons. Firstly, the issue involves a variety of contrasting groups, whereas in most issues groups find themselves pitted against the general public or against the lethargy of the political decision-makers.[2] Secondly, it is essentially a non-economic argument which nevertheless generates a good deal of heated debate.[3] The government therefore finds itself arbitrating between a range of social demands of a sort which would not ordinarily come under its scrutiny. Thirdly, because the issue has been a contentious one for many years, it is possible to observe group activity and society at several points in time and to make comparative, even developmental, statements about their interaction.[4]

Organised, unofficial and politically active groups have been given a variety of names and definitions by other writers.[5] In this book they will be referred to as 'pressure groups' and defined as:

> An organized combination of individuals bound together by shared goals or attitudes, who interact with other groups and with public institutions and who attempt to obtain decisions favourable

1 The study concentrates on England and Wales and makes no attempt to analyse developments the end of 1982.

2 Abortion is another 'cause' which has organised groups putting both sides of the argument. See M. Simms and K. Hindell, *Abortion Law Reformed*, Peter Owen, London, 1971. See also B. Pym, 'Pressure Groups on Moral Issues', *Political Quarterly* 43, July/September, 1972.

3 Hanging is a major 'non-political' issue which has been much debated inside and outside parliament. See J.B. Christoph, *Capital Punishment in British Politics*, Allen & Unwin, London, 1962.

4 The RSPCA has been making demands of society and politicians for over 150 years, and hunting has been an issue with political implications since the end of the 19th century.

5 'Organized Groups'; A. Potter, *Organized Groups in British National Politics*, Faber, London, 1961.
'Lobby'; S. Finer, *Anonymous Empire*, (rev. edn), Pall Mall, London, 1966.
'Interest Groups': D. Truman, *The Governmental Process*, A. Knopf, New York, 1951.
'Pressure Groups' has become the most generally acceptable name. See W.J.M. Mackenzie, "Pressure Groups in British Government", *British Journal of Sociology*, VI, 2, 1955.

to their preferred values by all means at their disposal but especially by gaining access to the governmental process.[1]

This definition is broad enough to include both the sectional or spokesman groups who operate on behalf of the sportsmen (BFSS) and animals (RSPCA), as well as the 'cause' or promotional groups whose main task is to influence legislation (LACS) or to stop it (BFSS acting on behalf of the MFHA, NCC and other hunting and field sports organisations).

Pressure groups are usually divided into two main categories: sectional groups who attempt to protect their shared interests, and cause groups who have a belief which they wish the public to share. Cause groups 'tend to seek to influence public policy by direct contact with parliament and the ministries or indirectly through appeals to public opinion'.[2] They may differ substantially from spokesman or sectional groups for, as Walkland says: 'By and large attitude or promotional groups are consulted much less frequently by governments contemplating legislation than are sectional groups. They lack most of the political and economic sanctions which sectional groups possess; they are usually smaller in size, weaker economically and have a more amorphous membership'.[3] The probable effects of these factors may be identified: cause groups may lack authority, or be denied access, or may resort to violent behaviour. Castles suggests a sub-division of cause groups into those who work on a rational basis within the political system, and those whose generalised demands would, if realised, be destructive of the system and who are therefore generally left to operate outside the mainstream of political life.[4]

Pressure groups are most usefully seen as autonomous sub-systems in a secular and differentiated society. They have a precise role to fulfil in the political process; they work at the boundaries of the political system but reflect and influence the cultural norms of that society;[5] they receive and transmit influence from the government to their supporters

1 This is an adaptation of the definition used by H. Ehrman in *A Dictionary of Social Sciences*, (eds) J. Gould and W. Kolb, Tavistock Publications, London, 1964.

2 D. Butler and J. Freeman (eds), *British Political Facts*, (3rd edn), Macmillan, London, 1969, p. 304.

3 S. Walkland *The Legislative Process in Great Britain*, Allen & Unwin, London, 1968, p. 41.

4 F.G. Castles, *Pressure Groups and Political Culture*, Routledge & Kegan Paul, London, 1969.

5 The systems approach and its language is explained in David Easton, *A Systems Analysis of Political Life*, J. Wiley, New York, 1965.

and from their supporters to the government.[1] They ar therefore, as organisations, as channels, and as sources of demands. Pressure groups interact not only with each ot with the decision-makers who aggregate their demands.

In this book there are three major areas to be investigated and analysed:

1 The social history of hunting and its relationship with the changing rural culture of England.
2 The pressure groups themselves which will be looked at in terms of their strengths and their tactics.
3 The public arenas and institutions in which the hunting issue is discussed.

Hunting and rural society

To understand how hunting has become a political issue it is necessary to investigate how and why hunting has developed, how it is conducted and what kind of people hunt. The members of the hunting community need to be placed in a context. Since hunting is a long-established sport, the primary context is historical, for the roots of hunting go back into the medieval period and beyond. For many the survival of hunting for such a long period is sufficient to justify it as an appropriate activity for countrymen today.

The nature of the rural society in which hunting has developed also needs to be discussed. The legal constraints on hunting and on those who have opposed hunting, the game laws, the pattern of land ownership and the class structure are all factors which have, over the centuries, influenced the development of hunting and are therefore relevant to its position today.

Further general questions about hunting also should be asked: does society view the sport as a legitimate one? How socially significant are its leading adherents? Have the social and economic changes which have occurred in British society over the last two hundred years had any effect on the social and economic viability of hunting? Information on these questions will provide insights with which to study the activities of individual pressure groups and the ways in which they perform in the political arena.

1 See R. Rose, *Politics in England*, Little Brown, Boston, 1964, p. 124.

The historical background and the key elements influencing the growth of hunting as a sport are described in Chapter 1. Chapter 2 concentrates on the significant changes in the social and economic environment in which hunting has operated, outlines the government's response to the more urgent political problems of the 19th and 20th centuries and shows how the natural alliance between hunting and the ruling élite has inevitably weakened. The effect of these changes on hunting itself and the responses within the sport to its altered circumstances are discussed in Chapter 3.

The pressure groups

Part II contains a systematic study of the people and pressure groups involved in the hunting issue. Chapter 4 outlines the historical development of the RSPCA in the wider context of animal welfare and looks particularly at the internal struggle in this organisation between the pro- and anti-hunting factions showing how the culmination of that struggle cleared the field for a more straightforward battle between the major pro- and anti-hunting groups.

Chapter 5 details the growth of the anti-hunting groups showing the variety of styles, structures and tactics used by the Humanitarian League, the League Against Cruel Sports, the National Society for the Abolition of Cruel Sports, the Hunt Saboteurs Association and the General Election Co-ordinating Committee for Animal Protection (GECCAP). The contrasts between these organisations show how difficult it is to orchestrate a social or political movement, for despite having exactly similar aims one of the points to emerge from the chapter is the extent to which anti-hunting energy has been dissipated by internecine rivalries.

Chapter 6 describes the development of the BFSS – the cornerstone of the pro-hunting lobby. A study of the style, structure and tactics of the BFSS facilitates comparisons with the anti-hunting groups and goes some way towards explaining the apparent success of the pro-hunting lobby.

Chapter 7 outlines and analyses a questionnaire on the background and attitudes of separate groups of highly committed activists on opposing sides of the hunting question. The data on the backgrounds of the protagonists enables deductions to be made about the legitimacy of the two sides and about their differing degrees of acceptability to the general public and to the political and administrative élite. The type and strength of opinions expressed make it easier to understand the entirely different *modus operandi* of the two sides and makes it clearer why there is so much heat and even violence in the issue.

Arenas and institutions

The hunting debate has taken place historically in a number of forums or arenas. The four major ones are discussed in Part III. The political culture is significant because of the effect it has on the attitudes of people towards hunting;[1] and public opinion, as it changes and develops, influences, if only indirectly, the political process. Political parties and parliament are arenas in the institutional sense. Parties have policies which can be influenced by pressure and parliament is explicitly the arena in which clashes of values and demands are moderated.

In Chapter 8 the elements of the political culture which have had an impact on the hunting issue are discussed. Class, while a salient feature, plays a paradoxical role. Strong 19th century antagonism to the élite and their sports has been ameliorated to such an extent that in the late 20th century the mainly urbanised working classes, while less deferential and more politically active than their forebears, are not particularly concerned with the class aspects of hunting. However, a growing environmentalism and a concern for the rights of the weak and unrepresented have provided a context in which anti-hunting sentiments can prosper.

Public opinion, the subject of Chapter 9, has become an arena in the sense that the anti-hunting community has used the medium of public opinion polls as a way of involving the mass in the hunting debate. It has enabled some evidence to be produced about the nature and extent of antagonism to hunting and can show whether the anti-hunting movement consists of a few sufferers from the 'cuddly-bunny syndrome' or has the support of a humanitarian mass. The publicity derived from the public opinion polls which are described and analysed in this chapter has also involved the media as a channel of communications for the opinions which have been expressed.

The opinions of political parties obviously provide a key to the likelihood of success of pressure groups. Without the active support of one or both of the major parties no legislative changes are likely to occur. Chapter 10 details the developments within the Labour and Conservative parties with respect to their attitudes, as parties, towards hunting and shows how they have responded to changes in the political culture and to pressure from politically active groups.

Ultimately the body which arbitrates between the conflicting demands of the pressure groups and of public and political opinion is parliament. Chapter 11 looks at how parliament has been used as an

1 Political culture is defined as 'the pattern of individual attitudes and orientations towards politics among members of a political system'. See G.A. Almond and G.B. Powell, *Comparative Politics*, Little Brown, Boston, 1966, p. 50.

arena for the struggle between the pro- and anti-hunting communities. There are three sections; first, a description of the major animal welfare bills and acts since 1800; second, an account of the demands made and the methods used in parliament by the two main protagonists, the BFSS and the LACS, discussing in detail their tactical manoeuvres with respect to legislation. The third section unravels, places in sequence and discusses the main pro- and anti-hunting arguments used, over the decades, in support of legislative demands. The chapter shows how the demands, tactics and arguments have all changed and developed over the years.

Part IV contains the two concluding chapters. Chapter 12 makes a comparative analysis of the organisational strengths and weaknesses of the main pressure groups; it compares group tactics, discusses the significance of access in the development and deployment of pressure group skills,[1] and outlines the process by which the hunting issue has become politicised. The conclusion asks a number of questions about hunting, pressure groups and politics and attempts to predict pattern developments.

1 Access is defined as 'the facilitating intermediate objective of political interest groups Truman, *Governmental Process*, p. 264.

PART I

HUNTING AND SOCIETY

1 Origins of hunting traditions

Introduction

One claim of the hunting community is that hunting must be preserved because it is part of the nation's heritage and as such is worthy of preservation on the basis of tradition alone. The evidence suggests that the origins of hunting lie in the Anglo-Saxon and Norman period. It was the conception of the Norman court that hunting was an exclusive and entertaining sport which required both ritual and etiquette in its practice. It is this conception which has provided the basis of the hunt as it is today. Hunting as a 'sport' is therefore foreign rather than English in origin, although the change from stag hunting to fox hunting is a feature that English conditions made necessary. If the claim is that hunting is traditional and that the length of its survival makes acceptable, even necessary, its preservation in its original and authentic state, then the hunting community can be well satisfied, for the traditions have shown a remarkable consistency over many centuries.

Moreover, the traditions of hunting can be seen to have fitted naturally into society when England was predominantly rural and agricultural. But that being so it must be asked: how did hunting survive when English society became both urban and industrialised? What were the changes that would have been expected to destroy the hunting scene? How has hunting adapted to the changing social environment, the differing availability of huntable animals and the changing membership of the hunting community?

The historical evidence shows that hunting very quickly became established as the exclusive occupation of the élite who preserved that exclusivity by harsh penalties for other classes indulging in the same activity. During the period between the Conquest and the Industrial Revolution the traditions and rituals of hunting were most assiduously observed by those who aspired to élite status, most particularly by the squirearchy which rose to prominence in the late Middle Ages. Its observation of the rules and rituals of hunting was an extension of its desire for power and social status, rather than a necessity of the sport itself. In which case the question arises as to whether the preservation of hunting owes more to its exclusive than to its traditional nature, limited access having enhanced its value.

Anglo-Saxon beginnings

The Anglo-Saxons differentiated between three different kinds of land: cultivated land, uncultivated open heath, and forest. The land they farmed surrounded the *burh* – or fortified settlement, and beyond this was the *westen* – uninhabited land which was, emotionally if not physically, felt to be waste, desert, and wilderness. The heath and the forest were parts of this *westenes* and both the stag and the wolf were hunted there – the stag either for food, for sport, or for the protection of crops, and the wolf mainly for bounty. The word *deor* at this time distinguished only the wild animal from the tame; therefore, in translations of passages of Old English reference to the hunting of deer could include wolves, boars, hares and foxes, all of which were wild. The heath and forest were owned by the leaders of the Anglo-Saxon tribes who invaded England in the 5th and 6th centuries, and it was the practice for heathland to be given to the élite of the *comitati* – the tested warriors who had served the leader well. The gift of land was only made to men of marriageable age; it was not given in perpetuity; it was dependent on the maintenance of the relationship between the lord and the warrior; and it was to be returned to the king if the warrior predeceased him. However, after the period of Anglo-Saxon migration was completed, landed man of mature years often preferred the life of a settled estate owner in the country to the life of a fighting man attendant on the lord in his hall. It was thus that a separate class of earls or thanes arose: lords who spent only part of the year at court and paid an annual rent to the king for the continued ownership of land.

The first hunting regulations were restrictions over the use of land, not a form of protection for the animals. Land legislation heralded the formation of large estates which became 'an inescapable feature of the political and the social system'[1] of the period. The laws of Canute in

1 M. Postan, *The Medieval Economy and Society*, Penguin, Harmondsworth, 1975, p. 86.

1016 made the first explicit statement about the protection of hunting rights. He stated: 'It is my own wish that every man is to be entitled to his hunting in wood and field in his own land' but 'everyone is to avoid trespassing on my hunting wherever I wish to have it preserved, on pain of full fine'.[1]

Any restriction on land uses has two corollaries: it requires enforcement, and it provokes resistance from those whose earlier freedoms have been curtailed. Canute denied access to his forests and estates in order to protect his own leisure. From that time onwards landownership was intimately bound up with privilege, exclusivity, and power over tenants' lives. The other landowners were the bishops and the king's administrative, judicial and military functionaries; 'both thegns and bishops were maintained by the revenues of large estates'.[2] The bulk of the population who were not landowners were forced into the category of 'dependent cultivators'[3] in order to supply the revenue for this aristocracy.

While all Anglo-Saxon men appear to have owned dogs, it was only the landowners who were also horse-owners, accordingly, the hunt in its earliest form consisted of a mounted élite accompanying dogs in pursuit of a wild animal and followed on foot by their *ceorls* who carried spears, spades and knives. The foot-followers assisted at the kill by helping to carry the animal, carve it up and cook it. Skill in the use of hounds during the hunt, the art of horsemanship and knowledge of the ritual of the hunt were the marks of royalty and of the class that hunted with the king.[4] King Alfred was described as a 'keen huntsman' who 'continued to practise every branch of hunting'.[5] Churchmen were keen hunters, from the bishops down to the lowliest monk. Even those

1 *The Laws of Cnut*, paras 80–80.1, in *English Historical Documents* (*EHD*), vol. I (ed.) D. Whitelock, Eyre & Spottiswoode, London, 1955.

2 Postan, *Medieval Economy*, p. 86. The church controlled perhaps one-third of all England's occupied surfaces, mainly in large units.

3 This is Postan's definition.

4 The Anglo-Saxon Poem 'The Arts of Men' lists the skills a man might possess:

> One is a pursuer in hunting of glorious beasts . . .
> One is well versed in horses, learned in the arts of steeds. . .
> One is a fowler, skilled with the hawk. . .
> One is daring on horseback. . .

Trans. R.K. Gordon, *Anglo-Saxon Poetry* (rev. edn) Dent, Everyman Library, London, 1954, pp. 316 and 317

5 Bishop Asser's *Life of King Alfred* in *EHD*, vol. 1, chs 76 and 22, pp. 266–7.

who were supposedly in monastic seclusion found themselves with the means to hunt because the king customarily granted large tracts of land to the church. Alcuin, writing in the 8th century, was forced to reprimand the monks of Jarrow and Wearmouth and urge them not to allow men under their supervision to dig out foxes or to course hares. He adds: 'How wicked to leave the service of Christ for a fox hunt'.[1]

The animals which provided the best chase were the more glorious animals to hunt; the stag, the boar, and the hare, therefore, are referred to as beasts of the forest. And it must be remembered that only kings could actually own an area which had been designated 'forest'. Both the stag and the boar had early mythological associations with royalty. The royal regalia found in the ship-burial at Sutton Hoo includes a standard with a stag on the top of it. And in the poem *Beowulf* the helmets of the warriors are described as bearing a representation of the boar on them.[2]

It was therefore established very early on in the hunting world that the aristocracy hunted for the chase, for the skill involved in managing horses, hawks and hounds, and because they were in pursuit of a noble animal. The peasant class was presumed to enjoy the kill and the subsequent spoils, and to be active participants in the hunt only when the animal had gone to ground and needed to be dug out and killed. They were, however, able to use their dogs to chase hares on open land.

Forest and game laws

William the Conqueror implemented a major afforestation policy; this did not necessarily involve planting trees but stated that once land had been declared 'forest' no subject could own it – only the king. William not only extended the Royal Forests, he also introduced penalties for killing the game therein. The Anglo-Saxon Chronicle reports on these hardships:

> A hard man was the king...
> He was sunk in greed
> And utterly given up to avarice
> He set apart a vast deer preserve and imposed laws concerning it
> Who ever slew a hart or a hind
> Was to be blinded.
> He forbade the killing of boars

1 Quoted by R.I. Page, *Life in Anglo-Saxon England*, Batsford, London, 1970, p. 166.

2 *Beowulf*, F. Klaeber (ed.), D.C. Heath, Boston, 1920, L.1111.

Even as the killing of harts.
For he loved the stags as dearly
As though he had been their father.
Hare also he decreed should go unmolested
The rich complained and the poor lamented
But he was too relentless to care though all might hate him.[1]

Game laws were those which concerned themselves with property and trespass. Game itself was never precisely defined; it included any animal which the landed aristocracy wished to preserve, use for sport or eat. Deer was historically the most significant game. Game laws as well as land laws, increasingly severe penalties, the beginnings of a forest law which was outside of the common law of the land,[2] and a succession of kings who hunted to excess, all are features of the establishment of Norman rule.

By the early 13th century 33 counties contained Royal Forests. The forest laws denied the peasant population the game which they had previously eaten, the timber they had used for houses and fires, and the land they had previously used as pasture.[3]

Barons who owned the land next to the boundaries of a Royal Forest could not hunt in it without the express permission of the king, at first rarely granted. The king could even revoke their right to hunt game on their own territory, although this absolute power had to be tempered by reality. Nevertheless, forest laws took precedence over the Common law for as long as the monarchy felt able to exercise this power. Even clergy committing forest offences were denied 'benefit of clergy'.[4]

The king could and did allow limited access to the Royal Forests. Some barons or bishops were granted a 'chase', and they might be allowed to fence a part of this chase and so create a 'park' in which rights of warren were allowed. Rights of warren did not include the right to hunt deer. Nevertheless the illegal taking of deer, or poaching, was common at all levels of society. 'Barons, bishops and knights poached indefatigably the king's, and one another's, deer'.[5]

1 G Garmonsway (trans.), *The Anglo-Saxon Chronicle*, J. Dent, Everyman Library, London, 1953, pp. 220, 1. Entry for 1086–7.

2 The earliest extant forest laws date from 1184 when existing regulations were consolidated at the *Assize of the Forest*, at Woodstock. For the text see *EHD*, vol. II (1042–189) (ed.) D.C. Douglas and G. Greenway, Eyre & Spottiswoode, London, 1953, pp. 416–20.

3 For a discussion of the earliest forest laws see J. Bagley & P. Rowley, *A Documentary History of England*, vol. I, Penguin, Harmondsworth, 1966. Section Four discusses the *Assize of the Forest* 1164 and forest laws in general.

4 Bagley & Rowley, *Documentary History*, p. 67.

5 C.C. Trench, *The Poacher and the Squire*, Longman, London, 1967, p. 71.

In order to prevent violations of the forest laws a network of courts and foresters were set up. Punishments for those caught by the foresters were severe. For poaching, either inside or outside a forest, blinding was a common punishment. To this Richard I added castration. Fines were sometimes levied on whole villages to avenge the unexplained deaths of deer.[1] When dead deer were found inquests were held. If the offender was a free man he was fined, if a serf he was executed. Barons and bishops could usually buy or bluff their way out of trouble. Bows and arrows were prohibited within the forest, and dogs, particularly mastiffs, were 'expediated', i.e. their claws and pads were removed and their feet reduced almost to stumps so that they could not effectively chase game. Not surprisingly 'a deep and smouldering resentment was felt against the strict enforcement of the forest laws'.[2] This resentment was shared by both the peasants and the barons, since in both cases the forest laws denied what the people concerned felt to be 'rights'.

Not until Magna Carta was the power of the king as expressed in his forest laws reduced. Clause 47 says: 'All forests created in our reign shall be immediately disafforested, and similarly river banks which we have reserved for our sport . . . shall be again thrown open'. Clause 48 says: 'All oppressive practices relating to forests, warrens and river banks and the malpractices of foresters, warreners and sheriffs and their officers . . . shall, in every county, be the subject of immediate inquiry be twelve sworn knights of the same county, elected by worthy men of the country and all abuses shall be stamped out, never more to be renewed'.[3]

From Edward III's reign the forest laws, while continuing to provide sport and income (by enforcing fines or selling immunity), ceased to be a major cause of grievance between the king and his nobles. In the late Middle Ages the kings continued to sell the rights over estates and forests, and the nobles and knights receiving these rights could hunt on their own estates, protect their own deer parks, and receive the fines levied against the transgressors of the forest laws.

All the written evidence of the time, which is in itself an embodiment of the prevailing aristocratic values, suggests that hunting was an occupation of the élite and that to join in the hunt in any capacity conferred status on the participants. Similarly to pursue a deer outside the hunt was not considered 'hunting' at all, but was 'poaching', an activity which was illegal even if economically profitable. The economic and financial motivations of the poor seem to have been a key factor in differentiating between the pursuits of the classes even when they

1 Bagley & Rowley, *Documentary History*, pp. 65–6.

2 D. Stenton, *English Society in the Early Middle Ages*, Penguin, Harmondsworth, 1951, p. 100.

3 Bagley & Rowley *Documentary History*, section six, pp. 91–113.

might, in fact, seem to be performing the same act. The definition of 'hunting' as opposed to 'poaching' segregated the participants into those whose leisure was involved and for whom the dispatched animal was insignificant, and those for whom sport was less significant than the desire to acquire food. The act of 'poaching' implied no enjoyment of the chase or of the rituals of the kill. It necessarily involved either pursuing animals to which the poacher had no right, or pursuing animals on land on which the poacher had no right to be. The criminality of the poacher's position was evident only to the élite who had defined it for themselves as such, but to the average villager, who did not perceive the values of the élite as the desirable norms, poaching was an established and useful rural activity. Farnham Park was regularly invaded by poachers who caught deer 'with nets, snares and hounds with bows and arrows and other mysteries'.[1]

This situation, which existed in the Middle Ages, did not radically change until the 19th century. If anything the rights of poor non-landowning countrymen were reduced and the quality of their lives deteriorated in the three hundred years after the accession of the Tudors. During the Civil War when hunting was abolished and the management of the parks disrupted poaching increased, the numbers of deer declined and the wild boar disappeared entirely. With the Restoration, the Royalists determined to reassert themselves, and the Parliament of 1671 passed a *Game Act* which reaffirmed the forest laws at their most vigorous, reinterpreting them according to 17th century customs. The *Game Act* prohibited all freeholders of under £100 a year, that is most yeomen and small landowners, from killing game, even on their own land. This act and its later extensions caused 'more bitterness and ill-feeling, at least among country people, than almost any other piece of legislation'[2] to that date. Trevelyan maintained that 'the interests of the yeoman and farmers were sacrificed in order that the squire should have plenty of partridges to shoot'.[3]

Poaching however continued, and in order to stop it the Black Act of 1722–3 was passed by Walpole and his government. The act was supposedly extant for three years only, in order to deal with particular unrest, but it was prolonged several times and made permanent in 1758.[4] It was an entirely brutal law, which emphasised both the total authority

1 E. Robo, *Medieval Farnham*, Langhams, Farnham, 1935, p. 96.

2 M. Brander, *The Hunting Instinct*, Oliver & Boyd, London, 1964, p. 100.

3 G. Trevelyan, *English Social History*, Longman, London, 1944, p.279. See also E. Bovill, *English Country Life*, 1780–1830, OUP, London, 1962, pp. 174–5.

4 This Act, the Waltham Black Act, is 9 Geo.I, C.22. The Act and its implications are dealt with in E.P. Thompson, *Whigs and Hunters; the origin of the Black Act*, Allen Lane, London, 1976, *passim.*

of the landed classes in parliament and the lack of concern for the welfare of the dispossessed rural poor of the period. It created 50 new capital offences mainly for offences against property: destroying trees, hunting deer, wounding cattle, and burning haystacks, as well as the unauthorised carrying of arms; all warranted execution.

The Act illustrates the total social and political dominance of the landowners for whom the preservation of game was more important than whether their tenants were adequately housed or fed. Attempts to repeal the Act in 1820 were vigorously opposed and the most that could be achieved by reformers was the reduction of some penalties. Most of the capital offences which concerned only property were made liable to transportation for life.

The landowners instituted game laws to keep the poor in their place, and, since they themselves were also magistrates, they tended to use the poor laws and game laws to their own advantage. For the poor, being illiterate, 'the legal process was a secret between the magistrate and landowner'. When conviction under the Game Laws (particularly the Black Act) seemed difficult, poachers were allowed to apologise and 'what was an irritating lack of power . . . could be presented to the poachers and villagers as magnanimity'.[1] No kind of hunting was legally available to the rural poor, not even ferreting for rabbits, an activity which the tenant farmer had no right to pursue until the *Ground Game Act* of 1880. There was therefore a vicious circle of repression and reaction. Burning ricks, poisoning deer and killing dogs were common activities in the 18th century as a protest against the rigorous application of the Black Act. 'Poachers were the common enemy of the landed ruling class, and the solidarity of the villages . . . was matched by a similar pact of honour among magistrates. In their minds the game laws had little enough to do with any abstract ideal of justice. Their real meaning lay in the peculiar social connotations of game itself'.[2]

Land ownership and enclosures

In the 13th and 14th centuries the knights and nobles gradually increased their power, their land holdings, and their access to the Royal Forests in order to enjoy their hunting. Freemen (but not peasants) were allowed to pasture their cattle and sometimes extend their holdings within the traditional boundaries of the forest.

1 D. Hay, 'Poaching and the Game Laws on Cannock Chase' in *Albions Fatal Tree: Crime and Society in Eighteenth Century England*, Allen Lane, London, 1975, p. 251.

2 Ibid., p. 244.

Agricultural developments and a rising population had their own effect on the forests. The people needed firewood, and the sheep (a major source of wealth throughout the Middle Ages) needed open land in which to graze. Rights of enclosure for the lord of a village became established in the 13th century as long as fresh lands were found for the existing tenants; this tended to be in the Royal Forests.[1]

After the Black Death of 1348, which reduced the population by a third to about three million, there was more land available per head. This fact, plus the impoverishing costs of the Hundred Years War for which the nobles had to pay, encouraged landowners to raise money by renting out land to free peasants. These people were the beginnings of a yeoman class: 'The developments of the 14th century fostered the growth of a prosperous farmer class on the one hand, and a rural proletariat on the other'.[2] The secure copyholder or leaseholders farmed their growing holdings more intensively and were able to invest energy and capital into what were virtual freehold rights over their land. In the 15th century, despite the political uncertainties caused by the Wars of the Roses, agriculture prospered and the wool trade particularly made many farmers and merchants into men of substance.

As the right to own land, to farm it and to hunt on it moved slowly down the social scale, it nevertheless created a growing rift between the 'haves' and the 'have nots'. By the time of the Tudors there was a large landowning class who gradually took control of the organs of power and used it for their own ends. The philosophy of individual, rather than collective, land tenure had come to stay.

One way in which the ambitious Tudor landowner improved his position was by enclosure and the eviction of the small copyholders. Initially there was resistance to enclosure by parliamentarians who feared agrarian riots. However, a general enclosure bill was passed in 1621 and no government after 1640 tried to prevent enclosure or fined those who had enclosed illegally.[3] In fact three-quarters of all enclosures took place before 1700.[4] This is not surprising since by this time parliament was controlled by just those 'knights of the shires' who had most to gain from the modern kind of farming and no particular interest in protecting the land rights of dispossessed peasants. These developments enabled new farming techniques to be better utilised and

1 Stenton, *Early Middle Ages*, p. 122.

2 A. Myers, *England in the Late Middle Ages* (rev. edn) Penguin, Harmondsworth, 1963, p. 48.

3 C. Hill, *Reformation to Industrial Revolution*, Penguin, Harmondsworth, 1969, p. 69.

4 E. Kerridge, *The Agricultural Revolution*, Allen & Unwin, London, 1967, *passim*.

helped to ensure that the rising population was well fed.[1]

Two important 17th century changes were the abolition of feudal tenures (and the Court of Wards) and the introduction of strict entail. The first enabled estates to remain secure, and strict entail enabled a landowner to be certain his heir would inherit; thus he was encouraged to build up and invest in his estates. Feudal tenures were not abolished downwards; accordingly copyholders (small tenant farmers) had no rights to their property and were subject to arbitrary death duties and eviction at the whim of their landlords. An Act of 1677 ensured that even freeholders unless they had written legal title, were no more secure than copyholders. These developments caused a major rift in the rural world, placing landowners and large farmers on one side and the small farmers and peasants on the other. The latter were legally and economically very insecure, depending for survival on good harvests and generous landlords. Even to be a landlord was not enough; many old-fashioned squires had to sell out at difficult times to those who were progressive, or tough, or rich enough to survive periods of slump or bad harvest.[2]

The 18th century was generally a period of prosperity for farmers and landowners; there was a marked tendency for estates to grow larger.[3] However, the enlargement of estates was at the cost of the small landowners, and enclosure was at the expense of the less efficient yeomen. While agriculture and the lucky few prospered, the majority of people who derived their livelihoods from the land found their social and economic position changing rapidly for the worse. Enclosures were both cause and effect of the breakdown of the medieval pattern of rural society. The three-tier structure of landlord, tenant and farm labourer had begun to emerge in the 17th century; it developed rapidly as enclosure continued, and at the end of the burst of enclosures in the period 1760–1815 it was the typical pattern of rural relationship. Over 1800 parliamentary enclosures were allowed between 1760 and 1815 covering seven million acres[4] and by 1850 almost all land was enclosed. Although the culmination of the enclosure process was almost entirely beneficial to agriculture and food production, it was destructive of the

1 The population of England and Wales was static at around 5¼ million in the 17th century. However it rose in the 18th century and doubled in the 50 years after 1780 and again in the 60 years between 1841 and 1901. See E. Hobsbawm, *Industry and Empire*, Penguin, Harmondsworth, 1969, pp. 42–3.

2 There was a period of economic prosperity during the Interregnum, but a major slump during the early part of Charles II's reign. See M. Ashley, *England in the Seventeenth Century* (rev. edn), Penguin, Harmondsworth, 1952, p. 24.

3 P. Mathias, *The First Industrial Nation*, Methuen, London, 1969, p. 54.

4 See Mathias, *Industrial Nation*, p. 73.

old rural social order. Enclosure was praised by the Board of Agriculture in the mid 18th century for it made labourers 'work every day of the year' and secured 'the subordination of the lower ranks of society'. However, more sympathetic contemporary writer, Arthur Young, wrote 'By nineteen out of twenty enclosure bills the poor are injured and some grossly injured'.[1]

Class formation and the rise of the squirearchy

At the time of the Norman invasion the class structure of England was temporarily frozen, as the Norman élite imposed themselves on the Anglo-Saxon system which they had conquered. The manifest separateness of the Norman barons obviously lessened as they became Anglicised and intermarried with the families of English gentry; nevertheless, as a class the major landowners remained important. Their numbers were never great;[2] but their power at Court and their military significance as providers of knights and soldiers for the Crusades was considerable. Although socially inferior to the barons, the knights of the shires had significant local as well as national duties and were needed by the monarchy, as the calling of a parliament in 1295 shows, to ensure that 'royal authority' was upheld throughout the country.

Even in the relatively static Middle Ages economic and social mobility was possible. Merchants, lawyers, the king's ministers and the clergy, whatever their origins, kept the class structure from ossifying and also kept town and country from being estranged. Younger sons had to enter trade or government service to survive and successful town lawyers and merchants marked their success by buying estates. Dick Whittington, who died in 1423, is an example from this period of a younger son of a yeoman who did well in business and became a country gentleman. Moreover, the monarchs of the Middle Ages no less than the Tudors were always looking for able and loyal administrators; successful public service in a profitable office could be rewarded by titles and estates.[3]

The power of the barons waned towards the end of the Middle Ages. Their economic position weakened partly because of falling rents and falling land values, and partly because of the traditional expenditure

1 Both quotations from Hill, *Reformation*, p. 270.

2 Professor Painter puts the number of barons in 1160–1220 at 160. Quoted in Postan, *Medieval Economy*, p. 185.

3 William de la Pole, a merchant from Hull, became a landed squire, his son became an Earl and his great grandson the Duke of Suffolk. Both son and great grandson became king's ministers and both were rewarded by an increase in both titles and landholdings. See Myers, *Late Middle Ages*, p. 52.

they incurred which included providing men for wars, attending court, and meeting the cost of keeping up the large baronial households. The blood-letting of the Wars of the Roses destroyed most of the great families and ended their effective power as a class.

The Tudor accession coincided with a period of political stability in which both population and wealth expanded. Poised to take advantage of this was a rising élite of merchants and yeomen whose ambitions were given a significant boost by the sudden availability of land which resulted from the dissolution of the monasteries. One of the reasons why there was no popular outcry against the dissolution was because so many people benefited. 'In the century and a quarter after 1530 land was more freely bought and sold than ever before'.[1] The king favoured the development of this secular landed class, the 'squirearchy' which could act as a counter-balance to the power of the old style barons and of the bishops.

Economically the squirearchy prospered in the Tudor period for 'there was a massive redistribution of income in favour of the landed classes'[2] in the years 1580 to 1620. Politically the squirearchy's rise to influence was aided by the Tudor policy of selecting local administrators and JPs from their ranks rather than from the aristocracy. In parliament the loyalty of the newly land-endowed was an important factor for the monarch when financial matters were under the vote. The key to the shift from the medieval to the modern pattern of society is to be found in this emergence of the squirearchy. Indeed, Habbakuk has written: 'The rise of the squirearchy has become the organizing conception of English social life between the dissolution of the monasteries and 1640'.[3]

The squirearchy was the dominant class from the 16th to the 19th century, and as long as England was primarily rural and agricultural and as long as power and income were derived from land ownership, then the authority of the squirearchy was secure. As a class the squirearchy got richer in the 16th and 17th centuries. Between 1530 and 1640 prices increased fivefold but rents in some areas increased eightfold.[4]

For 300 years, therefore, there existed a rural class whose preoccupation was its land and the enjoyment of it. The traditions of hunting were consolidated by the emergence of this newly landed, newly powerful group.

The break-up of the medieval pattern of society also saw the fall of significant numbers of unprotected people who were unable to take

1 Hill, *Reformation*, p. 64.

2 Ibid, p. 65.

3 Quoted in Ashley, *England in the Seventeenth Century*, p. 20.

4 Hill, *Reformation*, p. 65.

advantage of their relative freedom.[1] The problem of the 'sturdy beggar', the landless, jobless peasant, became a major one in the 16th century. England 'lived in terror of the tramp' and any charity was 'as much the offspring of fear as of pity, of hatred as of charity'; however 'savagery had reached its peak [by] the middle of the century and thereafter repression yielded ground steadily to reason in the handling of the problem'.[2] The Speenhamland decision of 1795 permitted outdoor relief, and enabled the poorest to have their wages supplemented by the parish. But although the Speenhamland system reduced the incidence of starvation, it nevertheless kept wages low, since farmers knew that wages could be supplemented. The ultimate effect of the system was a general reduction in the morale, mobility and independence of the labourer.

The hunting community

During the Middle Ages the Normans retained a tight control over their forests, but gradually it became expedient for Norman kings to allow barons, abbots and other nobles the rights of warren in Royal Forests. This was the result of a recognition by the monarchy of the increasing power of the nobility and of those whose loyalty the king needed in order to govern the country effectively. Since nobles hunted, hunting was ennobling. 'The passion for hunting is linked to excellence. Hunting had an ennobling effect upon its practitioners, and by the same token, adroitness in matters of the hunt was the mark of a noble person'.[3]

From Tudor times the monarchy and their noblemen regarded hunting as one of the key elements of their social duties and activities. Henry VIII as a young man reportedly 'cared nothing but for girls and hunting' and indulged in both for many years.[4] Queen Elizabeth I was 'excellently disposed to hunting, for every second day she is on horseback and continues the sport long'.[5] James I hunted daily during his journey south from Scotland to be crowned king of England. In his advice to his son contained in *A Kinge's Christian Dutie towards God*

1 'Villeanage ceases but the Poor Laws begin' R. Tawney, *The Agrarian Problem in the 16th Century*, London, 1919, p. 46.

2 S.T. Bindoff, *Tudor England*, Penguin, Harmondsworth, 1950, pp. 293–4.

3 From M. Thiebaux, 'The Medieval Chase', *Speculum*, vol. 43, 1967, p. 260.

4 Sabretache, (pseud), *The Monarchy and the Chase*, Eyre & Spottiswoode, London, 1948, p. 54.

5 S. Strutt, *The Sports and Pastimes of the People of England*, Methuen, London, 1801, p.9. A re-issued and corrected edition was published by Methuen in 1903.

he notes the merits of 'the hunting namelie with running hounds which is the most honourable and noblest sort thereof'.[1] Charles II was the first king to win a race at Newmarket,[2] and it was his enthusiastic promotion of both racing and hunting which has since enabled the two activities to be mutually reinforcing.

The Stuarts were the last kings for whom hunting was central to their social lives, but most subsequent monarchs hunted at least occasionally. George III hunted regularly with the Royal Buckhounds and George IV was the first monarch to prefer fox hunting to the rather tame carted stag hunting which his immediate predecessors enjoyed.[3] This gave fox hunting additional social cachet which it had been gradually acquiring in the last years of the 18th century.

While hunting and racing undoubtedly benefited from this Royal imprimatur, the waning power of the monarchy meant that their support, while helpful, was not crucial. Queen Victoria disliked both hunting and racing, and engaged in neither, although, for both activities, the early Victorian period was a 'golden age'.

The relationship between hunting and the nobility was similar to the relationship between hunting and royalty. After rights to hunt freely on their own estates and in nearby Royal Forests were established, the nobles set up their own small-scale courts in the country. They ran large households, maintained a staff of huntsmen, grooms and game keepers and hunted whatever and whenever they chose. This they continued to do as long as they existed as a class.

Lower down the social scale hunting facilities were curtailed by economic as well as political restraints. Only in the 14th century, when the non-landowning class began to split between the successful tenant farmer and the poor yeoman and labourer, did the possibility arise of this affluent farmer class joining his landlord in the hunt. Even then they would hunt only by invitation.

However in the 17th and 18th centuries the squirearchy gradually came to dominate the hunting community as indeed it still does today. The English squirearchy was unique in Europe, in that it was a country-loving class whose members had, in general, no great desire to become courtiers or soldiers. Sometimes individuals owned sufficient land or forest for hunting purposes; others joined together with two or three neighbouring squires to hunt a wider area, which might have included deer parks or parts of the Royal Forests no longer required by the king. They were not particularly concerned whether their hounds hunted

1 Strutt, *Sports*, p.5.

2 Sabretache, *Monarchy*, p. 87.

3 R. Longrigg, *The History of Foxhunting*, Macmillan, London, 1975, p. 57.

stag, fox or hare, although the stag, when available, was always preferred. Their leisure was centred around hunting; their behaviour on the hunting field was a demonstration of their social status. It is this which explains why Treatises on hunting were among the most popular books of the later Middle Ages.[1] These books were written for the newly rich, the yeomen, merchants and the lawyers who needed to acquire a knowledge of the correct forms and correct terms of hunting in order to move from the fringes to the main stream of the hunting community. Such people knew the basic methods of hunting but were largely ignorant of hunting etiquette since, not knowing Norman-French, they were excluded from aristocratic literature and aristocratic conversation. This wish for self-improvement and the desire to show by familiarity with all aspects of hunting that they had moved up the ladder of social respectability was not unique to the landowning classes. The Peasants Revolt of 1381 was less a symptom of the despair of the very poor than a sign of frustration by those who had some money and freedom, but were protesting against the remaining legal obligations and dues which affected status. Hunting was one of the things the peasants were debarred from doing and this they resented,[2] particularly those who had acquired the necessary income and leisure to make it possible.

In the Middle Ages senior churchmen, most of whom were sons of noblemen or gentry and who were therefore trained in horsemanship, were frequently keen hunters. Many Abbeys and Bishops' Palaces had deer parks and these were regularly hunted, both for food and for pleasure. Lesser clergymen, possibly sons of merchants or freemen were, despite occasional rebukes from disapproving Bishops, hunting people. They mainly coursed hares and dug out foxes, for only the rich ones had sufficient wealth and status to hunt deer, and that was usually on their own estates.

At the time of the Reformation in England the church, and its Bishops, were still major landowners. The destruction of the power of the church, however, fundamentally altered the relationship between church and state and between churchmen and hunting. If the parson was a younger son of a landed family he could use his social position to ensure access to hunting or he could be a landowner in his own right. But as power devolved upon the squirearchy so the parish priest depended for his hunting upon his relationship with the squire. Increasingly the impact of Puritanism and of attempts by the church to fulfil a socially responsible role meant that it was not safe to assume that a clergyman was a hunting man.

1 The Boke of St. Albans (1486) was reprinted more times than any other book of its time except the Bible. See Longrigg, *Foxhunting*, p. 31. It covers Hunting, Hawking and Heraldry.

2 Longrigg, *Foxhunting*, p. 28.

In the 18th century, however, ordinary clergymen frequently hunted and, as fox hunting became more popular, it reached a stage where 'scarcely a hunt in mid-eighteenth century England was without its hunting parson'.[1] The apotheosis of the hunting parson was the Rev. John Russell (1795–1883) of North Devon. He kept hounds from his school days until he was over eighty. Hunting parsons gradually faded from the scene in the 19th century, although they survived for much longer in the North and West of England where hunting was less socially exclusive, and, important for most parsons, less expensive.

Initially only the wives and daughters of the nobility were allowed to be members of the hunting fraternity.[2] Numerous medieval manuscript illustrations show women in the hunting field both as spectators and as mounted participants.[3] They also attended the 'battues', and shot arrows from them in the general direction of the deer.[4] Medieval manuscripts illustrate a strong if implicit connection between hunting and sex. The Devonshire Hunting Tapestry at Tournais illustrates the disembowelling of a deer, but shows in the foreground a nobleman fondling the breasts of a servant girl while a lecherous countryman looks on.[5] Dr Fouillaux's *La Veneria* suggests that the best way to make fox hunting bearable is to observe it from the back of a cart with a young girl.[6] The connection may be one of analogy or of allegory, but from Chaucer to the 20th century stories which involve the chase, both of foxes and of women, surround the heroes and villains of the hunting and literary scene. Chaucer's monk for example loved 'venerie . . . and hunting for the hare was al his lust'.[7] The sexual nature of the pun is clear for the word venery has always had both sexual and sporting connotations. Even in Victorian times when decorous behaviour was, in theory, essential the hunting field readily accepted 'poule de luxe' who brought skills in all the major forms of venery to hunting.

By the 19th century, more and more respectable, but still mainly aristocratic, ladies began to take an active role in hunting. Lady Salisbury

1 R. Carr, *English Fox Hunting*, Weidenfeld & Nicolson, London, 1976, pp. 175–6.

2 Isabella (1292–1358), Edward II's Queen, had her own pack of hounds. See Myers, *Late Middle Ages*, p. 64.

3 See *The Taymouth Hours*, c. 1325–40. Illustrated in J. Hartham, *Book of Hours*, Thames & Hudson, London, 1977, p. 47.

4 A 'battue' is the driving of game, sometimes into an enclosure, where sportsmen wait with bows and arrows (later guns) to kill them.

5 Illustrated in Longrigg, *Foxhunting*, p. 31.

6 Carr, *Fox Hunting*, p. 22.

7 F. Robinson (ed.), *The Works of Geoffrey Chaucer*, Houghton Mifflin, New York, 1951, p. 19.

hunted her own pack in 1793[1] and by the end of the 19th century a number of wealthy women had become Masters of Hounds.

Throughout history law and custom has kept the hunting community small and recruitment to it has been either by birth, or by a change in the fortunes of the family, or by a change in the fortunes of the social group to which the family belonged. The group at the margin of acceptability were substantial farmers who were sometimes able to hunt by invitation but rarely by right. Below them was the bulk of the population who were forbidden, by custom, the social pleasures of hunting and were forbidden, by law, access to the animals which gave the sport.

Rituals of the hunt

In Norman times the royal beasts or beast of venery were the red deer, the fallow deer, the roe deer and the wild boar. The roe deer lost favour because it drove other deer away and it was struck off the list of protected animals in 1338.[2] The hare enjoyed a changeable status; it was at certain periods and in certain areas put under the protection of the forest laws and became therefore a beast of royal venery. This variable status was largely a response to the availability of other beasts. Whatever the king decided to hunt became, at least temporarily, a royal beast.

The lesser beasts were at first unspecified, but,when rights of warren were granted by Henry I, they included the fox, wild cat and badger. The hare was sometimes mentioned as was the wolf, but the wolf was generally considered to be vermin and fair game for anyone.[3] The otter, polecat, pine martin and weasel were specified in later documents.

Part of the confusion over which list these animals belong to is explained by reference to the places in which they were hunted. The king could grant to a subject the franchise of a chase, i.e. part of the forest, which when fenced became a park. He could also grant the 'rights of warren' in that park or chase to a subject, invariably a baron or major landowner. These rights of warren might or might not specify which animals could be hunted, but they excluded the royal beasts, that is the stag, the boar and sometimes the hare.

Peasants and poor freemen who regularly poached deer were able to hunt the lesser animals on common land, but it would not have been

1 Strutt, *Sports*, p. 9.

2 Bagley and Rowley, *Documentary History*, p. 64.

3 Strutt, *Sports*, pp. 11–12 suggests that the wolf was a royal beast but, since King John was offering rewards to wolf-catchers, this is unlikely. It may have been hunted but it was not protected and was virtually extinct by 1400. See Stenton, *Early Middle Ages*, p. 104.

an everyday sport for a countryman since his surplus time would have gone into providing sustenance for his family.

The lesser beasts of warren were usually pursued on foot, whereas royal beasts of venery were pursued on horseback. This partly accounts for the changing status of the hare, for the élite, who were the only people to possess horses, occasionally hunted hare as well as deer and boar with horses and hounds. Hare hunting was certainly popular in the early 14th century for Twici, who was Edward II's huntsman, began his treatise on hunting with a description of hare hunting 'for she is the most marvellous beast which is on this earth'.[1]

Although the animals listed in the categories may vary from one source to another, most writers specify that there are three categories, beasts of the forest, the chase, and the warren, and therefore three 'classes' of animal. The three classes of hunted animals anticipate the different levels of society which ultimately became involved in hunting them. The more noble the animal, the more its capture conferred nobility on its pursuers and, therefore, not surprisingly access to the most ennobling forms of hunting was restricted.

The stag, the most noble of all, was very much a royal beast in the Middle Ages: accordingly much more is known about hunting techniques and about the rituals which developed around the process. The medieval hunt was divided into three major stages, all of which have echoes in today's methods of hunting.[2]

First the stag was 'harboured', that is identified and isolated by one man and his hound, while the others waited and ate their breakfast in the forest. The harbourer formally reported his findings and, following this, valets with relays of hounds were posted at likely parts in the forests. The second stage was the hunt itself; the followers finished breakfast and mounted, and the pack was laid on. Various cries (in modified use today) informed the field of the progress of the hunt. Ultimately the stag became exhausted and turned at bay.

The third stage involved the death and dispatch of the deer. It was shot with arrows, or sometimes hamstrung before the *coup de grace* was delivered by the huntsman who pierced the stag's neck with a knife or sword. When dead, the deer was elaborately and ritualistically carved up. This was called the Quarry. The first parts to be removed were the testicles, then the feet, and the right forefoot was given to the most eminent person present. The head was kept for the overlord. The deer was then carried to the Castle in pieces, accompanied by a great deal of shouting and horn blowing.

1 P. Chalmers, *The History of Hunting*, Seeley Service, London (n.d. probably 1936) p. 173.

2 Thiebaux, 'Medieval Chase', p. 260–74. He divides the process into ten parts; only a simplified version (with corroboration from other sources) is given here.

Until the Stuart accession the 'battue' form of stag hunting was common, and indeed preferred by monarchs such as Elizabeth I. It consisted of driving deer into an enclosure and either shooting them with bows and arrows or bringing them down with dogs. It was both a sport and a means of acquiring fresh meat in winter.

During the 16th and 17th centuries the relative importance of the deer, hare and fox, the three most frequently hunted animals, underwent major changes. The deer became less important and the fox rose in status, while the hare kept its place as an acceptable alternative to whichever animal was most favoured in a particular area.

Because the élite jealously guarded the stag for their own sport, lesser mortals chased whatever presented itself. Their first preference was undoubtedly the hare. Twici put the hare at the top of his list; so did other writers such as the squire who in 1733 'gave his vote for the innocent hare above all other game'.[1] There are several reasons why the hare gives good sport; it lives above ground and does not run to earth like a rabbit; hounds will chase it naturally whereas they have to be trained to chase a fox; it can run very fast, and jump over fences up to five feet high. When followed it will take a series of leaps to avoid leaving scent; it will mingle with sheep, swim down or across rivers, and run along roads, all of which practices require skilled hounds and huntsmen to find the trail again. When being hunted the hare only runs when the hounds are close, otherwise it rests between bursts of activity. It also tends to run in a circle back to its 'form' or lair. The hound which follows the hare, nowadays the beagle, is considerably slower than the hare but has superior stamina. The interest in hare hunting lies in watching the slower hound ultimately catch the tiring hare.[2]

The fox emerged from its social obscurity very gradually. It is hardly mentioned at all before the reign of Edward I. During the Middle Ages fox hunting was not even considered a true sport; certainly few rules or rituals governed the process. In *The Master of the Game*, written in 1406, the fox ranks seventh in the list and is to be killed as quickly as possible.[3] They were driven to earth, dug out and netted rather than hunted. However in 1581 Sir Thomas Cockaine demoted the hare and put the fox at the top of his list; he also indicated that red deer were becoming scarce.[4]

1 From *An Essay on Hunting by a Country Squire*, 1733, p. 28. Quoted in Carr, *Fox Hunting*, p. 25.

2 See I. Clarke, *An Introduction to Beagling*, J. Allen, London, 1973.

3 Quoted in Carr, *Fox Hunting*, p. 22, and Brander, *Hunting Instinct*, pp. 40–1.

4 Brander, *Hunting Instinct*, p. 78.

In Northern England a number of major landowners chased after the fox in Stuart times and there are records of long but not fast hunts.[1] Neither the horses nor the hounds were bred for a fast chase and the habit of hunting at dawn when the fox had a full stomach meant that he did not run very far.

As English society and land-use patterns changed in the 17th and 18th centuries, fox hunting changed as well. For the nobility the disintegration of deer parks and the gradual erosion of forests produced a relative shortage of deer and the fox became an inevitable substitute. This was particularly so after the attempt by the later Stuarts to restock the Royal parks failed to produce sufficient deer for hunting purposes. Landlords who were keen to revive park hunting in areas where numbers were low took to hunting carted deer. This involved keeping a few tame deer in a paddock, releasing one for a hunt and making sure that the hounds did not catch it so that it could be hunted another day. Carted stag hunting flourished in Southern England in the early 18th century, but in the 19th century it slowly faded away. Only the survival of the Royal Buckhounds until 1901 gave it any prestige.

As the availability of wild deer declined, the hare, which tested the hounds more than any other animal, had a period of pre-eminence. But increasingly in the 18th century it was unable to provide the long fast runs which gradually became popular with the 'field'. For the squire the changes meant that he gradually chased more foxes than hares and many, but not all, packs of harriers slowly became packs of fox hounds. For the nobility the depletion of the stock of deer meant that they also gradually became fox hunters, until, by 1800, the pre-eminent and predominant form of sport was fox hunting.

1 Carr, *Fox Hunting*, pp. 28–9.

2 Changes in British society in the 19th and 20th centuries which have affected hunting

Decline in the significance of the agricultural sector

The fortunes of agriculture in the last century and a half have been extremely varied. The painful emergence from the post-Napoleonic slump culminated in a generation of prosperity from 1850–70. During these years the rapidly increasing population needed and was supplied with home-grown food. The booming economy absorbed the excess rural labour and helped to alleviate, at least among the mobile, the worst of the rural poverty. This improvement was temporary and the problems of the farmers were largely ignored during the agricultural depression of the last quarter of the 19th century because free trade was philosophically popular and economically profitable for the country as a whole. Furthermore, the urban dwellers who now made up the majority of the population (and after 1887 the majority of the voters) were in no hurry to protect farmers. Indeed many of the landowners of the period who might have raised their voices were primarily businessmen and merchants who had acquired land for social rather than economic reasons. Some were keen huntsmen. In 1870 a Cunard was a MFH and another Liverpool ship-owner was Master of the Quorn.

The significance of agriculture steadily declined in the 19th century. In 1800 agriculture produced 40 per cent of the national product; by 1850 it was under 20 per cent[1] and in 1900, 6.6 per cent.[2] Its share in

1 Hobsbawm, *Industry and Empire*, p. 195.

2 J. Bowle, *The English Experience*, Weidenfeld & Nicolson, London, 1971, p. 418.

the national capital declined between 1800 and 1880 from over 50 per cent to under 20 per cent.[1] During the 1870s the land under wheat halved, arable land was cut by a quarter and more grass was grown to fatten sheep and cattle,[2] the prices of which remained relatively low. Farmers and landlords became bankrupt and more and more labourers emigrated to the towns or the dominions or to North America.

The fortunes of farming have fluctuated violently in the 20th century. A gradual revival at the beginning of the century was followed by great expansion during the First World War. Two million extra acres were brought under the plough and food imports were substantially reduced. After the war free trade in food was re-established and agriculture suffered from this and from the depression of the 1920s and 1930s. It took another world war to convince governments of the strategic value of farming and of the need for agriculture to be protected against the full rigour of world market forces. Since the late 1930s state support has helped to improve output and productivity. In 1939 one-third of the food consumed in Britain was produced internally, rising to over 50 per cent by the early 1970s, for a population nine million larger. In the same period net production at constant prices increased by almost 150 per cent with a smaller work force.[3] Farming is now less a way of life and more an efficient and capital intensive industry.

The relative decline in the agricultural sector has been of major significance to the hunting community. As the country became increasingly urbanised and industrialised, fewer people were recipients and transmitters of the rural values which implied historically an acceptance of the right of the squire to hunt. For the static rural poor this acceptance was forced upon them and was fostered by deference, always a powerful factor in rural societies. Away from the constraints of rural life the majority of the poor were susceptible to other influences and deferential to another set of masters.

The corollary to the increasing mechanisation and efficiency of agriculture was the rapid growth of the towns and the dramatic increase in the industrial work force. In less than a century Britain changed from being a predominantly rural society to being an urban society with major industrial and commercial centres. In 1851, just over half of the population of 18 million lived in urban areas, and by 1900 over three-quarters of a population of 32½ million were urban dwellers. Since the turn of the century the rate of population increase has declined, but

1 J.D. Chambers and G.S. Mingay, *The Agriculture Revolution: 1750–1880*, B. Batsfc London, 1966, p. 208.

2 The increase in grass was much appreciated by the hunting community.

3 *Britain 1977*, HMSO, London, 1977, p. 279.

urban areas have continued to grow so that conurbations have become the 'dominant type of British community'.[1] Now over one-third of the population lives in London and the six Metropolitan counties. For urban dwellers the nature and condition of rural society is a distant irrelevance, especially as most of their parents and grandparents were also raised in urban communities and brought up with urban values and attitudes.

As Britain has become urbanised a smaller percentage of the population derives its income and employment from the land. Between 1800 and 1900 the numbers in agriculture, while similar in absolute terms (about one million), declined as a proportion from 36 per cent to 12½ per cent. Nevertheless, until overtaken by the transport and metal industries around 1900, agriculture was still the largest single employer of labour.[2] In the 20th century the work patterns of the population show an increasing concentration in office and factory work, far removed from the traditional occupations of farming and fishing. In 1976 the employment breakdown was as follows:[3]

36 per cent of employees in professional and government services.
35 per cent of employees in manufacturing industries.
12 per cent of employees in distributive trades.
8 per cent of employees in the construction industry.
3 per cent of employees in agriculture, mining, forestry.

Landlords and farmers

The nature of land ownership has undergone significant changes during the last 150 years. In the period up to the Napoleonic Wars the relative prosperity of the agricultural sector allowed peasants and small farmers to survive – despite the general tendency for landlords to increase their holdings. Economies of scale and a marketable surplus allowed the substantial farmer to survive the bad harvests of the Napoleonic years and the slumps of the 1820s and 1830s.

The small farmer did not totally disappear, for in 1831 half of the farming families in Britain, whether owner-occupiers or tenants, used no non-family labour. However, on average, farm sizes grew larger and by 1851 farms over 300 acres occupied over a third of farmed land.

1 *Britain 1977*, p. 15. The 1981 Census showed the population of England and Wales to be 48,521,000.

2 Hobsbawm, *Industry and Empire*, p. 195.

3 *Britain 1977*, p. 18. The figure of those employed in Agriculture and Forestry in 1980 was under 2.6 per cent. *Britain 1981*, HMSO, London, 1981, p. 285.

Farms of this size employed labour, and the farmer, conscious of his social status, would generally attempt to send his children to school, and would expect to hunt with, although not be a member of, the local hunt.

As farm sizes gradually increased, a slight drop in the number of farmers was to be anticipated. In 1851 there were approximately 250,000 farmers in Britain; numbers declined during the slumps of the 1880s and 1930s, but were stable in more prosperous periods. In 1981 there were 257,000 farming units, of which about half were full-time businesses. Of these, 30,000 were designated large businesses capable of employing four men or more on at least 350 acres.[1]

Nineteenth century changes in agriculture affected the relationship between landlord and tenant, and finally created a clear distinction between the large and successful farmer, whether owner-occupier or tenant, who was acceptable on the hunting field, and the small holder whose lack of material success gave him no resistance against the bad years. The depression of the early part of the century and the 1870s conspired to ensure that the latter group had neither the leisure, the education nor the social graces to be acceptable on the hunting field.

The position of landlords has altered during the last century. In the 19th century there was a concentration of land into fewer hands as successful landlords, many with investments in the railways or in trade, added to their holdings. In 1851 4,000 landlords controlled four-sevenths of the cultivated land, and by 1873 a similar proportion of the land was owned by some 2,250 people.[2]

The concentration of land in the hands of fewer and bigger landlords was matched by the decline in the percentage of land which was owner-occupied. In 1800 about 20 per cent of the land was farmed by owner-occupiers but this dropped gradually to about 12 per cent in 1900.[3] Thus the grip of the landowning squirearchy over rural society seemed complete, and it is no coincidence that the 19th century has been referred to as the golden age of fox hunting. However, the squirearchy's decline was rapid; it was triggered by the depression of the 1880s and accelerated by taxation,[4] the depression of the 1930s and two world wars. Owner-occupiers who controlled under 10 per cent of the land in 1914 found their fortunes recovering; in 1926 they farmed 36 per cent

1 *Britain 1981*, p. 285.

2 E. Seddon, *Modern Economic History*, McDonald & Evans, London, 1966, p. 21.

3 Chambers and Mingay, *Agricultural Revolution*, p. 92.

4 Death Duties were payable on landed estates after 1894. Lloyd George introduced land taxes in 1909. The ensuing furore resulted in the Parliament Bill of 1911 which reduced the power of the lords and ended the ascendancy of the landed class.

of farmland and by 1980 65 per cent of the working farmers in Britain owned their own farms.[1] Although private landlords have declined in significance, institutional landlords have purchased those estates which were not sold to tenants. The largest institutional landlord was and is the Crown, whose Commissioners are government appointed. It, with the Forestry Commission, which controls over half the productive forests in Britain, is run as an independent but commercial organisation.[2] In recent years the Crown and the Forestry Commission have been joined as major landlords by city financial institutions such as Insurance Companies and pension funds. Indeed, collectively, these have overtaken the Crown as landowners and buy up 25 per cent of the farm land offered for sale.[3]

Institutional landlords have no obvious need to protect the traditions of the old squirearchy and, unlike the newly prosperous and independent farmer, cannot derive personal satisfaction or local prestige by joining the hunt. The nuisance of hunting may be outweighed for farmers by the enjoyment of taking part, but it is hard to see what would encourage institutions to fight for hunting should it come under attack.

Farm labourers and the urban poor

The late 18th century pattern of rural life, landlord, farmer and labourer, gave the labourer little chance of self-advancement but, whereas the farmer and the labourer had traditionally worked together, the 19th century created a situation in which their interests were separate and, indeed, antagonistic.

During the boom years of the Napoleonic Wars the traditions of resident labour declined. It became more usual for wage labourers to live in rented cottages. However, after 1815, wages did not keep pace with prices, the spread of enclosures reduced the labourer's access to pasture, and mechanisation resulted in the supply of labour exceeding the demand. In bad times farm workers, who had rent to pay and a family to feed, were left without any income. Within one generation the condition of the rural labourer changed from relative affluence to one of misery and starvation. The view of Lord Ernle was that

> 'The standard of life from 1800 to 1834 sank to the lowest possible scale; in the South and West wages that were paid by employers fell

1 *Britain 1981*, p. 286.

2 Ibid., p. 300.

3 'The New Squirearchy', *The Money Programme*, BBC2, 9 June, 1978.

to 3/- to 4/- per week . . . and insufficient food has left its mark in the physical degeneracy of the peasantry'.

In the 1820s, Cobbett, who was alive to the social implications of the divisions in rural society, was pained to see 'the troops of half-starved creatures flocking from the fields'.[2] Up to 1851 the need for more food and the impact of enclosure, drainage and crop rotation had the effect of increasing the demand for labour, but the spread of mechanisation allied with poor harvests even in generally profitable times dramatically decreased the need and encouraged the flight from the land. Farm employment was 1¼ million in 1851, but it dropped by over 100,000 a decade until 1914. It stabilised thereafter with the wartime and postwar protection of agriculture, but full-time employment was below half a million in 1977. Between 1977 and 1981 the number of full-time farm workers declined by 3½ per cent per year to 237,000, which is a smaller figure than the number of farmers and their working family members.[3] Although the conditions of farm workers have improved in the 20th century, they remain a low paid workforce, and were in the 1978–81 period the largest single occupational group claiming Family Income Supplements.[4]

Conditions for the urban workers in the early 19th century were little better than those of his rural counterpart. There was a surplus of cheap labour, mainly redundant farm workers, to work in the new factories, foundries and mines. Even established craftsmen suffered, for their skills were being overtaken by technology. In declining industries wages went steadily down to subsistence level; the wages of hand loom weavers, whose skills rapidly became obsolete, dropped from 23/– a week in 1805 to 6/3d in 1833.[5] For the poor there was little alternative but to accept the wages offered. The quality of life was such that increasing numbers of skilled workers were forced to emigrate, and in bad years 'starvation was driving the poor to wreck the machinery which seemed to them to be the cause of their misery'.[6]

1 Quoted in J. Burnett, *Plenty and Want: a Social History of Diet*, Penguin, Harmondsworth, 1966, p.30.
Ten shillings a week was considered a good wage and rents, regularly 1/– or 2/– a week, could be a quarter of the labourer's income.

2 *The Autobiography of William Cobbett*, (ed.) W. Reitzel, Faber & Faber, London, 1967, p. 185.

3 Lloyds Bank Economics Bulletin, 41, May 1982, p. 2.

4 *The Guardian*, 3 Nov. 1978 and DHSS spokesman 1982.

5 Hobsbawm, *Industry and Empire*, p. 93.

6 J. Plumb, *England in the Eighteenth Century*, (rev. edn), Penguin, Harmondsworth, 1950, p. 214. The worst years for 'Luddites' were 1811–12 and 1816.

Emigration was a major factor in the social evolution of the 19th century. 'The export of men and women increased at a tremendous rate during the first generation after Waterloo'.[1] In 1830 alone 60,000 emigrated and in three years during the 'hungry forties' (1847–9) three-quarters of a million people emigrated.[2] As transport improved the numbers leaving increased. Between 1853 and 1880 2.5 million people emigrated from Britain and between 1880 and 1911 7.8 million emigrated, 4.4 million of them to the USA.[3] These figures imply an immense amount of personal misery and social disruption.

The low standard of living of the rural and urban work force inevitably alienated its members from their employers. The period when poverty was at its worst, the early 19th century, was also the period when game laws were at their harshest, and when punishments were most severe for relatively minor offences. The radical press was prevented from voicing demands for reform by the passage of the Six Acts in 1819; these Acts in addition to the game laws and the Combination Acts show that the government was most concerned to 'repress brutally what it could not comprehend'.[4] It would be naive to expect poor people living under these laws to have much sympathy or respect for the traditional sports of the ruling classes which flourished at a time when the poor found it most difficult to survive.

The rights of landowners over game

The zenith of fox hunting coincided with the most brutal of the game laws. Only at the end of the 19th century when society was undergoing rapid changes were the game laws relaxed, and not until the 20th century did game animals themselves receive any protection from indiscriminate field sportsmen.

In the late 18th and early 19th century the rural class war intensified. Poaching increased, and the squirearchy stepped up the attempts to suppress it. There was 'a merciless struggle in which an infinitesimal privileged minority fought to retain an exclusive right to what the whole of the rest of the community were convinced was a gift from

1 D. Thompson, *England in the Nineteenth Century*, Penguin, Harmondsworth, 1950, p. 95.

2 Ibid., p. 95.

3 L.C. Knowles, *The Industrial and Commercial Revolutions in Great Britain during the Nineteenth Century* (4th edn), Routledge & Kegan Paul, London, 1926, pp. 228–9.

4 Plumb, *Eighteenth Century*, p. 214.

God to be enjoyed by all'.[1] In George III's reign 32 new game laws were passed.[2] Among them were the *Ellenborough Act* of 1803 which made armed resistance a capital offence, and an Act in 1816–18 which made carrying nets at night punishable by transportation.[3] Since virtually no-one ever returned from transportation that was felt to be the equivalent to the death sentence.

The bitterness of the war between poachers and the system, represented by gamekeepers upholding the game laws, was made worse by the real poverty of rural society in the early 19th century. A poacher could earn 5/– a night by his activities but had to accept under 1/– a day for 12 hours of farm labour. The law made no distinction between the semi-professional poacher and the poor cottager who took the occasional hare for food. Both sorts of people were equally likely to be hanged or transported. As the depression of the early 19th century worsened the poaching laws, however severe, were plainly inadequate to stop destitute men from killing game for food.

In 1831 when one-sixth of all convictions in England were for offences against the game laws,[4] a series of bills were passed which were designed to rationalise the situation without creating a poachers' charter. The property qualifications were abolished so that any landowner, not just the very rich ones, was able to shoot game on his own land. Trade in game was also legalised. These changes were of no help to the poor poacher for the *Day Poaching Act* of 1831 and the *Night Poaching Act* of 1828 confirmed the existing penalties and increased the penalties for trespass. The changes did, however, make it easier for gentlemen to shoot and sell game.

Eventually the severity of the law was recognised and changing social attitudes made juries less willing to convict for poaching offences. The number of poachers declined in mid-century particularly as the standards of life rose for most workers. Even so in the 1840s in Wiltshire there were many parishes where every labouring family was in receipt of poor law relief.[5] But not until later on in the century when farmers and eventually rural workers obtained the vote were rights over game expanded and penalties reduced. The first act actually to reduce penalties for poaching was the *Poaching Prevention Act* of 1862. After the *Ground Game Act* of 1881 it became possible for any occupier of land,

1 Bovill, *Country Life*, p. 174.

2 Ibid., p. 177.

3 Thompson, *Nineteenth Century*, p. 17.

4 Bovill, *Country Life*, p. 196.

5 Chambers and Mingay, *Agricultural Revolution*, p. 139.

particularly the tenant farmer, to destroy the rabbits and hares which were devastating his fields. However this Act was so successful in reducing hares that a *Hares Preservation Act* of 1892 put a close season on hares and made it illegal to sell hares from March to the end of July. In 1906, the shooting rights were further restricted by making it legal for only the occupier and one other specified person to shoot ground game.

In the 20th century there have been a number of additions or amendments to the game laws designed to protect the game itself and to restrict access to it. In 1948 the *Agricultural Holdings Act* extended the rights of the occupier who had for the previous sixty years been secure in his right to shoot only ground game. The *Protection of Birds Act*, 1954, protected nesting birds, and made it illegal to remove eggs of listed birds; in 1951 the *Salmon and Freshwater Fisheries (Protection) Act* increased the penalties for poaching, and the *Pests Act* of 1956 abolished the use of steel traps except in rabbit holes.

Laws against trespass and poaching were tightened again in the 1960s. In 1960 the *Game Law (Amendment Act)* gave police power to enter land in respect of trespass cases and, in 1963, the *Protection of Deer Act* was passed which attempted to reduce the 20th century poaching of deer in Scotland and the West Country. It instituted fines for shooting and selling the wild Red Deer; however, the high price of venison and the continuing willingness of butchers and restauranteurs to accept meat of dubious provenance has meant that poachers, particularly in Somerset, have remained active. Tightening of the anti-poaching laws in the 1970s have had little effect.

Most of these acts have supported the sportsman against the poacher, and have involved a step back into the 19th century, although some legislation has protected the animals themselves. *The Badger Act* of 1974 made unauthorised badger digging illegal. A *Rabies Act* of 1974 tightened up the controls on the importation of animals and gave powers to the authorities in case of an outbreak. In 1975 the *Wild Creatures and Wild Plants Act* became law and it was under this Act that Otters became a protected species in 1978. In 1981 a significant new enabling act the *Wildlife and Countryside Act* was passed. It had a major section on animals and amended and consolidated existing legislation. Future Acts will undoubtedly result from compromises between the desires of sportsmen and animal-lovers, but both will use the language of conservation to impress the public with the justice of their case.

The recognition by governments of the needs of the working classes

In the 19th century political activism grew at all levels of the social hierarchy. The mood for social reform became respectable when led by such people as Wilberforce, Bright and Robert Owen. It became obvious that unless reforms were made and conditions improved, the poor, in desperation, would support the Luddites and men of violence. The reforms which came were *ad hoc* responses to immediate pressures and were based more on expediency than humanitarian urges. Nevertheless, in less than a century, universal suffrage, powerful trade unions and the beginnings of a welfare state had begun the process of transforming society and had placed some power over the political apparatus in the hands of a previously powerless majority.

The economic condition of the poor steadily improved after 1850, particularly for urban dwellers.[1] Consumption of staples increased and 'in 1870 most working class families were absolutely better off by about 10 per cent than they had been in 1850'. However, the rural labourer lagged behind; low wages, irregular employment and the game laws kept him 'chronically under-nourished and economically inefficient' even until 1914. Paradoxically, however, the gap between rich and poor widened in the second half of the century for, with general prosperity, the opportunities to make money increased and fortunes could be made rapidly in the largely untaxed, *laissez-faire* atmosphere of the period. Conspicuous consumption and social imitation were features of the Victorian golden age, but only for the middle classes who had some marginal income to spend.[2]

The ruling class accepted reforms in preference to revolution and were clear-sighted enough to see that change was inevitable and that acceptance of it was the only way to retain their wealth and social position. Disraeli, who understood the essentially conservative nature of the urban working class, piloted the 1867 Reform Act in order to tap their votes for the Conservative party. It was done for parliamentary advantage rather than for philosophical considerations.

One of the first struggles was over the rights of workers to form Trade Unions. The Combination Acts of 1799 and 1800 attempted to suppress Trade Unions but the patient work of Francis Place led to their repeal in 1824. Despite setbacks, government interference and painfully slow progress, the Unions gradually increased their economic

1 See Burnett, *Plenty and Want*, p. 176 and Thompson, *Nineteenth Century*, p. 144.

2 See Burnett, *Plenty and Want*, pp. 76–8 and pp. 124–6 and G. Mingay, *Rural Life in Victorian England*, Heinemann, London, 1977.

significance. The Trades Union Congress began in 1869, but only a series of legal battles into the 20th century gave unions full legal rights including the right to picket and in 1946 the right to contribute to political party funds.[1]

The demand for and the rise of Trade Unionism has been matched by the struggle over the vote. Many traditionalists feared the power of the masses and wished to ensure that real power remained in the hands of the property-owning classes. Others, however, interested mainly in very gradual change, felt that the leaders of the industrial and commercial worlds would add weight to parliament and its deliberation. The first major Reform Act of 1832 was in response to major political upheavals; it was felt to be expedient to extend the franchise. The majority of the middle classes was not enfranchised. This led to increased pressure both from radicals who demanded universal suffrage and from an outraged middle class who had been denied the vote in 1832. Jointly they ensured that the process of enfranchisement continued, although parliament, and even those demanding reform, believed that property, not person, should be used as the main criterion for the vote. Property was put forward as a unifying and not a dividing force, for could not the poor aspire to, and by hard work achieve, the independence and status which property conferred? Property created a class which could be trusted to execute its duty in a disinterested way.

In the face of major discontent and under pressure from the Chartists another generation of parliamentarians expanded the electorate to include all householders in the *Representation of the People Act*, 1867.[2] Suffrage was further widened to include most adult males in 1884–5. Only in 1918 and 1929 were women given the vote.

A significant effect of the enlarged suffrage was the decline in parliamentary power of the landowning squirearchy. The Reform Acts of 1867 and 1885 began the transfer of effective political power into the new urban and industrial sectors, although it took a long time for any real changes to become apparent. Landowners controlled parliament well into the 20th century, for they were in an absolute majority until 1885 and landowning MPs could easily outvote other MPs until 1914.[3] This position did not change until MPs began to receive a salary in 1910 and until the power of the House of Lords, dominated by landowners, was curbed in 1911. The decline in landed power was margin-

1 The Conservative governments of Mr Heath and Mrs Thatcher have attempted, without conspicuous success, to curb these rights.

2 The Electorate almost doubled to nearly two million people, Bowle, *English Experience*, p. 426.

3 Hobsbawm, *Industry and Empire*, p. 196.

ally accelerated by the institution of Death Duties in the budget of 1894. Paying MPs was more significant for it enabled people without income from property to become MPs.

The potential influence of the vote was only gradually understood by the urban poor. This was not only because the task of satisfying basic needs was arduous enough, but also because the poor were insufficiently informed to make independent choices. The poor received virtually no education until the 1830s, and charity provided almost the only source of protection against ill health and unemployment. Major improvements in their own conditions were necessary before the newly enfranchised working class could be expected to develop sufficient social independence and intellectual detachment to make demands on behalf of animals.

From the government's point of view also, animal welfare was a very secondary consideration. Having decided, in response to a variety of pressures, to allow non-property owners the vote, the government had to cope with the consequences, which involved a vast expansion of government activity. Indeed a comparison between the 1880s and 1920s illustrates 'the unprecedented extent to which the government was participating in and affecting the direction of social change in the early 20th century'.[1] This rapid expansion in the role of the government constantly brought new ideas to its attention and inevitably drew it towards some commitment to the protection of animals, for as Freeman said in 1869, 'the difference between cruelty to man and cruelty to animals is one of degree not of principle'.[2]

The extent of social legislation grew in the 20th century, first in response to the Reports of Rowntree and Booth,[3] but more significantly in response to the Beveridge Report of 1942,[4] which called on governments to intervene actively in the areas of health, education, employment and housing. Since 1945, the welfare state has grown rapidly. It has been the focus of major legislation which has in turn created a demand for administrators and professional staff to run it.[5]

1 J. Roebuck, *The Making of Modern English Society from 1850*, Routledge & Kegan Paul, London, 1973, p. 189.

2 E.A. Freeman, 'The Morality of Field Sports', *Fortnightly Review*, XXXIV, 1 Oct. 1869, p. 356.

3 Booth's *Darkest England* described the poverty and squalor in London and in 1899 S. Rowntree's *Poverty: A Study of Town Life* surveyed the equally appalling conditions in York.

4 Entitled *Report on Social Insurance and Allied Services*, Nov. 1942.

5 *Britain 1981*, p. 327. In 1979 1.6 million people were in government service.

In the key areas of health and education developments were slow. The drive behind improving health care was more economic than humanitarian. The wealthy were prone to cholera[1] and typhoid[2] and only a national system of sewage, clean water and decent services would suffice to improve radically the environment and the health of the people living in it. Only in the 20th century has the focus of attention moved from providing an environment in which people take care of themselves to providing individual care and support services.

In the 20th century all classes have recognised education as a route to advancement, particularly after the buying of office and commissions ended. The poor have depended less on their children for economic support, and the government has realised that an educated industrial work force is needed in an increasingly complex age. It became understood that it was politically as well as economically desirable to tap and use rather than suppress the abilities of the working class.

In 1944, the Butler Act instituted a state system of varied, comprehensive and compulsory education for all children although it left the private fee-paying schools intact. In 1967, the Labour government, concerned that the middle classes enjoyed disproportionate advantages, even from state-funded education, instituted enforced comprehensivisation of secondary schools. By 1981, 83 per cent of the secondary school population attended comprehensive schools.[3]

More working-class people have gained access to universities and added to the number of those who are likely to be free from the constraints of deference and obedience to the old order.[4] Such people are not overawed by tradition and are capable of questioning and analysing on what had previously been accepted faith.

The working classes have laboriously acquired some status and influence over the last 100 years and have learnt how to manipulate the levers of power. They have also observed, by its effect on themselves, how much legislation is essentially based on the protection of class interests. The game laws and the protection of hunting and sporting privileges were among the most rigorously applied laws in the 19th century. The abolition of these laws and the privileges they protected would seem a natural target for any government wishing to right what it feels to be social wrongs.

1 Filth and overcrowding increased the urban death rate in mid-century. There was a major cholera outbreak in 1866.

2 Albert, the Prince Consort, died of typhoid in 1861.

3 DHSS spokesman, June 1982.

4 Students in full-time or 'sandwich' higher education increased from 222,000 in 1962 to over 500,000 in 1979. See *Britain 1981*, p. 164. This is five times the pre-war figure.

3 Modifications in the hunting world

The change to fox hunting

The records of many of the major 18th century landowners reveal the gradual concentration on fox hunting rather than stag hunting.[1] It was at this time that the breeding of fast horses and hounds and the active preservation of woodlands caused fox hunting to emerge as England's premier field sport. It was assisted by planting coverts, building artificial earths,[2] encouraging foxes to breed and protecting them while colonies established themselves.

Hunting itself developed. Hugo Meynell, Master of the Quorn from 1753 to 1800, and fellow hound breeders such as Peter Beckford,[3] introduced a new approach to the techniques of hunting, and made the application of these techniques exciting for the followers. Meynell developed a system which has remained the basis of hunting to this day; the key to his system lies in the speed and skill of the hounds.

1 The Dukes of Beaufort and Rutland switched to hunting foxes in the 1760s. See Longrigg, *Foxhunting*, pp. 73 and 76.

2 The coverts and earths remain, a feature of 20th century hunting.

3 Author of the first major work on fox hunting *Thoughts on Hunting*, London, 1781.

Meynell's system attracted two types of followers.[1] The first were keen hunters, those whose delight lay in watching hounds at work. The second were socialites, those who were attracted by the speed and excitement of the chase. Meynell started hunting at 11 o'clock in the morning so that the fox, having digested its overnight meal, would be able to keep running in front of the faster hounds. The young followers in Melton Mowbray, the headquarters of hunting, also enjoyed the 11 o'clock start, because they could then drink for most of the night and still have a good gallop during the day.

The Meltonian's heyday (1800–30) coincided with the final round of enclosures. Ultimately the spread of enclosures was an asset to hunting for it broke up the straight runs and introduced the practice of jumping fences at the gallop. By the beginning of the 19th century breeders were beginning to produce horses able to stand up to the long fast gallops which Meynell's style of hunting had introduced.

It was accepted in 19th century England that fox hunting was a major sport: 'Fox hunting is now the chief amusement of the true British sportsman [since] the pleasures of the fox chase are so well understood, and conducted on such purely scientific principles. It is considered the *beau-ideal* of hunting by those who pursue it. There can be no doubt that it is infinitely superior to stag hunting'.[2] Speed made hunting socially significant and enabled it to become the 'national sport' of the 19th century. From Meynell's day to this the social differences between the Shire packs, the farmers' packs and the suburban packs survive although the essential mechanics of fox hunting remain the same.

The hunting season starts with cub hunting after harvest in late August or September when young foxes are culled. In November, the season commences properly and continues until April. The hunting day begins early in some hunts when earth stoppers go out to the area to be hunted in order to close the entrances to a number of earths. This makes sure that some foxes will, after their night's feeding, lie up in kale, gorse or woodland rather than go underground.[3] The hounds, perhaps 20 couples (i.e. 40 hounds) are taken to the meet, generally in a hound van or horse box where the 'field' of mounted followers will be assembling. Shortly after 11.00 a.m. the Master instructs the huntsman to take the hounds and 'draw' a covert or a field of kale where a

1 Meynell's individual significance can be overstated. In 1750 there were 'some fifty men breeding foxhounds upon sound selective principles'. G.T. Burrows, *Gentleman Charles: A History of Hunting*, Vinton, London, 1951, p. 18.

2 W. Howitt, *The Rural Life of England* (1st edn 1838), reprinted by University Press, Shannon, 1971, p. 31.

3 It also ensures that the fox has fewer places to hide when being chased.

fox is thought to be 'laid up'. The field must wait at the edge of the covert and hope that the fox will leave, followed by the hounds 'giving tongue' to indicate that they have found and are following the scent. The ideal hunt is one in which a fox runs hard for an hour or more across country with the hounds and the field in full pursuit. The fox, although fast, will tire before the hounds and can offer no effective resistance if caught in the open. Sometimes the fox may be caught and killed by the hounds before it leaves the covert, or may give the hounds only a short run; at other times it may successfully elude the hounds and find refuge in an unblocked earth. The hounds may find the scent is faint because it is old or because it has been ruined by fertiliser or sheep, or they may cross another line of scent and switch their attentions to a fresh fox who may be able to outrun them. A good hound is one that can pick up and stay on the line of one fox, and a good huntsman is one who leaves his hounds alone until they have 'checked' or lost their way before assisting them by 'casting' them forward to find the line of scent again.

When a fox is caught in the open the huntsman may, if it has been a good hunt, cut off the mask (head), the brush (tail) and the pads (feet) to distribute as favours to members of the hunt. The remains of the fox will then be thrown to the hounds. If the fox goes to ground the Master may order it to be bolted, or dug out and shot, or if it has given a good run, and the local farmer does not mind, it may be left to be hunted another day.

The number of foxes killed by hunts varies considerably. In an 'average season in the 1970s between 20–25,000 foxes were killed by hunts. This does not include those shot by farmers and gamekeepers which could double this figure. Some hunts, particularly those who claim that the modern fox hunter is a conservationist, kill very few. Thirty per cent of hunts kill fewer than 36 foxes and only 25 per cent kill 50 foxes or over.[1] Some hunts, however, take the business of fox control more seriously, and three hunts from the sample claimed to kill over 150 foxes per season. The fox population, while nationally stable, is locally volatile. Twenty-one per cent of hunts claimed that they killed fewer foxes than 20 years ago, 39 per cent said they killed about the same, and 33 per cent said they killed up to double the figure of 20 years ago. These wide variations are repeated in the figures showing the extent to which foxes are killed in the open. Over 20 per cent claim to kill half of their foxes by digging them out and half in the open. However the spread is very wide: 12 per cent of hunts claim to kill at least 90 per cent of their foxes in the open, and 11 per cent admit to

1 This and subsequent data about contemporary fox hunting is taken from questionnaires administered to a sample of MFHs between 1974–7. The data was further checked and updated in 1982.

digging out at least 90 per cent of theirs. Whether or not a fox is dug out depends very much on the wishes of the local farmers, the susceptibilities of the followers, whether the hounds have tasted fox lately, and whether the country is riddled with artificial earths which make going to ground inevitable. A quarter of all hunts have over a dozen artificial earths with one hunt claiming over 100 of them. In areas where foxes are in short supply these earths may be stopped in order to deny the fox a refuge and to help ensure a good hunt.

The effect of the primacy of fox hunting on other forms of hunting

Stag

To the dismay of the aristocracy, stag hunting never recovered from the break up of the deer parks in the Civil War. In the 18th century, individual landowners continued to hunt red and fallow deer, but excessive poaching and the gradual rise of fox hunting reduced the major centres of stag hunting to Exmoor and to Windsor Forest where the Royal Buckhounds hunted red deer.

After 1800, the Royal Buckhounds hunted only carted deer, and the convenience and economy of this form of hunting led to a period of popularity for carted stag hunting, which did not decline until after 1870. The Royal Buckhounds disbanded in 1901 but there remained a dozen packs which hunted carted deer in South East England before the First World War. Four survived the First War and two the Second. The Mid Kent ended in 1962 and the Norwich Hunt in 1963.

In 1825 the Exmoor pack of hounds were sold to Germany, thus leaving no real staghounds in England. Until 1855 there were only intermittent attempts to hunt on Exmoor and during this hiatus the red deer population declined sharply. The revival of stag hunting started in 1856 when the New Forest Buckhounds began, in a small way, to hunt fallow deer, and in the following year the Devon and Somerset Staghounds began to hunt again on Exmoor. Both of these hunts have a continuous history of successful stag hunting.[1] There are now two other stag hunts which began as off-shoots of the Devon and Somerset Staghounds. One, the Tiverton Staghound, was formed in 1896, to help cope with the reviving deer population, and the other, the Quantock Staghounds, was formed in 1902 to hunt the red deer

1 In its first season the D & SS killed only four stags; its success was by no means certain. W. Dixon, *Hunting in the Olden Days*, Constable, London, 1912, p. 39.

brought from Exmoor to the Quantock Hills.[1] Together these stag hunts kill approximately 150 stags or hands in a season – fewer than the number culled by farmers or shot by poachers.[2]

Hare

Despite its gradual replacement by fox hunting, hare hunting has retained some popularity. The hare continues to be hunted in three different ways, (a) by harriers, (b) by beagles, and (c) by coursing greyhounds.

The early packs of harriers were mixed packs which hunted hare or fox indiscriminately, and many of the leading figures of hunting, including Meynell, trained young foxhounds by setting them to chase hares. In the 19th and 20th centuries many harrier packs have changed to hunting foxes, and others have closed down or amalgamated as their supporters deserted them for fox hunting. The number of harrier packs in the 20th century has dropped from 101 in 1905 to 40 in 1935 and 27 in 1981.[3] Some of these hunt only the fox. In most respects harrier packs and their supporters are similar to foxhounds and fox hunters.

Beagling has the similar aim of catching and killing hares. However, the hounds are a smaller (and hence slower) breed, not over 16 inches high and they are bred for their voices and 'nose'. Beaglers follow the hounds on foot and the pleasure consists mainly in the exercise and in watching the hounds work. With the decline of harriers many supporters have turned to beagling which is much less expensive and less exclusive. Private packs of beagles are relatively easy to start up and a number of schools, colleges and landowning families have maintained private packs since the last century. The number of public subscription packs has fluctuated over the years for their survival depends mainly on a few keen beaglers. In 1932 there were 69 packs in England and Wales, 61 in 1961, and 76 in 1981.[4]

Coursing is different from beagling in several important respects. Its function is to test the merits of two greyhounds in their competitive pursuit of a wild hare. The hounds chase it by sight only and the followers stand and watch. It is therefore a spectator sport in which the

1 For details of the hunts see the relevant entries in *Baily's Hunting Directory*, J. Allen, London, annually. See also E. Lloyd, *The Wild Red Deer of Exmoor*, Exmoor Press, Dulverton, Somerset, 1970.

2 See *Sunday Times*, 15 August 1982.

3 See the relevant *Baily's*.

4 See *Baily's*, 1977–8 and 1980–1. The BFSS publicity sheet *This is Beagling* mentions 90 packs in England and Wales. Some private or unaccredited packs can be added to Baily's official list.

hare is almost incidental. Only in the 18th century did coursing become organised and exclusive. The first coursing club was the Swaffham in Norfolk, founded by Lord Orford in 1776. Other clubs were founded in the next fifty years, but the boom in coursing only came in the mid 19th century after the Altcar Club, founded in 1825, inaugurated the Waterloo Cup. This event quickly became and remains the premier coursing event. In 1856 there were 382 coursing clubs in Great Britain, and coursing flourished until the *Ground Game Act* of 1881 was passed. This Act enabled occupiers of the land to kill hare and eat it without fear of prosecution. The number of hares in England rapidly diminished and there was a gradual reduction in the number of coursing clubs; by 1892 the number had dropped by two-thirds to 137.[1]

At the height of its popularity coursing became an extremely competitive sport, but differences of opinion arose about the way it should be conducted. Accordingly in 1858 the National Coursing Club was founded as the representative, rule-making and adjudicative body for coursing.[2] It holds this position today, and all competitive coursing under rules follows the rules of the NCC, although some ad hoc and private coursing continues without reference to the NCC.

Since 1945 there has been a continuous decline in coursing. In 1971 there were 22 clubs, dropping to 20 in 1978, and their net membership is around 800 people. Most of these clubs have one or two meetings a year, usually of one day, but the three largest have three-day meetings, so there are between 80 to 90 coursing days a year. Attendance ranges from a dozen at a small meeting to over 1,000 at the Waterloo Cup at Altcar.[3] The coursing fraternity estimates that they kill approximately 600 hares a year or around 25 per cent of those coursed. This is only a fraction of the hares killed in organised shoots.[4]

The social range of coursing enthusiasts is considerable and there is a heterogeneous range of occupations represented among members of coursing clubs.[5] Farmers and landowners predominate, however, making up over 25 per cent of the membership. Those with a rural background make up another 40 per cent of the membership.

1 Stable and Stuttard, *Coursing*, p. 11. Information in the next paragraphs comes from Stable and Stuttard, the NCC and interviews.

2 Stable and Stuttard, *Coursing*, p. 27.

3 C. Freud MP, formerly a sporting journalist, stated that the Waterloo Cup was attended by 38,000 people in 1936 but only 180 in 1973. *Hansard* (Commons), 1975, vol. 893, col. 868.

4 See R. Page, *The Hunter and the Hunted*, Davis-Poynter, London, 1977, p. 65. Page attended part of a three-day hare shoot in East Anglia where the tally was 1,622 hares.

5 For a list of professions and jobs represented by members of three clubs, see Stable and Stuttard, *Coursing*, p. 16. The validity of this list has been questioned by W. Price MP, who doubts whether coursing is really 'the sport of the working man'. See *Hansard* (Commons), 1972, vol. 830. col. 917.

This low key and informal attachment to coursing makes the support vulnerable to outside attack. In recognition of this fact the Coursing Supporters Club was founded in 1974 with the purpose of defeating attempts to abolish coursing. Within a year it had 1,000 members and, in early 1978, it had over 5,000 members. While not many people actually go coursing, a much greater number of people are keen for it to survive.

Otter

Otter hunting has existed alongside other forms of hunting for hundreds of years. It was listed as a beast of the chase in the Middle Ages and mentioned by Sir Thomas Cockaine in 1581.[1] Although remaining popular in Wales and the West Country during the 19th century otter hunting declined as fox hunting developed. Some fox hunters and fishermen were unsympathetic to the sport; indeed, Nimrod in 1826, likened it to 'a superior duckhunt'.[2] The modern techniques of otter hunting are simple: first the trained hounds follow the 'drag' or scent left by the otter, and then having found it, hunt it along the water's edge. When the otter tires or fails to elude the hounds by swimming under water, it may seek to escape down a drain or return to its holt. If it fails to find shelter it may take to dry land where hounds can easily catch and kill it.[3]

In the 20th century otter hunting declined. There were 19 otter hound packs in 1906, 19 in 1932, and 11 in 1972, to which can be added 5 hunts which remained as organised hunts but did no hunting. In the 1960s the sharp decline in the number of otters became a cause for concern for otter hunters and conservationists alike. Otter hunts amalgamated or ceased operations and tended to avoid killing otters in areas where numbers were low. In both 1975 and 1976 only 5 otters were killed by hunts.[4] In 1977 the ten remaining hunts adopted the policy of killing an otter only when asked to do so by the owner of the fishing rights.[5]

1 BFSS publicity material states that otter hounds were kept to protect the fish in medieval ponds. See *This is Otterhunting*, BFSS (n.d. probably 1975).

2 Longrigg, *Foxhunting*, p. 113.

3 The trident has not been used to kill otters since 1860. L. Pine, *The History of Hunting*, LACS, London, 1973, p. 111.

4 Eastern Counties Otterhounds, in contrast, killed 330 otters in the 1904–5 season.

5 Press Statement by BFSS on 1 April 1977. For full text see BFSS *Year Book*, 1977, p.30.

During the 1960s and early 1970s research was done on behalf of the Mammal Society, the Fauna Preservation Society and the Nature Conservancy Council which confirmed that the number of otters in England had dropped sharply.[1] The research did not show that the otter was in danger of extinction; nevertheless further action was recommended to protect it. The government decided in late 1977 to issue an order under the *Conservation of Wild Creatures and Wild Plants Act* 1975. This order protected the otter everywhere in England and Wales, not just in areas where it was scarce.

Despite the cessation of otter hunting, the major hunts have remained, theoretically, in existence and four hunts changed to hunting the predatory coypu and wild mink of East Anglia. In 1978 the Mink and Coypu Hunting Association was formed to coordinate and oversee the activities of mink and coypu hunters. The organisation is recognised by and affiliated to the British Field Sports Society. It has 8 member hunts although there were, in 1982, 12 packs of mink hounds.[2]

The expansion of the field

The social composition of the hunting field underwent a number of significant changes in the 19th century. It had been an almost exclusively rural sport until the early part of the century, but about that time rich city people began to acquire land and subsequently to take up hunting. Many of them remained city dwellers and brought their urban middle-class manners and values to the hunting field.

The mixture of subscribers and followers was different in each hunt. The more fashionable packs were supported by landowners, the social élite, and by others, including politicians and railway magnates, whose primary source of wealth was not the land over which they hunted. The less fashionable had a higher percentage of farmers, tradesmen and professional people such as doctors and parsons, all of whom behaved with suitable deference to the élite. Suburban hunts, which began as subscription packs, mainly in the London area, were dependent on their supporters in trade and were often objects of derision by the smart set. However, their influence on the development of hunting has been slight since the richer or more fanatical follower has long been able to travel to more fashionable hunts in less built-up areas. The acceptance by the hunting fraternity of these suburban hunts and their survival to this day has nevertheless encouraged the pervasive belief that hunting

1 Otter hunts sent annual reports on the location and estimated numbers of otters to the Mammal Society throughout the 1970s.

2 *The Field*, 23–9 June 1982.

is not an essentially rural sport despite the fact that over 95 per cent of today's Masters are of rural origins.

The social range of people who actually hunted in the 19th century was rather narrow but, even so, those hunting genuinely felt themselves to be more equal in the hunting field than elsewhere. Certainly an ability to gallop hard and jump well gave status. Nevertheless, the separate classes of landlord, tenant-farmer and tradesman tended to hunt in different packs and, when they hunted together, neither side forgot the nature of the relationship, which quickly reasserted itself off the hunting field. Even hunt activities were not generally integrated, for farmers were rarely invited to hunt balls or allowed to be members of the hunt club.[1] Indeed 'if the farming men now and then mix with the landowners in their field sports, it is upon a footing of understood inferiority . . . the difference in manners of the two classes does not admit of anything like social and family intercourse'.[1]

The coming of railways in mid-century added to the rising popularity of hunting. At first the railways were feared and resisted by hunting people, but in fact they helped to open up hunting to a wider membership. Railway lines did not, unlike canals, act as a barrier and the noise and smell did not put off horses or hounds. The railways enabled the hounds and horses to go to distant meets by train and similarly enabled would-be supporters to come from the city to hunt. The railway boom coincided with a period of agricultural prosperity and, during this period, 1850–80, hunting was also enriched through the desire of rich railway developers (or their sons) to acquire social prestige – and what better way to do this than by buying an estate and becoming an MFH?

The social make-up of the hunting field has not altered radically since the mid 19th century except in relation to the number of clergymen and women in the field. In the first case, as hunting became more popular and expensive, the number of hunting parsons gradually declined. The spread of education furthered the rise of evangelism which, in its turn, created a wave of protest against hunting parsons. In 1868 Trollope stated: 'There is a strong feeling against a clergyman who hunts', and added later: 'Their number and wholesome influence on the hunting field is rapidly diminishing'.[2] However, only in 1931 did the Rev. E. Milne give up his long tenure (31 years) as Master of the Cattistock. Since the Second World War hunting parsons have been rare. Indeed their presence has inevitably produced adverse comments

1 From W. Johnston, *England as it is*, 1851, quoted in W. Reader, *Victorian England*, Batsford, London, 1964, p. 46.

2 Longrigg, *Foxhunting*, p. 149.

from the anti-hunting community.[1] The church today is firmly against hunting and there are five Bishops or Archbishops among the Patrons of the LACS – the BFSS can claim only one ordained Honorary Local Secretary.

Before 1850, only the wives and daughters of aristocrats or land-owning Masters were acceptable in the hunting field. Gradually the numbers of women in the hunting field increased; the aristocrats were joined by the wives and daughters of farmers. Women made up perhaps 10 per cent of the mounted followers in Leicester in the 1890s,[2] but their full emancipation in the hunting field did not occur until the First World War when a number of women became Masters of hounds and were successful at it. Women have become increasingly involved in hunting since then. In the 1977–8 season there were 69 female MFHs and 77 in the 1981–2 season. Women now constitute a majority of subscribers and followers in 17 per cent of fox hunts, and they make up at least a third of subscribers and followers in the majority of hunts. Since many of them take their daughters hunting they are even more important as regular mounted followers; in 12 per cent of hunts, they make up over 70 per cent of the followers.

Professional people play a small but vital part in the hunting community. For over half of the packs surveyed professionals make up less than 10 per cent of subscribers and regular mounted followers, although for 7 per cent of packs they make up over 50 per cent of subscribers. Tradesmen are less significant, being under 10 per cent of subscribers and followers for around 70 per cent of hunts and in the majority in none. Nevertheless the exclusiveness of hunts has diminished and many hunts have tried to make 'hairdressers, garage proprietors, that kind of person' feel more welcome.[3]

The army has always been closely involved with the hunting world and, since Britain was mainly at peace in the 19th century, the officer corps developed its leisure activities rather than its military skills. Young cavalrymen and army officers of good family treated hunting as a social duty. They regarded 'hunting as a peacetime training for their traditional avocation: war on horseback'.[4] The very moderate success of the cavalry in the Boer War did not dent the comfortable acceptance of this relationship. Indeed, hunting taught reckless riding and the last thing it encouraged was thought and discipline. However, the relation-

1 The HSA demonstrated against two hunting clerics in 1977 and publicise the activities of all hunting parsons.

2 D.C. Itzkowitz, *Peculiar Privilege*, Harvester Press, Brighton, 1977, p. 56.

3 *The Observer*, 31 Oct. 1965.

4 Carr, *Fox Hunting*, p. 50.

ship was strengthened in the late 19th century by the growth of the county yeomanry regiments which were formed after the Crimean War. They needed good horsemen and recruited most of their officers and men from the hunting field. The mutually reinforcing connection between hunting and the martial arts did not end until the First World War when the development of more powerful weapons and armoured vehicles rendered cavalry obsolete. After the war an officer's ability to ride, while socially useful, was of no military significance.

Between the world wars the connection between hunting and the army was maintained; it was relatively easy for a young officer to get three months leave during the winter in order to hunt with army horses.[1] When serving overseas, in India and Kenya for example, hunting with imported packs was a popular form of recreation for British officers. In 1937 when militarism was in the air the *Daily Telegraph* stated 'Hunting will remain an excellent part of the training of a field officer'.[2] *The Times*, more concerned with appeasement, felt that 'hunting, most notably among human pursuits, allows the characteristic virtues of the fighting man to be exercised in peace and fellowship'.[3]

Hunting fields increased in the 1960s and 1970s and remain large with over 50,000 people hunting at least once during the season. A third of hunts have over 100 horses out at the major meets and a handful have over 200; only 10 per cent have under 50. On typical Saturdays over half the hunts have between 50–100 horses out.

Among people who hunt are some whose names or professions are part of the public domain and whose political or social influence has an impact on the public. Among them are a small group of Conservative MPs who obviously carry a disproportionate weight whenever hunting legislation is being debated. Among Conservative MPs the most important for huntingmen is Marcus Kimball, Chairman of the BFSS and an MFH from 1951–8. His predecessor as Chairman of the BFSS was Lord Margadale, formerly John Morrison, Chairman of the 1922 Committee (from 1955–64) and an MFH from 1932–66.[4] The last Labour MP who hunted regularly was Reginald Paget an eccentric squire from Northamptonshire, who was an MP from 1945 to 1974 and

1 Mr Lane Fox, discussing his army career between the wars on BBC2 programme *Living on the Land*, 23 May 1978. It was also revealed in 1976 that members of the Guards Riding Club used army horses, vehicles and stabling to hunt with Shire packs. See *Cruel Sports*, 42, Oct. 1976.

2 Quoted in NSACS *Bulletin*, 37, Dec. 1939, p. 2.

3 *The Times*, 4 Nov. 1937, leading article.

4 They are at the end, perhaps, of a long tradition. Beckford, Meynell, Osbaldeston and Mytton were MPs as well as MFHs; this was a common combination throughout the 19th century.

Master of the prestigious Pytchley from 1968–71. The Labour MP for Blyth in 1978 hunted occasionally and was soon coopted on to the Main Committee of the BFSS. He remains in 1982, an MP, a BFSS Committee member and its only active Labour supporter in Parliament. Other well-known hunting supporters, active in the hunting lobby, are the 10th Duke of Beaufort, Master of the Queen's Horse for over 40 years and an MFH for 55 years, Lord Denham, the Conservative Chief Whip in the Lords, and Sir Bernard Waley-Cohen, a city financier who was the Lord Mayor of London 1960–1 and has been Chairman of the Devon and Somerset Staghounds since 1953.

Members of the Royal Family have ceased to be regular and almost automatic members of the hunting field and have become hostages to their social position. All of the monarchs of this century have hunted when heirs to the throne, but neither King George VI nor Queen Elizabeth has hunted after their accession. Prince Charles and Princess Anne are the most regular hunting members of the Royal family. Their keenness is shared by members of the related equestrian world who believe that hunting is a way of keeping fit for show jumping and 'eventing'. This argument is weakened by the fact that it is rarely the valuable showjumping horse which hunts, merely the rider.[1] The horse and hunting world overlap to mutual advantage in the media. Dorian Williams and Raymond Brookes-Ward, who was the Public Relations Consultant for the BFSS, are both commentators for televised equestrian events and both are Masters of Foxhounds.

Hunting is accessible to a wider range of social groups than it was 100 years ago. Many packs have a relatively high percentage of urban and middle-class supporters who, if they can afford the uniform, horses and transportation are welcome to hunt with the pack of their choice.[2]

Today there are also many followers who come on foot, motorcycle and car. These supporters raise funds through the hunt supporters clubs and also help to give hunting its democratic image. It cannot be maintained that the man on the horse and the man on foot are in any way equal, but undoubtedly the physical, financial and moral support of the foot-followers is a major asset in the struggle to frustrate the anti-hunters.

Despite the protestations of the hunting community that their supporters are drawn as much from urban as from rural areas, the evidence shows that hunt supporters are overwhelmingly rural. For 60 per cent of hunts, over 70 per cent of their car and foot-followers are of rural origins, and for only 7 per cent of hunts, obviously those near large

1 Nevertheless the view is sincerely held by well-known show jumpers such as David Broome and Harvey Smith. See BFSS *Open Door Programme*, BBC TV, 31 October 1977.

2 A number of fashionable Shire packs are more selective and new members may join only at the invitation of the Master.

cities, are more than 50 per cent of their unmounted followers from urban areas. These figures are estimates by the Masters and, while they are only educated guesses, the essential point that hunt supporters are predominantly rural cannot be doubted. The rural nature of hunt support is emphasised by the assessment of 65 per cent of Masters that fewer than 10 per cent of their mounted followers are city dwellers. Less than 8 per cent of hunts state that the majority of their mounted followers are city dwellers. These all come from hunts which adjoin metropolitan areas. Ten hunts have a border with London, but no more than five of these draw more than 50 per cent of their mounted supporters from the city.

Since hunting requires money and leisure, the relative youth of the 'typical' mounted follower is perhaps surprising. A half of all hunts state that between 30 per cent and 50 per cent of their mounted followers are under 30; although less than 10 per cent claim a majority of youthful followers. More than half of the hunts claim that at least 50 per cent of their mounted followers are between 30 and 60 years of age; only 20 per cent of hunts suggest that more than 10 per cent of their followers are 60 or over. On weekdays the field would probably consist mainly of retired people and school girls on holiday, so that an 'average' age would give a false impression.

The changing status and rising costs of Masterships

In the early 19th century Masters were a law unto themselves; they ran the hunt as they wished and were answerable to no one. Hard riders were usually unconcerned about closing gates or protecting crops and many Masters were blind to the social effects of their passion for hunting. Some were eccentric, some brutal and some drunk. One famous master, Squire Osbaldeston 1787–1866, was a rich landowner and brilliant Master of Foxhounds, but he ruined himself by gambling and ended as a social outcast because of his connections with crooked racing and gambling.[1] John Mytton (1796–1834) was a brave and brilliant horseman but was permanently drunk. He retired bankrupt to France and almost burnt himself to death while trying to cure a fit of hiccups. He died shortly afterwards, of drink, in a debtors' prison.[2]

Many Masters were, of course, sober and serious men. Some were traditional aristocrats who continued and still continue to hunt what were essentially family packs; others were squires or sons of land-

1 Carr, *Fox Hunting*, pp. 92–3, and Burrows, *Gentleman Charles*, pp. 68–70.

2 Nimrod, *Memoirs of the Life of John Mytton Esq.*, 1837, reprinted by Methuen, London, in 1903 and 1915.

owners who hunted in a less grand style.[1] Some Masters were of non-rural origins; they were people who had made money in trade and industry and who enjoyed the prestige attached to hunting in the shires. They might, if rich, take over a large and important hunt, or they might, like Mr Jorrocks,[2] take over a hunt whose members were farmers and the urban nouveau riche rather than the rural élite. There were also a few hunts dominated and even run by farmers, although these were rare and confined to Yorkshire and the West Country. Even so, their Masters were usually landowners rather than tenant farmers. Their lack of social significance tended to keep their hunting fields small.

As hunting became more expensive few landowners willingly paid to provide sport not just for fellow gentlemen and farmers but also for outsiders. The cost of running a hunt has varied enormously. Trencher-fed packs in the early 19th century could be maintained very cheaply, but even a small pack in kennels would have cost at least £500–£600 per annum. It is probable that in the 1830s a shire pack, such as the Meynell or the Atherstone, hunting 4 days a week during the season would cost between £4,000 and £6,000 a year. This is an estimate of the real costs rather than just the figures which appear in the accounts.[3]

In the 1977–8 season 193 packs of foxhounds were recognised by the MFHA. Their Masters were generally experienced men; only 10 per cent had hunted for less than 15 years and 20 per cent had hunted for over 50 years.[4] Masterships, while conferring prestige,[5] are still expensive, for inflation has meant that guarantees seldom keep up with real expenses. In 1974, two-fifths of guarantees were between £2,000 and £6,000 with another 10 per cent between £12,000 and £15,000. A few hunts incurred even greater expenses but were subsidised by farmers who gave hay and grain and sent 'flesh', in the form of dead sheep and cattle, to the kennels. In 1974, a third of all hunts estimated that this free feed and flesh was worth over £1,000 a season. Costs have risen sharply since then. In the 1977–8 season the average cost of running a hunt, including an estimate of the subsidies from farmers and money put in by affluent Masters, worked out between £6,000 and £8,000 for a pack that hunted one day a week. A large four day a week pack

1 Squire Weston of Fielding's *Tom Jones* was an early literary example of this type.

2 R.S. Surtees, *Handley Cross, or Mr Jorrocks's Hunt*, E. Arnold, London, 1845.

3 Itzkowitz, *Peculiar Privilege*, p. 79 and Carr, *Fox Hunting*, p. 116. This was half the annual income of the average peer.

4 This and much subsequent information is from questionnaires.

5 They confer less prestige than they did in 1885 when it was stated that 'an MFH is like a Member of Parliament, in a public position'. Itzkowitz, *Peculiar Privilege*, p. 173. Quoting a newspaper report.

would therefore cost in the region of £30,000.[1] Even a small West Country farmers' pack hunting two days a week cost around £12,000, although only half of this would be collected by the hunt as a guaranteed income for the Master.[2]

In the period between 1978 and 1982 costs have continued to rise. Many hunts have found paying their way difficult although the continuing activities of hunt supporters clubs have ensured the solvency of most hunts. The pressure of inflation which caused the Retail Price Index to rise 64 per cent between 1978 and 1982 gave hunts a continuing headache; labour and fuel costs rose dramatically and hunts sought to reduce staff whenever possible. By 1982, fashionable four day a week packs were costing £50,000 a year to run; smaller farmers' packs needed to raise at least £15,000 to stay in operation. Nevertheless, one hundred and ninety four hunts were recognised by the MFHA in 1982, one more than in 1978.

Most Masters come from hunting families. In 1978, 73 per cent had parents who hunted, and over 20 per cent had a parent who was an MFH. The expense and the organisational pressures of being Master encourage a tendency towards joint Masterships of fairly short duration. Sixty-eight per cent of Masterships are joint; 30 per cent have been in office for four years or less and 65 per cent for ten years or less. Nevertheless, in 1982, five stalwarts had been Masters for forty years or more!

One method of finding adequate funds which began in the 1850s and became increasingly common as the century wore on has been to charge the followers for the privilege of hunting. Subscriptions for the season, or a daily 'cap' have changed the face of hunting. No longer can Masters hunt when and where they choose, nor can they sell the pack when they get bored with the country or when foxes are in short supply, for packs have tended to become the property of the Committee rather than of the Master. For the first time hunting has had to be organised for the enjoyment of the subscribers. If these are mostly young bucks, a fast hunt has to be provided; if they are farmers, foxes have to be killed even if long hours are spent digging them out. Gradually it has become the norm for packs to be controlled by committees and financed by subscriptions, although Masters have never lost their power over hound breeding and the actual procedures of hunting; nor have Masters ever been relieved of the necessity to put in some of their own money to

1 Stag hunting is even more expensive partly because they have a longer season. The guarantee for the Masters of the Devon and Somerset Staghounds in the 1977–8 season was over £30,000 to hunt 3 days a week. This rose to £55,000 in the 1982 season.

2 This is corroborated by comparing the 1977 questionnaires with those issued in 1974. Fell packs which hunt on foot cost less; in the region of £5,000 a season for a pack that hunts 2 days a week.

ensure good sport. Indeed, many packs have been saved by the infusion of money and enthusiasm by outsiders wishing to establish themselves as gentlemen. Although certain families maintain close links with formerly private packs,[1] all need and accept subscriptions today which can be over £200 to hunt no more than one day a week during the season.[2]

Some of the money from subscriptions goes to pay for the kennelling of hounds and the purchase of horses, but much of it goes on labour and other costs. Labour costs are considerable; hunt staff are paid on the same scale as agricultural workers whose wages, while still relatively low, have increased sharply in the last decade.[3] Most hunts (55 per cent) employ between two and four people and stable between four and seven horses. The larger and more expensive establishments (10 per cent of the total), employ seven or more people and keep twelve or more horses for the Master and his staff.

Wire can be a major expense if the hunt expects to cross fields where farmers have used wire to control their livestock. Hunts have needed to allocate a special wire fund in order to pay the farmer to remove the wire from round his fields at the beginning and end of the season.

As the proportion of arable farming land has increased fewer hunts have needed to allocate a special wire fund. However, 10 per cent of hunts still have a wire fund in excess of £2,000, and past figures indicate the extent of the payments. The Pytchley estimate the cost of wire at over £3,000 in 1977,[4] and the Heythrop spent over £4,000 on wire in 1974.[5]

A few hunts still employ a full-time man to attend to the wire. He is aided by dozens of volunteer helpers at the beginning and end of the season. One man, use of a Land Rover and materials (some of which may be donated) inevitably involve a figure of between £3,000 and £4,000 per year.

Hunts also incur expenses for damages and poultry losses. Much of the damage done to fences and gate posts is mended by hunt staff, although some hunts make a small payment for damage or poultry losses out of general funds. A third of hunts made no payments for

1 The current Duke of Beaufort, like all his ancestors, hunts the Beaufort and Mr Berkeley hunts the Berkeley.

2 See *Baily's*, 1981–2 *passim*.

3 Basic agricultural wages were around £50 per week in 1978 and £70 in 1982. Hunt staff, particularly the kennel huntsman, can effectively double this with his 'perks'. These include free uniforms, free accommodation and the money from the sale of hides and skins from the 'flesh' used to feed the hounds.

4 Conversation with one of the Joint Masters.

5 Interview with the Master, Capt. R. Wallace.

damages in 1977, but 10 per cent of the rest said they paid out over £100 a year.[1] A conscientious Master and careful fields can keep damage costs down, but large numbers of mounted followers mean that some damage is inevitable.

The acquiescence of farmers in hunting

Convention and even the law seemed to be on the side of the fox hunter, for in 1788 a court stated that chasing a fox on to another person's land was acceptable if this was necessary to catch the fox. However, in 1809 Lord Essex and his half-brother, the Hon. William Capel, had a feud which came to a head when Capel smashed his way through locked gates in pursuit of his fox, and his field, consisting mostly of Londoners, followed. Essex sued Capel for trespass and the case hung on whether the 'governing motive' of the hunt was to act 'as vermin killers or as sports men'.[2] Gamekeepers were produced who testified that trapping and shooting were better ways to reduce foxes, and the defence did not deny that sport was the main reason for hunting nor that the hunt was keen to preserve enough foxes to make hunting worthwhile. The case went against the hunt, and was followed by seven similar suits which established the right of all landowners to warn off hunts, and to sue them and their followers for trespass and for damages if the warnings were ignored. These rights were rarely exercised and hunting people in practice continued to be cavalier in their treatment of other people's property. Another case in 1878 was needed to remind the hunting community of the error of their supposition that 'fox hunting may be exercised over the land of any person without his consent'.[3]

By the mid 19th century, when the social acceptance of fox hunting was complete, farmers who had for centuries killed bothersome foxes began to preserve them for the hunt. During the agricultural boom more and more farmers became regular followers, and gradually the commission of vulpicide was regarded as a heinous social crime and non-hunting farmers were threatened with eviction by landlords if it was suspected that they killed foxes. No one apparently doubted the landlord's right and even duty to do this.[4]

1 From questionnaires.

2 For a discussion of Essex v. Capel, see Bovill, *English Country Life*, pp. 233–40.

3 Bovill, *English Country Life*, p. 229.

4 Itzkowitz, *Peculiar Privilege*, pp. 116–17. Even in the 1980s some landlords keep the sporting rights and insist that their tenants allow hunting over their land.

The agricultural depression of the late 19th century radically affected the relationship between farmers and hunting. Farmers had less spare time and money and, in many cases, ceased to hunt; protecting their stock and growing crops became more important to them than encouraging the hunt. Technical developments such as steam ploughs and chemical fertilisers ruined scent and further estranged farmers from hunting people. Most important of all was the spread of wire. First introduced in mid-century it had not spread because a combination of goodwill, pressure from landlords and rural prosperity had encouraged farmers to grow hedges. However it took 20 years for a newly planted hedge to become an effective barrier for keeping in sheep and cattle, whereas wire could be put up with a few stout rails in a matter of hours. Wire was frequently the cause of bad falls and, when zealous huntsmen took to cutting it down, it became the cause of major antagonism between farmers and the hunt. During the depression landlords could no longer effectively stop farmers from erecting wire fences since farmers could afford no alternative. Barbed wire appeared in England in 1882; it was cheap and effective and even more dangerous to the hunt than ordinary wire fencing.

The mainstay of hunting in the 20th century has undoubtedly been the farmer, particularly the substantial owner-occupier who has enjoyed a rising standard of living since the Second World War. For over 20 per cent of hunts farmers make up between 31 per cent and 50 per cent of subscribers and regular mounted followers, and for 12 per cent of hunts they make up over 51 per cent. Small farmers are less important: for 40 per cent of hunts they make up only 10 per cent of subscribers, and for a third they are less than 10 per cent of regular mounted followers. The difference between the percentage who subscribe and the percentage of those who follow is accounted for by the fact that hunts do not necessarily expect farmers who hunt to pay a cash subscription. Some form of payment in kind is expected, either by giving grain or flesh to the hunt, or by rearing lambs for sale. Similarly, hunt animals, hound puppies or horses, may be cared for together with the farmers' own animals on the farms where the conditions and costs of keeping them are relatively easy and inexpensive.

Horses, which once provided essential transportation and muscle power, have remained in significant numbers on farms at least partly because the costs involved in buying and caring for a horse can be claimed from the farm as business expenses. There are, therefore, generally sufficient numbers of horses available on the farm to make hunting a practical proposition, not only for the farmer himself, but for any member of his family who wishes to hunt. A person without land who owns a horse purely for sporting purposes must expect to pay £1,500–£2,000 for a good hunter, and £40 a week to keep it stabled and fed.

Farmers have not only become important as breeders and users of horses, they have also become increasingly important economically as the number of landlords has declined. Many of them own capital intensive farms, and have a life-style which has enabled them to accept influential positions in rural society. Their professionalism and relative affluence in the past generation has removed both the old deferential relationship with the remaining squires and the barriers which kept farmers from prominence in the hunting community. Their ability to afford the sport and their pattern of life which permits it are two of the critical factors which have enabled hunting to survive.

Appendix 3.1

In March 1983 The Standing Conference on Countryside Sports comprising 51 mainly pro-hunting organisations issued a report entitled *Countryside Sports: Their Economic Significance*. It clearly demonstrated the close economic relationship between hunting and the rural community. It suggested (p.40) that £1 billion are spent annually on field sports in Britain. It also suggested that '214,000 people hunted with hounds' (p.40). However, this figure is made up of those who ride to hounds (about 50,000) *and* those who follow on foot or by car. This is not quite the same as 'hunting with hounds'.

PART II

PRESSURE GROUPS

4 The beginning of organised support for animal welfare: the RSPCA

The early years

In the early 19th century those who campaigned on behalf of animals were also campaigners for the rights of people. Evangelical and utilitarian principles led them to wish to end slavery and to emancipate Catholics, as well as to reduce the effects of the game laws. But like their spiritual descendants in the 20th century, their causes were not generally popular ones, for their struggle was contrary to the prevailing morality of the time.[1]

The first society to extend its interests to animals was The Society for the Suppression of Vice which campaigned against baiting on the grounds that it corrupted those who indulged in it. In 1808 The Society for Preventing Wanton Cruelty to Brute Animals was formed in Liverpool. It submitted one report that warned against 'intemperance in benevolence' and 'precipitancy of judgement' and sank virtually without trace.[2]

The first law giving some protection to animals was passed in 1822; however the protection it offered was limited, nor was it easy to police. For these reasons, in 1824, a group of a dozen people formed the Society for the Prevention of Cruelty to Animals. Among the founders

1 The success of the anti-slave trade movement in 1807 was the first major humanitarian measure which infringed property rights.

2 See E.S. Turner, *All Heaven in a Rage*, M. Joseph, London, 1964, pp. 116–18.

were Richard Martin, William Wilberforce and the Rev. Arthur Broome who, as its first secretary, kept it going through the first difficult and impecunious years and was even imprisoned for debt on its behalf in 1826.[1] Its earliest aims were to generate publicity for the cause of animals and to try to enforce and extend the 1822 Act.

By 1834 the Society had begun to achieve respectability. The Earl of Carnavon became its first president and was succeeded by a long line of Earls, Dukes and Heirs to the throne. In 1835, Princess Victoria became a Patron and in 1840, when Queen, she gave it a Royal warrant. The Society was by then known, respected and financially secure. It was not, however, particularly at peace with itself. Arthur Broome resigned in 1828 because of some internal disharmony, and in 1832 the Society's next Secretary, Lewis Gompertz, resigned because of 'religious differences' and started his own short-lived organisation.[2]

For the first 50 years of its existence the RSPCA concentrated on alleviating the suffering of horses, farm animals and domestic animals. In order to do this it established a corps of mobile inspectors and developed local branches which were and still are semi-autonomous, making future centre-branch conflicts inevitable.

Educational programmes soon became a major part of the RSPCA's activities. A junior movement was founded later in the century, and essay-writing competitions were held annually. As the Society became more established it set up animal hospitals and clinics and started a Veterinary section to do research, to help with the clinics, and to give advice on prosecutions with which the legal department became involved.

While its educational programmes undoubtedly helped to bring gradual changes in the general attitudes towards animals, progress on the legislative front was slow. However, the animal welfare movement continued to grow. In 1889, with RSPCA backing, the Royal Society for the Protection of Birds was formed. Numerous other specialist societies were established to protect dogs or horses, to protest about vivisection and to vocalise religious concern about the mistreatment of animals.

The domination of the RSPCA by its pro-hunting members is threatened

While the animal welfare movement slowly gained support and respect-

1 See Turner, *All Heaven*, p.142.

2 See E. Fairholm and W. Pain, *A Century of Work for Animals*, J. Murray, London, 1924, p. 68.

ability in the 19th century, hunting remained unscathed. The reason was obvious; the very people who gave the RSPCA its respectability and support were the affluent leisured class who were themselves supporters of fox hunting. Richard Martin hunted on his Irish estate; the 7th Duke of Beaufort, who was an active supporter both inside and outside parliament, was an MFH. The magistrates who reprimanded and fined illegal cock-fighters or cruel cab-drivers had to hurry home from the hunting field in order to do so.[1]

By the late 1880s the strains in the hunting world were duplicated within the membership of the RSPCA. Support for the Society from both the sportsmen who professed to love animals and abhor cruelty, and from the radical-intellectual community which felt that hunting was as abominable as cruelty to dogs or horses made conflict inevitable.

As early as 1891, the Rev. J. Stratton wrote; 'What has become of the Society for the Prevention of Cruelty to Animals that it seems never to have made a persistent stand against barbarity in high places?'[2] In 1908, a motion at the AGM of the RSPCA directed that a committee be formed to draft and present to parliament a bill to abolish otter hunting.[3] The motion was passed with only two dissentients but no steps of any kind were taken.

Throughout this century the RSPCA has been struggling to resolve the dilemma caused by the hunting activities of many of its leading members. It has continued to work most effectively at expanding and enforcing the legislation which protects tame, captive and domestic animals, but has failed to grasp the logical nettle of expanding this legislation to include wild and hunted animals. Even now a fox, if tame, is protected when in its owner's garden, but unprotected when over the fence in a farmer's field.[4]

After the 1914–18 war the link between royalty and the Society, which had been continuous from 1840 onwards, was strengthened when the Prince of Wales, a keen fox hunter and shooter, became Patron and later President of the Society. This did not stifle the complaints of the anti-hunting rank and file, many of whom also joined the League for the Prohibition of Cruel Sports (LPCS) when it started in 1924 in order to fight more effectively against hunting. In 1929, a poll of RSPCA members voted by 3,125 votes to 1,142 in favour of the abolition of wild deer hunting with hounds,[5] and in 1939 there was a

1 For an example of judicial hypocrisy, see Turner, *All Heaven*, pp. 228–9.

2 J. Stratton, *Royal Sports*, William Reeves, London, 1891, p. 1.

3 *Cruel Sports*, 1927, p. 29. A report by the Hon. Stephen Coleridge, Second President of the LPCS.

4 This is one of the anomalies caused by the 1911 *Protection of Animals Act*, the main consolidating Act during the 20th century. For details see Chapter 11.

5 *Manchester Guardian*, 19 April 1929.

vote of 2,657 to 323 in favour of taking action to abolish coursing in all its forms.[1] However the Society's leadership, while noting these decisions, took no action and promoted no anti-hunting bills.

In 1928, the Manchester Branch unanimously agreed to take steps to put a stop to blood sports, while in the same year a letter from the General Secretary of the RSPCA was read out at an anti-hunting meeting in Minehead (Somerset) which said, *inter alia*, that the RSPCA had no intention of working for the abolition of stag, fox or any other kind of hunting.[2] A decade later, the RSPCA successfully prosecuted the Master of the Zetland Hunt for tying up a fox after digging it out and, it then being a captive animal, throwing it to the hounds. In the same year, however, the Harrogate Branch Secretary 'referred with satisfaction to the patronage of Lord Bingley, joint Master of the Bramham Moor Hunt'.[3] In 1926, the Council refused a bequest of £10,000 because the bequest was made on the condition that the Society actively oppose blood sports and vivisection, and this the Society was unwilling to do.[4] In 1931, a local RSPCA committee member was asked to resign from the committee because her anti-hunting attitude upset hunting members.[5] The central organisation made no attempt to intervene on her behalf.

The RSPCA was active on behalf of animals during the war[6] but did not become involved with questions of hunting. However, in 1949 the hunting issue had emerged again. In this year, a Private Members' bill which attempted to abolish all forms of hunting except fox hunting was debated. It was, to many peoples' surprise, defeated, and the Home Secretary of the time, C. Ede, appointed a committee under the chairmanship of J. Scott Henderson KC to investigate the issue of cruelty to wild and hunted animals. Its report, in 1951, opposed the abolition of hunting or coursing.[7]

Its decision to do so was, at least in part, influenced by the leadership of the RSPCA for the report stated: 'It is significant that the RSPCA consider that the cruelty involved in shooting foxes is such as to make it an unsatisfactory substitute for hunting, and that they

1 A. Moss, *Valiant Crusade*, Cassell, London, 1971, p. 145.

2 *Cruel Sports*, 1928, pp. 93 and 109.

3 *Cruel Sports*, 1938, p. 36.

4 *Cruel Sports*, 1927, p. 17.

5 *Manchester Guardian*, 29 June 1931.

6 The Society established homes for Army horses and rescued animals during the blitz.

7 *Report of the Committee on Cruelty to Wild Animals*, HMSO, London, 1951, Cmd 8266, afterwards called the Scott Henderson Report.

would therefore prefer hunting to continue if its abolition were likely to lead to an increase in the amount of shooting'.[1] Further, RSPCA members 'regard fox hunting as an effective and traditional method of control, and they also feel that, if hunting were to be abolished, greater cruelty would be caused to foxes'.[2]

Following the Scott Henderson Report the RSPCA issued its own policy statement on hunting which, after minor amendments, was adopted at the 1958 AGM of the Society.[3] It began: 'The RSPCA cannot approve of hunting for sport'. The statement was against all forms of hunting except fox hunting because, although alternative methods existed for the control of other animals, the control of foxes by methods other than hunting were more cruel. The RSPCA's position on fox hunting had three main elements: (a) that control was necessary, (b) that hunting was the least cruel method, and (c) that cruelty not ethics or politics was the primary consideration. There were weaknesses in all of these arguments. Firstly, for the last 100 years the rationale behind fox hunting had been that it was a sport, and it was to provide this sport that foxes had been protected, bred and bagged, giving nature no opportunity to provide its own balance. Secondly, it was purely a matter of opinion whether shooting was more or less cruel than hunting; a hunted fox might know that he was being chased, whereas surprise was of the essence if a fox was to be shot. Thirdly, while claiming that cruelty and not politics must be its chief criterion the statement justifies inaction on the political not moral grounds that parliament would reject any anti-hunting measure which the Society promoted.

This statement of official policy clarified the Society's position, but had the undesirable effect of also more clearly establishing the battle lines and ensuring a long period of almost continuous internal dissension.

In 1960 the activists managed to secure an Extraordinary General Meeting to discuss whether the policy should be amended. The Council was strongly opposed to this on the somewhat élitist grounds that the membership was not competent to decide; it felt all policy decisions should be left to experts.[4] This view is still held and occasionally expressed by Council members, as the stance taken by Janet Fookes

1 The *Scott Henderson Report*, para. 162.

2 Ibid., para. 170.

3 See the RSPCA's policy statement published in 1958.

4 *Against Hunting*, (ed.) P. Moore, Gollancz, London, 1965, pp. 67–8.

and others at the 1982 AGM has made clear.[1]

An attempt to get a poll of members on the hunting issue failed. Nevertheless, the LACS, at the request of some RSPCA 'dissidents', conducted a postal poll (which the RSPCA refused to recognise). Seven thousand nine hundred and seventy-five questionnaires were returned showing that members were between 8 and 9 to 1 against coursing and stag and otter hunting, and 5 to 1 against fox hunting.[2]

Further motions in 1960 and 1961 also failed. In 1961, the Council proposed and had adopted a resolution stating that no special meetings could be called to discuss a matter which had been discussed within the three previous years. This was an attempt by the Council to limit further discussion on hunting; in the resulting furore a group of anti-hunting members were expelled from the Society.[3]

These anti-hunting activities inevitably brought a reaction from the pro-hunting community. In the early 1960s pro-hunting members of the RSPCA were encouraged to make their presence felt and to get hunting colleagues to join. The Earl of Halifax, Chairman of the MFHA, said in 1960: 'It is, in our opinion, absolutely essential that we should try to get fox-hunting people to join the RSPCA so that they are in a position to vote'.[4] All Masters of Foxhounds were sent a memorandum urging them to join the RSPCA for the purpose of stopping an anti-fox hunting resolution. At another special meeting in early 1961, the Duke of Beaufort, an RSPCA member and the President of the BFSS, spoke against a motion making the RSPCA totally opposed to fox hunting. In 1962 Dr Rattray, the Vice Chairman and pro-hunting member, declared that 'members of the British Field Sports Society joined the RSPCA and out-voted them', i.e. the anti-hunting group.[5]

The anti-hunting members gained small victories in 1963 and 1964 when anti-stag-hunting and anti-hare-hunting motions were passed at consecutive AGMs of the Society. However, in 1965 an anti-fox hunting motion was passed only after an amendment had rendered it innocuous. Following this debate almost half the audience left causing the *Guardian* to comment: 'it was difficult to avoid coming to the conclusion that for 157 members the day's business had ended with the debate on fox hunting'.[6]

1 See Reports of 1982 AGM, *The Times*, 25 Jan. 1982.

2 See NSACS *Bulletin*, 136, Mar. 1962.

3 Moore, *Against Hunting*, p. 71.

4 *Horse and Hound*, 2 July 1960.

5 Quoted by P. Moore in *Against Hunting*, p. 70.

6 *Guardian*, 10 June 1965.

The victory of the pro-hunting members was not complete, for in 1968 the hunting issue came to the boil again. Masters of Foxhounds were advised by Halifax at the AGM of the MFHA in May 1968 that: 'All of you and all supporters of Field Sports who are members of the RSPCA should attend the meeting (of the RSPCA) and be prepared to vote on what may be an important division of the Society, hoping that a decision may be taken to revise the newly published policy which is so strongly opposed to Field Sports'.[1] During the subsequent AGM of the RSPCA the Annual Report containing the attack on hunting was rejected. A subsequent postal vote, however, showed that the majority of members were firmly anti-hunting. Nevertheless, the Council pushed through a motion allowing it to reject any motion which had been discussed within the last 3 years.

At the AGM of June 1970 Mrs Vera Shephard, a veteran campaigner, was prevented by the Council from informing the meeting of the evidence she had collected on the 'take-over' of the RSPCA leadership by the hunting community.

This so incensed a group of young radical RSPCA members (25 in number) that they immediately formed a Reform Group to bring organised pressure to bear on the Society in order to establish its active opposition to hunting. To do this they had to remove those Council members who were sympathetic to the values of the hunting community and to force the leadership to take note of the wishes of the ordinary members.

A representative leadership is elected

The contest between the Reform Group and the RSPCA establishment was fought with a maximum amount of acrimony and hyperbole. The Reform Group was motivated primarily by the hunting issue, but was also concerned to try and enforce some existing RSPCA rules which it felt were being ignored or misapplied. It was of dubious legality, for instance, for the Council to demand a three-fifths majority vote on some issues (hunting for example) but not on others. The Reform Group was also motivated by a desire to turn the RSPCA into an active pressure group willing to campaign hard on an issue. Its present function as a polite but moribund club for 'do-gooders' offended its own more radical members.[2]

1 *Baily's*, 1968–9, p. 357.

2 A point made in interviews with several members of the Reform Group.

The initial impact of the RSPCA Reform Group was slight. In late 1970 the Chairman of the RSPCA, John Hobhouse, a non-hunting member of a hunting and shooting family, wrote to the house magazine of the hunting world, *Horse and Hound*, suggesting that readers join the RSPCA. His argument was that 'education is better than seclusion', a statement which the Reform Group claimed was a cynical attempt to ensure the continuing strength of the pro-hunting faction. The Reform Group further declared, using Mrs Shephard's evidence, that there had been a plot by hunting people to take over the RSPCA. In reality the existing pro-hunting members had recruited others to help them put up a long and successful rearguard action in order to keep the RSPCA silent on the hunting issue.

In 1971, a meeting between the Reform Group leaders and members of the Council failed to resolve matters and relations became steadily worse. An article in the RSPCA Journal *Today* gave the official view that the Reform Group 'consisted of about 100 dissident members'.[1] It stated that none of the 200 branch secretaries sympathised with the Reform Group, and explained that the reason why Richard Meade, a keen fox hunter, had been co-opted to the 45 strong Council was in order to strengthen connections with the British Horse Society. The article concludes by quoting a letter to Brian Seager, the Chairman of the Reform Group, criticising his 'obsession with plots' and stating that 'further communications from the Reform Group will remain unanswered'.[2] In 1972, a second article in *Today* referred to 'dissidents' who were attempting to 'create confusion and doubt'.[3] At this stage the Council attempted to expel Brian Seager and a group of his supporters from the Society. However, the move failed when Brian Seager obtained 7,500 votes during the voting for membership of the Council in the Spring of 1972 and threatened to call 500 witnesses to speak on his behalf if an expulsion meeting took place. Not surprisingly the RSPCA preferred to avoid the publicity that such a trial would generate. The number of votes which Seager obtained was insufficient for election, even although it was only 150 votes fewer than John Bryant, Seager's predecessor as Chairman of the Reform Group, was elected to the Council. Also elected were five out of the eight people standing for the Council with Reform Group support, and

1 *Today* (The RSPCA Journal), 4, Autumn 1971, p. 10.
Daily Telegraph, 21 Nov. 1972, suggested 500, which is under 1 per cent of the membership. In fact the Group remained at its original 25 but received donations from hundreds of sympathisers.

2 *Today*, 4, 1971, p. 10.

3 *Today*, 7, 1972, p. 2.

Seager himself was elected to the Council two years later.

The prodding of the Reform Group influenced a significant number of the Society's members. It persuaded some that the cause of hunting was lost within the RSPCA, and accordingly many hunting supporters left the Society despite attempts by the Chairman of the MFHA to discourage them from doing so.[1] The Master of the Goatland Hunt said in 1972: 'The more fox hunters we have in the RSPCA the more we have the Society on our side. If more (hunt) members join them we will have the right sort of people in the Society and we won't hear so much from the wrong sort'.[2] Some anti-hunting members were, on the other hand, persuaded that the Council was too powerful and, as a result, candidates supported by the Reform Group did well in the 1972 and subsequent Council elections.

The struggle within the Society clearly related both to the division of opinion over the hunting issue and to the nature and style of the leadership. The debate was vociferous and, in 1973, it was decided to hold an independent Inquiry, under the chairmanship of Charles Sparrow QC, into the affairs of the Society. This was an admission that the split within the Society and within the Council[3] was insoluable. The main part of the Inquiry took place in January 1974, and the Report was published in November 1974.[4] On the key issue of relations between the Council and membership it states: 'Members of the Council must limit themselves to questions of principle and policy' and recommended that there should be a 'reduction in the number of members of the Council' from 44 to 22.[5]

The Report was particularly scathing in its remarks about both the Reform Group as led by Mr Seager and the Chairman of the RSPCA, Mr Hobhouse. It mentioned 'repeated and inexcusable errors of judgement by the Chairman himself' and felt that, since a leader will attract his own supporters, 'it is at least partly his fault that we have not been impressed by the performance of some Council members'.[6] In his evidence to the Inquiry Mr Hobhouse told them that he was irreplace-

1 *Baily's*, 1971–2, p. 361.

2 *Cruel Sports*, Oct. 1972, p. 4.

3 The split within the Council was exacerbated by a libel action taken by one Council member against another.

4 *Report on the Affairs of the Royal Society for the Prevention of Cruelty to Animals*, C. Sparrow QC, Sir D. Barratt, P. Hunt CA, RSPCA, Nov. 1974.

5 Ibid., Recommendations 5 and 4, p. 14.

6 *Sparrow Inquiry Report*, paras 180, 181, 190.

able, and that the panel members were against him.[1] However the Panel in its unanimous feeling 'that the Society must have a new Chairman'[2] said that they had 'been brought to the verge of understanding why some people believe that the Society must be reformed violently'.[3] The vigour of its attack on the Chairman was reinforced by its belief that he had forged a letter of praise about himself purporting to come from the Vice-Chairman of the Society and a number of leading members of the Council. However, such was the nature of RSPCA internal politics that one Council member has said of this incident that the Panel was deceived and that Mr Hobhouse was 'stabbed in the back'.[4] Moreover there was sufficient sympathy for Mr Hobhouse at the Council meeting called to discuss the Inquiry Report on 21 December 1974 that every recommendation except the removal of Mr Hobhouse was accepted. Even this was only achieved reluctantly after Lord Houghton (then Mr D. Houghton) spelt out the folly of inaction, and after Richard Ryder, who proposed the motion to accept all the recommendations, withdrew the recommendation about Hobhouse.

Hobhouse, however, chose to defend himself both against the Report and against the Vice-Chairman F. Burden MP who felt, more strongly than most, that he should go. Following this confrontation many previously neutral Council members who wished to discontinue the drama turned against him.

In 1975 there were elections for the 20 places on the revised Council. Mr Hobhouse did not stand and the result was in essence a repudiation of his leadership. John Bryant and Brian Seager, the first and second Chairmen of the Reform Group, as well as a number of Reform Group sympathisers, were elected and as a group made up about a third of the Council. This was despite the severe criticisms made by the Panel of Inquiry concerning the methods and manners of some of the Reform Group leaders.

Since 1975, the bulk of the reforms suggested by the Inquiry have been put into effect. On most issues the 'middle of the road' Council members sided with the Reform Group team. The Reform Group disbanded itself within a year after the Sparrow Inquiry Report for by then it was already achieving its aims from within. The 'take-over' of the Council by the Reform Group was, like the attempts by the fox-hunting members of the Society to avoid a policy commitment against

1 Ibid., para 195.

2 Ibid., para 201 and Recommendation 1.

3 Ibid., para 200.

4 Interview with a source who wishes to remain anonymous.

hunting, more a result of individual initiative than a conspiracy. Nevertheless it was successful. When the policy statement on hunting came up for a debate at a Council meeting in early 1976, the suggested policy was passed unanimously, without discussion. It was published in June 1976 and read: 'The RSPCA is opposed to any hunting of animals with hounds'. In an explanatory note it said: 'Hunting is taken to include otter hunting, stag hunting, fox hunting and coursing and the hunting of hares and rabbits. The RSPCA is not persuaded that fox hunting is an effective method of control in any circumstances'.[1] The final round in this particular struggle came in June 1977 when Richard Ryder, author of a book against animal experimentation,[2] a campaigner since 1969 against otter hunting and hare coursing, and an early supporter of the Hunt Saboteurs Association, became Chairman of the RSPCA.

In 1978, the RSPCA was officially but not actively against hunting. Its new and younger Council members caused the Society to rethink, debate and publish its priorities in a way which it had never done before. The major campaigns with which the Society became involved were the revival of the concept of animals rights,[3] and the separate issues of cruelty to laboratory animals, the export of live farm animals, the slaughter of seals, and the problem of feral cats. Hunting itself was no longer such an important issue although at the 1978 AGM one of the few statements to arouse any emotion was a demand from a young member (who also belonged to the HSA and LACS) that, since members of the Royal Family hunted, the Queen should be removed as Patron of the Society.

Organisational crises reoccur

At the end of 1979 the hunting issue was quiescent, awaiting the possibility that the radical members of the Society would attempt to make anti-hunting activism a priority for the Society. This was unlikely because the anti-hunting activists, with the RSPCA now officially on their side, could direct their energies towards the media and the political process. Indeed it has become apparent that those sympathetic to hunting made a tactical error in their attempts to defend hunting. If the anti-hunting policy had been quietly adopted in the early 1970s the subsequent publicity generated by the Reform Group and the Sparrow

1 Later published in a booklet *RSPCA Policies on Animal Welfare*, Feb. 1978, p. 4.

2 R. Ryder, *Victims of Science: The Use of Animals in Research*, Davis-Poynter, London, 1975.

3 The RSPCA held a Symposium on 'Animals Rights' in Cambridge during August 1977.

Inquiry would not have occurred, nor would a strongly anti-hunting group led by Ryder, Bryant and Seager have so quickly gained effective control of the Council. In the internal crisis the 'young turks' tested and defeated the 'old guard' and this gave them the confidence to believe that if hunting re-emerged as a key issue their leadership on the matter would be acceptable to the members. The revised organisational structure and the smaller Council were now more efficient tools for mounting campaigns, and the collapse of the pro-hunting group within the Society removed any major internal obstacles.

Intellectually the Society was also more secure. The violence of the debate had made the combatants think out their position with considerable care. This could, in time, produce a different kind of arrogance among the new leadership, but at least the policies and goals of the Society continued to evolve. This flexibility and willingness to discuss new ideas and arguments was a product of the increasing intellectual security of the animal welfare movement as a whole. Arguments against vivisection, for example, were now mounted at a scientific level rather than at an emotional one[1] and four recent books dealing with the moral implications of man's treatment of animals have been written by academic philosophers.[2]

The new intellectual respectability of the RSPCA made it willing and able to join with other animal welfare societies and with politicians in attempting to bring the whole range of animal welfare issues into the political arena. In April 1978, after prodding from Ryder and Clive Hollands (a leading anti-vivisectionist), the RSPCA took a leading role in establishing, under the chairmanship of Lord Houghton of Sowerby, the General Election Co-ordinating Committee for Animal Protection (GECCAP).[3]

Nevertheless having survived the Reform Group crisis and settled back into a more productive routine the RSPCA was not quiet for long. Richard Ryder was Chairman for two years until 1979 and he was followed by Janet Fookes MP and then by Mr A. Hart. None of them were able to defuse the tensions within the Society between the younger radicals and the more conservative members. At every election the balance changed slightly as disagreements over first one and then another issue surfaced. However at no time was any serious attempt

1 Ryder, *Victims of Science*. Ryder is a clinical psychologist.

2 *Animals, Men and Morals*, (eds) S. and R. Godlovitch and J. Harris, Gollancz, London, 1971. Ryder was among the contributors to this book.
P. Singer, *Animal Liberation*, Cape, London, 1976. Singer is a Professor of Philosophy.
Animals in Research, (ed.) D. Sperlinger, Wiley, London, 1981.
S. Clark, *The Moral Status of Animals*, OUP, 1977.

3 See below, Chapter 5.

made to retract the Society's official view on hunting and a *modus vivendi* was found on most issues.

The main problems within the Society, while exacerbated by policy, personality and even political differences, stemmed from the way the Council related to the bureaucracy. This point was raised by the Sparrow Inquiry but despite structural changes the problems did not go away. One strand of the story which was much reported, particularly by the *Daily Mail*, began with the appointment of Mr Hopkins as Executive Director in 1978. Soon allegations of overspending, low staff morale and general mismanagement at the RSPCA headquarters filtered to the Council.

These administrative problems ran parallel with Hopkins' desire to enlarge the cadre of conservative Council members. The Council elections in 1980 when Janet Fookes MP was Chairman changed the complexion of the Council and placed the Radicals once more in a minority position. Debates on serious issues within the Council (as distinct from squabbling) were thus curtailed and the power of the Executive Director was correspondingly increased since he was left relatively unchecked to make wide-ranging decisions.

In 1980, Richard Ryder and Richard Course, two of the leading Radicals on the Council, demanded, with others, that an Inquiry should take place. Ryder was threatened with removal from the Society for passing on to other Council members allegations which he had received and Course was removed from the Society for walking out of the Council chamber with a copy of the internal Inquiry's report.[1] The Inquiry, conducted by the Society's own auditors, and described as 'somewhat elliptical' by a Council member, neither exonerated nor condemned Hopkins. However, further inquiries by the Treasurer and Chairman (a previous Treasurer) found that a degree of financial mismanagement was apparent. This, combined with a letter by a senior staff member to each member of the Council claiming that all the accusations about Hopkins were true, ensured that action of some kind had to be taken. In March 1982 it was decided that the Financial Controller and the Executive Director should be dismissed.[2]

This did not, of course, solve the Society's problem as the 'shambles' of the 1982 AGM shows. The Society had no Executive Director, a divided Council and had lost several of its senior staff. The members were livid about the mismanagement of their Society, and the active ones passed a vote of no confidence against the Chairman and the Vice-Chairman at the 1982 AGM. However the President, despite general

1 His concurrent attacks on the Royal Family and their hunting activity would not have helped his case.

2 *The Times*, 5 March 1982.

sympathy with the Radicals, felt unable to take note of this vote, because, on the basis of a postal ballot conducted throughout the membership as a whole, the Chairman and his deputy were deemed by him to be confirmed in their posts.

However, the President, Richard Adams, tired both of the arguments within the Council and of the 'institutional lethargy' of the organisation, resigned on 29 September 1982.[1] This was designed partly to pre-empt a move to trim his Presidential influence and partly to seize the opportunity for him and three of the Vice-Presidents who resigned with him, Lord Houghton, Clive Hollands (of GECCAP) and Lady Dowding (of Beauty without Cruelty), to align themselves firmly and explicitly with the radical members of the Society.

These constitutional crises damaged the Society's image and showed to the public at large as well as the membership that not only was the Society ill managed and thus in danger of losing many of its better staff but also that Council divisions over tactics and personalities consumed so much of its time that the necessary checks on the management were inadequate. Indeed Fookes and Hart were strong supporters of the dismissed Executive Director. However the fact that the accusations made by the radicals had been substantiated did little to sooth tempers or smooth relationships among Council members – all of whom were collectively responsible for the Society's mismanagement.

Strong personalities with strong disagreements could have worked together if in general the Society had been prospering. However, the radicals found the Conservative government unhelpful while the Conservatives, led by Janet Fookes, a Conservative MP, naturally wanted to establish good relations with the government. On almost every issue which required government action the Council was fundamentally divided. One example of the effects of this division occurred in 1980 when the Radicals led by R. Ryder decided that Hopkins and the Chief Vet should not join the government's farm animal welfare council on the grounds that it would probably be a whitewash body. The 'old guard' thought this was 'a snub to government – and more particularly a Tory government and altogether typical of the young, trendy "leftiness" they abhorred'.[2] When the Radicals lost their majority on the Council in June 1980 they found that their influence on RSPCA affairs almost totally evaporated.

This lack of direction and control over the organisation, some financial mismanagement, overspending in general and the hiring of over 200 inspectors and other new members of staff has helped to cause the

1 *Guardian*, 30 Sept. 1982.

2 *The Times*, 25 Jan. 1982.

current major financial crisis within the Society.[1] Because of its dependence on legacies, a fluctuating source of income, the Society has frequently had deficits in the past. In 1958, the Society received £416,355 from legacies, of which £250,412 was used to meet the deficit on current account. In 1974 a 'financial crisis' during a period of major internal squabbling was overcome by a fortuitous increase in legacy income. This amounted to £2.6 million in 1975 and £3.3 million in 1977, or 87 per cent of total income.[2] In 1978 and 1979 there were surpluses of over a million which encouraged Hopkins, unchecked by the Council, to spend money both on expanding the Society's staff and awarding himself and other senior staff generous 'expenses'.

In 1980, income was £6,749,000 of which 71 per cent or £4,791,000 was derived from legacies. However, expenditure was £7,991,000 giving a deficit of almost £1.25 million. There was a further deficit of over £1.5 million in 1981; income was £7,782,000 while expenditure was £9,307,000. The increasing expenditure was largely the result of the high costs of recruiting and supporting extra staff. In the words of the Treasurer: 'The expansion of the Inspectorate continued in 1981, giving marked increases in employment and telephone costs.[3] The financial crisis was a product of excessive expenditure rather than of the failure of legacy income to materialise. The financial crisis came to a head when the Treasurer hitherto a 'conservative' member of the Council refused to sanction a deliberate deficit in the 1982 budget, particularly since over £3 million worth of investments had already been sold to keep the Society going. It was the Treasurer's determination to inquire into the quality of the Society's financial mismanagement and her disturbing findings which led to her joining with the radical members of the Council in their eventually successful demand to dismiss the Executive Director.

In late 1982 the Society was at a crossroads; it had recently appointed a new Executive Director, had attempted to make substantial savings on staff and expenditure on staff, and was battling to reduce its mounting deficit. This had set the staff against the Council since they felt they were being made to pay for the bad management foisted upon them. As the national staff side secretary of the Society said, 'Unless something is done to get some proper management in the RSPCA,

1 In Jan. 1979 the RSPCA employed 597 people in England and Wales. By Sept. 1981 this had increased to 797.

2 See relevant Annual Reports.

3 Annual Report and Accounts 1982, Treasurer's Foreword.

the organisation will crumble'.[1] Undoubtedly the Council will try to solve the Society's organisational problems but first it needs to solve the financial crisis and then to rebuild the morale of the staff, neither of which are simple matters.

The morale of the membership and its willingness to invest in the Society's future by giving subscriptions or leaving legacies cannot be taken for granted. Membership dropped in the late 1960s and early 1970 during the internal squabbling over hunting from around 55,000 to 47,000 in 1980.[2] A good number of these were hunting supporters voting with their feet, others were members who felt that they could not be bothered to support a Society which spent so much of its time on internal argument. Others were actively discouraged from joining by some of the staff and Council members who preferred a controllable membership of conservative old ladies to one of younger and more radical people who would demand action and monitor the results.[3] A further drop in membership to under 30,000 in late 1982 was as much a result of general economic difficulties and a rise in the price of a subscription as of dissatisfaction, for by this time some of the staunchist radicals had thrown in their lot with the LACS or other more radical groups and the committed hunters had long since withdrawn. This may be a temporary low; hunting people may begin to rejoin in large numbers if they feel the current crisis of confidence in the RSPCA provides an opening for a recolonising attempt on the Society.[4]

Despite its recurring financial crises, internal political crises and a period of poor management the RSPCA continues with its 'good works'. In 1980 the organisation had *inter alia*:

57 Animal homes
38 Welfare centres
50 Clinics
316 Inspectors

It treated over 166,000 animals and humanely destroyed 184,000 ill, injured or unwanted animals. It found homes for 48,000 dogs and 37,000 cats and handled 254,000 animals at its Hostel at Heathrow. Its long history of attempts to investigate and prosecute cruelty to animals continued. It investigated 28,740 complaints and, in addition to issuing cautions and warnings, obtained 1,454 convictions for cruelty or maltreatment. It is these activities which will probably ensure

1 *Guardian*, 28 June 1982.

2 Accounts 1980, Treasurer's Foreword.

3 The view of a recent Chairman.

4 See BFSS *News*, Spring 1982.

that the organisation will survive; however the shape it survives in will depend on a restoration of confidence, adequate management and financial good health.

The main contribution of the RSPCA to the hunting issue has been to remove it from the fringes to the centre of the debate. In the 19th century the Society and its leadership were primarily concerned with working-class cruelty to cab-horses, dogs and farm animals. But even within a decade or so of its establishment the Society was supported by royalty and by the establishment, and was therefore quickly afforded a high degree of legitimacy. Although as social changes occurred in Britain more and more of its intellectual members questioned the continuation of hunting, the Society was unwilling to fight against the prevailing social norms which accepted hunting because of its desire to maintain its legitimacy. However, it was not allowed to opt out of the debate because the Society was a significant arena in which the struggle between the pro- and anti-hunting communities took place. Both sides wanted RSPCA support and used the basically neutral mechanism of the RSPCA to deploy their skills and test their strength.

The inevitable split within the RSPCA which had been rumbling since the 1890s only surfaced after the Second World War, when by a long and internally damaging process the largely anti-hunting membership took control of the Society from the pro-hunting leadership. They did this without forfeiting the legitimacy which the Society had continued to earn by virtue of its good works in other areas of animal welfare. As a Society it continued to be granted access to the civil service and to the legislative process. So, when it added hunting to the animal welfare questions about which it was concerned, it helped to place hunting on the 'official agenda'. Since 1976 the RSPCA has been officially against all forms of hunting and has thereby added its influence and prestige to the anti-hunting side. This, while noted by the media and decision-makers, is less significant than it might appear for, in ordering its priorities, the RSPCA has in practice deemed hunting to be a relatively minor source of cruelty.

This may change again in the near future for in 1981 the RSPCA conducted a major survey of public attitudes not only towards hunting but also on other animal welfare issues.[1] It was also concerned to discover public attitudes towards the Society. The survey produced a number of significant findings.

1 *Public Opinion and Animal Welfare in Britain*, Gallup Polls for the RSPCA – Survey in 1981, published in 1982.
For further details on public opinion and hunting see Chapter 9.

Issue	RSPCA's legislative proposals for (%)	against (%)
Ban export of live animals	71	18
Ban fox hunting	72	18
Ban hare coursing	77	15
Ban the clubbing of seals	86	10
Ban animals in circuses	31	31
Ban the sale of pets in markets	73	16

The key point to arise from this part of the survey[1] is that antagonism to hunting and coursing is a significant issue with the public at large,[2] and that the RSPCA is, if anything, following rather than leading public opinion on this issue.

Certainly the RSPCA is not considered particularly forceful even by those who rated high on a 'concern for animals scale', although it is generally well thought of by those for whom animals are a matter of concern rather than of deep significance. As the Report states, 'the high scoring category might reasonably be regarded as the Society's target group' but in many cases 'those who share the Society's concerns and aspirations in animal welfare, but do not readily accord it their support, regard the Society as an ineffective, or insufficiently active, vehicle of change and reform'.[3] The tension between animal welfare activists and 'do-gooders' is apparent and during the 1980s the RSPCA will once again have to decide whether it is the complacent repository of kindliness towards animals or an active and reformist pressure group.

1 RSPCA/Gallup, p. 8.

2 More so than vivisection for example when only 52 per cent supported the RSPCA's will to reduce it, p. 8.

3 RSPCA/Gallup, p. 46.

5 The anti-hunting lobby

The beginnings of organised opposition

Organised opposition to hunting began in 1891 when two leading RSPCA members, H. Salt and H. Williams, founded the Humanitarian League. In 1927, *Cruel Sports* on the first page of the first issue stated: 'The most effective organised effort we know against blood sports was that made by the Humanitarian League from 1891 to 1919'.[1]

The Humanitarian League was not devoted solely to the hunting issue. Williams and Salt were keen Fabian pamphleteers who wrote in favour of women's rights, prison reform, pacifism, vegetarianism, free thinking and socialism; they also wrote against hunting, cruelty to animals, vivisection and capital punishment. Their range was their downfall; their association with vegetarianism caused them to be classed as cranks, and their pacifism and free thinking in the First World War turned established and 'respectable' opinion against them. These factors were the primary causes of the demise of the organisation in 1919.

Nevertheless, in its brief but stimulating existence the Humanitarian League did have some affect on the hunting issue. The League's first pamphlet was an attack on the Royal Buckhounds emphasising the

1 *Cruel Sports* (Journal of the League against Cruel Sports), 1927, p. 1.

cruelty of hunting a half-tame deer.[1] It was also revealed that £6,000 was paid for the upkeep of the pack from the civil list.[2] Lord Randolph Churchill supported an earlier attack on carted stag hunting in 1883 because it was not a 'true sport' like fox hunting, and because its practitioners were 'the counter-jumpers of London – that class of persons who were dominated by the generic term of "Arry" '.[3] In 1892 the class nature of field sports was made specific by two melodramatic pamphlets; one suggested drag hunting as an alternative to fox hunting, and another suggested football and skittles as an alternative to rabbit coursing – the classes were not expected to join together in their substitute leisure pursuits![4]

In 1902, the Humanitarian League launched a publicity campaign against Eton College, the only major school at that time to have a pack of beagles. The Headmaster and Provost were both members of the Windsor branch of the RSPCA and felt that having a pack of beagles was perfectly acceptable since, as the Headmaster wrote to the League: 'I have never been given to understand that the Society has condemned the hunting of animals'.[5] He added, quite correctly, that if it did it would lose a great many subscribers. Despite this and subsequent attacks, the Eton Beagles survive to this day.

The Humanitarian League's last important contribution to the hunting debate was to publish *Killing for Sport*,[6] a collection of anti-hunting essays. To this G.B. Shaw wrote a lengthy preface which for the first and almost the last time injected some wit into the debate. He suggested that seasonal child hunting would be beneficial; it would provide sport, the children would be well fed and the survivors would help to build a better nation. He also stated: 'I know many sportsmen and none of them are ferocious. I have known many humanitarians and they are all ferocious'.[7] His main (serious) argument was that he could understand killing for profit, hatred or revenge, but felt that killing for pleasure or for social reasons was degrading to the participants. *Killing for Sport* represented an attempt to marshal the arguments against

1 Rev. J. Stratton, *Royal Sports*. The stags were generally castrated and therefore harmless. Some carted stag hunts stabled the deer in kennels and gave the deer pet names.

2 Turner, *All Heaven*, p. 242.

3 *Hansard* (Commons), 1883, vol. 276, col. 1686.

4 R. Jude, *Rabbit Coursing: an appeal to working men*, William Reeves, 1892 (Humanitarian League Publication, no. III), p. 7, and Lady F. Dixie, *The Horrors of Sport*, William Reeves, 1892 (Humanitarian League Publication, no. IV), p. 7.

5 See Turner, *All Heaven*, p. 243.

6 *Killing for Sport*, (ed.) H. Salt, Humanitarian League, London, 1915.

7 Ibid., see preface.

hunting. It emphasised the cruelty involved in hunting and discussed humanity's duties towards lesser creatures. It also stated firmly the class arguments: 'Hunts are recreations for the wealthy classes only, and this mainly results from their expensiveness'.[1]

It would be unwise to over-estimate the importance of the Humanitarian League. Nevertheless, it had some impact; its publications were regularly quoted in subsequent books and articles; its leading members were interesting characters and it started what has proved to be a very long debate. But it was small, relied very much for financial survival on the personal fortunes of its main figures, and was dismissed by main stream opinion for its embrace of so many diverse causes. Undoubtedly its most important functions were to act as a ginger group within and alongside the RSPCA, and to keep the animal welfare issue in front of parliament and the general public.

Organisation around a cause: the LACS

Membership and income

For five years after the demise of the Humanitarian League in 1919 there was no organised anti-hunting lobby. This changed in 1924 when two stalwarts of the animal welfare world, who were members of the RSPCA and former members of the Humanitarian League, formed the League for the Prohibition of Cruel Sports. They were Henry Amos and Ernest Bell, both of whom felt that the RSPCA was insufficiently active on the hunting issue.

Membership of the new Society grew steadily; by 1927 there were 500 members, mostly disgruntled RSPCA supporters. The formation of the NSACS and the Second World War caused membership of the LACS to dip but it was boosted again by the promise of legislation in 1948–9 and by the Scott Henderson inquiry of 1950–1. Since then internal disputes and lengthy periods of inaction have caused membership to fluctuate.

However it rose slightly in the 1970s and reached a figure of around 13,000 in 1978 before levelling off and stabilising at between 11–13,000 in 1982.[2] In exciting times those who die or drop out are readily replaced by new members. In quiet times, such as during a period of Conservative government, new members are harder to find.

Membership fluctuations have not adversely affected the Society's

1 Ibid., p. 62.

2 There is no accurate membership list. However adding about 4,000 life members to those subscribing and giving donations implies a figure of around 12,000.

financial position for since the war legacies have played an increasingly prominent role in the Society's budget. From 1960, legacies have produced more income than subscriptions; by the early 1970s the amount raised by subscriptions fell to under 10 per cent (6 per cent in 1977) of that contributed by legacies. In the 1981 financial year subscriptions contributed under 3 per cent of total income whereas legacies contributed 62 per cent (76 per cent in 1980) and donations, interest on investments and sales each contributed between 8 per cent and 10 per cent.[1]

Organisational development

In its attempts to be an active and radical organisation the League has rarely been free from internal conflict. In 1931 the Hon. S. Coleridge, who was the President, resigned over 'dissatisfaction with the conduct of some members of the League'.[2] His resignation was followed by that of E. Bell, the Treasurer and Co-founder. In July 1932, Coleridge's successor, Lady Cory, also resigned, and on 8 July of that year these dissidents held the inaugural meeting of the NSACS. The crisis was caused by policy disagreements, particularly over the hunting exploits of Royalty, which went unresolved because of the inability of the personalities involved to compromise and co-operate. The return of Amos from a period of illness provided the catalyst for the final break since Amos claimed that he and his supporters stood for the 'old standards' and refused to compromise over hunting. As old friendships collapsed under the strain of the arguments and accusations, Amos stated the central question:

> The larger and truer issue, however, is whether the League shall continue to stand for the principles, the spirit, the method and the policy it was founded to promulgate, or whether it shall tone down its spirit and water down its policy and become, to all intents and purposes, a branch of the RSPCA, and thus be in the pocket of the fox-hunting party.[3]

The publicity generated by the split attracted sufficient membership for both the LACS and NSACS to survive. Local semi-autonomous branches of the League in the South-West, Oxford and Bristol which started in 1927 and 1928 expanded during this period of the Society's internal struggles. By 1939, there were eight active local branches.

1 See Annual Report, 1981, for details.

2 *Cruel Sports*, 1931, p. 33.

3 *Cruel Sports*, 1932, p. 73.

Table 5.1
LACS

Year	Income		Approximate membership
1927	£1,350		1,000
1931	£1,286		1,500
1934	£ 900		1,200
1935	£1,160		1,400
1938	£2,133		3,000
	of which subscriptions	£1,547	
	legacies	£ 435	
1939–45	*Total* Income £11,741, of which legacies £6,570. The average annual subscription income was around £600 p.a., well under half the pre-war figure.		Membership was around 1,000 during the war.
1947			2,500–3,000
1948			5,000–6,000
1950			3,000
1965	£23,168		8,000
	of which legacies	£6,272	
	donations	£7,515	
	subscriptions	£5,455	
	(There was also an accumulated fund of £44,869)		
1969	£34,371		10,000
	of which legacies	£13,235	
	donations	£9,791	
	subscriptions	£7,006	
	(Accumulated fund	£46,013)	
1973	£71,711		9,000
	of which legacies	£36,321	
	donations	£18,653	
	subscriptions	£5,911	
	(Accumulated fund	£120,335)	
1977	£146,651		Not over 12,000
	of which legacies	£107,954	
	donations	£23,027	
	subscriptions	£6,147	
	(Accumulated fund		
	1975	£210,219	
	1977	£379,875)	

A single legacy of £50,000 was given to the League in early 1978 and one of £200,000 in 1981.

.../Table 5.1 continued.

Year	Income		Approximate membership
1980	£311,316		
	of which legacies	£237,166	
	subscriptions	£8,167	
	donations	£21,156	
	Bank Interest	£29,586	
	Sales	£9,075	
	Surplus Income over Expenditure	£169,337	
	(Accumulated fund	£716,980)	
1981	£275,331		
	of which legacies	£171,391	12,000
	subscriptions	£9,308	
	donations	£27,063	
	Bank Interest	£23,647	
	Sales	£26,139	
	Surplus Income over Expenditure	£58,683	
	(Accumulated fund	£770,502)	

Achievements, however, were few and during the war the League was forced to mark time and hope that the post-war period would bring some kind of success. The League used the continuation of hunting during the war as justification for its own activities, just as the BFSS justified its own reactivation on the grounds that its opponents had not ceased operations. The League's affairs were left almost entirely in the hands of its Secretary, Mr J. Sharp, whose single-minded devotion enabled the Society to survive. He attacked hunting as an unpatriotic activity and was supported by a number of papers, among them the *Daily Express, Daily Herald* and *News Chronicle*. He encouraged people to write letters and letters continued to stream from him. In 1942, he sent 556 letters to the press of which 110 were published.[1]

Letters to the press were one of the few ways of beginning a debate in the war. A complaint that Lord Halifax, the British Ambassador in Washington, and a former MFH, had gone hunting moved Carl Sandburg to write to the *New York Times*, 'Are we going to war for the

1 *League Doings*, Jan. 1942 and Winter 1942. (*League Doings* replaced *Cruel Sports* from 1940 to 1958.)

sake of a lot of English fox hunters?'[1] Letters were published complaining, accurately, that the Wartime County Agriculture Committees were packed with hunting people and were, as a result, doing nothing to stop hunting. At least 100 packs continued hunting during the war and their activities gave the League scope to continue its attacks.[2] Friendly MPs gave support by asking questions in parliament.

During the war, hunting was looked on with less favour than usual by the government, especially since fox and stag shoots has been shown to be relatively effective means of control. In 1940, the Ministry of Agriculture stated that, despite the continuation of hunting, two-thirds of the deer killed on Exmoor during that year were shot.[3]

Because of this the Society faced the post-war period optimistically, but the failure of the 1948–9 Bills and the certainty that the Conservative governments of 1951–64 would not encourage anti-hunting legislation caused the League to sink into an organisational gloom. As far as the media was concerned, hunting was a dead issue and the League a spent force. Finding ways of getting media attention involved protesting about relatively trivial matters. In 1954, the League complained about cruelty to the horses involved in the Grand National and objected to the way the BBC handled a programme on Myxomatosis. However, the cultivation of the media was, from the mid-1950s, in the hands of a journalist, E. Hemingway, and thanks to his skills, 36 newspapers published reports of the 1956 AGM, the year in which he became Chairman.

Hemingway's success as a publicist and his enthusiasm for disrupting hunts and annoying hunting people enabled the Society to avoid facing the fact that it was further from its avowed goal in 1960 than it had been in 1950. It had a radical image and sufficient financial independence for it to ignore the demands of its ordinary members, but could not disguise the fact that it had failed to gain support in the arenas where decisions about hunting were made.

Both Hemingway and Sharp, secretary since 1930, died in 1963, and effective control of the Society moved into the hands of Mr R. Rowley who continued the Hemingway tradition of strong, energetic and personal leadership. However, as successive attempts to abolish coursing failed in the late 1960s and early 1970s, the membership not unnaturally asked whether the leadership were doing sufficient to help this legislation through parliament. In 1972, during a Conservative government, *The Economist* felt that 'the abolitionist cause has now passed

1 *League Doings*, Autumn 1941, p. 3.

2 See *Baily's*, 1939–49.

3 *League Doings*, Autumn 1944.

its peak'.[1] The disappointment of the membership was even more keenly felt when further legislative attempts against coursing failed in 1975 and 1976. The independent and cavalier leadership style of Mr Rowley had not met with success and a backlash from the membership was inevitable. The crisis came to a head in 1977; the AGM of May was adjourned in chaos and at an Extraordinary General Meeting in November the arguments continued both over the interpretation of the rules and over the policies of the Chairman, Mr Rowley. He was opposed for the first time since 1963 but the EGM failed to resolve the conflict and both candidates withdrew.

During this internal crisis the League, like the RSPCA in 1974, was riven by a dispute between the Chairman and his opponents within the Society. The central ingredients of the saga are somewhat bizarre. Mr Course, a member of the Executive Committee of the LACS and a member of the HSA, was charged in September 1977, with receiving confidential documents stolen from the BFSS in March 1977. He maintained that they were left on his doorstep and that Mr Rowley or his supporters put them there and later tipped off the police.[2]

In fact they were stolen by members of the ALF who on seeing, among other things, evidence of a BFSS spy in the League's office handed some of the documents over to Course, who went to Rowley with the evidence. Rowley, it was claimed by his enemies, then told the BFSS and they not surprisingly told the police. Certainly Rowley was advised by Lady Follett, a Committee member, that he should inform the BFSS 'So that they can if they wish invoke the assistance of the police. . . Disclosure of these facts to BFSS could result in the public exposure of Richard Course's associations and his possible prosecution'.[3] Whatever the facts of the case some members of the League believed that the Chairman, in order to undermine the position of the militants and in order to protect his own position, was more concerned to expose his fellow Committee member than to consider the implications of the information which Course had shown him. He was, in Lady Follett's words, concerned to 'ensure that whatever the differences of opinion between the League and the BFSS at least they are conducted in a civilised manner'.[4] When the case came to court Course was acquitted; however intra-group relations did not improve.

1 *The Economist*, London, 6 May 1972, p. 5. In an article on coursing.

2 For details see *Howl*, 9, Autumn 1977, p. 2. Further details from interviews 1977–82.

3 Letter from Lady A. Follett to R. Rowley, 6 Apr. 1977.

4 Ibid., 6 Apr. 1977.

In order to resolve the crisis Lord Soper, the League's President, was able to prevail upon Lord Houghton, the 79-year-old ex-Chairman of the Parliamentary Labour Party, to stand for the post of Chairman. He was elected unopposed at the adjourned AGM of December 1977, and was re-elected (unopposed but heckled by Rowley supporters) at the AGM in 1978. He was acceptable in 1977 and 1978 for three main reasons. The first was the fact that Lord Soper, the President, had personally recommended him during a period of considerable strain within the Society and members were pleased to find a person of repute willing to take on the task. The second was that a movement away from Rowley's style and methods was inevitable and such was the tension between members of the League's Committee that an insider would have been inevitably a 'friend' or an 'enemy' of the regime; Houghton as an outsider was neither.

The final reason was the most important. Houghton was a veteran politician who offered a new policy – to bring hunting into politics. He claimed that only legislation would end hunting. This was opposed by a vocal minority at the 1978 AGM, but its leader, Lt Col. P. Kerr, failed to gain election to the Council and was heartily booed at the AGM. Despite the continuing acrimony it was apparent that Lord Houghton's commitment to political activities was supported by the LACS Committee and by the bulk of the membership.

Houghton's period as Chairman coincided with a period of great activity on the political front. When the Conservatives won the 1979 election he, being well over 80 years old, wished to conserve his energy for other fights and so stood down as Chairman. He was replaced by Richard Course.

After the 1979 election the League spent two years in turmoil. Its members had for five years been expecting legislative developments which they realised only a Labour government was likely to enact. Enthusiasm was therefore at a low ebb and the Society needed aggressive leadership, 'otherwise it would have folded by now'.[1] This was, to a large extent, provided by Course himself and a number of his fellow Committee members. However they in turn needed but generally did not have an efficient administration to support them. The Executive Secretary, J. Allen, left in 1979, was replaced on a caretaker basis by A. Shaw MP for just over three months; his successor Miss M. Denby left in under a year. Following this the Executive Committee attempted to act as a Management Committee with each member responsible for a part of the Headquarters operations. It was soon realised that this was unworkable, and in June 1981 Richard Course, the Chairman, accepted the post of Executive Director. Mark Davis, who ten years before had been the Secretary, took on the post of Chairman.

1 Interview with a Committee member, Aug. 1982.

Course's energy and enthusiasm and his willingness to take on all-comers ensured that the League did not become somnambulant. However the clashes between him and other Committee members did not end. On almost every issue of policy the Committee's endless arguing regularly drove Committee members to the brink of resignation. In August 1982 John Bryant, for example, was persuaded to withdraw his resignation which was prompted by a Committee split over the policy of extending their sanctuaries. Course's position in early 1983 was by no means secure. He inspires deep loyalty and deep antagonism by his determination and drive. If he fails to generate significant changes he will be expendable; more probably he will decide that the pleasure to be derived from 'banging his head against a brick wall while being stabbed in the back' is limited and will therefore withdraw from his highly vulnerable position before he is pushed. Course himself, having given up a business to become Executive Secretary of the League, is clear that he cannot spend more than a few years doing the job before either a major breakthrough or total failure makes it time for him to move on.[1]

Patronage and privilege

In the 1930s, the League's attacks on the RSPCA and Royalty, two pillars of the establishment, were admirably suited to the purpose of generating publicity and establishing its credentials as a radical organisation. Nevertheless, the Society had to take care not to alienate other important sections of society and to keep intact its links with other organisations.

As part of a campaign to achieve respectability, the League acquired patrons or Vice-Presidents with prestigious names or titles. By 1938, it had 74 patrons and of these 26 had titles, 11 were churchmen and 9 had military ranks; 28 of the 74 were women. The number and changing occupations of its patrons gave some indication of the League's fortunes. In the rebuilding period after the war the League lost most of its patrons, and there were still only 27 in 1965, although the number rose steadily to 60 by 1977. Of these 10 were churchmen, 25 were 'personalities' of stage or screen, and 23 were women. The decline of titled patrons and the increase in 'personalities' show a clear desire on the League's part to seek publicity and support at all levels of society rather than to concentrate on establishment respectability. This trend was reinforced in 1982 when it was decided actively to seek more

1 Interview with Course, August 1982.

patrons and Vice-Presidents from the media and entertainment world.[1]

In particular the sympathy of the farming community was thought to be vital to the success of the League. During the depression an increasing number of farmers had begun to protest in the farming journals about the damage done to the poultry industry by predatory foxes. The League, who claimed that hunting served to preserve and not reduce foxes, demanded that the government should organise shoots. In 1929, a Poultry Council spokesman claimed that £239m had been paid for imported poultry and eggs between 1901 and 1928 'which might have been earned by home producers but for the preservation of foxes'.[2] The MFHA was sufficiently worried by this to hold an investigation, but the problem faded as the depression ended. Egg prices rose and farmers were more tolerant of losses; they were also, because of their higher income, able to fence their chicken pens more effectively. After the war, the clash of interests between poultry farmers and hunts became less acute mainly because of a steady growth of battery hen egg production. This development was of no propaganda value to the League, who therefore let the issue drop.

In the early years the League lost no opportunity in criticising the established church for its acceptance of hunting. However, after the war the church seemed in general to be more sympathetic to the League's viewpoint; there were no ordained MFHs after 1945 and in that year two Bishops signed a petition against coursing. Relations with the church improved further when, after 1957, the League decided to seek support from rather than to attack the church.[3] In 1963 the League's new policy was partially rewarded by a letter from Michael Ramsey, The Archbishop of Canterbury, which stated his, rather than the church's, view on coursing. He said: 'You are free to quote me as being strongly against the practice of coursing as a cruel one'.[4] They were further rewarded in 1970 when the National Assembly of the Church of England passed a strongly worded resolution against hare coursing.[5]

Throughout its history the League has been consistently anti-establishment, and has used class-consciousness as a necessary ingredient in its programme. Its most successful leaders, Amos, Hemingway, Rowley and Course, have all been most at home when attacking the establishment. The 1965 Annual Report summarised this approach:

1 From interview, Aug. 1982.

2 *The Times*, 14 Feb. 1929.

3 A policy decision along these lines was made at the 1957 AGM. See *The Times*, 26 Mar. 1957.

4 *Cruel Sports*, Winter 1963, p. 1. It was widely quoted in the national press on 9 Jan. 1964.

5 Quoted in *House of Lords Debates*, 1972, vol. 330, col. 663.

'The blood sportsman whether he be the suave "gentleman" in his top hat and scarlet coat, or the despicable, ragged, grovelling earth stopper, must be treated as an outcast of society'.[1] The BFSS could not be negotiated with since it was described as 'the evil brotherhood, the Ku Klux Klan of the countryside'.[2]

The élitist tendencies of the hunting community have been regular targets of criticism by the League. In 1964, the League discovered that there had been no elections to the Badmington Parish Council for 17 years. There were seven seats and always seven candidates – the Duke and Duchess of Beaufort and five estate officials employed by them, one of whom said 'we always consult his Grace first'.[3] This example of local democracy at work was matched by a report in 1970 from the Duke of Beaufort's hunt when the joint Master, Major Gundry, dismissed an odd-job man. The ex-employee stated: 'Everyone around here bows and scrapes to Major Gundry – he has tremendous influence'.[4]

Under Hemingway the League continued its pre-war policy of attacking members of the Royal Family, both for their hunting exploits and for the social cachet that royal support gave to field sports. At the League's AGM in 1957 Hemingway, when attacking 'debased and spurious forms of sport', stated that 'it is only the patronage of the Queen which keeps hunting within the law in Britain today'.[5]

The League's strictures against hunting may have had some effect, for not until 1972 did a member of the Royal Family, Princess Anne, go hunting. The League voiced its displeasure and commissioned an opinion poll which revealed that 48 per cent of the population felt she should not hunt, while 37 per cent felt that she should be allowed to do so. *The Times* stated that 'the Princess should be granted the widest freedom to follow her own bent and shape her own life'.[6] Royal involvement in other horse and field sports has also come under the League's scrutiny.[7] The League has condemned royal shooting and has criticised the cruelty involved to horses in the Horse Trials in which

1 LACS Annual Report, 1965, p. 17.

2 Ibid., p. 17.

3 *Cruel Sports*, 2, 1964, p. 2.

4 *Cruel Sports*, 1, 1970, p. 3.

5 *Guardian*, 27 Mar. 1957.

6 *The Times*, 14 Dec. 1972.

7 *The World Tonight*, BBC Radio, 25 April 1974, carried a report on the LACS's attitude to royal involvement in field sports.

Princess Anne was taking part.[1] The Princess of Wales was censured for shooting a stag at Sandringham in 1981.

While criticism of the Royal Family is an excellent means of generating publicity it cannot claim to be successful as a way of stopping royalty from hunting. Princess Anne has continued to hunt occasionally and Prince Charles has hunted with at least 42 different packs.[2] Indeed, he has hunted more in the early 1980s than in previous years, and in 1983 was reported as hunting twice a week.[3] Nevertheless, the publicity has been most useful and, every time a royal hunting exploit is attacked, the League claims a sharp increase in membership.

The LACS denies that either its position or its rhetoric exacerbate class antagonisms. However members do admit that some public antipathy to hunting can be attributed to the fact that hunting is a pursuit of the 'idle and aristocratic'.[4] They feel, therefore, that the League is justified in using class antagonism if it can be turned to advantage. It became easier for the League to play down the class or privilege element of the hunting debate when successive public opinion polls showed clearly that social class and political affiliation had a significant impact on peoples' attitudes to hunting. In other words the League does not need to stir up Left-wing working-class antagonism to hunting because to a certain extent it already exists,[5] since 'League supporters are mostly on the Left'.[6] A more fruitful source of converts for the League are urban middle-class people who know little about the details of hunting, but who abhor cruelty and violence and may, with luck, disapprove of privilege. While this type of supporter may improve the League's image with decision-makers, it cannot abandon radical and aggressive behaviour, for it is this which has kept it going in hard times and appeals to its most dedicated supporters.

This is the paradox which confronts the League. It must be radical with its natural constituents and exploit their emotions, and it must be aggressive in order to be newsworthy; but if it is going to influence leaders of opinion and decision-makers, it must at the same time adopt a 'sensible' posture and learn the art of negotiation and compromise.

Luckily for the League its financial independence releases it from the need to attend slavishly to the demands of its members; it has neverthe-

1 *The Times*, 7 Jan. 1971.

2 Baily's, 1981–2, p. xi.

3 *Daily Mail*, 4 Jan. 1983.

4 Interview with G. Barter, LACS Committee member for 10 years, Mar. 1974.

5 Ibid. and interviews with three LACS Secretaries/Directors 1973, 1978 and 1982.

6 Interview with LACS Secretary, Apr. 1973.

less found it difficult to steer a clear path between its conflicting goals. When anti-hunting legislation was doomed to fail, during Conservative administrations for example, it needed to concentrate on generating publicity, but when legislative change was possible the Society needed to develop an aura of respectability with the media and decision-makers. Such flexibility was not always easy; in 1964 when a Labour government took office, the HSA, while working independently from the League, was confused by many with the League and reinforced the League's image as a Society with a taste for violence. In contrast, during the Conservative government of 1970–4, the League's failure to generate legislative changes and its reluctance or inability to resort to headline catching activities produced a drop in membership, because the members could only see that the 'politics of respectability' were not producing tangible results. In 1982–3, the League is hoping that the enthusiasm of Richard Course will sustain them until a friendly government is elected.

Tactics

The early tactics of the League were designed to generate publicity for its cause; the written word was one of the most important methods. Pamphlets against various types of hunting were produced, and letters and articles appeared in local and national papers signed by leading members and officials of the Society. *Cruel Sports*, the Society's journal, encouraged the faithful to write to the press and collected together snippets from sympathisers, particularly if they were farmers, clergymen or people with titles.[1] Some reports such as those entitled 'Women's Witness against Blood Sports'[2] introduced an evangelical note into their publicity. *Cruel Sports* also mounted campaigns against hunting and publicised the activities of other anti-hunting groups.

Pamphlets and leaflets were the main thrust of the League's drive for publicity in its early years. With Ernest Bell's help the Society had, by the end of 1929, distributed 'five hundred thousand leaflets and journals . . . to MPs, preachers, teachers, editors, farmers, national welfare, higher thought [sic] and allied workers all over the country'.[3] During and after the war pamphlets were regularly produced and circulated, although this became a decreasingly significant activity for the Society as time went on.

1 *Cruel Sports*, 1929, see pp. 12 and 19.

2 *Cruel Sports*, Aug. 1927.

3 *Cruel Sports*, 1929, p. 146.

The League has always carefully monitored the BBC and has generally managed, by being persistent, to get its views heard. In 1933, the League was invited to take part in a debate about hunting and, in the same year, it managed to squash a proposal to broadcast the opening meet of the Quorn.[1] In 1936, the League complained about a broadcast on hunting but the BBC's Controller of Public Relations replied that hunting was a deep-rooted tradition about which many listeners wanted to hear.[2] Since it was this very tradition which the League was battling against, continuing disagreement with the BBC was inevitable. From time to time 'balanced' debates took place in which the League participated, but generally the League felt the BBC to be 'the organ of the class which is devoted to blood sports'.[3] It was not until the post-war period that the League managed to establish stable and friendly relations with the BBC. Gradually the Society earned the reputation of being the premier anti-hunting organisation so letters to the BBC tended to be answered and, whenever 'balanced' debates occurred, its representatives were asked to take part.[4]

The League was always keen to publicise 'incidents', either those which put the hunting community in a bad light or those in which human or political angles could be exploited. Many of the incidents reported occurred in Somerset and Devon, for it was here that Hemingway and Rowley established their base. An early incident occurred in 1927 when Hemingway was thrown, twice, into the sea at Minehead during a hunt dance at a sea-side hotel. A subsequent court case kept the issue alive for months.[5]

Successful exposure in the media undoubtedly had an impact on the hunting world, for the BFSS issued a leaflet in 1961 advising Masters of Hounds on how to deal with the media if an incident occurred, and on how to write hunt reports for local newspapers. It recommended that local editors were, whenever practicable, to be given complimentary tickets to Hunt Balls and that foxes were no longer to be 'killed', they were to be 'accounted for'.[6]

In the period 1968–72 the League identified 114 noteworthy

1 *Cruel Sports*, 1933, pp. 27, 82 and 90.

2 *Cruel Sports*, 1936, p. 30.

3 *Cruel Sports*, 1938, p. 2.

4 The LACS was represented at a BBC TV '*Talk-in*' on hunting on 24 Nov. 1972. The Chairman was Robin Day.

5 *Cruel Sports*, 1927, p. 128.

6 Circulated privately to Masters of Hounds and referred to in NSACS *Bulletin*, 136, Mar. 1962, p. 1.

incidents and circulated details to the press.[1] One incident during 1968 concerned the Master of the Devon and Somerset Staghounds. He was fined for assaulting a female protester while out hunting.[2] The League arranged for a parliamentary question to be asked by Marcus Lipton,[3] and as a result, the Master, a local magistrate, was removed from the list of Magistrates for a year.

Another case, this time with a human angle, caught the attention of the press in March 1973, when an 18-year-old girl tried to stop the Quantock Staghounds from killing a stag which had taken shelter in her parents' stables. The family's landlord arrived saying 'I have the sporting rights'. The deer was then shot in front of the weeping girl and gutted in a nearby field. The landlord's retention of the sporting rights caused the *Daily Mail* to talk of feudalism in its comment on the matter.[4]

In November 1981 the *Daily Mirror*, always a reliable supporter of the LACS, published major hunting stories on consecutive days. On the first day there were several centre page pictures of hounds killing a fox in a village street. On the second the paper published an editorial and a 'close-up special' on this 'grim exercise'.[5]

Hunt Balls and high living have always brought out the puritan element in the League's leadership. It has a straight-laced sense of morality and frowns at indulgence of all kinds. It was exceptionally horrified by events at the Tiverton Staghounds Hunt Ball in 1972. It reported that 'when the band played a pop number called "Jump up and down and wave your knickers in the air", a young woman hunt member did just that'.[6]

Hemingway used his chairmanship of the Society to develop two major policies. The first was the practice of demonstrating against and sabotaging hunts. Poster demonstrations and mildly disruptive activities were the essence of this policy which achieved little except publicity. Poster 'demos' had been used since before the war but Hemingway produced cadres of enthusiasts who enjoyed teasing hunts and who gradually increased the efficiency of these disruptive tactics. They introduced, in 1958, a 'secret weapon' – an aniseed trail designed to confuse the hounds.

1 'Incidents', LACS, 1 Nov. 1972.

2 *Daily Mail*, 21 Dec. 1968.

3 *Hansard* (Commons), 1969, vol. 781, cols 30–1.

4 *Daily Mail*, 31 Mar. 1973. For a detailed description of a kill, see the *Sunday Mirror*, 11 Mar. 1973.

5 *Daily Mirror*, 26 Nov. 1981 and 27 Nov. 1981.

6 *Cruel Sports*, Jan. 1973, p. 5.

On balance the 'secret weapon' was a failure, although it did generate publicity. In 1957, Hemingway decided as an alternative policy to buy up a small but strategically placed piece of land on Exmoor and to deny hunting people access to it. He knew, being a West Countryman, the difficulties that this would create for hunts since it introduced the notion of trespass on land over which they had traditionally hunted. Exmoor was ideal from Hemingway's point of view; it is the home of at least 6 packs, and land there is easier to acquire than in the hunting shires since it is both cheaper and tends to come in smaller lots. In the autumn of 1959 the Devon and Somerset Staghounds crossed the League's property and the League's response was dramatic. First it demanded police protection; then it sought a High Court injunction against the Staghounds and placed armed guards around the sanctuary. This, of course, created a vast amount of useful publicity for the League. The success of this first land-buying venture encouraged the League to buy more, and purchases were increased during the chairmanship of Mr R. Rowley, who succeeded Hemingway. By 1970, the League had 8 small properties and, by 1976, they owned 24 lots amounting to over 1,500 acres. Further substantial holdings of over 600 acres were added between 1975 and 1982 bringing the total number of lots to 33.[1] As acreage increased, each purchase became more significant for while a hunt can fairly easily avoid one small sanctuary, it cannot easily hunt if the whole area is dotted with pieces of land which the hunted animal may enter but which the hunt may not. The purchases are concentrated on Exmoor, and in recent years the League, as an established landowner, has been able to purchase whole farms and then lease them to commercial but non-hunting farmers. In certain cases the League has purchased only the sporting rights and not the land itself.

The hunts on Exmoor claim that the acquisition of land is of little importance, but privately they accept that it can be a considerable nuisance. They do not relish the publicity or the costs of fighting a trespass action, nor do they enjoy stopping the hunt near a sanctuary when hounds are running well.[2]

The sanctuary policy, despite originating as a tentative alternative to the League's 'secret weapon', has been a success at three levels; it protects a number of animals from the hunt; it provides regular and continuous publicity for the League whenever a sanctuary is invaded; it gives the organisation a way of spending its increasing legacy income.

1 See *Cruel Sports*, Oct. 1976; *West Somerset Free Press*, 31 Dec. 1975, Annual Report, 1977, p. 13, Annual Report, 1981, pp. 7–8.
See also *The Times*, 3 Sept. 1982.

2 Confirmed in conversation with a number of West Country Masters of Hounds during the period 1976–80.

From its experience in dealing with the legal implications of having sanctuaries, the League has developed another activity. It offers free legal advice to landowners who wish to sue or get injunctions against hunts who trespass on their property. The service was only an occasional one; the League won three cases for clients in 1972 and six cases in 1974.[1] However, Course, first as a Committee member and later as Executive Director, strengthened this policy. In the 1981–2 season he involved the League in 58 cases mainly for trespass and damage. His aim was to not only worry the hunting community but also to extract some recompense for the considerable number of people whose pets were killed by hounds. One case resulted in £400 being paid to the owners of a cat which was killed, and in another case £1,200 in damages were paid for injuries to a horse.[2]

In 1981 the League developed, almost by accident, another major publicity generating tactic. Since the League's early days it has regularly asked landlords such as the National Trust and the Crown to ban hunting on its land, and of course purchased land itself in order to deny hunts access to it.

A number of urban councils such as Northampton had never allowed hunting on their land and others such as the London Boroughs of Enfield and Haringay had banned it in the 1970s but none was a significant landowner.[3] However in late 1979 the Cooperative Party in Croydon was addressed by Richard Course who persuaded a Mr Mani to take up the League's cause within the Cooperative movement. The Coop, through the Cooperative Wholesale Society, owned 50,000 acres of farm land.[4] Mr Mani as an insider was able with the League's help to start a process which organised itself into a group called 'Cooperators against Bloodsports'. Their activities and the pressure they were able to exert both locally and nationally within the Cooperative movement culminated in the CWS banning hunting from the beginning of the 1982 season on all the farmland which it owned.

This move, highly significant in itself, stirred local League members into action and numerous requests were made to local councils to ban hunting on land which they controlled. The League organised petitions, sent speakers, usually Richard Course, to address council meetings or meetings held to encourage local authorities to take action. From mid-1981 (after the county council elections in May) to mid-1982 many

1 *Cruel Sports*, Oct. 1972 and Annual Report, 1974, p. 2.

2 Interview, Aug. 1982.

3 *Cruel Sports*, 7, 1982.

4 *Cruel Sports*, 6, 1982.

councils were forced to take a vote on this issue and it soon became clear that the chances of success depended almost entirely on the political complexion of the council. In Labour strongholds such as Mid-Glamorgan, Humberside and Derbyshire motions to abolish hunting on council owned land were passed. In Conservative counties such as Lincolnshire and Dorset motions were defeated. In Waverley (Surrey) the local league and HSA supporters organised a petition and encouraged a Labour and Liberal initiative to get hunting banned on Waverley land. Despite passionate speeches in favour of the ban, the Conservative flavour of the area made it inevitable that all abolitionist moves would fail. This inevitably did not stop local meetings from being well attended and rowdy, nor did it deter dozens of people from filling the letters pages of the local paper for weeks on end.[1]

The close correlation between the success or failure of these motions and the political complexion of the council persuaded the League to be a little more discriminating in its approach. It decided to give all possible help to Labour or Liberal controlled areas, but wherever possible it discouraged its supporters in Conservative strongholds by making the point that a failure to ban hunting was a 'victory' for the hunting community. Any boost to the morale of the BFSS was felt to outweigh the advantages of adding perhaps 2,000 acres to the total of prohibited land, particularly where this land was little used by foxhounds. The value of this public relations approach was illustrated when the Conservative controlled East Sussex Council passed a motion of opposition to hunting but did not prohibit it — the resulting publicity was most gratifying for the League, especially as the distinction between disapproval and prohibition was generally blurred in press reporting of the vote.

The success of this new strategy by the League can be measured by the very powerful response it evoked from the BFSS, the MFHA and local supporters of hunting. The MFHA in collaboration with the BFSS declared its intention of setting up a 'task force' in each country 'to investigate the position and take action as necessary'.[2] One memorandum ended 'We are now in a battle situation such as we have not faced since the parliamentary bill directed against hunting in 1949. Please will you give the conduct of this battle your prime attention'.[3]

The Coop ban produced a variety of reactions; hunting people were encouraged to visit their local Coop and make a personal protest to

1 See *Farnham Herald*, Nov. 1981 to May 1982 *passim.*

2 MFHA Memorandum, 30 Mar. 1982.

3 Ibid., 30 Mar. 1982.

the manager,[1] information was sought on any potentially embarrassing links between Coop branches or individuals and any business or sporting contacts they might have with hunting people. Some attempts were made to get the decision reversed, and the Fernie Hunt (with hounds) picketed delegates to the Cooperative Congress at Brighton in June 1982.[2]

When local councils were debating motions to abolish hunting in their areas the BFSS branch teams adopted a variety of approaches; they attended meetings, sent letters to the press, made personal calls on councillors and even stood for elections to the councils themselves. All of this, as in Waverley, enlivened village hall and local council meetings throughout the winter of 1981–2.

By mid 1982 over 25 councils, including a number of county councils, had taken a vote on hunting; at least 15 councils, all Labour controlled, had voted to ban hunting on their land. The amount of land owned by the sympathetic councils totalled not more than 40,000 acres and affected relatively few hunts. However, the publicity value to the League was enormous. Both the League and the BFSS realised that the dramatic surge of motions, debates and arguments could not last. Indeed *Horse and Hound* claimed 'Anti-hunting moves in the county councils show signs of running out of steam, thanks to the victories of hunting folk in so many areas'.[3] Certainly the BFSS, having failed to spot the trend when it started, was quickly and efficiently mobilised to defend field sports when local authorities debated them. It soon realised that the political complexion of the council was likely to be the major factor and saw that in rural areas, where in some cases significant amounts of land were council owned, the councils were predominantly Conservative.

Nevertheless the League had found a most valuable policy which gave them scope for future initiatives. They began to look for other large institutional landlords such as the National Trust upon whom to exercise their influence for they realised that only large scale landowners (such as the Coop) could significantly affect the availability of hunting land.

In 1982, the League had four major policy areas all of which had been at one time or another predominant. The sanctuary policy was no longer as significant as it had been although it still provided both a useful source of publicity when sanctuaries were invaded and a safe haven for the legacies which continued to keep the organisation financi-

1 MFHA Memorandum, 17 Feb. 1982.

2 *Guardian*, 1 June 1982.

3 *Horse and Hound*, 3 Sept. 1982, p. 3.

ally buoyant. The second policy, to prosecute for trespass and damage, derives from the first and had a similar function: to generate publicity to annoy the hunting community and almost coincidentally to provide sanctuary for a few animals. The third policy, to encourage landowners to ban hunting on their land, obtained a sudden and dramatic dominance in 1981–2 although it had long been one of the League's policies. The fourth policy, by far the most important and the one to which all league activity in theory is directed, is to promote and help pass legislation which will abolish hunting.

The League committed many of its emotional and financial resources in the 1970s to facilitating anti-hunting legislation.[1] Despite this activity all attempts have failed and if there are no legislative successes in the 1980s internal strife will occur again for the League cannot fall back on the same old themes. The RSPCA is now officially if not actively anti-hunting; the media, including the BBC, are increasingly antagonistic to hunting, so is the church and public opinion in general. The League cannot continue merely pointing out these facts; it needs a significant breakthrough in order to keep morale high and to avoid turning in upon itself once more.

The inevitable clash between strong leaders and incurably optimistic members has involved the League (like the RSPCA) in a series of internal but well publicised power struggles. The damage has been more apparent than real for while the publicity has harmed the public image of both societies, it has kept them in the public eye. Internally at least the violence of the debates has had a cathartic effect. The societies may have lost members but they retain the cushion which legacies give them.

The continuing and public struggles within the League are a product of two factors: a leadership independent of the necessity of earning subscriptions, and a membership with a cause. Gradual changes in policy have been inevitable but it has usually taken a push from the membership or major divisions within the Executive Committee for these changes to take place. Strong leaders such as Hemingway, Rowley, Houghton and Course have been necessary to keep the organisation going and to give it its drive, but when the tactical hobby-horse of the leader, whether 'demos', 'sanctuaries' or 'politics', has been ridden as far as it will go, the change in emphasis from one strategy to another has rarely been smooth. The League's leadership earnestly hopes that its subsidiary tactics of generating publicity through a variety of means will sustain it until a genuine breakthrough is achieved.

1 For details see below, Chapter 12.

The public activism of the HSA

In 1963, the LACS began to withdraw from 'field work' and to eschew confrontational techniques, partly because of the failure of the secret weapon and partly because the new Chairman, Mr Rowley, wanted to improve the League's image. The leading 'field workers', however, enjoyed their 'sport' and felt that their activities both protected animals and aided the anti-hunting cause. As a result, an *ad hoc* organisation, the Hunt Saboteurs Association (HSA), was formed by groups of League members who wished to continue sabotaging hunts. Although membership has continued to overlap with the LACS, there are no administrative or financial connections between the two organisations.

The aims of the HSA have remained clear throughout its existence: 'To save the lives of hunted animals by legal, non-violent, direct means and to bring to the attention of People and Parliament the barbaric cruelties involved in the hunting of animals until such time as these practices are banned by law'.[1]

To achieve this objective the HSA has been guided by four major principles: firstly, to keep the organisation informal; secondly, to concentrate on sabotaging hunts; thirdly, realising that this will not of itself end hunting, to encourage other animal welfare organisations to press for legislative change; and fourthly, to remain within (if only just within) the law. The HSA cannot claim to have held rigorously to these principles, but they remain its essential tenets.

The central organisation of the HSA developed slowly, and then only in response to the need for separate groups to share information, discuss tactics and allocate their limited funds. Lack of money was the main reason for the slow evolution of an HSA structure; another was the desire of activists to concentrate on their own individual field work. In 1963, the first HSA group was formed in Devon and its prime targets were the otter hunts of the area which, being conducted on foot, were easier to sabotage. Sabotaging otter hunts was also a relatively easy way of generating publicity for, by the 1960s, the media were aware that otters were in danger of extinction.

A London group was formed in 1964 and this concentrated on attacking the suburban fox hunts in South and East England. Newspaper reports of its activities generated publicity for the cause, and local activists created new groups. By 1972, 17 active and 58 'potential' groups of two or more people had been identified; almost all the active groups were in Southern England, the largest being in University towns. Tentative developments in the North were based on the Universities of

1 A statement of principle quoted in each edition of *Howl*, the magazine of the HSA.

Leeds and Newcastle. By 1982, they had developed a 'contact list' of 86 people and groups.

The publicity created by HSA activities gradually produced an influx of funds. These were, initially, only sufficient to pay for the expenses of a part-time honorary secretary and the cost of the occasional bulletin. A biannual newsletter began in 1971 and, in July of the same year, the first recorded HSA General Meeting of 25 local leaders took place. Officers were elected and their legal position discussed. It was decided to keep things as informal as possible; a constitution was 'approved' but not 'adopted'.[1] Lines of communication were drawn and the largest group, in London, was established as the Headquarters which would deal with publicity and recruitment. Demonstrations and fund raising were to remain the prerogative of the local groups. In 1972 an unpaid press officer and an unpaid legal adviser were appointed.[2]

The development of the organisation was aided by donations of over £500, resulting from a major *Guardian* article of July 1972.[3] This money, with further income from a higher membership level, encouraged the HSA to begin an official glossy *Newsletter* in 1973.[4] Its aim was to inform the faithful about the work of other organisations, both sympathetic and unsympathetic, and to encourage members of the HSA to be active against seal culling, coursing, badger digging, vivisection and other activities with which the animal welfare movement is involved.

HSA finances and membership received a further much-needed boost[5] when, on 22 November 1975, the BBC 'Open Door' programme featured the Society. Membership immediately doubled and increased steadily as further newspaper articles and television items appeared.[6] The combination of this publicity and a few advertisements in weekly magazines brought the membership to nearly 3,000 in mid-1977.[7] It also gave the organisation, for the first time, a healthy surplus bank balance, £3,632 in May 1976,[8] from which publicity and legal fees

1 From interviews in 1973, 1976, 1978 and 1982 with D. Whetton (HSA Hon. Secretary) and other HSA members.

2 Ibid., see also *Newsletter*, no. 1, 1971.

3 'Otters' Hell', Jill Tweedie, *Guardian*, 3 July 1972.

4 *Howl* or 'Hands off our wildlife'. It is the only magazine or journal concerned with hunting which manifests a sense of humour.

5 Total income for 1973–4 was only £458, Annual Report 1973–4.

6 Southern TV and London Weekend TV broadcast items about the HSA in 1977.

7 HSA Annual Report, 1976–7, p. 3. Advertisements appeared in *Time Out, New Statesman* and *The Vegetarian*.

8 Statement of Accounts, 1976–7.

could be paid without driving the Society into debt. Another BBC programme in March 1981 gave it further publicity and more members.

In 1982 the HSA mailing list rose to around 4,000 of whom 'well over 3,000' were paid up members (at £3 per head per year).[1] Income in the early 1980s was between £10,000 and £15,000 a year, the fluctuations depending less on membership changes than on the level of subscriptions and donations.

The HSA has remained, in essence, a collection of local groups dedicated to the sabotage and disruption of hunting and coursing. The techniques have included: spraying 'Anti-mate' to spoil scent; making a noise in coverts to encourage foxes to go to earth; blowing hunting horns to attract hounds away from the huntsman; blowing dog whistles which only the hounds can hear; giving false directions to hunt followers.

The number of 'strikes' or 'hits' have varied from year to year, depending on the enthusiasm and size of the active groups. Some have hit a hunt every weekend during the 30 week long hunting season, others only venture forth occasionally. The Midland and Anglian group managed to send out 90 teams in 1972 mainly to 'fashionable' hunts in the shires. Groups in the South-West focussed their attentions on otter hunts in the early 1970s; the Bucks and Courtney Tracy Otterhounds alone were visited 20 times in 1972.[2] The HSA sent the long-suffering huntsman a Christmas card and a St Valentine's card for 'good sportsmanship'. Groups in the South East widened their net and hit 27 different hunts in the 1970–1 season.[3] By 1970, when the HSA was well established, the total number of 'hits' per season ranged from between 150 and 200 and continued at this level throughout the 1970s and early 1980s. Since members arrange their own transport and pay their own expenses their enthusiasm is the chief determinant of their level of activity.

In 1974, the leadership discussed but resisted attempts at the AGM to extend HSA activities to include the disruption of shooting and fishing. Members were unanimously against shooting, but were divided over angling; in the end the meeting agreed to concentrate on hunting and coursing – with the emphasis on coursing since it was 'the most likely blood sport to be banned by law'.[4] Some action has been taken against shooting. A grouse shoot was successfully stopped in August

1 Interview with Secretary, 1982.

2 *Newsletter*, no. 4, Mar. 1973.

3 *Newsletter*, no. 1, June 1971.

4 Minutes of 1974 AGM.

1978. It was a 'gesture' and no further demonstrations against shooting were planned. However, in many areas unofficial 'hits' have been arranged on each 'glorious 12th' of August at the beginning of the shooting season.

The problems of divergent interests have repeatedly troubled the HSA. In 1977 and 1978 the rules were revised and made binding on members, partly to protect the Society from its less responsible members. Matters, however, continued to arise at meetings which were not strictly relevant to sabotaging hunts. In 1978, a National Front member was expelled since it was felt that his politically unacceptable views had brought the Society into disrepute.[1] Similarly, a motion was passed allowing the HSA to associate itself with campaigns against environmental abuse.

In the 1970s the HSA allowed some extensions of its tactics in the field. Distributing leaflets at agricultural shows has become a popular activity so have 'run-ons' at gymkhanas and horse shows. These tactics produce valuable local publicity but do little to bring the HSA's goals any closer.

From the beginning of the 1970s the more politically active members of the HSA have accepted the limitations of HSA policy and have sought to work within the LACS and the RSPCA in order to make these bodies more politically active. A number of HSA members, particularly the leadership, belonged to the RSPCA Reform Group and were among those who gave evidence at the Sparrow Inquiry. During the struggle to change RSPCA policy the HSA advised those of its members who were also RSPCA members which RSPCA Council candidates were worthy recipients of their vote. Partly thanks to their efforts, at least four members of the HSA were on the RSPCA's Council by the time the RSPCA formally stated its opposition to hunting in 1974. The official change in RSPCA policy was a relief to all HSA members, who felt that they could then concentrate on converting the opposition, and since 1974 many HSA members have joined or have declared an intention to join the RSPCA. The intention to join was added (unasked) to almost 10 per cent of the questionnaires returned by HSA members. *Howl* in 1976 stated 'We now have no hesitation in advising members to join the Society'.[2] Their position in 1982 is more equivocal now that conservatives control the RSPCA Council; however they have not rescinded their official approval.

Relations with the LACS have been more complicated. The League's sanctuary policy was felt to be only a limited success, but such was the

1 Discussion at 1978 AGM, and Memorandum from expelled HSA member.

2 *Howl*, 6, Spring 1976.

commitment to it of Mr Rowley that any criticism of it appeared to him to be a personal attack. It was inevitable, therefore, that a clash would occur between those who favoured action on the political and legislative fronts and those who favoured the policies of Rowley. The major clashes occurred in 1977 at the LACS AGM when activists, many of whom also belonged to the HSA and the RSPCA, tried to change the policies of the League. They criticised the lack of effective publicity, the expense of the sanctuary policy, and the unsympathetic reactions of Rowley. The meeting itself showed a broad division between the mainly young activists who were 'united in their common determination to end blood sports in their lifetime',[1] and the older animal welfare people who had joined the movement because it was, according to the activists, socially the in-thing to do.[2] One activist at the 1977 AGM reported 'an elderly woman boasted that she had been "in Animal Welfare" for 35 years – I would be ashamed to make such a claim'.[3]

The 1977 AGM and Extraordinary General Meeting of the League did ultimately result in changes in the League's policy, although at the expense of further major and public ruptures within the animal welfare movement. The HSA made an attempt to improve inter-group relations by suggesting a meeting with the LACS and NSACS. However, the LACS failed to reply, and the NSACS stated that its constitution barred such a meeting.[4] The LACS's refusal was undoubtedly because Rowley felt that HSA members were part of the 'gang of young hoodlums who are after the League's money'.[5] Since the HSA believed that this response was attributable to 'Rowley's megalomaniac desire to retain the Chairmanship of the LACS',[6] it was not unduly upset. Nevertheless, it did feel that Rowley's attacks on fellow anti-hunting workers, his willingness to ignore LACS rules and policy decisions, and his retreat after 1975 from the parliamentary front rendered him unfit to remain Chairman.[7] Having helped in the process of removing Rowley, the HSA was also instrumental in stopping the return to influence of his

1 *Howl*, 9, Autumn 1977, p. 3.

2 The activists believe that all 'they' do is 'discuss how terrible blood sports are at coffee parties'. Ibid., p. 3.

3 Ibid., p. 3.

4 HSA Annual Report, 1976–7, p. 2.

5 LACS AGM, 12 May 1977.

6 HSA *Newsletter*, June 1977.

7 Ibid., June 1977.

supporters at the 1978 AGM of the LACS. They recommended a number of candidates for the LACS Committee and urged LACS members to attend their AGM and vote accordingly.[1]

While some HSA members concerned themselves with the problems of allied organisations and with helping the LACS in particular to increase the level of its political involvement, others were determined to continue with direct action. Many of them joined the Animal Activists,[2] a society which began as an off-shoot of the HSA when the HSA decided it wanted to avoid the 'wrong kind of publicity' and would concern itself only with hunting.[3] Animal Activists was formed in 1975 with the explicit policy of applying direct tactics against all forms of animal abuse. It is strictly vegetarian, as is the amorphous Animal Liberation Front (ALF), begun in 1976 with the policy of destroying laboratories using animals for experimentation, and of attacking hunt kennels. In just over a year ALF claimed 37 hits and did damage amounting to £300,000.[4]

Its founder, R. Lee a student solicitor, was jailed for three years in 1974 and jailed again in 1977 for further attacks on breeding establishments. He withdrew from illegal activity after these two periods in jail but remained an activist, and left behind a relatively flourishing organisation which claimed over 2,000 members with over 300 actively involved with illegal activity.[5] The true figures are probably nearer 500 and 50; nevertheless strong sympathy for the activists does exist within the animal welfare movement.

The fringe groups changed their tactics in the 1980s. Their activities remained unofficial and their membership loosely structured, as individuals were caught and imprisoned or as they recruited new members. One group, the Northern Animal Liberation League, decided to arrange 'break-ins' at animal experiment or animal breeding centres in broad daylight. On occasion they took and distributed photographs to ensure maximum publicity.

In 1982, a series of raids on breeding establishments, fur shops and farms with battery hens were mounted. Some actions received a sympathetic hearing in the press; others, particularly the release of mink from mink farms, worried both countrymen and ecologists.[6]

1 See HSA Internal Memorandum, June 1978.

2 *Howl*, 5, Autumn 1975.

3 HSA *Newsletter*, 3, 1972, p. 12.

4 *The Times*, 12 Apr. 1978. Article by M. Duffy. Confirmed in conversation with active (but necessarily anonymous) members in Sept. 1978.

5 *Sunday Times*, 5 Sept. 1982.

6 *Guardian*, 12 Aug. 1982.

This activity had, for the ALF, one highly satisfactory outcome. It realised that its known militancy constituted a threat to establishments which conducted animal experiments whether or not it raided the laboratory. Many Medical Research Council laboratories were disrupted by threats but few were actually raided.[1] Indeed, ALF activities, however deplorable to research scientists, did make many question the need to use animals in research and work to reduce the numbers involved. One researcher who used animals in his experiments stated 'there is much more consciousness about the way animals are treated today because of these people than there used to be'.[2]

The activities of these groups, one operating consciously outside the law, have, in a sense, left the HSA free to pursue its own stated goals. However, most of the activists who indulge in illegal activity have kept their HSA membership; and so even if Animal Activists or ALF members actually claim responsibility for strikes against laboratories and hunt property, blame is nevertheless attached to the HSA, affecting the attitudes of the public and of decision-makers towards the Society. The HSA has tried throughout the 1970s to restrict its members to non-violent actions which do not offend the law. In 1974, they turned down a request that 'the immobilisation of hunt vehicles'[3] should be included as an acceptable tactic. The publicity gained by the peaceful annual sit-ins at the BFSS offices between 1974–8 was cancelled out by the damage done to their image by the destructive raids on the BFSS offices in March 1977. Responsibility for these raids was claimed by the ALF, but the three people charged for the break-in were also HSA members. Inevitably this and other actions have severely damaged relations with the police.

Until the mid 1970s the problem of violence was largely confined to the hunting field. Confrontations with 'hunt heavies' were frequently unpleasant although the resulting court cases brought welcome publicity and donations from sympathisers. Many hunters continue to feel, along with a joint Master of the Essex Union Hunt, that 'Horsewhipping a hunt saboteur is rather like beating a wife. They are both private matters'.[4] As early as 1964 a group of four Culmstock Otter Hunt supporters and seven HSA members were bound over to keep the peace because of a well-publicised scuffle in which a saboteur's jaw was broken.[5] As a result of this court case the HSA became newsworthy

1 About 6,000 people marched to and demonstrated outside research laboratories in Carshalton on 24 April 1983.

2 *Sunday Times*, 5 Sept. 1982.

3 1973–4 Annual Report. This became a policy of the ALF. See *Howl*, 8, Spring 1977, p. 3.

4 *Howl*, 8, Spring 1977, p. 1.

5 *Daily Telegraph*, 30 Sept. 1964, gave 22 column inches to the court case.

and relatively trivial incidents became major stories. It is, for example, unlikely that the *Daily Mail* would have spent 48 column inches discussing the Protection of Deer Bill unless its reporters had not felt that the anti-hunting movement was news.[1] Similarly all the Sunday papers reported that a man had been knocked down by a horse in November 1976; the story has significance only because a member of the Cowdray Hunt attempted to ride down a saboteur.[2]

Not only was violence used against HSA members; the law also was invoked by HSA opponents in their attempts to suppress the Society. In December 1971 when the HSA was very active, Francis Bennion, a well-known right-winger, tried to get the Director of Public Prosecutions to charge the HSA Committee with 'conspiracy to disrupt lawful events'.[3] The BFSS gave Bennion temporary support but withdrew it after a few months.[4]

More recently and, for the HSA, more significantly a member made legal history in 1977. Mrs V. Waters was a witness at a case concerning violence at a meet of the Atherstone Hunt.[5] The defending solicitor, when his clients were bound over, asked under the Justices of the Peace Act 1361 that Mrs Waters should also be bound over on the grounds that she, as a well-known HSA member, might be troublesome in the future. Mrs Waters not surprisingly said that, as she was a witness called by the police to help with the case, she would not be bound over. She was nevertheless sent to prison for a month and initially treated like a criminal rather than a civil prisoner. The fines of the guilty men were paid for by the BFSS and the Master of the Atherstone Hunt declared: 'I'm very glad she's in prison. She was a bloody nuisance'.[6]

This was not the first occasion on which an HSA member had been threatened by the application of an obscure law. A member in Swindon was charged under an Act of 1847 for laying carrion in the street.[7] His crime was to display the remains of a fox killed by the Old Berks Hunt; killing the fox was legal, but attempting to draw critical attention to its death was apparently not. In the same year another HSA member

1 *Daily Mail*, 19 Feb. 1965. A full-page 'Newsight' Report.

2 See particularly the *Sunday Mirror, People, Sunday Telegraph*, 21 Nov. 1976.

3 See *Newsletter*, no. 3, p. 2. Bennion also prosecuted Peter Hain in an attempt to stop Hain's successful campaign in 1970 to cancel the tour of the S. African cricket team.

4 Confirmed by the BFSS Public Relations Officer in an interview in Sept. 1973.

5 *Sunday Times*, 21 Aug. 1977. The report covered 70 column inches of print.

6 Ibid., 21 Aug. 1977. The 1361 Act was applied again to sufferers of an attack in Sussex in Dec. 1979.

7 *Howl*, 8, Spring 1977, p. 1. The charge was later dropped.

was threatened with prosecution for unblocking earths in the Duke of Beaufort's hunt country.

HSA members are aware that when they are charged with a 'breach of the peace' when attempting to sabotage a hunt or coursing meeting the proclivities of the judge or magistrate who hears their case will be of great significance. In February 1977, 31 saboteurs were bound over for disrupting a coursing meeting.[1] The HSA was advised to appeal and made a request for legal aid which in all cases was refused, even though a number were either students or unemployed. The judge who turned down their applications and who would have heard their appeals, Judge W. Openshaw, was a member of the BFSS and, of his two sons, one was a former Master of Hounds and the other a BFSS honorary local secretary. Openshaw did not declare this fact and it was not known until after the case was over. However three saboteurs managed to obtain the free services of a solicitor; he took the appeal to another judge who dismissed the police evidence and the case without bothering to hear evidence for the defence. It is cases like this, however insignificant in themselves, which lowers the trust of HSA members in the impartiality of the establishment.

Since 1977 the HSA has been worried by the revised *Criminal Trespass Law* which came into effect in the middle of that year. The purpose of the law is to protect property from squatters, but the HSA fears that merely being on farmland 'with intent to sabotage the hunt' could be construed as criminal trespass.[2]

The HSA has always been conscious that relationships with the police were likely to be difficult. In general the HSA leadership felt that the police were a neutral body and advised members: 'At all times be courteous to the police – generally they are fairly unbiased and occasionally, particularly on otter hunts, openly on our side'.[3] Unsympathetic policemen can nevertheless arrest people 'for actions likely to cause a breach of the peace' and even Anti-mate spray can be classified as a 'harmful weapon'.[4] The *Newsletter* of 1976 stated: 'At all costs avoid direct antagonistic confrontation'.[5] This more urgent state-

1 Details in *Howl*, 19, Autumn 1981.

2 *Howl*, 9, Autumn 1977, p. 2. The law has not, at time of printing, yet been applied to a member of the HSA.

3 HSA *Newsletter*, no. 1, June 1971, p. 2.

4 Ibid., p. 2.

5 *Newsletter*, no. 4, Mar. 1973, p. 1.

ment was an indication of the fact that the police were becoming less sympathetic to the HSA and more tolerant of the violence inflicted on saboteurs and their vehicles by 'hunt heavies'.[1]

Relations with the police have gradually worsened in the 1970s. It was disclosed in 1977 that the Police National Computer had details of HSA activists and their cars.[2] The police had obtained a membership list and added the details to their computer. This became known when a number of HSA members, stopped for traffic offences, found that the police had details of their HSA membership. In 1977, the police were able to show that HSA supporters were in the vicinity of John Peel's grave when it was desecrated in January of that year. The police have used this case and the subsequent attacks on the BFSS offices and on hunt kennels to justify having private information about HSA members on their computer. They felt totally vindicated when two members of the HSA were imprisoned for desecrating Peel's grave and three members were jailed for breaking into the BFSS offices. This extra-legal activity by a few over-eager individuals has caused relations with the police to deteriorate to the extent that the Executive Committee has stated: 'The police have been putting a lot of undue pressure on some members over the past year'.[3] The Committee accepts that recent publicity has been damaging to the HSA and has reminded its members 'that they should take the utmost care' when attempting to sabotage a hunt, not least because 'The opposition play dirty and will twist any little incident to their own purposes'.[4]

Undoubtedly this perception of police harrassment has a self-fulfilling quality and mutual antagonism between the police and saboteurs is bound to build up. One result of this deteriorating relationship is that many saboteurs feel that, since the police are actively against them anyway, there is no particular harm in taking the law into their own hands. For this reason there is greater acceptance at all levels of the HSA of the need for violence,[5] and, indeed, at least three members of the 1978 Committee were either members of, or expressly sympathetic to, the ALF.[6]

1 This has continued. See *Howl*, 7, Autumn 1976, and *Howl*, 8, Spring 1977. The much visited Enfield Chase Hunt started a Hunt Protection Association whose task was to sabotage the saboteurs. See *Howl*, 9, Autumn 1977, p. 4.

2 *Datalink* (for programmers and systems analysts). See the issues of 24 and 30 Oct. 1977; 7 and 21 Nov. 1977; and 5 Dec. 1977.

3 HSA Memorandum, Nov. 1977.

4 Ibid., Nov. 1977.

5 The HSA has issued advice on what to do when arrested and on how to cope with police questioning.

6 From Internal Memorandum, 1978.

The HSA in 1982 finds itself in the same position as the LACS in the 1960s. It has turned away from a total reliance on direct action and field work, and is attempting to find new channels for its energies. It can see plainly that hunting will not cease because of its activities, and so it has decided to adopt, as a second major channel for its activities, the policy of politicising the anti-hunting movement. This is not the same as taking the lead in political matters. It has encouraged the larger and more respectable organisations such as the RSPCA and the LACS to press more actively for legislative change. The HSA leadership was delighted with the policies and actions of Lord Houghton and, indeed, 40 per cent of HSA members belong to the LACS.[1]

Despite keeping sabotage as its primary aim the HSA has, like the League in the 1960s, become a more mature organisation. It now has a constitution, a set of rules and leaders, many in their late 30s, who have achieved a certain amount of respectability. They have survived without being dull; however their official decision to discourage illegal behaviour has partially forfeited the loyalty of a number of their activists who are willing to contemplate violent and illegal acts.

Indeed, the ALF has attracted many of the HSA radicals and other members with a less violent and more political perspective have moved closer to the LACS. Dave Whetton, the HSA Secretary throughout the 1970s, has reduced his commitment to the HSA and become a Committee member of the LACS. His successor as Secretary was, in 1982, on a suspended sentence for activities conducted under the aegis of the ALF. Had the HSA been a more bureaucratic and centralised organisation it would undoubtedly have been racked by dissent. As it is, local groups make their own way; some, with a strong radical element, have become involved with militant anti-vivisectionists; others, while equally keen to sabotage hunts, have decided to use their surplus energies to assist the LACS.

The HSA has to hope that legislation against hunting will materialise within the next few years. If it does not, the leadership's decision to work within the system will, in the minds of its most active members, have been the wrong one.

The respectable failure of the NSACS

Organisation

In 1932 the unity of the LACS was split by an internal row. Disagreement arose because of the League's attacks on 'the supineness of the

1 From questionnaire. Seven out of the ten 1978 Committee members belonged to the LACS and at least five to the RSPCA.

RSPCA',[1] and some members' criticisms of royalty. The split assumed serious proportions since the leading members were unable to reach a compromise, and in early 1932 the President and Hon. Treasurer resigned. On 8 July 1932, these two, together with many friends and allies from the League, set up the National Society for the Abolition of Cruel Sports (NSACS). Those that joined the new Society did so largely through the resentment caused by Henry Amos, the League founder, who suggested that some League members suffered from a 'compromising, time-serving spirit' which attempted to 'deflect the League from the aggressive, challenging spirit and policy' to one which 'plays into the hands of the RSPCA and the hunting party'.[2] Many of those who resigned from the Council felt that continual criticism of the RSPCA was pointless. Equally Amos's attacks on their probity were more than they were prepared to tolerate.

The NSACS grew rapidly at first. Many of its early members were defectors from the League, including Henry Salt, who became a Vice-President, and Ernest Bell, a co-founder of the League. The Oxford Society for the Abolition of Cruel Sports immediately removed its affiliation from the League and joined forces with the NSACS. It remained a separate Society until 1971 when it became fully integrated into the NSACS.[3]

The Society's membership, excluding the Oxford Group, has fluctuated over the years as Table 5.2 shows:

Table 5.2
NSACS membership

Year	Approx. number of members
1933	300
1935	450
1938	550
1940	250
1950	2,000–2,500 (maximum of 3,000 in 1948–9)
1960	1,500
1970	1,200
1978	under 1,000
1982	5–600

1 *Cruel Sports*, 1932, p. 75.

2 *Cruel Sports*, 1932, p. 11.

3 The Oxford Branch, never more than 120 strong, had the same Secretary, Mrs Muriel Chapman, throughout its existence. She disapproved of the attacks on the RSPCA, accepted that the split was largely over personalities, and still belonged to both the LACS and the RSPCA. Interview in Sept. 1973.

The gradual growth of the Society before the war ceased in 1940 when, but for the work of the Oxford Branch Secretary, the Society would have foundered. After the war the prospect of legislation against hunting stimulated recruitment and caused a steep rise in the total membership; indeed the Scott Henderson Committee suggested that the NSACS had about 6,000 members.[1] However this is highly unlikely and is not even claimed by the Society itself. Indeed, in 1950 the Society admitted that 'membership has fallen and funds have sharply declined because of administrative neglect caused in turn by our activities on behalf of the Bill'.[2] Since then membership has declined further, and the Society has failed to attract sufficient new supporters to replace its ageing membership. Publicity derived from the anti-coursing measures of the 1970s, however, helped to bring in sufficient new members to stabilise the membership at around, but not above, 1,000 people. The absence of major parliamentary debates in the 1980s contributed to a further decline to around 600 in 1982.

Financially the Society has been relatively secure. Its income during the first year was £557 and by 1938 it was over £800, of which legacies accounted for £350. From the war period to this day legacies and dividend income have played a major role in keeping the Society alive, for these sources of income have continued to increase even during periods when membership has declined sharply. Since the early 1950s legacies have been the major source of income and these in turn facilitated the purchase of a portfolio of shares. Income from these shares overtook income from subscriptions in 1973–4. This trend has continued as the figures for 1976 and 1978 show. There was, at the end of 1978, an accumulated fund, which included the investments, of £52,421 and a surplus of income over expenditure of £6,073 for the year.

Expenditure during the 1970s was minimal; the Secretary's salary and printing and stationery accounted for half the total expenditure and the rest was accounted for by such items as a press cuttings service and the hire of rooms. Each year the accumulated fund grows larger and larger, for there have been no significant initiatives or major projects which have, in the Society's opinion, been worthy of their support.

This extreme caution largely results from the nature of the mainly elderly, female and middle-class leadership which has been extremely concerned to uphold decent and civilised values. The majority of the Council and of those who attend AGMs are women, all but one of its

1 *Scott Henderson Report*, para. 130.

2 Annual Report and Accounts, 1949–50, p. 2.

Table 5.3

Income	1976	1978
Subscriptions and Donations	818	858
Legacies	14,099	7,433
Investment income	2,169	3,243
Miscellaneous	381	550
Total	£17,467	£12,084

recent secretaries have been women and three of the seven post-war Chairmen have been women. Of the others, one was a musician, one a master at a leading public school and two were clergymen. In 1978, the leadership was also relatively elderly, the average of the Committee being around 60; in 1973 three Council members had belonged to the Society since it began over 40 years earlier. By 1982, the major changes in the Committee were caused by the deaths rather than the withdrawals of Committee members and the average age remained high.

Throughout its existence the Society has been concerned with status and respectability. Among the early Vice-Presidents were Bertrand Russell, J.B. Priestley, H.G. Wells and five professors, including H.J. Laski. Reverends and writers featured strongly in their membership list; in 1934, the report stated 'a considerable proportion of our new members are authors'.[1] Since then the Society has maintained its links with important people from all walks of life but especially with academics, churchmen and authors. It is justifiably proud of its literary and intellectual tradition and offers Vice-Presidentships to people who succeed in these fields. Vice-Presidents in 1982 included Patrick Moore, Lord Soper and Iris Murdoch. Collectively they gave a stamp of respectability to the Society but did little to advance its cause.

Aims and tactics

Since its inception the aims of the NSACS have been consistent. Its manifesto, as amended in 1936, reads:

> The Society's ultimate aim is to secure the legal protection and state control of British wildlife and the legal abolition of all forms

1 Annual Report, 1934, p. 3. This contrasts sharply with the early membership of the LACS.

> of killing for sport; its immediate object will be to educate public opinion to demand the suppression of the hunting and coursing of our native wild animals – Deer, Fox, Otter, Badger, Hare, etc.[1]

In subsequent years the objective was refined but not altered. Its manifesto in 1978 stated the same primary goal but added three secondary points: (a) that it seeks to obtain the co-operation of naturalists, (b) that it is opposed to all killing for sport, and (c) that it wants to reach its goals by peaceful and educational means. This last part was added to the Society's articles of association in 1975, when it emphasised that it advocated 'peaceable, non-violent and non-aggressive methods. . . It does not favour practices that can distress, disrupt or confuse animals connected with hunting and coursing'.[2] It was explicitly rejecting the methods used by the Hunt Saboteurs Association and by the more active members of the LACS.

The Society has emphasised educational and publicity-seeking campaigns from the beginning. It issued 15 pamphlets in its first two years and quickly launched campaigns against the Eton College Beagles and against the National Trust for allowing hunting on their properties.[3] These campaigns were mounted by issuing leaflets, writing letters to the papers, and holding meetings of the faithful in various parts of the country. By 1935, 120,000 leaflets had been circulated to about 3,000 schools and, by 1937, 600,000 leaflets had been sent to 11,000 elementary schools.[4] When war broke out in 1939 all 30,000 elementary schools in the country had received parcels of leaflets. While this was a splendid achievement and may well have influenced a number of people, it did not generate publicity or have any identifiable short-term influence on the public at large.

After the war the presses were even busier; they produced 86,000 pamphlets in 1946, 336,350 in 1948 and 115,600 in 1950. They were widely distributed to the public at large, and to 2,000 head teachers, 20,000 clergymen and 20,000 farmers.[5] Since 1950 no large-scale printing has occurred, although the Society keeps its major publications in print and occasionally adds to them.[6]

1 See Frontispiece of Annual Reports, 1935 and 1937.

2 NSACS *Policy and Principles*, Leaflet n.d. (probably 1977).

3 It was joined in this by the LACS. See inter alia *Cruel Sports*, 1931, p. 37.

4 Annual Report, 1937, p. 5.

5 Annual Report, 1949–50, p. 2.

6 The most significant of which are *Foxhunting* and *A Master of Hounds Speaks*.

Letter writing has been the second continuing thread in the NSACS's activities. The Council has encouraged all members to write as many letters on animal welfare themes as possible, particularly to newspapers who were willing to publish them. The *Daily Herald* and the *Manchester Guardian* were, in the 1930s, 'generous in allowing discussions on blood-sports — in striking contrast to most of the other dailies'.[1] The Society felt that the publicity created by letters 'has been of the greatest value to our cause in the last three years'.[2]

During the rebuilding period after the war letters were again the main outlet for their energies. In 1946, 119 newspapers, local and national, either published letters from, or wrote reports about, the Society.[3] Letters and articles were usually written in response to an external stimulus. When, shortly after the war, the NFU poultry committee was 'concerned about the damage done to poultry stocks by foxes' and urged that 'legislation should be introduced to provide for the continuance of adequate control for foxes',[4] the Society sensed a chance to get support from farmers and distributed 5,000 leaflets entitled 'Eggs or Foxes'. Letters were also written in support of Bills presented to parliament: for example, 45 letters were written by the Press Secretary and published during 1958 while the *Protection of Deer Bill* was under discussion.[5]

Letters and articles were not always motivated by events in the hunting world or because a debate was pending. One letter calling for a reform of parliament used the failure of anti-hunting legislation as an illustration of how easy it was for 'popular' legislation to be thwarted.[6] Despite the impossibility of measuring the success of such low-key activities as letter-writing campaigns, the Society continues to feel that publishing letters and articles, cultivating journalists and writing sensible and factual pamphlets are the best ways for it to proceed. It is content to adopt the role of supporting agency, and is equally happy to leave the initiative to other societies.[7] Such a policy is understandable when it is realised that most of the leading members belong to the RSPCA or the LACS.

1 Annual Report, 1933, p. 8.

2 Annual Report, 1939, p. 4.

3 Annual Report, 1946, p. 4.

4 NFU Yearbook, 1946, quoted in NSACS Annual Report, 1946, p. 5.

5 Annual Report, 1958.

6 Letter from Mrs M. Chapman, *New Statesman*, 5 Oct. 1973, p. 474.

7 From interviews with NSACS Secretary in 1973 and 1978.

Not all the media have been helpful. Before the war the NSACS managed to get its views heard on radio in a number of discussions,[1] but generally felt the BBC to be unsympathetic. Even in 1950 the Society was moved to say: 'The BBC have broadcast frequent hunting propaganda but have refused all requests made by the NSACS to be allowed to put the case against hunting'.[2] By the time the BBC was more willing to hold general debates on the hunting issue the Society had diminished in influence and had forfeited its leadership of the anti-hunting movement to the LACS. It was not, as a Society, asked to contribute to Robin Day's '*Talk-in*' on field sports in 1972.

Only twice since the war has the NSACS taken the lead on an anti-hunting issue. In 1947, it published a Bill to Protect British Wild Animals from Cruelty, which it claimed was the first strictly anti-hunting Bill to be published by any Society. The Society was encouraged by the prospect of Labour government support for the Bill and so promoted it vigorously. It started a petition in conjunction with the LACS and obtained 50,000 signatures within six months. With the help of Anthony Greenwood a modified version of this Bill[3] was debated in the 1948–9 parliamentary session but was defeated when the Labour front bench withdrew its support. This was a severe blow to the entire anti-hunting community for they had assumed that the Bill would go through. The government offered as a palliative a Committee of Inquiry to investigate cruelty to animals. When, however, the composition of the Committee was announced, the Society issued a protest for none of the anti-hunting bodies had been contacted, nor even had 'neutral' ones like the RSPCA. The Committee did, however, contain a Master of Foxhounds, a hunting veterinary surgeon and two contributors to sporting journals. A Trade Unionist had been included, but he was from the TGWU rather than from the union which represented most farm workers, the National Union of Agricultural Workers. In its protest the Society quoted the words of Mr Beadle, the founder of the BFSS, who said 'it all depends who is put on the Committee as to what they will find out'.[4] Like Mr Beadle the Society concluded that there was 'very little chance of any form of hunting being condemned by the Committee as a whole'.[5] Despite an 89 page submission to the Inquiry and further lengthy oral submissions by the Society, its doubts were justified. The Scott Henderson Committee dismissed the submissions of

1 'Should Blood Sports be Abolished', BBC Radio, 19 May 1937. Reprinted in *The Listener*.

2 Annual Report, 1949–50, p. 3.

3 *Protection of Animals (Hunting and Coursing Prohibition) Bill.*

4 NSACS *Bulletin*, 107, Oct. 1949, p. 3.

5 P. Moore, in *Against Hunting*, p. 140.

the anti-hunters and gave its approval to all types of hunting. The report has been in the forefront of the BFSS's defence since then.

The second major flurry of NSACS activity was the publication in 1965 of *Against Hunting*, a collection of essays edited by the astronomer Patrick Moore. Its aims, as expressed in the preface, were quite clear: 'To combat the deluge of hypocritical pro-hunting propaganda, to enlist the unemotional support of the RSPCA', and to 'introduce legislation in parliament'.[1] The book was favourably reviewed in the *Sunday Times, Observer* and the *Sunday Telegraph*, and received reviews in 22 newspapers and magazines.[2] It did not, however, sell many copies.

The writing, publicising and selling of this book was the last major initiative undertaken by the Society. It mounted minor campaigns against various forms of hunting, particularly when legislation was in the offing, and it criticised Pony Clubs, now affiliated to the BHS, claiming that its most important function was 'to instruct children in the art of hunting animals to death'.[3] These activities, however, were conducted mainly within the Society, either at meetings or in comments in the *Bulletin*. Since moral and educational goals are not of themselves newsworthy, the Society found itself reduced to commenting on the activities of others. They gave moral support and encouragement to the HSA in the early 1960s and, in 1971, they invited the Chairman of the RSPCA's Reform Group to speak at their AGM. But even these activities caused dissension within the Society; while on the one hand they said of the HSA 'whatever may be thought of their activities, they are stout-hearted opponents of hunting',[4] on the other hand they added a commitment to peaceable and non-violent methods to their articles of association in 1975,[5] and removed leading members of the Reform Group and of the HSA from the Society.[6]

Attempts to decide how aggressive their activities should be inevitably split the Society. In 1953, the struggle to find a new role after the failure of the 1949 Bill led to the resignation of the Chairman and Secretary and to an almost complete halt in the Society's activities.[7] In 1967, the Chairman, the Rev. A. Jones, resigned because 'a group of Council members have been able to enforce their wishes against the

1 See *Against Hunting*, pp. 10–11.

2 *Bulletins*, 147 and 148, Oct. 1965 and Feb. 1966.

3 *Bulletin*, 142, May 1964. Pony Clubs were started in 1929.

4 *Bulletin*, 142, May 1964.

5 *Bulletin*, 167, Oct. 1975.

6 From questionnaire, and from interview with two expelled persons in June and Aug. 1978.

7 From an interview with a contemporary Council member, Sept. 1973. Noted also in the BFSS Annual Report, 1953–4.

Chair'.[1] This dissension further weakened the Society and put pay to new initiatives which might have resulted in the wake of the small, but to the Society significant, amount of publicity generated by *Against Hunting*.

In the 1970s, the NSACS gradually faded from the scene. Its members were reluctant to accept the fact that well-written pamphlets no longer have much effect, and that their attempts to influence public opinion were no longer of great significance. Its unwillingness as an organisation to become politicised and fight hard and noisily for legislative change has rendered it, as a society, almost irrelevant. Younger and more radical enthusiasts have the option of joining the LACS, the HSA or the RSPCA to fight for the same causes. It is only the continuing influx of legacies and the persisting belief in the value of education and good sense which gives the Society any reason for continuing in existence.

Both its friends and its opponents saw the Society as a spent force in 1980. The last two Directors of the BFSS affect not to have heard of the organisation, and the Executive Director of the LACS had no dealings with the Society in the two years after he joined the League in 1976.[2] Only a small proportion, under 6 per cent, of HSA members also belonged to the NSACS, and only 3 per cent of HSA members thought that the Society was an effective organisation.[3] This degree of membership overlap is unusually small, considering that the HSA and the NSACS are seeking exactly similar goals. Both membership overlap and mutual regard have decreased in the years between 1976–82 because the NSACS has decided not to allow HSA members or known radicals to belong to the Society and refused two invitations to discuss with the HSA and LACS joint publicity drives in favour of anti-coursing legislation. It was further evidence that the Society is neither feared by its enemies nor respected by its friends. Its high moral tone has caused it to commit strategic suicide.

GECCAP: some political co-operation is achieved

The need for co-operation between societies has always been clear to members of the animal welfare movement, but only after the RSPCA

1 Letter in *Bulletin*, 152, May 1967.

2 From an interview, June 1978.

3 From questionnaires administered to a sample of HSA members in 1976 and 1977.

had undergone its catharsis, changed its leadership and condemned cruel sports, could any meaningful collaboration take place. In 1976, on the hundredth anniversary of the law controlling vivisection and during a period of Labour government, Animal Welfare Year (AWY) was declared on the initiative of Clive Hollands and Richard Ryder.[1] The President of the organising Committee was Lord Houghton, who was known to be sympathetic to the welfare of animals and was soon to become Chairman of the LACS. AWY did not include the anti-hunting organisations and so neither the LACS, nor the NSACS, nor the HSA benefited directly from the publicity generated by AWY activities.

The year was primarily a publicity exercise and was described by C. Hollands, its Chairman, as 'the greatest opportunity ever presented to animal societies in Britain to get their message across to the public, press and parliament'.[2] The Committee considered that 'the most important contribution made by Animal Welfare Year was, however, the bringing together, for the first time in history, nearly seventy organisations to work in harmony for a common purpose'.[3] At the end of the year the success of the venture and the realisation 'that greater strength lies in unity and collective action'[4] encouraged over fifty societies to continue their liaison with each other. Six joint consultative bodies were formed, covering the major areas of concern – pets, horses and ponies, farm animals, laboratory animals and wildlife in general. Some organisations became members of more than one of these joint bodies and the RSPCA joined all six.

The joint consultative bodies decided that they would continue to work together in a new organisation in order to make direct approaches to politicians and political parties, and in order to 'put animals into politics'. The LACS was able to join this collection of committees when the committees recombined as the General Election Co-ordinating Committee for Animal Protection (GECCAP) in April 1978. The admission of the League to GECCAP was facilitated by the fact that Lord Houghton was chairman of both, and because Hollands and Ryder, two of the most significant members of the AWY Committee, felt that the League should be included.

GECCAP expected to have six hectic months preparing itself for an autumn 1978 general election. It saw as its primary task the need to

1 Respectively Director of the Scottish Society for the Prevention of Vivisection and Chairman of the RSPCA.

2 SSPV Annual Report, 1977, Section C on Animal Welfare Year, p. 28.

3 Ibid., p. 28.

4 Ibid., p. 43.

obtain a commitment from political parties on three points. First, it wanted political parties to develop an animal welfare policy so that governments would themselves promote animal welfare legislation rather than leave the initiative to private members. Second, GECCAP urged the creation of a standing Royal Commission on Animal Protection which would codify the existing law and indicate where further action was needed. Third, GECCAP wanted parties to make a policy commitment in each of the six areas of concern, which now included blood sports, defined as 'live hare coursing and hunting with hounds'.[1]

During its first month of existence GECCAP began the process of stimulating political debate by writing to the Chairmen of the six mainland political parties. When it was realised that no election was going to be held in 1978, GECCAP mounted vigorous lobbies at the three major party conferences in October 1978. At each Conference an exhibition and information centre was set up, delegates were given literature and special meetings were held. At the Labour Conference an audience of 70–80 people, including 12 MPs, came to the GECCAP meeting and at the Conservative Conference their meeting was attended by 120–30 delegates, including eight MPs. The Liberal Conference organisers gave the GECCAP meeting, which was addressed by Lord Houghton, semi-official status. After it, over 50 people signed a resolution calling (unsuccessfully) for an emergency debate on animal welfare.

GECCAP had hoped that when its aims were successfully realised it would be able to dissolve, leaving behind effective sub-groups in the animal welfare world who would tend to work as independent bodies. Because of this expectation GECCAP was set up as an *ad hoc* Committee with no legal or fund-raising status, and its income depended upon donations from constituent charities. In its first six months it received £38,000, including £20,000 from the LACS and £10,000 from the National Anti-Vivisection Society, most of which was quickly spent on advertising and on promoting and distributing a booklet entitled 'Putting Animals into Politics'.[2] Other organisations, including the RSPCA and the NSACS, offered funds but only under certain conditions, thus leaving the future of GECCAP at the mercy of organisations which were themselves divided over the wisdom of co-operating with other animal welfare charities and of politicising the animal welfare movement. The longer GECCAP remained in existence

1 *Letter to the Political Parties*, GECCAP, Apr. 1978, p. 4. Shooting and fishing were omitted.

2 £28,000 was spent on advertising and £6,500 on printing. 45,000 copies of the brochure had been distributed by mid November, 1978. Interview with Clive Hollands, Secretary of GECCAP, Nov. 1978.

the more complicated its own status, funding, internal organisation and relations with other charities would become.

GECCAP undoubtedly had the effect of making the animal welfare issue more political. This was partly because of the enthusiasm and skill of Lord Houghton, but also because the most active members of GECCAP were those organisations whose ends could only be achieved by legislative change. The anti-vivisectionists and the anti-blood sports groups needed to influence political opinion so that legislation or executive orders could be introduced to stop the activities of which they complained. It was no coincidence that the teams of GECCAP people lobbying and leafleting at the 1978 party conferences were led by Committee members of the LACS and NAVS. They were assisted by Committee members of the HSA and RSPCA.

GECCAP, in late 1978, was faced with a series of problems, the first of which was to clarify its legal status. It also needed to work out and get agreement on its tactics for the 1979 general election and to decide on its future as an organisation. It had to decide whether to be politically active or whether to restrict itself to advertising in 'journals of opinion where people are influencing the thoughts of others'.[1] If it were instantly successful, it could dissolve itself into its constituent parts but, if it were totally unsuccessful, it would disintegrate because, as Lord Houghton stated, 'charitable bodies contain the most uncharitable people – the nearer they are to God the more vicious they can be'.[2] GECCAP predicted that they would meet with partial success and tentative commitments, making it inevitable that their goals would not quickly be met. If some promises were made during the 1979 election campaign, the organisation expected to remain dormant until the next election, leaving the task of lobbying for individual pieces of legislation to the joint consultative committees of which GECCAP was constituted.

Throughout 1978 GECCAP was planning for the 1979 election. It could not move with maximum authority until funding was assured and strategy was decided, but it could nevertheless seek to extend its range of contacts. In November 1978, the Secretary, Clive Hollands, wrote to 11,300 student unions and sent details of GECCAP to a variety of Trade Unions in the hope that some would support GECCAP and make statements on its behalf. The rewards of this kind of activity tend to be small and hard to measure; however, Lord Houghton was sure that the General Secretary of the National Union of Teachers would help GECCAP because 'he is very indebted to me'.[3]

1 Meeting of GECCAP, 16 Nov. 1978. Remarks by the Chairman, Lord Houghton.

2 Ibid.

3 Ibid.

Other animal welfare societies gradually accepted the leadership shown by GECCAP; the RSPCA sent a letter complimentary to GECCAP to all its branch secretaries in October 1978 and the NAVS ordered 10,000 copies of 'Putting Animals into Politics' for distribution to its members.

GECCAP quickly began the process of making itself better known in parliament. Uncommitted MPs were lobbied and Lord Houghton had an open letter to MPs published in the House of Commons magazine which spelt out the aims of GECCAP. He also suggested that GECCAP's constituent committees might use friendly MPs to mount a campaign of Parliamentary Questions on animal welfare matters. In the past questions have tended to increase when a Bill was being debated, but Houghton felt that questions were more useful as a means of keeping interest alive during periods when no Bill was under consideration.[1]

GECCAP's attempts to generate publicity within parliament were aided by a stroke of good fortune. In one of the last Private Members Debates before the Election,[2] a supporter, Jeff Rooker, introduced a motion on animal welfare which he linked with the need to 'Put Animals into Politics'. During the debate the government responded by outlining its commitment to setting up a Council for Animal Welfare.

Even before this boost GECCAP activities had caused considerable concern to the hunting community. The BFSS wrote a warning letter to all its members and *The Field* commented 'If Lord Houghton keeps his disparate crew together for the general election he will have a lobby of formidable resources. . . . Lord Houghton's initiative is a serious challenge to all who are concerned with hunting hounds'.[3]

Although GECCAP continued with its publicity campaign until the eve of the 1979 general election and mounted a major advertising campaign funded by the RSPCA in March 1979, it could not intervene directly in the election by supporting or advertising its support for particular candidates, since to have done so would have contravened the Representation of the People Act, 1949. However, it could and did let the public know where the individual parties stood on particular issues and encouraged local enthusiasts to ask questions at political meetings. It became clear that while all major parties had made promises to extend animal welfare legislation only Labour had clearly committed itself to the abolition of coursing and hunting.

1 In the 1960s 20–30 Parliamentary Questions a year on hunting and animal welfare were commonplace.

2 See *Hansard* (Commons) 1979, vol. 964, cols. 1873–1966, 23 Mar.

3 *The Field*, 29 Nov. 1978.

Following the general election in May 1979 GECCAP took steps to wind up its activities. However, before it did so it published a final newsletter, organised 'ginger' groups within each of the three main parties at Westminster and with the consent of GECCAP constituent members devised a way of ensuring that its work continued. At its final meeting in July 1979, GECCAP was formally dissolved and the National Consultative Committee for Animal Protection was born. Lord Houghton was its first Chairman and it was charged with the task of ensuring that animals remained in politics.

In June 1982 Lord Houghton with Clive Hollands began the process of reviving GECCAP in time for the next election. They held a number of meetings in the summer and autumn of 1982 and decided on a two-stage campaign. The first part involved ensuring that anti-hunting commitments were inserted into as many party manifestos as possible; The second and equally important stage involved a decision to scrutinise the contents of any manifesto commitments and to encourage their supporters to vote for whichever party gave the clearest and fullest promise of support for animal welfare causes.[1] The second part of the strategy was decided upon in the light of the findings of a poll in 1975 and confirmed by the poll conducted by the RSPCA in 1981 which showed that 13 per cent of the electorate would consider switching their vote in favour of candidates or parties which declared a commitment to animal welfare and anti-hunting policies. GECCAP, prompted by the League, decided to form a register of people willing to vote for animal welfare policies in the hope that, at election time, these people would form a cadre of activists in each constituency. The League was prepared to fund this register and also declared its willingness, in principle, to donate funds to any political party which made a commitment to abolish hunting.[2]

Although GECCAP itself remained an *ad hoc* body throughout its existence it did leave behind an important legacy. It had shown that the 'disparate crew' of animal welfare activists could not only cause concern to the hunting community but also that it could, given purposeful leadership, work successfully together. The work of GECCAP was unlikely to bear fruit during a period of Conservative government but by its very existence it gave notice that the animal welfare movement had learned a number of key lessons which would in time, it predicted, enable it to be more than a match for its pro-hunting (and pro-vivisectionist) opponents.

1 In Dec. 1982 R. Course formed the Animal Protection Alliance consisting of the LACS, BUAV and Compassion in World Farming. Its purpose was to co-ordinate these political initiatives.

2 Interview with LACS Executive Director, Aug. 1982.

6 The pro-hunting lobby

The beginnings of organised support

Until almost the end of the 19th century the hunting community felt secure and could see no need to organise any defence against its growing number of antagonists. Much more serious, particularly for fox hunters, was the growing number of internal disputes. Most significant were the ones over the rights of access to coverts since coverts had become more precious as hunting countries became smaller and boundary problems more frequent. An informal committee of MFHs, all belonging to Boodles Club, was established and became a source of arbitration in 1856. In 1881, the Duke of Beaufort persuaded the Boodles Committee to disband in favour of a formal organisation of all Masters to be entitled the Masters of Foxhounds Association (MFHA). It was to have a committee and a set of rules, essentially the same as those of the Boodles Committee, and all the rules were to be binding on every hunt. In 1886, it took over the assembly and publication of the *Foxhound Kennel Stud Book* and thus became the authoritative source of information on hound pedigrees. The MFHA became the governing body of the fox-hunting world and was used by Masters to solve disputes, advise on problems and make rules of behaviour for the hunting community. In 1891 the Association of Masters of Harriers and Beagles was formed in conscious imitation of the MFHA.

The MFHA was essentially an inward-looking organisation, and it became clear, when urban and evangelical opponents of hunting received support during the agricultural depression, that something more was needed. In 1884, the National Sports Protection and Defence Association was formed. It became in 1885 the Field Sports Protection and Encouragement Assocation.[1] and restricted its aims to the protection of hunting, shooting, horse racing, fishing and coursing. It determined 'to so link together sporting interests that, on any sport being attacked, full inquiry may be made by a committee of leading sportsmen, and, should such sport be found to have been properly conducted, to render assistance in opposing such attack, and that the sporting public may not be left unprepared to resist these aggressive measures'.[2]

This Society did not remain active for long and its existence has left no impression on the hunting debate.[3] It was succeeded by the equally inactive Field Sports & Game Guild which was, in turn, incorporated into the BFSS in 1932.[4]

In defence of a sport: the BFSS

Membership and income

It was inevitable that the increasing organisation of the anti-hunting movement would produce a backlash from within the hunting community. When, in 1930, the RSPCA gave its backing to a Bill to outlaw deer hunting, Fred Beadle, a West Somerset businessman and farmer, whose cousin has been Master of the Devon and Somerset Staghounds, attempted to rally local hunting people to the hunting cause. Lord Bayford, an ex-Master of Staghounds and a recent Minister of Agriculture (1922–4), was persuaded to become Chairman of a proposed pro-hunting society. A correspondence was started in *The Times* by Lord Fortescue who wrote to defend hunting against the RSPCA.[5]

The inaugural meeting was held on 4 December 1930, in London.[6] Most of the initial backing came from the stag-hunting community in Somerset and Devon, but the involvement of the Duke of Beaufort, who became its first President, induced national support. Many joined because they were aware that the abolition of stag hunting would put fox hunting at risk.

1 *Baily's* Magazine, XLIV, Aug. 1885, p. 324. This magazine preceded the *Hunting Directory*.

2 Quoted in Itzkowitz, *Peculiar Privilege*, pp. 145–6.

3 It receives no mention in the literature of the Humanitarian League, the LACS, or the BFSS.

4 It handed over 1,000 2½ per cent consols to the BFSS and ensured that it started with a number of shooting members. See first *Year Book* and second Annual Report, 1932.

5 *The Times*, 28 Mar. 1929, and 20 May 1929. See also a correspondence during June 1930.

6 *The Times*, 5 Dec. 1930, p. 21.

The Society flourished, thanks to the public response to the RSPCA poll, the warning implied by the anti-deer-hunting bill, the active support of the MFHA and the publicity given to the new Society by the sporting press. Within six months of its inaugural meeting the BFSS had attracted 3,450 members and a year later the number rose to 8,548.[1] The response was as a result of the 'intensity and frequency of attacks against sport'.[2]

The membership rose steadily until the war and then dropped sharply;[3] indeed the Society disbanded in 1940. It was re-established six months later because its opponents did not follow suit. After the war revival was rapid, for most hunting people believed that the Labour government would allow or even encourage a Private Member to present some kind of anti-hunting bill. In mid-1948 the BFSS launched a major publicity campaign to attract funds and membership, knowing that Private Members' time was shortly to be restored. The BFSS launched this campaign on the recommendation of its parliamentary advisers and in under six months collected over 100,000 members and almost 1.2 million signatures for a 'Countryman's and Sportsman's Pledge'.[4]

This well-timed operation provided the Society with both membership and sufficient income to run a campaign against the Bill to abolish stag hunting and coursing,[5] but, after the battle against it was won, the new membership evaporated. Eighty-thousand people failed to renew their membership in 1950 and in five years the Society was reduced to its pre-1948 size. Only in the 1960s when anti-coursing legislation became a regular feature of the parliamentary year did membership begin to improve.

More importantly for the future of the BFSS an increasing amount of support came from people who neither hunted nor shot. The trade membership scheme begun in the late 1960s gave the Society additional contacts with the business and commercial world and the affiliation membership scheme brought members of small local societies, often of fishermen,[6] into the BFSS alliance. The willingness of the BFSS to support coursing, and its firm espousal of the 'thin end of the wedge' argument, convinced many coursing enthusiasts that the BFSS deserved

1 BFSS, Second Annual Report, 1932.

2 Ibid., 1932.

3 See Table 6.1.

4 *Year Book*, 1949, pp. 17–19.

5 *Protection of Animals (Hunting and Coursing Prohibition) Bill*, 1948.

6 In 1973, the 4,481 members of the York and District Amalgamation of Anglers became affiliated to the BFSS. *Year Book*, 1974, p. 15.

Table 6.1
Membership of the BFSS

Month	Year	Number of members	Notes
May[1]	1931	3,450	
March	1932	8,548	
[2]	1938	10,000 approx.	'1,000 increase' reported at AGM
	1939/45	down to 4,000	
	1946	4,986	up by 804 during year
	1948	17,907	with membership of affiliated clubs the total was over 65,000
	1949	118,357	an increase in full membership of over 100,000
	1950	36,230	
	1952	22,983	
	1955	17,869	
	1956	16,000 approx.	
[3]	1960	18,000	
	1965	under 20,000	
	1970	25,000 approx.	including affiliate membership – 108,670
	1975	38,650	
[4]	1978 1980	45,000	with affiliate membership and including 1,300 trade memberships (a scheme which started in 1969), the total is 130,000
[5]	1982	62,630	including over 1,700 trade members

1 The figures quoted are either the official or estimated figures at the end of the financial year, i.e. 31 March. 1931 figures are for the year ending 31 May. All figures are from the annual *Year Book* and Annual Report.

2 Estimated figures are derived from internal evidence in the Annual Reports and checked against subscription income.

3 The lowest membership figures occurred during the period of Conservative government. 1955–60 marks the nadir; however, in the following decade membership almost doubled (see Annual Report, 1971, p. 33).

4 From interviews with the Director (formerly Secretary) of the BFSS, May 1978.

5 Figure for 30 June 1982 Affiliated Hunts & Clubs each count as one member. *Their* individual membership when totalled came to 360,380.

support.[1] Indeed 'to support and assist the BFSS'[2] is among the aims and objects of the Coursing Supporters Club.

Unlike the anti-hunting societies the major source of income for the BFSS has always been its current membership.[3] In the 1930s and 1940s over 90 per cent of its annual income was derived from subscriptions and donations. Income dropped sharply during the war years and recovered only slowly afterwards. Significantly, in the year of anti-hunting legislation, 1949, subscriptions shot up to over £50,000: however, few of the new members retained their membership, and total income dropped to £23,448 in 1950.

Both income and membership reached their lowest ebb in 1956, but thereafter, despite a static membership, income rose gradually, mainly because money was coming from other sources. Sales of badges, maps and publications made a small but increasing contribution. Bequests, although erratic, enabled the BFSS to build up a small portfolio of investments, and increased the Society's funds by £1,000 in 1954, £3,712 in 1960 and £11,962 in 1963.

In the early 1970s, it was apparent that to survive the onslaught of inflation and the growing strength of the anti-blood sports supporters, ways of increasing income would have to be found. In 1969, a system of trade membership was started; in 1974, ordinary membership fees were increased to £2 (and to £5 in 1977), and in 1976 life membership was increased from £50 to £150.[4] Nevertheless, despite a successful membership drive in the 1970s subscriptions and donations have declined as a percentage of total income from 82 per cent in 1970 to 71 per cent in 1978.[5] Subscriptions represented just under two-thirds of total income in 1981.

Sales of goods and services have had an increasingly significant effect on the Society's income. The presence of one of the BFSS caravans at horse shows has been responsible for the increase in direct sales, although as a percentage of total income they have declined from 11 per cent in 1970 to under 8 per cent in 1978.

1 See Public Relations Report in *Year Book*, 1975, p. 7, and *Year Book*, 1976, p. 7.

2 Aims and Objects, no. 2. From their literature (undated).

3 See Table 6.2.

4 In 1977–8 the life membership scheme contributed £17,100 to central funds compared with a total of £14,980 for the previous four financial years.

5 For details see Table 6.2.

Table 6.2
BFSS income (from Annual Reports)

Year[1]	Income[2] (£)	Of which: Subscriptions and donations	Bequests	Sales	Deficit
1932	4,524	4,300			
1939	5,820	4,300			
1946	4,278	3,980			
1948	11,304	9,460			
1949	53,582	50,791			
1950	23,448	17,724			
1955	16,649	12,688			
1956	15,683	11,830			
1960	22,698	15,133			
1965	28,436	20,772			
1970	52,159	43,054	600	5,985	848
1974	95,258	68,978	4,351	16,706	6,044
1978[3]	235,968	167,798	8,391[4]	34,071	4,316
1981[5]	364,362	321,127	650	29,078	

Bequests have become more numerous in the last decade; indeed the Treasurer of the BFSS has stated: 'Legacies have been our salvation over the years'.[6] Between 1969 and 1978 bequests amounted to £63,888 – a considerable sum.[7]

Another recent source has been the income from the Fighting Fund. In 1975, a special fund-raising drive was undertaken to fight the legislative attempt to abolish coursing and other forms of hunting. The

1 The 'Year' covers the preceding 12 months ending on 31 March.

2 The accounts also contain miscellaneous items; therefore the figures for subscriptions and donations, bequests and sales do not add up to the total income.

3 In the four years between 1974 and 1978 the Retail Price Index increased by 90 per cent. The Society therefore enjoyed a substantial increase in *real* income during this period, a trend which has continued in 1982.

4 1977 was a record year for bequests – the total was £21,899.

5 In 1981, the financial year was changed to coincide with the calendar year.

6 B. Waley-Cohen at the 1978 AGM, 8 July 1978.

7 In comparison, this figure is only 60 per cent of the LACS's legacy income for 1977 alone, and is under 2 per cent of the RSPCA's legacy income for the same year.

target of £250,000 was quickly reached in two years. Some of the income (about £100,000 between 1975 and 1981) has been transferred each year to the main account in order to subsidise the Society's PR work.[1] The fighting fund's net value in 1978 was £252,624; in 1981 it had fallen to £231,818. The fighting fund is important for two reasons. It shows that, if necessary, field sportsmen will supply considerable amounts of cash at short notice if it is convinced that a crisis is at hand, and it also gives the BFSS some readily available capital to supplement its investments which were valued at £25,482 in 1976, £11,377 in 1978 and at £232,504 at the end of 1981. The fighting fund like the LACS's Accumulated fund is used only when a moment of crisis occurs; however both funds are most useful as supplements to general income while the moment of crisis is awaited.

Organisational development

The smooth running of the BFSS has depended on the achievement of a successful balance between the interests of the local membership and those of the central organisation. Initially, the BFSS concentrated on reaching its potential membership and, to this end, it issued within its first year 30,000 leaflets through the mail or at agricultural shows and point-to-points. The response to this enabled the Society to build a network of Honorary Local Secretaries based on hunt countries. In 1945, there were 125 Local Secretaries, 246 in 1955, and nearly 300 in 1960. By 1977, there were 308 in England alone and over 400 in the UK.[2] They were led by Regional Secretaries who liaised directly with the London office and who received a small salary for their services. The advantage of this system is that it has enabled the BFSS to expand beyond the confines of the West Country hunting community, and it has encouraged non-hunting field sportsmen to join. In areas where shooting or fishing is more popular than hunting Honorary Secretaries can be recruited who are knowledgeable about the most popular local sport.

The small Headquarters staff have rarely been able to put all their energy into dealing with the public, the politicians and the anti-hunting movement; they have always had to exercise care in their dealings with their own followers. In practice, they have been faced with disruptions between different sections of the membership rather than membership dissatisfaction with the leadership. The major internal differences have

1 Source: Interview with Director 1982. See also Annual Accounts.

2 See 25th Annual Report, 1955, *Baily's*, 1960–1, p. 298 and 47th Annual Report, 1977.

always been between the shooters and the hunters. The BFSS has made strenuous attempts to convince both shooters and hunters that their sports can co-exist by arranging demonstrations and by making appeals for unity.[1] The importance of this continuing source of disunity was recognised by Marcus Kimball who has been Chairman of the Hunting/Shooting Advisory Committee since he became Chairman of the Society. Although in some areas a *modus vivendi* has been found, in 1981 the point was made again:

> Shooting coverts *can* be managed so that sufficient foxes may be left unmolested . . . [but] debarring the local hunt access to shooting estates until the end of the shooting season is too often the practice. When the Hunt is allowed to draw the coverts they are blank, or virtually so, owing to ruthless 'pest destruction' methods of the keepers employed by the shoots.
>
> With all field sports under attack, it is a pity that fellow field sportsmen all too often spoil hunting far more effectively than so called 'hunt saboteurs'.[2]

Although the hunting/shooting debate has been the major source of dissension within the Society, there are nevertheless other minor problems beneath the surface. In its enthusiasm to become the umbrella organisation for all field sports, the BFSS has successfully attracted the support of wildfowlers, falconers and hare coursers; these sports are not viewed with any great enthusiasm by the hard core of hunting men. Coursing is the only victim of regular attack and a substantial section of the hunting community would be quite undisturbed if coursing were abolished. However, the 'official' view of the BFSS is that to fail to support coursing would be the 'thin end of the wedge' which would seriously undermine all other sports. The Questionnaires showed that 84 per cent of MFHs would object if coursing was abolished. However, of a dozen MFHs asked to give a private rather than official view on coursing, only two remained firm in their defence of coursing. Reginald (now Lord) Paget MP, an ex-MFH, was not even publicly committed to coursing when interviewed.[3] The 1975 Report stated that they must 'unite all lovers of country sports under the BFSS umbrella. It is no good anyone any more saying "I don't go coursing, that battle is nothing to do with me". Everybody must be made to realise that it could be their sport under attack'.[4]

1 For a Report on a number of experiments, see *Shooting Times and Country Magazine*, 7 Apr. 1973.

2 *Baily's*, 1981–2, p. vii.

3 On 15 Nov. 1973.

4 *Year Book*, 1975, p. 7.

Attempts to make members of the hunting, shooting and coursing community aware of the need for all field sports men to work together were not immediately successful for, in 1976, the public relations officer stated: 'It is a sad but true fact that people tend to live in watertight compartments. Unfortunately this is sometimes true of those who take part in country sports. So much so that at one time it looked as if we were fighting each other – an unexpected bonus for those who would wish to destroy our sports'.[1] Today, however, the response to the fighting fund appeal and the narrow escape from anti-coursing legislation in 1976 has convinced an increasing number of the value of sticking together. The BFSS is not naive in its approach and does not wish to court danger by adopting sports which it feels unable to defend. In this way badger digging, a very traditional sport, was not recognised as a field sport[2] since its practitioners were neither numerous nor significant. When otter hunting ended in 1978, many otter hunts took to hunting coypus and wild mink in East Anglia. In 1978, the BFSS referred dismissively to coypu hunting as 'organised ratting'; however, the BFSS later helped in the formation of the Mink and Coypu Hunting Association. The Association is now affiliated to the BFSS and has a rapidly improving image among the hunting fraternity.[3]

Gaining the support of anglers has proved difficult for the BFSS to whom they are significant because they are numerous (about three and a half million), from all classes and frequently urban – Birmingham Anglers Association has over 60,000 members.[4] In 1970, the BFSS declared itself to be 'increasingly active in fishing affairs',[5] and has concerned itself with the problems of fishermen ever since. However, it has made relatively little impact on the fishing community and few have joined the BFSS.[6] Indeed in 1976 the National Federation of Anglers declined to be associated with the fighting fund.[7] This standoffishness continued until 1982 when, following an RSPCA report by Lord Cranbrook which claimed that fish did feel pain and some unguarded but much reported remarks by Richard Course of the LACS that if fish *must* be killed it should be for food rather than for sport,

1 *Year Book*, 1976, p.7.

2 Annual Report, 1973, p.6.

3 *The Field*, 23–9 June 1982.

4 Noted in the BFSS *Year Book*, 1974, p.14.

5 Annual Report, 1970, p.36.

6 Interview with the Director of the BFSS, May 1978.

7 *Year Book*, 1976, p.7.

the National Anglers Council issued a lengthy press release.[1] It stated:

> Some minor pressure groups have openly declared their opposition to angling and are actively engaged in an anti-angling programme. The NAC is firmly opposed to any interference with legitimate rural or urban recreational activities, including field sports which are open to participation by the general public. (Anglers) will continue to act to preserve the rural environment in co-operation with other interested organisations and will oppose any attempts to take away the freedom of the individual to take part in the legitimate rural or urban pursuit of his choice.

This was music to the ears of the BFSS leadership and has ensured that in future co-operation will be much closer although the LACS has since made it clear that it is not against fishermen who throw the fish back in, merely those who kill fish for fun.

One area which has caused some strain within the Society is, ironically, the one which externally has been one of its greatest strengths: that is the aristocratic nature of its leadership. The founder, Fred Beadle, was not an aristocrat, but the people he and his friends asked to help launch the Society were. Lord Bayford was educated at Harrow, Balliol and the Inner Temple; Lord Fortescue and the Duke of Beaufort were from well-established landed families, and Toby Fitzwilliam, the Secretary from 1931 to 1953, was a direct descendant of Earl Fitzwilliam and 'could expect a welcome from most of the great houses in England'.[2]

This situation has not changed markedly since the war. The Duke of Beaufort has remained President; the two most important Chairmen have been John Morrison (now Lord Margadale) and Marcus Kimball. Both are owners of large estates and both long-serving members of parliament, Kimball since 1956 and Morrison from 1942–64, the last ten years of which he was Chairman of the 1922 Committee.

The Vice-Presidents of the Society who are appointed for their prestige alone have usually been aristocratic landowners and politicians. In 1932 of the 19 Vice-Presidents there were two Dukes, seven Earls and seven Lords; in 1947 only four of the 23 Vice-Presidents did not have titles.[3] By the 1970s the number of Vice-Presidents had been reduced because their role was no longer particularly significant; nevertheless only one out of the six in 1982 did not have a title.

1 Dated 5 July 1982. The NAC includes the National Federation of Anglers, National Federation of Sea Anglers and the Salmon & Trout Association.

2 S. Beadle, *The Beginning*, BFSS Publications, 1971, p. 7.

3 See relevant *Year Books*.

Retired army officers have also played a key part in the development of the Society. In 1955, seven of the nine members of the General Purposes Committee had a military rank and so have all of its Secretaries (Directors) who have been appointed since the war, the last two being retired Generals. Four of the eight senior staff at Headquarters in 1982 retained a military rank, and of the twelve Regional Secretaries in 1977, nine were retired officers.[1]

This military and aristocratic combination has undoubtedly given the BFSS a high degree of legitimacy, both within the organisation and among the governmental agencies with which it deals. This has not, however, necessarily been the best combination of forces with which to impress the ordinary hunting person. To the extent that deference still exists in rural England, an appeal by the local magnate to join the BFSS would undoubtedly have an effect. However, the hunting community has always made much of the classless nature of hunting and coursing and inevitably, just as there was a social gap between the shire packs and farmer packs, there was a social gap between the leaders of the BFSS and those they wished to lead.

The gap is wider in coursing. Stable and Studdard have taken pains to show that over 70 per cent of coursing supporters were neither rich, nor farmers, nor landowners;[2] and a spokesman for the BFSS has also claimed that 60 per cent (out of 5,000) of the members of the Coursing Supporters Club are Trade Unionists.[3] Therefore it is unlikely that the leadership of the BFSS in 1982, a Duke, a General and a Squire, had much in common with the average courser, except a desire to keep the sport going.

Lack of enthusiasm for the Society among ordinary field sportsmen is hard to quantify. It manifests itself in the young, professionally-trained commercial farmers who belong to Hunt Supporters Clubs but who do not bother to join the BFSS, and among labourers who will willingly pay a 'cap' to follow the Devon and Somerset Staghounds in a car, but who assume that 'they' will provide the money and the energy to ensure that hunting remains secure.

Within the Society complaints are always discreet and usually pointless. The Committee is essentially self-selecting; there are never more candidates than positions for the Main Committee, hence elections which involve having to make a choice between candidates are never held, and if a Committee member wishes to be re-appointed this is usually arranged. However, there is the occasional Committee member

1 *Year Book*, 1977.

2 *Review of Coursing*, p. 14.

3 BFSS AGM, 18 July 1978.

with strong views who may find himself at odds with the majority of the Committee. He may persuade the Committee to accept his point of view or arrange a compromise, but if this fails he will find that he is not encouraged to seek re-election and will not be appointed to the Advisory Committees or the General Purposes Committee where most of the policies are decided. If the Society particularly wants an outsider to join a Committee he does not have to be elected. He can be co-opted, either on to the Main Committee or to an Advisory Committee. In this way John Ryman, a Labour MP in the 1974–9 parliament,[1] was co-opted to the Main Committee and Jimmy Hill, a fox-hunting footballer and TV personality, was co-opted on to the Public Relations Committee. Even Marcus Kimball was initially a co-opted rather than an elected member, when he showed 'promise' as an MP in 1962. This somewhat closed electoral system does have its advantages. It keeps dispute to a minimum, it saves the Committee from the kind of factional in-fighting which has racked its opponents and, since competitive elections are never held, competitive appeals (and promises) to the membership at large do not have to be made and any underlying divisions are thus kept from the public.

The dangers of creating a gap between the local organisation and Headquarters are recognised by the Society. It has three Field Secretaries whose job, while technically Headquarters-based, is to visit local areas to rally the faithful and to attend shows with a BFSS caravan in order to attract new members and sell BFSS goods. The BFSS Chairman and Director frequently visit the regions to make speeches about the progress of the Society and they are conscious that this activity enables them to be aware of local problems and to keep the existing membership loyal, informed and quiescent.[2]

In recent years the increasing significance of the regions has been recognised and structural alterations have been made to ensure that local voices are heard at head office. Each county and each major sport has a representative on the Regional Committee, and the Regional Chairman is now automatically a member of the Main Committee. This ensures smoother communications, and has had the effect of devolving a great deal of executive power over local matters to the regions. In 1981–2, the numerous battles to stop local authorities from banning hunting on council land were conducted regionally rather than from Head Office.

1 Ryman remains, in 1982, their only active supporter on the Labour benches.

2 See Regional Reports in 1977, 1978 and 1981 Annual Reports.

Tactics: from defence to offence

Public relations

Gaining the sympathy of the media and counteracting the propaganda of the anti-hunting community has been a most important activity for the BFSS. In 1931, the Society counted 140 letters and articles in the Press which attacked hunting. The BFSS felt that these attacks were 'well organised, well financed and carefully planned (and) in many cases they contain outrageous statements calculated to appeal to the sensibilities of city-bred people'.[1] The report added that the BBC had been broadcasting talks which were 'prejudicial to sport'. In response the BFSS mounted its own carefully planned campaign and sent articles to 192 different papers, many of which were published.[2] It also sought and received 'assurances' from the BBC.

This counterattack engaged a major proportion of the BFSS's energies in the 1930s. In 1933, 777 copies of articles were sent to the press, and 1,161 were sent in 1936.[3] The BFSS maintained that this activity influenced editors, and reduced the number of erroneous and harmful articles published about field sports. By 1937 the Duke of Beaufort felt that the BFSS had been most successful in 'combating anti-sport propaganda'.[4] Certainly in the pre-war period the BFSS succeeded in persuading a number of neutral papers that the case for hunting had not been abandoned. During the war the Society was able to declare: 'The Press has made considerable use of the facilities offered by the Society to supply reliable information on sporting topics'.[5]

The attacks on hunting became more numerous and more virulent in 1947 and 1948. The BFSS complained that the 'antis' were portraying them as the 'idle rich', 'spivs and drones . . . riding roughshod over the fields and against the wishes of the agricultural community'.[6] However, these attacks had one beneficial side-effect for the 'antis have stirred up the slumbering wrath of the countryman who hitherto, relying on a righteous cause and a clear conscience has been inclined to scoff at the idea that there was anything serious in these threats'.[7]

1 Second Annual Report, 1932, p. 29.

2 Ibid., p. 31.

3 From Annual Reports, 1933 and 1936.

4 Annual Report, 1937, p. 7.

5 Annual Report, 1943, p. 2.

6 Annual Report, 1948, p. 26.

7 Ibid., p. 26.

After the excitements of the 1949 campaign the nature of the BFSS's relationship with the media changed. It no longer had to advertise its existence although it did have to work hard to counteract the work of its opponents who 'continue to bombard the press with numerous letters full of inaccuracies and time-work fallacies'.[1] In defence the BFSS distributed 35,000 copies of *Field Sports: the Truth*, a compilation of extracts from the Scott Henderson Report which was described as 'the most valuable publication the Society has ever produced'.[2] It also set up a network of Correspondence Page Members to 'cover every provincial newspaper of any importance and [to] ensure that anything more dangerous than spinsterish hysteria receives a prompt reply'.[3]

The main response of the BFSS to the campaign mounted by their opponents was to embark, in the mid 1950s, on a public relations campaign, an attacking rather than defensive move. It attempted to convince journalists and the public that hunting had a positive contribution to make to society. By 1959, the number of attacks on hunting dropped sharply and the BFSS thought the campaign was already won. In 1961 they declared that the unfavourable publicity generated by 'incidents' was 'a thing of the past'.[4]

It was true that the BFSS was increasingly taking part in radio and television debates on field sports,[5] and that its films and teams of lecturers were appearing all over the country; however, the hiatus was temporary. Although undoubtedly the BFSS had become effective at countering the sometimes exaggerated tales of its opponents, it still had to 'manage' its allies in order to reduce the number of newsworthy incidents. Outspoken and arrogant hunting people were difficult to control, and the LACS under Hemingway had learned how to capitalise on unguarded statements. The rise of the HSA also generated a variety of incidents which the press was willing to report and no amount of PR work by the BFSS could entirely silence the angry reactions of the more short-tempered members of the hunting community.

In 1961 the BFSS issued a pamphlet entitled 'You and the Press' which advised Masters of Hounds on how to deal with press or television interviews and on how to reply to what they considered to be false reports. Masters involved in an incident were also encouraged to contact the London-based Public Relations Officer (PRO) who would

1 Annual Report, 1953, p. 20.

2 Ibid., p. 20. It was their 95th publication.

3 Noted in *Baily's*, 1960–1, p. 297.

4 Annual Report, 1961, p. 16. An 'incident' is any occurrence in the hunting field which could be used by the LACS to embarrass the hunting community.

5 The BFSS was invited to provide speakers for three television discussions in 1960.

ring up editors or journalists friendly to the hunting cause and suggest that they use their influence to ensure that a 'balanced' story appeared.[1]

This positive approach became more general after 1969 when Raymond Brookes-Ward was appointed as the PR consultant to the BFSS. He and Marcus Kimball, who became Chairman in 1967, believed in an open approach to the press and decided not to treat media-men as antagonists. Local press officers were appointed: three in 1969 and seven by the end of 1977.[2] Their role was 'to take a firmer and less defensive line in answering critics'.[3] An occasional Bulletin was issued to newspapers, friendly journalists and sporting magazines;[4] editors were wined and dined in conjunction with the MFHA, as they had been in the 1960s;[5] local papers were monitored for anti-hunting letters and articles and suitable replies sent.[6] The increasing attention of the media in the early 1970s also led the Society to organise training for selected speakers in radio and television techniques. This scheme was started in 1973,[7] and revived in 1977.

The BFSS expressed its PR policy in 1971: 'To maintain good relations with the press and television, to fight back immediately when attacked; and consistently to make supporters of country sports aware of the Society's work and aims'.[8] The first aim has been central to the Society since it began, the second became explicit when R. Brookes-Ward became the PR consultant in 1969, and the third has become an increasing part of the PR function in the 1970s. In 1975 the PR report began: 'Our principal aim in the coming months is to unite all lovers of country sports under the BFSS umbrella'.[9] In 1977, a full-time PRO was appointed partly to facilitate the drive to double membership and partly to start a 'major effort in education'.[10] The targets for the effort in education were schools, the adult public and, of course, the latent

1 Interview with R. Brookes-Ward, Sept. 1973.

2 Annual Report, 1977–8, p. 16. The key one for the Exmoor area was Jim Butcher, Agricultural Correspondent of the *Western Morning News*.

3 Annual Report, 1969–70, p. 37.

4 Ibid., p. 37. The sporting press began to solicit articles, not just accept them.

5 See Annual Report, 1962–3, p. 17; 1963–4, p. 16, and *Year Book*, 1971, p. 38.

6 *Year Book*, 1972, p. 11.

7 *Year Book*, 1973, p. 8, and Annual Report, 1977–8, p. 16.

8 Annual Report, 1970–1, p. 39.

9 Annual Report, 1974–5, p. 7.

10 Annual Report, 1977–8, p. 15.

membership. In 1981 an Education Advisor was appointed to initiate and to respond to requests for information from schools and colleges.

The cornerstone of the policy of constructive and positive relations with the media and the public was the belief: 'After all, we have nothing to hide, we should be proud of our heritage and of the very real contribution we make towards the conservation and economy of the countryside'.[1] The theme of 'hunters as conservationists' had emerged quietly in the 1950s. It began when the parallel with myxomatosis was drawn. Myxomatosis was introduced into Britain as a means of rabbit control in the 1950s, but was soon seen as a cruel method of virtual extermination. A similar 'final solution' to the fox problem was unacceptable both on the grounds of cruelty and because extermination of foxes was ecologically undesirable. In the 19th century the hunting community had admitted that it preserved foxes for sport by breeding them. It became defensive about this in the 20th century, but after the support given to it by the Scott Henderson Committee it felt justified in proclaiming not only that hunting was a humane form of control but also that without hunting foxes would disappear. Thus they were able to preserve foxes under a new name; previously they had been controllers of noxious vermin; now they were 'conservationists'.

The rise of the movement for a balanced ecology found fox hunters in the vanguard. In 1965 the BFSS declared itself to be concerned with the 'wider aspects of the countryside', and to be 'playing an ever-growing part in the conservationist world'.[2] By 1972 the Society felt that since the 'majority of the nation is not aware of the part that field sports play in conservation' it must continue to explain

> that hunting provides the best and most humane methods of controlling the numbers of foxes, deer and otters, the alternative to hunting being the extermination of the species; that but for shooting interest(s) a large amount of habitat for all wild life would be destroyed; and that, thanks partly to the millions of fishermen, the pollution battle has at last made real progress.[3]

In 1974 a conservationist clause was added to the objects of the Society, and since then the Society has emphasised its commitment to conservation on every possible occasion. It considers that its future role in ecological issues is crucial to its survival, for without the tacit or explicit support of conservationists hunting would disappear with the

1 Annual Report, 1974–5, p. 8. See also a 1983 Report entitled *Countryside Sports: their Economic Significance*, published by a Standing Committee dominated by the BFSS and its supporters.

2 Annual Report, 1963–4, p. 16.

3 Annual Report, 1972, p. 11.

animals which are hunted.[1]

The hunting world's embrace of the conservationist cause and its active involvement in ecological good works goes some way towards ameliorating the effect of public hostility towards all kinds of hunting. However, society and its values have changed in the 30 years since the Scott Henderson Committee gave the pro-hunting community its valuable support, and the BFSS has found it difficult to mount an adequate defence for certain sports. Indeed, it only engages in a full and active public defence when it feels that it is strategically imperative for it to do so.[2]

The defence of otter hunting has had to be mounted on intellectual grounds rather than on the grounds that otter hunting was useful or necessary. The BFSS accepted that Gavin Maxwell and others had succeeded in making the otter a 'popular' animal and that the decline in the otter population, while not caused by hunting, meant that hunting could not easily be justified. The BFSS realised that it could not persuade the media or public opinion that otter hunting was desirable and so, as an organisation, it did not object when the otter was added to the list of protected animals, although it did press for regional rather than national protection of the species. It would have objected, however, if an attempt had been made to abolish otter hunting. As the law now stands, there is no otter hunting in 1983, but it would be a simple matter, if otters were withdrawn from the protected list, for hunting to recommence. Although the hare has not found a Gavin Maxwell to defend it, hare coursing has been attacked by an Archbishop of Canterbury, the General Assembly of the Church of England[3] and by a Labour Prime Minister. Despite this, and despite the willingness to make a tactical retreat over otter hunting, the BFSS still defends coursing.

It is arguable that the hunting community would buy more time and allies for themselves by abandoning hare coursing. This, however, is unlikely to happen in the short run for it would conflict with the BFSS's image of itself as a principled defender of a worthy 'cause' and as an upholder of a glorious tradition. It would also dismay the supporters of other fringe sports and reduce their trust in the BFSS's willingness to fight for them.

1 The significance of this new approach was confirmed in interviews with R. Brookes-Ward, Sept. 1973, and M. Kimball, May 1978.

2 The general arguments in favour of hunting are detailed in Chapter 11 (C).

3 The resolution quoted by Baroness Bacon in the *Lords Debates*, 1972, vol. 330, col. 722, states that it is part of people's 'Christian profession and responsibility to make plain their opposition to activities of this sort'.

However, the radical change in its self-image from a hunting protection society to a conservationist organisation illustrates how clearly the BFSS understands the value of expedient behaviour as a tactic, and if a new image is of greater public relations value in today's society the BFSS would probably be prepared to abandon old principles in favour of new ones.

The formation of alliances

(i) *Coping with opponents*. The BFSS has been involved with a wide range of other organisations and its response to them has depended on whether they were basically 'friend' or 'foe'. The activities of 'unfriendly' organisations such as the LACS were early stimulants of BFSS activity. In 1933, money was needed 'to fight an opponent, whose activities are increasing and whose funds appear inexhaustible'.[1] This theme, that 'the antis are accumulating large reserves', was regularly repeated[2] and ultimately used to launch the fighting fund in 1975.

Since the League's members were most useful as bogey men, only their more extreme exploits were reported to BFSS members. When the LACS was in breach of parliamentary privilege in 1936 the BFSS was moved to comment that this was 'an admirable example of the mentality of the opponents of sport'.[3] However, the League's exploitation of hunting incidents in the 1960s made the BFSS improve its public relations effort and concentrate more on combating the League's influence. Turner has suggested: 'If much of the arrogance for which fox hunters were notorious has dwindled in the last 30 years, the credit may perhaps be divided between the BFSS which has discouraged acts of provocation and the LACS which has ever been on the lookout for them'.[4]

In their PR battle with the League the BFSS was content to have Rowley as its main opponent for it was convinced that since he was 'an underhand and mean-minded individual' and 'a bit of a crank' he was as likely to damage his own cause as to advance it.[5] The BFSS was more worried by the political initiatives of Lord Houghton, the Chairman of the League, and the publicity generated by Richard Course's 'blunt, honest street-fighter' approach than by Rowley's tactics which it

1 Annual Report, 1933, pp. 23–4.

2 Annual Report, 1943–4, p. 4. See also 'Who is for Country Sports: Who is Against?', BFSS (n.d. probably 1948). This listed the opposing societies and their funds and ended with a plea for money for the BFSS.

3 Annual Report, 1936, p. 36.

4 Turner, *All Heaven*, p. 286.

5 Interview with the BFSS PRO, Sept. 1973.

was always able to dismiss as a product of 'social jealousy' and 'townee ignorance'.[1] After his departure the BFSS stopped suggesting that Rowley was 'small-minded', and 'deceitful'[2] and expressed regret that the 'left wing' of the LACS had defeated him.[3]

At first the BFSS tended to ignore the 'exhibitionist antics of the HSA'[4] and felt that 'followers of hunts have shown remarkable forbearance in face of provocation' largely because '[HSA] activities have in no way spoilt the day's hunting'.[5] Only in 1977 when the HSA was linked, through its connections with the ALF, to a series of violent and illegal acts did the BFSS editorialise about the HSA: 'At first the antics of its supporters made . . . it possible to be amused',[6] now however society in general had turned against these protesters, 'trumpeting their message of intolerance and coercion'.[7]

This official view was not entirely realistic. When the HSA first became active, the BFSS, the MFHA and the Masters of Otterhounds had to discourage hunting people from beating up saboteurs and riding them down.[8] M. Kimball has expressed the view that, like the suffragettes in their attempts to get the vote, the activities of saboteurs have probably delayed the abolition of coursing and hunting.[9]

Relations with the RSPCA were delicate during the early years of the BFSS. Anti-hunting tendencies were noted by the future leaders of the BFSS in the 1920s,[10] and the official stand by the RSPCA against stag hunting and coursing was greeted with alarm.[11] After the war the situation was improved by the essentially pro-hunting stance of the RSPCA spokesman at the Scott Henderson Inquiry. Relations were generally good throughout the 1950s and early 1960s, but 'the friendly relations that now exist between the Society and the RSPCA'[12] came to an end

1 Interview with R. Wallace, Chairman of the MFHA.

2 Interview with BFSS Secretary, Sept. 1973.

3 Interviews with BFSS Director and Chairman 1978. The HSA considered it 'very strange that the hunting press have come down strongly in favour of Mr Rowley staying on as Chairman – this surely must indicate that they do *not* consider him to be a threat'. In the HSA Notice of its 1977 AGM, June 1977.

4 BFSS Annual Report, 1963–4, p. 16.

5 Annual Report, 1972, p. 11.

6 Annual Report, 1976–7, p. 9.

7 Ibid., quoting Auberon Waugh, *Daily Mail*, 22 Mar. 1977.

8 Interview with BFSS Secretary and PRO in 1973.

9 Interview with BFSS Chairman, May 1978.

10 Beadle, *The Beginning*, p. 9.

11 Annual Report, 1939, p. 41.

12 Annual Report, 1962–3, p. 25.

with the success of the Reform Group in 1974. The BFSS commented: 'Hunting has always been a subject on which the RSPCA has tried desperately to avoid committing itself. Now pushed by the hot heads, it has condemned it. Nor do shooting and fishing escape'.[1] The BFSS felt that the problems for the RSPCA were not over and continued: 'The RSPCA will have only itself to blame if it finds its country branches depleted. There are, after all, other charities concerned with the welfare of animals'. In the early 1980s the BFSS observed with relief that the RSPCA while being officially against hunting was not actively so. Since the BFSS was able to support most of its activities it recommended membership to its own members and further suggested that they encouraged their 'RSPCA branch to put up a resolution in favour of field sports'.[2]

(ii) *Cultivating alliances*. Its dealings with the RSPCA have made the BFSS increasingly aware of the importance of establishing and keeping good relations with other organisations. These organisations fall into three categories: first, those concerned with other field sports; second, those, mainly connected with horses, whose co-operation is essential if the field sports themselves are to prosper and, third, organisations with social, economic or political goals which have been identified by the BFSS as potentially helpful to their cause.

The BFSS attempted to form the widest possible alliance of all field-sports men but was at the outset most closely identified with stag hunters and with the MFHA.[3] Its involvement with other sports is at two different levels: first it consults with the sporting body concerned,[4] and second it has its own Advisory Committees of BFSS members and outside experts. The degree of co-operation varies from sport to sport. On coursing, 'all matters connected with coursing are dealt with in consultation with the Committee of the National Coursing Club',[5] but the decisions about BFSS policy on coursing are decided by its own Advisory Committee which contains NCC representatives. Effectively the same procedure is followed on matters concerned with shooting, but on questions of fishing the BFSS tends to act after consultations with, but separate from, fishing organisations.

1 Annual Report, 1975–6, p. 7–8.

2 BFSS *News*, Spring 1982, p. 6.

3 Toby Fitzwilliam, Secretary of the BFSS, was also Secretary and/or Treasurer of the MFHA from 1936 to 1954.

4 In 1982 there were 18 organisations represented on the Main Committee whose concern was to kill and/or preserve wild animals. There was also a representative of the Clay Pigeon Shooting Association.

5 BFSS Annual Report, 1955–6, p. 4.

On hunting matters the relationship between the BFSS and the relevant organisations is, although unspecified, extremely close. R. Wallace, the Chairman of the MFHA, is a Vice-Chairman of the BFSS; B. Waley-Cohen, Treasurer of the BFSS from 1954 to 1978, is Chairman of the Devon and Somerset Staghounds and their PRO Raymond Brookes-Ward was until 1978 on the Main Committee as the representative of the Masters of Basset Hounds Association. These three, together with M. Kimball, Lord Margadale and the Director, were, to the public and parliament, the effective leadership of the BFSS throughout the 1970s and into the 1980s.

The British Horse Society, its affiliate the British Show Jumping Association and the Hunter Improvement Society (HIS) are the major horse organisations. They could exist without hunting, but hunting would be hard put to exist without their support. They are in an enviable position for not only are they free from organised opposition, but also the sports they serve – riding, racing, show jumping and cross country 'eventing' – are increasingly popular.[1]

In practice, relations between these Societies and the BFSS are close but informal, and an overlapping membership ensures that developments in one Society are quickly known to the others. Informality is desirable for the horse societies because they can remain non-contentious and are able to discuss matters affecting horses with other organisations who are against hunting.[2] Informality is acceptable to the BFSS because they know that they can rely on the sympathy and support of these organisations, the most significant of which is the BHS.[3] Many of its previous Chairmen and Presidents have been leading members of the BFSS and its 1982 President was Dorian Williams, MFH, for eight years its Chairman and a personal friend of the leadership of the MFHA and BFSS.[4] In order to keep day-to-day relation-

1 In 1981 there were 12,400 race horses in training, over 30,000 members of the BHS to which Pony Clubs are affiliated, and 16,000 members of the British Show Jumping Association. The HIS was formed in 1885 to improve the quality of race horses and hunters. The Queen is Patron, the Committee consists of the rural aristocracy and it had, in 1980, over 10,000 members. Each of these figures shows a 15 per cent increase over the last 3 years.

2 The BHS is a member of the National Joint Equine Welfare Committee which includes the RSPCA.

3 Both the BFSS and the MFHA appear on the BHS list of 'Horse and Pony Breeding and Administrative Societies' (n.d.). During the 1948–9 campaign to abolish hunting the BHS wrote, in protest against the Bills, to the Prime Minister, the Home Secretary and the Minister of Agriculture. See *Baily's*, 1948–9, p. 36.

4 Post-war Presidents or Chairmen of the BHS include, J. Morrison MP, MFH; the Duke of Northumberland MFH; Viscount Knutsford MFH; the Earl of Halifax MFH; the Duke of Beaufort MFH, and the Earl of March, owner of Goodwood.

ships secure, the BFSS sponsors prizes at many 'equitation' and show-jumping events[1] and sends a publicity caravan to as many horse shows as possible.

The third category of groups with which the BFSS wishes to remain friendly are those with joint areas of concern. Some have an overlapping membership and are predictably on the side of the BFSS; others, mainly in the field of conservation, are more unreliable partners.

The National Farmers Union (NFU) and Country Landowners Association (CLA) fall into the first category; obviously without their active support the BFSS would not have prospered, and hunting would not have survived. The CLA was the most obvious ally, given the historic connections between hunting and the squirearchy. The relationship continues although it was not close in the 1970s since the CLA, as spokesman for the squirearchy, was 'somewhat moribund'.[2] However the relationship improved in the 1980s when, in order to combat local government initiatives against hunting and other field sports, the CLA encouraged its members to stand in local government elections themselves. Throughout this period, at annual CLA Game Fairs the BFSS has been given a 'generous allocation of space'[3] which usually includes a stand and a supporters' tent.

The relationship between the BFSS and farmers has evolved since the 1930s. Initially the BFSS relied on the deferential support, by farmers, of the aristocratic leadership of the hunting community. Ordinary farmers had no authority within the organisation and their needs were quite secondary to those of the landowners with whom they were not always in agreement. Traditional landowners have been precise about the distinction between owner-occupiers and tenant-farmers to the extent that tenant-farmers who took over hounds have been known to be refused permission to hunt on their land. Only during the war, when fox hunting survived because of the farmers did the BFSS pay 'a tribute to thousands of farmers who have contributed so much' and who by 'taking over the hounds themselves . . . have proved to be the backbone of the sport'.[4]

This recognition of the farmers' role was by no means premature; the 1948–9 Bill was defeated largely because the Labour front bench feared the wrath of the farmers who, through the NFU, had expressed their profound displeasure at the attempts to abolish hunting. The NFU

1 See *inter alia*, Annual Report, 1972, p. 7.

2 From interview with M. Kimball, May 1978.

3 Annual Report, 1970–1, p. 41.

4 Annual Report, 1943–4, p. 8.

declared themselves ready to fight the Bill 'locally and nationally'[1] and a major collaboration took place between local NFU staff and local BFSS Honorary Secretaries.[2] It was this collaboration which helped to produce the 1.2 million signatures for the 'Countryman's Pledge' and the 100,000 new members for the Society. Further representations by NFU leaders persuaded the Minister of Agriculture to oppose the Bill on several grounds, not least that in the post-war reconstruction period the nation depended upon 'the good will of all classes of the rural population' and that by enacting this Bill 'we should risk the loss of willing co-operation in a great national effort'.[3] The Minister was also convinced that field sports were not 'the exclusive preserve of the leisured classes [but] a traditional feature of country life patronised by very large masses of the rural population'.[4]

Since 1949 the BFSS has taken care to keep its relations with the NFU in good repair and has, of course, encouraged as many farmers as possible to join the BFSS. To do this it has defended the farmer and his sports against 'urbanisation and industrialism [which] have had much to do with the growth of Anti-ism',[5] and have through its system of local representatives kept up a continuing presence in rural areas.

The hunting community knows that, given the changing economic and social conditions of rural life, support by farmers for hunting cannot be guaranteed; the National Union of Agricultural Workers will not defend hunting,[6] and many farmers are uninterested in it. In 1973, a bad summer for farmers, the Chairman of the MFHA stated more as a hope than as a description: 'It says much for the good relationships which exist between the farming community and the fox hunters that regular hunting commenced on schedule . . . and that Hunts are welcomed'.[7] The formal relationship between the NFU and the BFSS is also carefully nurtured for the NFU is seen as hunting's 'greatest ally'.[8]

Since its conversion to a more active stance and to the conservationist cause the BFSS has involved itself in joint ventures with a variety of organisations. It has always been aware of the value of prestige gained by association with other organisations, but initially these associations

1 BFSS *Year Book*, 1948–9, p. 18.

2 See *Baily's*, 1948–9, p. 37.

3 *Hansard* (Commons), 1949, vol. 461, col. 2228.

4 Ibid., col. 2227.

5 Annual Report, 1958–9, p. 18.

6 *Lords Debates*, 1972, vol. 330, col. 663. Confirmed by Jack Boddy, their General Secretary.

7 BFSS Annual Report, 1974–5, p. 9.

8 Confirmed in interviews with the Chairman and Secretary of the BFSS in 1978 and 1982.

were in areas concerned with sport. As early as 1934 the Society co-operated with ICI and Oxford University over a study into game bird diseases,[1] and it decided that it was its 'unique prestige'[2] which encouraged others to ask it to join in research projects. In practice, the BFSS's connection with all field sports gave the Society, through its members, access to a fund of knowledge about habitat, animal diseases, pollution[3] and the effects of chemicals on agriculture.[4]

However, only with the rise of the ecology movement were they able to put the knowledge of their Specialist Committees and of their members to active rather than internal and defensive use. In 1955, several members of the BFSS were invited to join the Birds Protection Advisory Committee – although as private citizens.[5] By the 1960s it was, as an organisation, ready to be actively involved in the conservationist cause. When the *Deer Bill* (1963) was discussed, it joined in negotiations with the concerned hunting and landowning bodies as well as the Nature Conservancy, the Forestry Commission, the Council for Nature and the Fauna Preservation Society. In the same year the Society had representatives at a Conference chaired by the Duke of Edinburgh on 'The Countryside in 1970' and was represented at a European Conference on Wildfowl Conservation.[6]

A major co-operative exercise occurred in 1965 when representatives of the BFSS and MFHA were invited with others to join a working party convened by the Council for Nature, the Fauna Preservation Society and the Society for the Promotion of Nature Reserves. The working party also included representatives of four government bodies, the Home Office, the Nature Conservancy, the Forestry Commission and the Ministry of Agriculture. A report entitled *Predatory Mammals in Britain* was published in 1967 and such was the success of the co-operation that the BFSS organised another working party of nine organisations on avian predators and invited the same four civil servants to attend.[7] The co-operative nature of these studies and the balanced reports which emerged gave the BFSS a desirable boost in the eye of the conservationists and civil servants with whom they had been work-

1 Annual Report, 1934, p.35.

2 Annual Report, 1937, p. 7.

3 Papers on game birds, 'heather beetle' and pollution of rivers were published during and shortly after the war. Annual Report, 1948–9.

4 In 1963 a representative attended a symposium on Agricultural Chemicals.

5 Annual Report, 1954–5.

6 Annual Report, 1962–3.

7 The report was entitled *Predatory Birds in Britain*, BFSS, and Council for Nature, n.d. (1970).

ing. Professor Hewer wrote: 'Sportsmen and naturalists look at nature from differing points of view and it might appear that small scope existed for a common approach to problems of wild-life management', however 'the measure of common interest and agreement found among the 18 organisations was encouraging'.[1]

In the 1970s and early 1980s the BFSS has given active support to a variety of research projects. It assisted the Mammal Society's research into the number and spread of otters;[2] it provided funds for a research project into the problems of pheasant rearing in 1973[3] and more recently sponsored studies on foxes,[4] on salmon fishing,[5] on the problem of lead poisoning in swans and on the number and distribution of hares.[6]

The BFSS believes in expanding its network of contacts as widely as possible. Its keenness to work on committees and sponsor joint research projects derives from a belief that 'it is essential that officials are known to each other' since 'few problems are new and all of them can be solved if the right allies are found'.[7] It is thought important for the BFSS to build up a network of friends in a variety of organisations for 'BFSS strategy, which is inevitably a defensive one, must be based on alliances which are strong enough to deter, or, if necessary, defeat, those who would destroy our country sports'.[8]

This thinking has led the BFSS into Europe. It has been a major contributor both in finance and in personnel to the establishment of a permanent body, the Federation of Field Sports Associations of the EEC whose job is to work on behalf of field sports throughout the European community and to safeguard against the possibility that legislation against hunting might come from Brussels rather than Westminster.[9]

1 *Predatory Mammals in Britain*, (ed.) P. Gouldsbury, Council for Nature, London 1967 and 1973, from Preface, p. 7.

2 Annual Report, 1973–4, p. 10.

3 Ibid., p. 8.

4 Interview with Chairman of BFSS, May 1978.

5 Annual Report, 1974–5, p. 9.

6 BFSS *News*, Spring 1982.

7 Annual Report, 1977–8, p. 12.

8 Ibid., p. 12.

9 Annual Report, 1976–7, pp. 11–12, and Annual Report, 1977–8, p. 15.

(iii) *Friends in the administration.* From the beginning the BFSS has understood the importance of establishing a working relationship with Whitehall – particularly with the Home Office and the Ministry of Agriculture. It was therefore keen to deploy the skills of its members on behalf of government inquiries, and was delighted when, in 1934, the Home Office invited the Society to give evidence before an Inquiry into Game Laws and Gun Laws.[1]

During the war a series of questions antagonistic to hunting were raised in parliament. The Society provided detailed information on the questions to the government departments concerned and, while these questions undoubtedly provided some unfavourable publicity, the Society felt that 'in practically every instance' its view of the matter prevailed.[2] Certainly in 1943, the BFSS declared that 'very valuable contacts have been made with a number of Ministries and the friendly relations thus created have built up an atmosphere of mutual confidence which is most helpful when our opponents are using their best endeavours to injure us'.[3] By 1944, despite the continuing parliamentary questions, 'Ministers have made it clear that hunting is not a handicap to the war effort'.[4]

These warm relations with government departments showed their value during the debate on the 1949 Bill to abolish stag hunting and coursing, for it was mainly the intervention of the Minister of Agriculture acting on the advice of his civil servants which won the day for hunting. The civil servants undoubtedly had some influence for most of the Labour front bench voted against the Bill despite the personal hostility of some of them towards hunting. Since then the BFSS has assiduously cultivated the good will of civil servants by providing information and answering questions as helpfully as possible.[5] Contacts were not particularly significant during the period of Conservative government but, after the mid 1960s the interaction between the BFSS and the civil servants increased. This was not a result of a policy change but was primarily caused by the government's involvement in environmental concerns. The Society aided the Ministry of Agriculture with an

1 Annual Report, 1934, p. 34. Also mentioned in the 1935 Report.

2 Annual Report, 1942, p. 2.

3 Annual Report, 1943, p. 2.

4 Annual Report, 1944, pp. 4–5.

5 Confirmed in interviews with civil servants.

inquiry into the control of pigeons by narcotics,[1] and was among the organisations which drew attention to the dangers to wildlife of the uncontrolled use of Aldrin and Dieldrin. The Ministry of Agriculture responded by banning these pesticides.[2]

The two working parties on Mammalian and Avian Predators in the late 1960s were of considerable significance because, besides having representatives of sporting and conservationist bodies on it, the team included representatives from government departments. The good impression made by the sporting community on these government officials was to be of direct benefit to sporting interests. Government departments such as the Ministry of Agriculture were able to use the BFSS as a source of knowledge when inquiring into pest control, rabies and foot-and-mouth disease.[3] This enabled the BFSS to influence the decisions made and to ensure that sporting interests were not forgotten.[4] The second advantage derives from the mere fact of working together successfully with government officers. The particular Home Office official who was on the working parties was, since he dealt with questions concerning wild animals, also responsible for providing answers to parliamentary questions about coursing and hunting and for providing briefs for Ministerial speeches when anti-hunting legislation was being discussed. Although in the early 1970s the civil servant mostly involved was bound to prepare a brief according to instructions, he was personally, as a result of his dealings with both sides of the hunting issue, firmly pro-hunting and instrumental in keeping the government neutral on a number of coursing Bills in the years preceding 1975.[5]

These benefits were potent for a number of reasons. Firstly, government departments increasingly looked to the BFSS for advice on all sporting matters and the BFSS has slowly become, like the NFU, a part of the consultation process without which orders and enactments do not occur.[6] Secondly, since the government's stance was neutral

1 Annual Report, 1962–3.

2 Annual Report, 1963–4.

3 These topics were under discussion in 1973. Interview with Sir Richard Goodwin, Secretary of the BFSS.

4 The 1977 *Year Book* lists (p. 10) nine topics on which the Society was active in Westminster and Whitehall during the year.

5 Interview with an official at the Home Office in 1973. Confirmed by the BFSS.

6 See P. Self and H.J. Storing, *The State and the Farmer*, Allen & Unwin, London, 1962.

until the mid 1970s, the sympathy of officialdom for the BFSS tended to undermine Labour government attempts to push an anti-hunting stance. A Home Office Minister in the late 1960s wanted to set up another Inquiry into cruelty to wild animals, believing that Scott Henderson's Report was biased and out-of-date. However, the official bureaucratic view was that Scott Henderson was quite adequate and so the Inquiry did not take place.[1] Thirdly, having identified and got to know the civil servants involved in animal welfare issues, it was quite easy for the BFSS leadership to develop the relationship at a social and professional level. It saved time being able to approach a civil servant directly as a friend and to know that you could rely on his advice and his discretion. Normally MPs must ask permission from the Minister concerned whenever they wish to talk with a civil servant, but it was a simple matter for the Chairman of the BFSS to obtain a general clearance to check things with a fellow member of a working party.

From the civil servant's point of view a number of genuine benefits accrued; since it was desirable to have a deeper knowledge of the subjects and organisations concerned in the area for which they were responsible, it was helpful to know that any questions put to the BFSS would be promptly and accurately answered. It was also pleasant to be asked to join a group for an occasional meal at the House of Lords. For Home Office and Ministry of Agriculture officials this state of affairs was preferable to dealing with the LACS office which did not answer questions, and with R. Rowley who was 'unfriendly and unhelpful'.[2]

The return of a Labour government in 1974, although a minority one, changed the significance of this relationship in one important respect; the Labour party and government had decided previously to attempt to abolish coursing and to ignore other field sports until that had been achieved. Accordingly the focus of attention moved from the civil service to parliament and representations made to the civil service were of little consequence. However, old habits die hard and the BFSS made a courtesy visit to the new head of the animal welfare section of the Home Office in 1975, after the government had declared its intention of introducing an anti-coursing bill during the 1975 session.[3]

Since 1974 the questions concerning animals have been divided between three ministries; the Home Office is concerned with cruelty, the Department of the Environment is concerned with conservation, and the Ministry of Agriculture with pest control. The BFSS has, unlike the LACS, attempted to establish a working relationship with individual

1 Interview with Home Office official.

2 This paragraph paraphrases part of a conversation with a Home Office official in Sept. 1973.

3 Interview in 1978 with the Head of the Animal Welfare Section 1975–8.

civil servants in all of the relevant Ministries, for it sees the advantages to be gained from on-going and friendly contacts with government. The Society made representations to the Department of the Environment while the Wildlife and Countryside Bill was under consideration from 1979–81 and has occasional discussions with the Ministry of Agriculture about pest control – particularly when foxes and deer are involved. The BFSS admits that it finds contacts at all levels easier during periods of Conservative government.

7 The activities compared: the background and attitudes of the pro- and anti-hunting communities

Background and life-style of MFHs and HSA members

Pressure groups have had an obvious impact on public and political opinion, but so also have the behaviour and values of the leading members of the hunting and anti-hunting communities. Data has been collected and analysed on those who lead the fox-hunting community (MFHs) and on those (in the HSA) who are in the front line of the struggle against hunting.[1] Since fox hunting is the core sport, any findings about the behaviour and attitudes of the fox-hunting community will necessarily be illuminating for those wishing to learn more about other field sportsmen. Fox-hunting people are for the time being, willing to protect the weaker sports and so their ability to protect their sport from attack and to present a good image of themselves to the outside world is of significance to all field sports. Similarly the HSA contains many of the most active and aggressive members of the anti-hunting movement who, by virtue of their individual memberships of other animal welfare organisations, have a disproportionate effect on the hunting debate.

The education and career profiles of MFHs show that they come from a rather narrow socio-economic section of society. Sixty-five per cent attended a public school, and nearly 6 per cent received other forms of education including private education at the hands of tutors.

1 Questionnaires were administered to MFHs in 1973 and 1977 and to HSA members in 1977.

Just over half have had some third-level education; 40 per cent have attended university and over 40 per cent have received professional training. The careers followed by MFHs cover an essentially middle-class spectrum. A third are farmers, nearly another third have combined farming with business or military careers, and nearly a third have experienced a significant amount of military service. Seventeen per cent have professional jobs, and 5 per cent claim to be housewives. A third claim to be full-time Masters; over a half state that they are only part-time.

A demographic profile of Masters does not provide any major surprises. Over a third are in the 45–55 age bracket and nearly three-quarters are between 35 and 65 years of age; 85 per cent are married and around 10 per cent admit to having been divorced. They are essentially active and outdoor types, for nearly 70 per cent of those answering the questions on leisure gave sports other than hunting as their major leisure activity.

The evidence on wealth and class is less clear cut. Thirty-eight per cent of the sample felt that they were comfortably off and 43 per cent felt that they were 'averagely' well off; of the remainder 7 per cent declared that they were rich and 6 per cent that they were poor. However the feeling by 43 per cent of the whole sample that they had average incomes is either self-delusion or a witticism. Except in rare cases, to be an MFH requires a large income or the backing of substantial amounts of capital. Sixty per cent of those who answered the question in early 1977 had incomes of over £6,000 and almost all felt that they belonged to the middle or upper class.[1]

The anti-hunting world does not often interfere with the lives of Masters of Foxhounds. However, almost 22 per cent of Masters have had brushes with the Hunt Saboteurs Association although rather fewer (15 per cent) had been involved with the League Against Cruel Sports. Much of this involvement has been occasioned by the LACS's attempts to help individuals press trespass charges against erring hunts.

Nearly 30 per cent of Masters believe that the HSA and LACS pose a threat to hunting and over a third believe that their efforts will cause the abolition of hunting in the near future. Eighty-four per cent of Masters would object if coursing were to be abolished and do so because they object to government interference in what they view as a private matter. Forty-two per cent see attacks on coursing as the thin end of a wedge which could eventually topple fox hunting.

The growth of anti-hunting sentiments in the rural areas, particularly among farmers, is a source of concern to MFHs. One hunt in the sample had over 25 per cent of its country in the hands of anti-hunting

1 The average annual income for *non*-manual adult male full-time workers in late 1976 was £4,250. *Britain 1978*, p. 317. A comparable figure in 1982 would be not less than £12,000.

farmers and landowners; 10 per cent of Masters have 10 per cent or more of their country controlled by anti-hunting farmers. A few also see a weakness in one of the traditional defences of hunting for, although 80 per cent do not consider hunting to be cruel, almost 20 per cent accept that it is.

A small sample was asked about their perception of the attitudes towards hunting of parliament, press and the public. Of those replying 68 per cent felt that parliament was generally sympathetic to their point of view, 58 per cent felt that the press was sympathetic and 88 per cent felt that the general public was on their side. If these perceptions can, however tentatively, be transferred to the hunting community at large, it indicates how little it trusts opinion polls. It also shows why many members of the hunting community consider it their duty to stop administrative and legislative attacks on what they believe to be a popular sport.

It is for this reason that Masters have become much more conscious of the world outside hunting and of the need to protect and promote hunting. All the respondents belong to the BFSS and nearly half belong to the RSPCA. Twenty-eight per cent belong to organisations allied to hunting, such as the BHS, and to organisations which represent shooting and fishing.

Almost 20 per cent of MFHs describe themselves as active in local or national politics and many are Chairmen of the local Conservative party. This activism and interest compare very sharply with the 0.3 per cent of the population who have held local office, and the 3 per cent of the population who took part in any electioneering in 1964.[1] Forty-five per cent of Masters actually belong to the Conservative party. When asked which party they would vote for in a general election, 81 per cent chose the Conservatives and 14 per cent gave no choice; one person in the sample chose the Liberals; none chose Labour.

In late 1977, when the questionnaires were administered, the HSA had in the region of 2,800 members; 54 per cent had joined since 1976 and over 80 per cent within the previous four years. Despite this upsurge in membership support has been mainly passive for only 43 per cent of those responding to questionnaires described themselves as activists. Nevertheless a third of the members went on 'demos', 40 per cent wrote to the press and 32 per cent attended meetings at which they could express their antipathy to hunting. Fox hunts received by far the largest amount of attention from saboteurs; 55 per cent of all

1 D. Butler and D. Stokes, *Political Change in Britain*, Penguin, Harmondsworth, pp. 41 and 504–5.

demos were against fox hunts and just over half of these (55 per cent) were described as 'fashionable' hunts. Farmer and fell packs were demonstrated against by less than 10 per cent of the activists.[1]

HSA supporters were evenly divided in their opinion over which type of hunting was 'worst' and which therefore should be abolished first. Otter hunting obtained the vote of 28 per cent, hare hunting of 20 per cent and stag hunting of 19 per cent. A further 22 per cent felt that most or all forms of hunting were equally disagreeable.[2] Two-thirds believed that if coursing were to be abolished it would be 'the writing on the wall' for fox and stag hunting.

HSA members do not, like many MFHs, inherit their role or their convictions. Only 3 per cent have followed parents into the organisation and only 14 per cent have a spouse who is also a member. None have close relatives who hunt and against whom they might be wishing to protest. Since a mere 14 per cent have had dealings with Masters of Hounds or with the BFSS their knowledge of the hunting world is rarely profound – confrontation rather than conversation being the preferred mode of contact. This does not stop HSA members having strong feelings about hunting people who they describe as 'snobs', 'sadists', 'social climbers', and 'hard, cruel people', 'concerned with their virility', who enjoy 'senseless brutality and destruction' and suffer from 'blood lust'.[3] Given this strength of feeling it is not surprising that HSA members reject wholesale the arguments put forward by the hunting community.

HSA members are divided in their views about the amount of support they have. Sixty per cent believe that parliament is generally sympathetic to their stand on hunting, while 30 per cent believe that it is not; 47 per cent believe that the press is generally sympathetic, 36 per cent do not; 11 per cent feel that the press is divided. The figures indicate more conviction, however, about public opinion; 84 per cent believe they have public sympathy for their views, whereas only 11 per cent believe they do not. Given this degree of sympathy from outside, HSA members are unconvinced that their own side is sufficiently active. Only 10 per cent believe that the LACS is really effective, 19 per cent believe it to be ineffective, and 56 per cent feel that it only reached a medium level of effectiveness. Similarly over 56 per cent feel that the NSACS is ineffective, and 93 per cent feel that the RSPCA could do

1 Since the demise of otter hunting attention has further concentrated on fox hunting. HSA Committee members when shown these figures in 1982 felt that they remained valid for that year.

2 None singled out fox hunting for special opprobrium.

3 Quotations from questionnaires.

more to help the abolitionists' cause,[1] even though the Reform Group had two years earlier won its battle to make the RSPCA anti-hunting.

HSA members are actively involved with other organisations; 25 per cent belong to the RSPCA, despite feeling that it could be more effective, and over 40 per cent are members of the LACS. Twenty per cent belong to Friends of the Earth, 15 per cent to other animal welfare organisations and 56 per cent belong to organisations based on social or environmental issues. Twelve per cent of the total replying to the questionnaires specified that they belong to vegetarian organisations, and 18 per cent state that they belonged to anti-vivisection groups. Since they were not asked if they belonged to vegetarian or anti-vivisection societies, the true figure is probably higher. Four respondents to the questionnaire listed their membership of over ten animal welfare or allied organisations.

The demographic characteristics of HSA members differ sharply from those of the fox-hunting community. Men slightly outnumber women by 54 per cent to 46 per cent, and their age profile suggests a youthful membership:

46 per cent are under 25
28 per cent are between 25–35
11 per cent are between 36–45
10 per cent are between 46–65
5 per cent are over 65.

Almost exactly half (49 per cent) are married, 43 per cent are single and the rest either widowed or divorced. Their places of origin are evenly spread, 33 per cent are from cities, 37 per cent from towns and 30 per cent from rural areas.

In terms of income and class identification HSA members are heterogenous; 56 per cent of those who answered the question felt themselves to be members of the middle class, 4 per cent felt they were of the upper class and 38 per cent were of the working class. Their income profile suggests that their class identification is reasonably accurate.

Income during 1977:	Under £1,500	38 per cent
	£1,500–3,000	25 per cent
	£3,000–4,500	21 per cent
	£4,500–6,000	10 per cent
	Over £6,000	4 per cent

The large group whose income is under £1,500 consists mainly of students, old-age pensioners and the unemployed. Students account for

1 R. Ryder, Chairman of the RSPCA in 1978 and a member of the HSA, also felt that the RSPCA could do more.

19 per cent of the HSA membership with the unemployed providing another 8 per cent – a figure which has increased since 1980.[1]

The educational background of HSA members is also mixed. Eighty-two per cent went to state schools and 12 per cent to public schools. Fifty-nine per cent have had third-level education, and of those 25 per cent went to university, 26 per cent have had technical training and 15 per cent professional training. Since their education or training,

28 per cent work at professional jobs
12 per cent work at clerical jobs
6 per cent work at technical jobs
6 per cent work at manual jobs
5 per cent are housewives.

The remaining 16 per cent (of those working) claim to work at jobs which are a combination of the above.

HSA members engage in a wide variety of leisure pursuits in addition to their involvement with animal welfare organisations. Fifteen per cent put sport as their major leisure activity, 17 per cent mention TV and books, and 8 per cent specify cultural activities; 30 per cent mention a combination of those three, and another 20 per cent mention either nature pursuits or a combination of other leisure activities with nature pursuits.

Politics does not play a substantial part in the lives of HSA members. Only 30 per cent state that they are involved in local or national politics, and 70 per cent definitely state that they are not. Even fewer, 15 per cent, belong to a political party; 7 per cent are members of the Liberal party, 5 per cent are Conservatives and 3 per cent are Labour party members. One member did belong to the National Front (NF), but during 1978 he was removed from the HSA since the Committee was disturbed by the presence of an NF activist in their ranks. Given a choice of political party in the event of a forthcoming election, 20 per cent were unwilling to state a preference;[2] however 29 per cent of the total plumped for the Liberals, 23 per cent for Labour and 18 per cent for the Conservatives. The remainder stated a preference for either a Social Democratic party (several years before one came into existence) or the Communists.

1 Confirmed by HSA Secretary, 1982.

2 One stated that he would vote for 'none of the buggers'.

Values and attitudes

The evidence from the questionnaires shows that MFHs are a relatively homogeneous group of mainly middle-aged and middle or upper class country dwellers. Hunts saboteurs on the other hand are much more heterogenous, being a more equal mixture of classes and age groups. They are also more evenly divided between the sexes and between urban and rural dwellers.

With respect to values and attitudes, it is known that Masters and saboteurs represent extremes of opinion on the question of hunting and coursing. However the evidence from questionnaires administered between 1974–8 shows that on most social issues the two groups are deeply divided. Indeed of the 31 questions in the questionnaire at least 25 answers show significantly different opinions between saboteurs and hunt Masters. The questions which correlate with each other can be reduced to a number of groups or 'super questions' and compared not only with each other but with a 'normal' population. The definition of the super questions and the data on the normal population derives from the work of Prof. H. Eysenck.[1] The results of these comparisons, between the hunting and anti-hunting groups and 'normal' peer groups, are indicative and tentative rather than absolute, for the populations being compared do not exactly overlap. Nevertheless the comparisons are important for they show that the HSA and the MFH, while more like their 'normal' peer groups than like each other, have strong but very different opinions on most questions.[2]

Eysenck identifies six primary factors; they are authoritarianism, religion, ethnocentrism, humanitarianism, sexual morality and tough-mindedness. The factors are 'rotated', both in this study and by Eysenck, to create a statistically more powerful and intrinsically more rational alignment between pairs of these factors. This exercise produces a continuum on which the two populations are placed, enabling comparisons to be made between them. Factor I, which in theory can 'explain' 26.2 per cent of the difference between the two groups, is the authoritarian – humanitarian dimension. In this study the two factors of tough-mindedness and authoritarianism correlate highly and share the same relationship with humanitarianism.[3] Factor II which 'explains' another 10.5 per cent of the variance Eysenck entitles 'religionism', and opposes attitudes favouring religion and sexual probity with those in favour of sexual permissiveness and anti-clericalism. Factor III is

1 H.J. Eysenck, *The Psychology of Politics*, Routledge, London 1954, and H.J. Eysenck, 'Social Attitudes and Social Class', *British Journal of Social and Clinical Psychology*, 10, 1971, pp. 201–12.

2 For details of the questions and of the statistical processes used see Appendix A on pp. 171–6.

3 See Table 7.3(c) on p. 175.

clearly concerned with attitudes to other colours and races. Eysenck does not discuss this factor but here it will be called 'ethnocentrism'.

Factor I contains all the important political and economic and some of the social questions. What is remarkable about the two populations under scrutiny is the size and predictability of their differences. The MFHs are, for example, less against the death penalty and more in favour of military service than HSA members, and MFHs feel that their country right or wrong is an acceptable credo, whereas saboteurs do not. On economic questions saboteurs tend slightly to the view that capitalism is immoral, whereas Masters of Hounds emphatically do not; interestingly both agree that nationalisation leads to inefficiency and bureaucracy, but MFHs hold the view with much greater strength. They are also more concerned than saboteurs to keep production and trade free from government interference. Hunters are significantly more authoritarian in their views on the way to treat criminals. They strongly disagree that criminals are treated too harshly and are considerably more sympathetic to the idea of flogging sex criminals. On question 9 the mean for MFHs is 4.02 and the standard deviation 1.03; this suggests that few people from this survey have a score below the median of 3 and indicates a strong and general lack of sympathy for the criminal.

Factor II concerns religious and sexual matters. Here the differences are almost equally strong. The views are not necessarily opposed, for both groups accept the idea of trial marriages, but the saboteurs do so with greater enthusiasm; both are hesitant about free love, but the MFHs are more so than saboteurs. MFHs are considerably more in favour of religion than HSA members. The populations disagree over whether religious people are hypocrites. The MFHs do not feel that God is an invention of the human mind, whereas the HSA members are evenly divided. Both agree that Christ was divine and both disagree with the suggestion that there is no survival after death. However, the MFHs feel much more strongly about religion than the saboteurs.

On Factor III, ethnocentrism, the two populations are significantly different except on the question of Jews, where their views virtually overlap. The saboteurs are nevertheless significantly more enthusiastic about coloured people and are more opposed to discrimination; indeed, their three highest scores are on questions of race. Even though they are less positive in their views than saboteurs, the MFHs remain on balance against discrimination and do not, by a small margin, accept that coloured people are inferior. This point is important, for while MFHs are undoubtedly more racist than saboteurs they are not, on balance, positively racist.

On the basis of this evidence it is possible to give tentative answers to the 'super questions' which are derived by combining the basic factors into three major factors. It is apparent that MFHs are considerably more authoritarian, more religious and more ethnocentric than saboteurs, and that saboteurs are, in their turn, more permissive, more humanitarian and less ethnocentric than MFHs.

Eysenck has attempted to relate these factors to two other primary factors which have become a valuable technique for distinguishing between groups of people. The first factor, R, opposes conservatism with radicalism and the second, T, opposes tough-mindedness with tender-mindedness. Eysenck superimposed these two dimensions on a diagram which juxtaposes the two major factors produced in his study.[1] By rotating the axes four quadrants are produced; authoritarian beliefs appear in the tough-minded conservative quadrant and humanitarian beliefs, such as disapproval of the atomic bomb, appear in the tender-minded radical quadrant. From the evidence of this study, it is apparent that MFHs are essentially tough-minded conservatives and that saboteurs are radicals, although some are tough- and some are tender-minded.

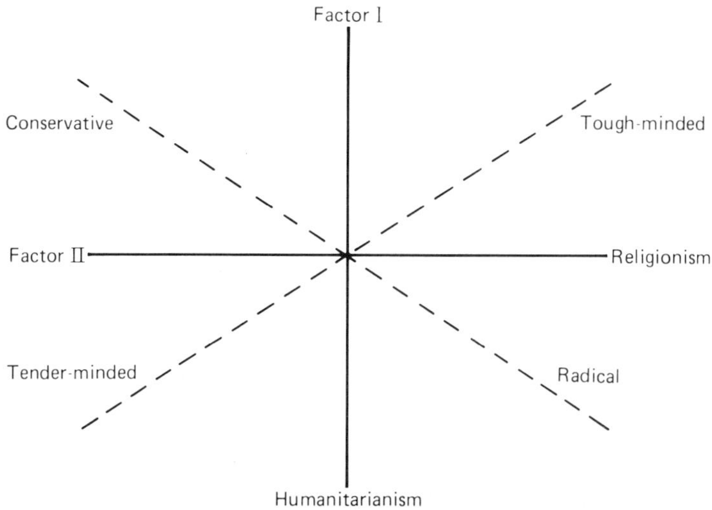

Figure 7.1

This characterisation, while significant in showing the extent to which saboteurs and MFHs disagree on the broad principles as well as on almost every individual question, is less powerful than it seems for, as Eysenck makes clear, age correlates with conservatism and the male sex with tough-mindedness. He also shows that women and young people tend to be both more radical and tender-minded.[2]

1 For the theoretical justification of this approach, see Eysenck, *Social Attitudes*, pp. 210–12, see Fig. 7.1.

2 In Eysenck's study, however, 'different social classes share identical attitude structure'. See *Social Attitudes*, p. 209.

Eysenck establishes this by breaking down his population into a series of sub-groups on the basis of age, sex and class. HSA and MFH populations are too small to be subdivided without losing a high degree of statistical reliability; however the typical MFH is, by Eysenck's definition, middle-class, male and middle-aged; 97 per cent are over 25 years old, which, for him, is when middle age begins. By averaging the means of the middle-aged and elderly middle-class men in Eysenck's study, a peer group is thereby produced against which the middle-class and middle-aged huntsmen may be compared. A similar but more complicated process is followed in an attempt to produce a peer group with which the mainly young HSA members may be compared. The peer group for the HSA has been constructed by averaging the skilled young men, the professional middle-aged (i.e. 25–45) men, the skilled middle-aged females, and young unskilled females, which includes students and housewives. The internal evidence of the HSA questionnaires supports this mixture of sub-groups; it corresponds as closely as possible to the heterogenity of the whole HSA population.

Table 7.4 in Appendix B shows the mean scores for the MFH and the HSA and the scores for their 'normal' peer groups. It shows also the differences between the two pairs of populations and makes clear that neither the HSA nor the MFH are entirely 'normal' in their distribution of values and attitudes.

The relationship between the HSA and its 'normal' peer group shows that HSA members are relatively more tender-minded and more radical. On every question which contributed to Factor I they are more 'extreme' than their peers, that is, their replies tend to be more politically radical or socially humanitarian.

On questions of sex and religion, the collective stand of HSA members is compatible with their position in Factor I. They are more in favour of trial marriages and free love than their peers and are more likely to believe that religious people are hypocrites. They disagree with the notion that the church should increase its influence on society but accept, although less whole-heartedly than their peers, that Christ was divine. The picture for Factor III is similar, saboteurs are on every question considerably less ethnocentric than their peers, even though on every question their peers are relatively sympathetic to Jews and coloured people.

Masters of Foxhounds are in general closer to their peers than the HSA, although, in every case where the mean scores are substantially different, the MFHs take a more extreme view in the direction of conservative tough-mindedness. Whatever their feelings they have no hesitation in expressing it strongly. On Factor I they believe, with their peers but more strongly, that governments should not interfere, and that capitalism is not immoral. They feel again more strongly than their peers that it was not necessarily right to abolish the death penalty and that we do not treat criminals too harshly. While their peers are cautious about the slogan 'my country right or wrong', MFHs are not; it is the question on which the two mean scores are furthest apart.

On Factor II there is a significant division between their attitudes to religion and their attitudes to sex. Although they are firmly on the side of the church and of religion, on the questions relating to sexual morality they are more liberal than their peers. They accept that trial marriage might be a good idea and are less disapproving than their peers of free love and of sexual relations outside marriage. Whether hunting stimulates or sublimates sexual passion is uncertain but there exists a popular belief that hunting people are sexually promiscuous. As Paul Johnson writes: 'The hunting fraternity are notoriously lascivious and, in the season, the night air of Melton Mowbray is loud with the sighs of adulterers'.[1] And Maureen Duffy has described hare hunting as symbolic rape and hunting in general as a two-part masturbation fantasy of 'the hunt and the kill; the build up and the orgasm'.[2] Whatever the reason which explains the 'excitement of the chase' its followers exhibit a tolerance in sexual attitudes which is in marked contrast to their attitude on other issues.

Factor III reveals an interesting point. Two questions concern or mention Jews and on both of these (Questions 6 and 25), the hunting community were a little more tolerant than their peers, but on questions relating solely to coloured people (Questions 11, 15 and 23) they were a little less so. The differences are small but are interesting, because they possibly result from the pattern of recruitment into hunting over the last one hundred years. The tradition whereby scions of successful business houses have ensured their respectability by buying country estates was exemplified by the Jewish community and many Jewish families have become pillars of the hunting establishment.[3] This is not true of coloured people.

There are, of course, individual questions in the questionnaire which do not correlate with others or provide loadings for major factors, but which nevertheless show up interesting contrasts between the various populations. The notion that a person's greatest obligation is to his

1 *New Statesman*, 12 July 1963.

2 In *Animals, Men and Morals*, pp. 117–18.

3 The best known being Sir Bernard Waley-Cohen, Chairman of the Devon and Somerset Staghounds, Treasurer of the BFSS for fourteen years, and a city financier.

family is strongly felt by MFHs. They feel this more strongly than their peer group, and predictably much more so than HSA members.

The MFH feel more strongly on Question 3 than on any other; the question suggests that an occupation by a foreign power would be better than war. They disagree with this more strongly than their peers who, in turn, feel it much more strongly than the HSA and their peers. Neither MFHs nor their peers have strong feelings about suicide, but HSA members are much more willing than their peers, and than MFHs, to accept that a person has the right to take his own life. The question suggesting that freedom is less important than internal order (Question 28) divides the four major populations in a predictable way; the HSA peers are more concerned with freedom than the MFHs' peer, but both these groups are outflanked – the HSA is firmly on the side of freedom and the MFH is strongly on the side of order.

The most interesting of the questions on which there is broad agreement between the two populations concerns the right to privacy 'on matters such as birth control'. Whatever their views on birth control Masters of Hounds are firm upholders of the right to privacy for they feel strongly that attacks on hunting are an invasion on their own privacy. The only other question on which they virtually agree – the non-contentious question of telling white lies – is significantly the only question on which the HSA, the MFHs and both their peer groups are in complete agreement.

Most statistical analyses of attitudes require relatively sophisticated techniques and often founder on the question 'How large must a difference be before it is significant?' – an unanswerable question because there is no statistical way of defining political or social significance. In this case the question is not appropriate; the two populations being compared are grossly different in their values and attitudes. Although there is considerable overlap in their ages and social classes, there is almost none in their attitudes. On almost all social, economic, political and moral questions the two populations sharply disagree.

This has a number of implications. First, it explains why in practice the two communities are permanently at loggerheads, for almost no common ground exists to act as the basis for a compromise between them. Second, the HSA's relative acceptance of a person's right to involve himself in another's affairs (Question 5) helps to explain why, officially at least, the organisation accepts some police harrassment as a necessary price to pay and also why it finds it hard to understand why legislative and administrative changes with respect to hunting are so slow. Third, the hunting community's intolerance of HSA activities is partly a product of its inability to understand what HSA members think as well as a reflection of its desire for privacy and its desire to keep out prying eyes. The authoritarianism and tough-mindedness of the hunting community is also essentially unsympathetic to any group which disagrees with it.

Two further points arise from the comparison between both populations and their peer groups, both of which work to the advantage of the hunting community. The first is that the HSA is relatively extreme even when compared with its peer group. This places its values at the margins of social acceptability and raises the possibility that society will label it as an extremist organisation because of both its behaviour and its views. For the HSA and other animal welfare societies this problem is compounded by their historical attachment to vegetarianism. R. Ryder of the RSPCA, Lord Soper, R. Rowley and R. Course of the LACS and W. Price MP are all vegetarians. In 1978, over one-third of the RSPCA's Council and LACS Committee were vegetarians. By 1982 these figures had increased to over 50 per cent for the RSPCA and 100 per cent for the LACS. Indeed half of the LACS Committee in 1982 were vegans.[1] The HSA is even more closely involved with vegetarianism; all of the HSA Committee in 1978 were vegetarians or vegans, and by 1982 all but one of the Committee were vegans. This naturally influenced their policies, and the HSA's AGM in 1978 passed by a three to one majority a motion offering support to an organisation to be called 'Vegetarians against the Nazis'. The strength of these beliefs, some of which, like vegetarianism, clashes sharply with rural English proclivities, exacerbates an already deep division. It produces the ironic result of enabling hunters to class the ideas of HSA members as doubly worthless for 'not only are they anti-hunting, they are also vegetarians', and on both counts therefore are cranks. HSA members, of course, maintain that their stand is both logical and sensible.

The second point also favours those who lead the defence of hunting. Their members are essentially middle-aged, upper middle class, tough-minded and Conservative. This description does not perhaps fit the 'man in the street' but it is almost a caricature of the political and administrative establishment. The MFHs' deviations from the 'normal' peer group with which they have been compared make their values more rather than less like the politicians, civil servants and leaders of establishment opinion with whom they have to negotiate. The HSA members, on the other hand, have pursued the logic of some of their radical and tender-minded values and have thereby increasingly alienated themselves not only from leaders of opinion, but also from the essentially young middle-class community from which they come.

The radicalism of the HSA on most issues is not a new extremist development, it is the continuation of a lengthy historical pattern. The early attacks on hunting were launched by evangelicals and by radicals

1 Interviews with Committee members, 1982.

before being taken up by two organisations, the Fabian Society and the Humanitarian League, who shared both policies and members. The radical beginnings of the anti-hunting movement have tended to be forgotten by the membership of the societies which set out to abolish hunting. The middle class sentimentalists who have joined the cause have disguised the radical underpinnings of the original purpose and have suppressed the class and, by extension, the party political aspects of the debate.

Hunting is a minor issue for most people and for some is of no consequence at all, but for a few it is among the most salient of all political issues. For them and for those who have strong feelings about hunting there is a correlation between their attitudes on hunting and their attitudes on other issues. In other words, if it is known where a person stands on the hunting issue it is possible to predict his attitude towards, for example, nationalisation or racial issues. Thus have opinions for and against hunting been absorbed into two conflicting universes of complementary values; those for and those against humanitarian, radical and tender-minded principles.

This point was confirmed in 1982 by the RSPCA poll a part of which focussed on the relationship between support for animal welfare issues and a number of other social and political issues such as the desirability of giving aid to the Third World, of having sporting links with South Africa and of protecting the environment. The survey showed clearly that those supporting the RSPCA's position on animal welfare questions were more likely than those who rejected or were unconcerned about the RSPCA's policies to support government action in pursuit of radical political causes particularly those concerned with the environment. As the Report of the Survey states: 'What is clear, however, is that those who express concern for animal welfare and, or, support the RSPCA are far from withdrawn from other, more general, issues in British political life. They are not exclusive in their concern for animal welfare, but are generally reformist across a wide range of issues'.[1]

1 RSPCA/Gallup, 1982, p. 50.

Appendix A

An analysis of the attitude survey contained in the questionnaire has involved a number of steps.[1] First the answers have been tabulated and the mean scores and standard deviation have been computed for both populations.[2] From Table 7.2 it can be seen that there are substantial differences between the mean scores on all the questions except questions 10, 14, 20, 30 and 31. The difference between the means on question 21 is at the margins of statistical significance (at the 95 per cent confidence level),[3] but essentially both groups disagree (the HSA a little more emphatically) with the contention that underdogs deserve little sympathy.

Table 7.1
Attitude survey

Attitude statements

1	People should realise that their greatest obligation is to their family.
2	Production and trade should be free from government interference.
3	An occupation by a foreign power is better than war.
4	Men and women have the right to find out whether they are sexually suited before marriage (e.g. by trial marriage).
5	Nowadays, more and more people are prying into matters which do not concern them.
6	Jews are as valuable citizens as any other group.
7	The death penalty was barbaric and it was right to abolish it.
8	Most religious people are hypocrites.
9	Our treatment of criminals is too harsh, we should try to cure them, not punish them.
10	Sex relations except in marriage are always wrong.

1 See Table 7.1.

2 See Table 7.2.

3 Statistical significance at the 95 per cent confidence level is assessed by the following formula

$$\sqrt{\frac{50^2}{n} + \frac{50^2}{n}} \times 2$$

The difference between the two means being compared is then established and, if the result of the equation above is greater than the difference between the means, then the difference is *not* statistically significant.

Table 7.1 continued/...

11 It would be best to keep coloured people in their own districts and schools in order to prevent too much contact with whites.

12 Compulsory military training in peacetime is essential for the survival of this country.

13 Sex crimes, such as rape and attacks on children, deserve more than mere imprisonment, such criminals ought to be flogged, or worse.

14 Persons with serious hereditary defects and diseases should be compulsorily sterilised.

15 It would be a mistake to have coloured people as foremen over whites.

16 My country, right or wrong, is a saying which expresses a fundamentally desirable attitude.

17 The idea of God is an invention of the human mind.

18 A person should be free to take his own life, if he wishes to do so, without interference from society.

19 Free love between men and women should be encouraged as a means towards mental and physical health.

20 A white lie is often a good thing.

21 The so-called underdog deserves little sympathy or help from successful people.

22 The Church should attempt to increase its influence on the life of the nation.

23 Coloured people are innately inferior to white people.

24 The dropping of the first atom bomb on a Japanese city, killing thousands of innocent women and children, was morally wrong and incompatible with our kind of civilisation.

25 All forms of discrimination against the coloured races, the Jews etc., should be made illegal and subject to heavy penalties.

26 Capitalism is immoral because it exploits the worker by failing to give him full value for his productive labour.

27 Christ was divine, wholly or partly in a sense different from other men.

28 The maintenance of internal order within the nation is more important than ensuring that there is complete freedom for all.

29 The nationalisation of the great industries is likely to lead to inefficiency, bureaucracy and stagnation.

30 Matters such as abortion and birth control are private and should be left up to the person concerned.

31 There is no survival of any kind after death.

The scoring for this survey was 1 = strongly agree
2 = agree
3 = don't know or no opinion
4 = disagree
5 = strongly disagree.

Table 7.2
Analysis of questionnaires

Question	HSA Mean	HSA Standard dev.	MFHs Mean	MFHs Standard dev.	Differences between means
1	2.71	1.17	1.67	0.85	1.04
2	3.25	1.23	1.99	0.97	1.26
3	3.30	1.26	4.32	1.08	1.02
4	1.78	1.03	2.88	1.38	1.10
5	2.94	1.27	1.71	0.91	1.23
6	1.45	0.71	1.71	0.63	0.26
7	2.39	1.44	3.85	1.17	1.46
8	2.79	1.29	3.85	1.00	1.06
9	3.35	1.29	4.02	1.03	0.67
10	3.88	0.95	3.53	1.13	0.35
11	4.52	0.84	3.59	1.05	0.93
12	4.12	1.28	2.70	1.30	1.42
13	3.38	1.47	2.44	1.39	0.94
14	3.25	1.34	2.91	1.30	0.34
15	4.29	0.89	3.38	1.05	0.91
16	3.71	1.17	2.38	1.09	1.35
17	2.95	1.46	3.67	1.15	0.72
18	2.53	1.25	3.02	1.10	0.49
19	3.11	1.18	3.82	1.01	0.71
20	2.21	0.85	2.15	0.79	0.06
21	4.13	1.01	3.83	0.97	0.30
22	3.51	1.43	2.38	1.00	1.13
23	4.59	0.73	3.45	1.94	1.14
24	1.93	1.18	3.53	1.18	1.60
25	2.05	1.23	2.73	1.17	0.68
26	2.99	1.34	4.21	0.94	1.22
27	2.87	1.28	2.00	0.84	0.87
28	3.09	1.24	2.03	1.02	1.06
29	2.53	1.28	1.39	0.60	1.14
30	1.99	1.25	1.77	0.91	0.22
31	3.45	1.30	3.61	1.09	0.16

The next step in the analysis was to correlate the scores to see which questions appeared to relate to each other. The results of this correlation were then subjected to a factor analysis, which highlighted the questions which help to 'explain' the key factors.[1] What the key factors themselves explain or describe is a matter of intuitive judgement.[2] This process collects together the questions which help to explain the differences between the sets of attitudes of those completing the questionnaire. Factor I in Table 7.3 (a), for example, 'explains' 14.3 per cent of the variance of the attitudes expressed by HSA members.

Factor analysis is more useful when the two populations are combined for this enables comparisons to be made between the two populations, not only with respect to individual questions but also in relation to the key factors.[3] The high scores emerging from the factorial analysis indicate clearly the questions on which the two populations are most seriously divided. The high scoring questions have then been combined into groups (i.e. factors, or super questions), so that an analysis of all 31 questions was avoided.[4]

Table 7.3 (a)
MFH Factors (after Varimax rotation)

	Questions	Amount of variance 'explained'
Factor I (Questions with a score of 0.5 or above)	4, 8, 17, 19, 27 and 31	14.3%
Factor II	7, 12, 13, 14 and 15	11.6%
Factor III	2, 5, 12, 16, 23, 24, 26 and 29	6.8%

1 See Tables 7.3 (a) and 7.3 (b).

2 Eysenck's terminology and definitions will be used.

3 See Table 7.3 (c).

4 Reference to Tables 7.1 and 7.2 provides the data for such a comparison.

Table 7.3 (b)
HSA Factors (after Varimax rotation)

	Questions	Amount of variance 'explained'
Factor I (Scores of 0.5 or above)	2. 7, 9, 12, 13, 26 and 29	19.8%
Factor II	4, 8, 17, 19, 22 and 27	12.3%
Factor III	6, 11, 15, 23 and 25	6.8%

Table 7.3 (c)
Joint HSA and MFH Factor analysis (after Varimax rotation, scores of 0.55 or over)

Question		Factor loadings
Factor I		
2	Government should not interfere with business	0.71
7	Death penalty is barbaric	0.69
9	We treat criminals too harshly	0.55 (negative)
12	Military service is essential	0.69
13	Sex crimes deserve severe punishment	0.62
16	My country first	0.69
23	Coloured people are inferior	0.55
24	Atom bomb was wrong	0.59 (negative)
26	Capitalism is immoral	0.71 (negative)
29	Nationalisation was wrong	0.72 (negative)
Factor II		
4	Trial marriage is OK	0.60
8	Religious people are hypocrites	0.66
17	God is an invention	0.71
19	Free love is OK	0.59
22	Church should increase its influence	0.67 (negative)
27	Christ was divine	0.66 (negative)
31	No survival after death	0.58
Factor III		
6	Jews are valuable citizens	0.66 (negative)
11	Keep coloureds separate	0.56
15	Coloured foremen are a mistake	0.60
23	Coloured people are inferior	0.57
25	Discrimination should be illegal	0.60 (negative)

Table 7.4
Data for peer group comparison (from Eysenck)

Question	(a) HSA mean	(b) Mean of comparable normal population	(c) Differences between (a) and (b)	(d) MFH mean	(e) Mean of comparable normal population	(f) Differences between (d) and (e)
1	2.71	1.79	0.92	1.67	1.88	0.21
2	3.25	2.54	0.71	1.99	2.65	0.66
3	3.20	3.76	0.56	4.32	3.91	0.41
4	1.78	3.11	1.33	2.88	3.18	0.30
5	2.94	2.36	0.58	1.71	2.48	0.77
6	1.45	1.84	0.39	1.71	1.78	0.07
7	2.33	3.56	1.23	3.85	3.38	0.47
8	2.79	3.51	0.72	3.85	3.59	0.26
9	3.35	3.78	0.43	4.02	3.66	0.36
10	3.89	3.38	0.51	3.53	3.29	0.24
11	4.52	3.79	0.73	3.59	3.84	0.25
12	4.12	3.08	1.04	2.70	3.23	0.53
13	3.38	2.36	1.02	2.44	2.74	0.30
14	3.25	3.06	0.19	2.91	2.95	0.04
15	4.29	3.46	0.83	3.38	3.69	0.31
16	3.71	3.27	0.44	2.38	3.47	1.09
17	2.95	3.47	0.52	3.67	3.24	0.43
18	2.53	3.03	0.50	3.02	3.09	0.07
19	3.11	3.79	0.68	3.82	3.94	0.12
20	2.21	2.18	0.03	2.15	2.22	0.07
21	4.13	3.60	0.53	3.83	3.85	0.02
22	3.51	2.79	0.72	2.38	2.57	0.19
23	4.59	3.98	0.61	3.45	4.04	0.59
24	1.93	2.77	0.84	3.53	3.03	0.50
25	2.05	2.76	0.71	2.73	2.85	0.12
26	2.99	3.34	0.35	4.21	3.87	0.34
27	2.87	2.62	0.25	2.00	2.60	0.60
28	3.09	2.81	0.28	2.03	2.33	0.30

Note

Some of the differences in Table 7.4 between one population and its peer group are so large that the arguments in favour of the sub-groups chosen to make up the peer groups need to be tested. On a straightforward humanitarian/social question such as the use of the atomic bomb (Question 24), it would be hypothesised that the HSA and its peer group, consisting mainly of young and female people, would be more against the use of the bomb than the older, middle-class MFHs and their peers. It would also seem reasonable to suggest that the peers of the HSA would be more against the bomb than the peers of the MFH. It can be seen from Table 7.4 that these hypotheses are substantiated. A mean of 2.35 *could* be produced by averaging Eysenck's scores for unskilled females of all ages, but the mean of this obviously unsuitable grouping would still be 0.43 from the HSA's mean of 1.93. A similar exercise which further justifies the composition of the peer groups can be conducted with a politico/economic question. No. 26 on the morality of capitalism, shows that both the HSA and the MFH are relatively close to their peers while their means are 1.22 apart.

PART III

ARENAS AND INSTITUTIONS

8 The political culture

As the political, economic and social structures of a society change so do the values of the people who live in that society. As these values change the political culture – the ideas, expectations and attitudes of the people towards the political system and the political process – changes as well.

Alongside the changes which produced in 19th century Britain an enfranchised, literate, urban working class, and a more philanthropic approach to social problems, there arose a humane concern for the welfare of animals. Its beginning was tentative, and its roots lay in the philosophical rather than the political past. Long before any arguments could be deployed against hunting, society had to develop to a point where it was convinced that the way individuals behaved and the way in which they treated animals was a suitable and worth-while subject for discussion and ultimately for legislation.

The early philosophical arguments turned on whether animals had souls. Aquinas believed that they did not; Descartes believed that since animals could not think, they could not feel, and therefore there could be no cruelty.[1] Post-Renaissance thinkers, however, considered that gratuitous cruelty to animals was unworthy as well as unnecessary. Sir Thomas More condemned the infliction of suffering for sport,[2] and

1 C. Niven, *History of the Humane Movement*, Johnson, London, 1967, pp. 32 and 45–7.

2 M. Hutchings and M. Caver, *Man's Dominion*, Hart-Davis, London, 1970, p. 69.

Pepys described bull-baiting 'as a very rude and nasty pleasure'.[1]

The 17th century Quaker movement was one of the first to include in its platform a belief that animals had rights which should be respected. The Quaker influence when combined with that of the Puritans was sufficient to abolish bear-baiting and cock-fighting for the period of the Puritan interregnum. These activities were banned partly 'because it was considered that these barbarities had a bad effect on the common people',[2] and partly because the Puritans were against pleasure. This has left, according to Brander, 'a narrow-minded minority who throughout subsequent generations have remained consistently anti-hunting and anti-sport'.[3]

In the 18th century, the people who wished to stop the worst types of cruelty to animals drew supporters from the increasing number of Methodists and Non-Conformists. Many of them, including Wesley, believed that animals had souls and that as God's creatures they had certain rights. In the second part of the century articles appeared supporting the cause of animals,[4] and at the same time a more humanitarian mood began to permeate certain sectors of society. Jeremy Bentham gave the early animal welfare movement some philosophical respectability. He asked on the animals' behalf: 'The question is not, *Can they reason?* nor, *Can they talk?* but, *Can they suffer?*' He felt that the day might come 'when the rest of animal creation may acquire those rights which never could have been withholden from them but by the hand of tyranny'.[5] He spelt out the point more fully in the *Principles of Penal Law*:

> Cockfights, bull-baiting, hunting hares and foxes, fishing and other amusements of the same kind, necessarily suppose either the absence of reflection or a fund of inhumanity, since they produce more acute sufferings to sensible beings and the most painful and lingering death of which we can form any idea. Why should the law refuse its protection to any sensitive being?[6]

1 *The Illustrated Pepys (from the Diaries)*, ed. R. Latham, Bell & Hyman, London, 1978, p. 118. Entry for 14 Aug. 1666.

2 Moss, *Valiant Crusade*, p. 12.

3 Brander, *Hunting Instinct*, p. 97.

4 One of the earliest was Dr Hildrup, *Free Thoughts on Brute Creation*, 1742. One of the most important was Dr H. Primatt, *A Dissertation on the Duty of Mercy and the Sin of Cruelty to Brute Animals*, 1776 (this book had a profound influence on the founders of the RSPCA).

5 J. Bentham, *The Principles of Morals and Legislation*, (ed.) L.J. Lafleur, Hafner, Connecticut, 1970, pp. 310–11.

6 Quoted in Carr, *Fox Hunting*, p. 197.

In the 19th century the radical movement became increasingly concerned with the plight of animals and its members joined or supported the RSPCA when it was formed in 1826. Hunting itself was rarely attacked until after the middle of the century.

At the dawn of the 20th century it was clear that the anti-hunting movement was growing and that it was dominated by middle-class Fabians, moralists and townspeople. The extent to which it commanded rural or mass support was unknown.

Values and expectations changed in the 19th century with respect to people as well as towards animals. However, as long as satisfying basic needs fully occupied most people, the mass, if they thought of it at all, believed that improvements in their position would only occur through good luck or through the intervention of the land-owning members of parliament. This was the source of Disraeli's belief that a natural alliance existed between the upper and working classes against the economically aggressive middle classes, and it was particularly true in rural areas where the values and behaviour of the landowners influenced their workers. The common interest in the land ensured a similarity of loyalties and values, and, since changes resulted from forces beyond their control, the poor mass of the population continued to maintain traditional patterns of deferential and obedient behaviour towards their social superiors. Furthermore, by the time these traditional attitudes and values had changed, society was urban and industrial rather than rural and agrarian. Therefore, since the landed gentry were no longer causing mass unhappiness, field sports were no longer a dominant source of class friction, and the issue of hunting was for many no longer a crucial one. In the 19th century few of the poor had the leisure to consider such time-consuming activities and in the 20th century a variety of urban activities has pushed hunting into the background so that the mass have neither wished to join the hunting field nor resented those who do.

Nowadays in urban areas hostility to hunting is a product of the folk memory of once rural forebears and is kept going by anti-hunting publicity, whereas in rural areas feelings about hunting are much more likely to be based on some knowledge of the activity. In both cases the hostility felt towards the hunting community in the 19th century has lessened in the 20th, for the vote, the welfare state and generally rising standards of living have diminished some of the 'deep-rooted and bitter divisions in English society'.[1] Ironically as democratic ideals have spread and as the mechanics of testing public opinion have been perfected, class antagonism has decreased. The hostile mass, who were power-

1 Bowle, *The English Experience*, p. 419.

less in the 19th century, have gained limited access to the levers of power in the 20th, and have, by and large, ceased to be hostile at least as far as hunting is concerned.

A major study by Newby has established that the rural worker today is no longer deferential although he remains powerless. Accordingly, the 'largely quiescent social and political behaviour . . . must be seen to result from the agricultural worker's dependence rather than his deference'.[1] In farming communities deferential behaviour may emerge because a worker understands that he is subordinate. Newby shows that this does not mean that the worker accepts the moral principles of deference or behaves deferentially in other social interactions. Undoubtedly the acceptance and even the rightness of inferiority which deference implies is of declining significance in both rural and urban areas. Nevertheless neither it, nor class consciousness,[2] nor class differences in the degree of access to key positions in society have disappeared. In the hunting context: 'The cleavage [is] now deeper and more radical, between town and country, between knows and don't knows. Previously opposition to hunting and shooting had been based primarily on envy with a sound background of knowledge. Now it [is] based on emotion with no real understanding of the issues involved'.[3] Since urban life has been the norm for most people in 20th century England the issues which arouse most class hostility are those which spring from an urban context. Fox hunting appears to most urban dwellers a distant and insignificant issue, a fact which works on balance to the benefit of the hunting community, for, if the anti-hunting community successfully convinced people that hunting was a manifestation of class oppression, it might quickly become a casualty of the class war. Nevertheless the exclusiveness of hunting makes it important both for snobs and for the socially mobile.[4] The fact that they hunt confirms to the world at large that both groups have risen to or are already members of the dominant class. Since the days when status was conferred rather than earned, to go hunting has been an indication of status.

This is particularly so when one of its followers is the Prince of Wales, who nevertheless believes that hunting enables him to 'meet more farmers, and more ordinary British blokes than in any other

1 H. Newby, *The Deferential Worker*, Penguin, Harmondsworth 1977, p. 414.

2 Butler and Stokes, *Political Change in Britain*, ch. 4, esp. pp. 120–4.

3 M. Brander, *Hunting and Shooting*, Weidenfeld & Nicolson, London, 1971, p. 127.

4 'Snobbery belongs rather to the situation where one class melts imperceptibly into another and where fairly free movement from one into another is possible'. A. Sampson, *The New Anatomy of Britain*, Hodder & Stoughton, London, 1971, p. 202.

exercise or sport that I have ever done and . . . to keep in touch with what actually happens in the British countryside'.[1]

Since snobbery is most rife when classes are confused and when class mobility is possible, hunting as a leisure activity has been able to attract a new kind of élite. It has managed to do this without becoming commercialised or losing its traditional aura and at a time when the breaking down of rigid class barriers has produced a group eager for social advancement. Thus it has remained an élite sport even though the nature of that élite has altered radically. Occupation and income rather than land and leisure are the main determinants of social status today and hunting remains significant for those who live in rural areas and who wish to measure their social position against an old standard. There are other leisure pursuits which demand wealth, such as yachting, but few which have such a heritage. Also, while the hunting community is based on the rural élite, the changes in British society and in landownership patterns have removed the control of rural affairs and of hunting from the hands of the great landowners. Hunting, although remaining an élite sport, has become accessible to farmers and to professionals and to businessmen from the towns. It has avoided being too restrictive and at the same time is able to confer some social cachet on its followers.

These developments, have, in general, had the effect of reducing overt class antagonism to a minor issue, so that it is rarely mentioned by either side when hunting is being debated. However, the pro-hunting community sometimes accuses its opponents of exploiting class consciousness, while in fact the anti-hunting community strenuously avoids doing so. Only the most thoughtful of hunt saboteurs consider that class conflict motivates their activities, and the majority sincerely believe that their concern is with conservation and avoiding cruelty. Similarly the majority of MFHs believe that they are conserving traditional sports against townee interference. Most believe that antagonism to hunting stems partly from ideological roots but relatively few consider this to be a function of overt class hostility. The class issue inflames the emotions on both sides without becoming a substantive issue; it is essentially a part of the political culture and is significant because of its hidden impact on the political process.

Hunting has become an essentially middle-class sport in the 20th century; however, it can never become a classless sport. It will continue to be enriched by its rituals, its language and its echoes of the past, and these echoes will be a reflection of its traditional associations with the

1 Speech at the 100th Anniversary Dinner of the MFHA, June 1981. Quoted in *Baily's*, 1981–2, p. ix.

political and economic élite. Property was power in the 18th and 19th centuries, during which period the poor could only rebel against 'the class nature of laws and justice'.[1] Nowadays property and capital provide both an entrée into the hunting community and remain, as they always have, the factors which give social groups political and economic leverage. But for the mass of those involved in the hunting issue, class is not of conscious significance. This does not, of course, mean that antipathy to hunting has decreased but rather that the causes of the antipathy have gradually changed.

The social, political and economic changes of the 19th and 20th century have fundamentally altered the balance of power within society and have influenced the nature and style of the political process. There has emerged a militant trade unionism and a Labour party committed to a radical restructuring of the British economy and society.

While the more radical goals of the founders of the Labour party have not been achieved, a number of changes have taken place. Working-class literacy, the spread of radio and television and almost a century of political participation have ensured that public issues are debated nationally and openly. This encourages the emergence of sub-groups in society and these sub-groups make demands on the political process thus creating in the minds of both governments and the governed a tacit acceptance of an increasingly interventionist role for governments. In the last half century the state has become active in areas which were traditionally considered private or unsuitable for legislation. This legislation has been both restrictive and permissive; it has, for example, placed speed and alcohol limits on drivers and removed restrictions on homosexuals and given the right to women to choose an abortion.

This general increase in governmental and sub-group activity has led to a growing feeling of political competence. In the 1960s Almond and Verba found that 78 per cent of the population felt that it was competent to influence local political questions; and almost two-thirds felt nationally competent.[2] Two-thirds also felt both willing and able to discuss politics. Almond and Verba summarised their findings: 'The participant role is highly developed. Exposure to politics, interest, involvement and a sense of competence are relatively high. There are norms supporting political activity as well as emotional involvement in elections . . . there is general system pride as well as satisfaction with specific government performance'.[3] Paradoxically because of British

1 Hill, *Reformation*, p. 238.

2 G.A. Almond and S. Verba, *The Civic Culture*, Little, Brown, Boston, 1965, pp. 142–3.

3 Almond and Verba, *Civic Culture*, p. 315.

people's belief in their own competence, an absence of deep cleavages within society, and a feeling that society was moving in more or less the right directions, the level of actual involvement in political activity has been relatively low. The British people expect to be able to leave politicians and civil servants to make acceptable decisions. Nevertheless, the willingness to be involved, when stirred, remains.

In the 1960s and 1970s the rise of the ecology movement and the work of conservationists have been of increasing significance in the anti-hunting debate. Just as early vegetarians were dismissed as cranks, so were early conservationists and ecologists. However a seminal work by Rachael Carson in 1963[1] alerted the world to the dangers of pollution and to the ease with which natural habitats can be irretrievably destroyed. In the 1960s there was a 'new and rapidly mounting concern with environmental issues . . . 'Conservation' and 'Pollution' were becoming topics of daily discourse.[2] In 1970, an independent standing Royal Commission on Environmental Pollution was established and in 1975 the Conservation of Wild Creatures and Plants Act was passed as an enabling act to protect wildlife and plants from man's excesses. The Wildlife and Countryside Act of 1981 represented a continuation of this process.

The anti-hunting community was enabled by the development of the ecology movement to adopt a less strident tone, for the views it expressed were no longer at the margins of public acceptability. In this same period the 'crime' of speciesism has been identified. A speciesist, like a racist, 'allows the interests of his own species to override the greater interests of members of other species'.[3] The view of those opposed to speciesism is that 'we require *now* to extend the great principles of liberty, equality and fraternity over the lives of animals',[4] or more prosaically that humans should no longer 'inflict suffering on non-humans for trivial reasons'.[5] Some of those opposed to speciesism such as Singer and Godlovitch are vegetarians, and they are also opposed to vivisection, battery egg production and all activities which exploit animals. For them hunting is an almost incomprehensible activity defying basic morality since they believe that animals, having rights, impose obligations on their human masters.

These obligations would be severely questioned even by conservationists if an outbreak of rabies or hydrophobia occurred in Britain.

1 R. Carson, *Silent Spring*, Hamish Hamilton, London, 1963.

2 J. Ryder and H. Silver, *Modern English Society*, Methuen, London, 1970 and 1977, p. 291.

3 Singer, *Animal Liberation*, p. 28.

4 *Animals, Men and Morals*, (eds) S. and R. Godlovitch and J. Harris, p. 238.

5 Singer, *Animal Liberation*, p. 217.

Strict quarantine regulations have so far kept rabies out of Britain even though 30 cases of rabies have been recorded in quarantined animals in the last 50 years. Before that rabies was an occasional hazard; indeed between 1886–1903 some 173 people and 3,056 animals died of rabies in England and Wales. The threat today is a real one, for the disease, which is always fatal to both men and animals, is endemic in parts of Continental Europe and outbreaks occur near Channel ports virtually every year. In Germany, in 1980, there were 6,500 recorded cases of animal rabies, mainly in dogs, cats, foxes and wolves.[1]

An outbreak in England, however minor, would have major repercussions. It is possible (but neither simple nor painless) to vaccinate people and pets against rabies, but it is not possible to vaccinate wild animals. If a wild cat or some urbanised fox was to catch rabies, perhaps from a pet smuggled into the country, it could in a short time infect other wild animals and could easily infect children or adults by licking or biting them. Even if the outbreak was restricted to animals it could then only be contained by restricting the movement of animals over a wide area and by the eradication of all foxes and other potential carriers. During this period all hunting would cease in the region as it does when an outbreak of foot and mouth disease occurs. Sporadic outbursts around the country would similarly disrupt hunting, as would the fear of an outbreak at a hunt kennels. If rabies became endemic in Britain all hunting would stop, thousands of animals, most of them 'innocent', would have to be destroyed and people would be at risk. This is a prospect which both the hunting community and its opponents view with equal dread.

The effects of the conservationist and ecology movements have been profound. Both pro- and anti-hunting groups, and the animal welfare world in general, have claimed to be working as conservationists from the 1960s onwards. Whatever the merits of these claims it has ensured that hunting has become part of a more widespread and increasingly important debate about the relationship between man and nature. The problems implicit in this relationship have entered the political consciousness of British people and have thereby added to the topics which are deemed to belong in the political arena. This is a reflection of changing political values and suggests that the public at large now accepts that animal welfare issues, including hunting, should be a part of the political process and are legitimate targets for legislative action. This throws the onus for producing data, arguments and counter-arguments on to the pressure groups which concern themselves with animal issues. By so doing the pressure groups themselves become more legitimate and are encouraged to take a responsible role, particularly at times when legislation is under consideration.

1 Figures from 'The Risk to Great Britain from Rabies', *RSPCA Today,* Summer 1982, pp. 42–3.

9 Public opinion

Opinion and the media

The 19th century changes in Britain's social, economic and political structures had a gradual but cumulative effect on the values of the people and their leaders. Universal suffrage implied that the feelings and opinions of everyone were of equal political importance, and from this basis grew a belief in the power of public opinion. In the 19th century public opinion in the sense of aggregated mass opinion had little impact on political affairs; the opinions that mattered were few and were those of the owners of property. They were transmitted to members of the élite through the media, particularly *The Times* which, like all important newspapers of the period, had full-time hunting and coursing correspondents. Its views give an insight into the collective opinions of the élite with respect to animal welfare issues. In 1800 *The Times* congratulated those who had succeeded in defeating the attempt to abolish bull-baiting since the legislation was an 'undue interference with private life'.[1] In 1809 *The Times* was more sympathetic to an attempt to stop cruelty to domestic and farm animals and supported the establishment of a system of rights and privileges for animals.

Attacks on sport, however, it could not comprehend and until the mid 20th century *The Times* gave extensive coverage to all field sports,

1 *The Times*, 25 Apr. 1800.

particularly hunting. It assumed that opening meets,[1] hunt balls, hound breeding policies and problems with the supply of horses were all significant news items of interest to the élite.[2] This remained the case until the Second World War after which the social and sporting side of hunting gave way to an emphasis on the politics of hunting. By the 1950s the majority of reports in *The Times* concerned 'news' items such as parliamentary debates, pressure group activity or violence on the hunting field. Photographs of hunting members of the Royal family appeared from time to time in the 1960s and 1970s but hunting as an activity had little news value unless it was in trouble.[3]

The reporting of coursing in the 20th century has followed a similar pattern. The Waterloo Cup in particular was widely and extensively reported at the beginning of the century but in 1970 the event received only one mention in *The Times.*[4] Public hostility towards the sport has increased to such an extent that coursing enthusiasts, far from wishing to popularise their sport, have, since the 1960s, attempted to keep their activities private and to avoid any contact at all with the media.[5]

The growth of the radical press in the 20th century added another dimension to the debate by providing a forum from which attacks on field sports could be mounted. The *News Chronicle* and the *Guardian* were early supporters of the anti-hunting movement and of the pressure groups which promoted it; they were joined in the 1960s by the *Daily Mirror* and the popular Sunday papers. These papers published stories in which the themes of cruelty, snobbery and class antagonism could be exploited in order to discredit the supporters of hunting and coursing.

The effect of changes in the media's view of field sports on public opinion is difficult to gauge. It is certain that the lot of animals has improved in the last 150 years. This is partly because more people believe that they should be treated better, but primarily because the economic gains to be derived from treating animals harshly have largely disappeared. Meat from animals flayed alive has ceased to be considered a delicacy; over-galloped coach horses have been replaced by trains,

1 It listed all the meets of certain hunts. See *inter alia The Times Index* Jan–March, 1920, which lists every meet of the Beaufort Hunt.

2 The activities of 86 different hunts were mentioned at least once during the first quarter of 1930. See *The Times Index*. However this dropped to 11 hunts in 1950. *The Times* published two collections of its own articles on hunting in the 1930s.

3 In the second half of 1970 only one report in *The Times* out of five did not imply a criticism of hunting.

4 This compares with 23 separate reports of the same events in 1910.

5 Even *The Times* has editorialised against coursing, on 5 Nov. 1969.

refrigeration has reduced the need to ship live animals to distant markets. It has been economics, not kindness, which has initiated the major improvements in the lot of animals in the late 19th and early 20th centuries.

Nevertheless, these developments encouraged further cumulative changes in attitudes to animals. It became at first acceptable and then respectable to indulge pets and to be sentimental about animals. Anthropomorphic children's books, stories about tame otters, films such as *Bambi* have reinforced the general assumption that animals not only have rights and privileges but also that they possess almost human feelings and sensibilities. Some people have viewed this as sentimentality (the cuddly bunny syndrome) but others have seen it as a step forward for a civilised society.

While changes in attitudes have undoubtedly occurred, public opinion could not overwhelm other, more potent, values; accordingly not all animals benefited from the growth of the humane movement. Hunted animals in particular remained undefended and unprotected because it was accepted by those in power that foxes were vermin, that the sport continued a noble tradition and that opponents of hunting were ignorant or jealous or both.

For similar reasons public opinion was not likely in the 19th century to become a force for change unless those who had the power to initiate change agreed with mass opinion. The social status of the sport concerned was crucial to its future. Thus, when Lord Randolph Churchill declared in 1883 that trap pigeon shooting, of which he disapproved, 'was recognised by a large body of public opinion in this country to be objectionable and cruel' it was clear that its end was imminent.[1]

Public opinion, particularly before it could be adequately measured, could also be used to defend hunting. In 1920 the Home Secretary expressed his conviction that there was 'no evidence of a predominating demand for the suppression of stag hunting'.[2] He thus declined to give government support to a Bill which was attempting to abolish it. At the end of 1928 when the prospect of a Labour government unsympathetic to hunting seemed imminent, *The Times* stated: 'The truth is that hunting, like so many other good things, is an anachronism which survives only because it is securely based on public opinion and sustained by the good will of all affected and concerned'.[3] Even in those days good will was more significant than public opinion for two reasons: firstly, the

1 *Hansard* (Commons), 1883, vol. 276, col. 1684.

2 *West Somerset Free Press*, 31 Dec. 1927.

3 *The Times*, 17 Nov. 1928, leading article.

government was not keen to intervene in areas which were not important sources of disputes and, secondly, the actual state of public opinion was entirely unknown.

As the LACS, NSACS and BFSS joined battle in the 1930s, the government, wherever its sympathies lay, was forced to take an interest. Although dormant during the war, the debate re-opened with a vengeance once it was over. By 1949, the dispute reached such a pitch that *The Times* was moved to declare that the abolitionists were attempting 'to invade the sphere of the individual conscience'.[1] The paper decided that 'opinion and morality will have to change before these bills become law'.[2] The unspoken corollary to these arguments was that, if opinion and morality did change, anti-hunting legislation would be more acceptable.

Public opinion polls

The first independent poll against hunting was conducted in 1958, when Sir Frederick Messer's bill to abolish stag hunting was down for debate. The poll showed clearly (see Table 9.1) that a majority, 65 per cent in the case of stag hunting, and 53 per cent in the case of fox hunting, approved of abolition. Women were more unsympathetic towards both these sports than men. Among the rich (groups AB) a substantial majority were *not* in favour of the abolition of fox hunting and were only just in favour of the abolition of stag hunting.

Table 9.1
1958 Gallup poll on hunting

Would you approve or disapprove if parliament were to make laws forbidding (a) the hunting of deer, or (b) fox hunting?

	Total %	Men	Women	Rich	Middle class	Working class	Poor
Hunting of deer							
Approve of prohibition	65	60	68	53	66	65	63
Disapprove	16	21	12	38	22	15	8
D.K.	19	19	20	9	12	20	29
Fox hunting							
Approve of prohibition	53	49	57	35	49	55	53
Disapprove	24	31	17	59	31	21	19
D.K.	23	21	26	6	20	24	28

Source: *News Chronicle*, 21 Feb. 1958. Conducted by Gallup Polls.

1 *The Times*, 25 Feb. 1949, p. 5.

2 Ibid., p. 5.

During 1968 the National Committee for the Abolition of Deer Hunting, under the chairmanship of E. Hemingway of the LACS, attempted to discover the feelings of the communities most closely concerned with deer hunting. The Committee asked local authorities in North Devon and West Somerset for their views which, since they represented community leaders rather than mass opinion, were important. The results clearly showed that the more rural the council and the closer it was to the centre of Exmoor (the home of stag hunting), the more it was in favour of hunting.[1] The Dulverton RDC in the middle of Exmoor voted almost unanimously for hunting; the Bridgwater UDC, 25 miles away, voted against.

This finding was corroborated by a regional poll in 1966 conducted in Devon and Somerset only (Table 9.2). It shows that 78 per cent of those asked disapproved of stag hunting; however, there was a 17 per cent difference between those living in urban boroughs and those in purely rural areas. The figures do not support the argument put forward by the BFSS that rural West Countrymen are strongly in favour of hunting, for only 18 per cent explicitly were; however neither do they prove the claims of the LACS that even inhabitants of Exmoor are against stag hunting, for rural dwellers in Devon and Somerset could easily live 30 to 40 miles away from Exmoor. The 1966 poll nevertheless shows a strong rural-urban difference, and it is reasonable to argue that the inhabitants of Exmoor are more sympathetic to stag hunting than their counterparts, whether rural or urban, at the other end of Devon or Somerset.

Table 9.2
Regional poll in Devon and Somerset only[2]

Do you approve or disapprove of deer hunting with hounds?

	All	Urban	Rural	Municipal county boroughs
Approve	13	18	18	7
Disapprove	78[3]	89	70	87
D.K.	9	13	12	16

1 NSACS *Bulletin*, 123, Mar. 1958. Confirmed during conversation with the Chairman (during the 1950s) of a local rural district council.

2 Conducted by NOP in 1966.

3 In the age group 16–34, 83 per cent disapproved.

A further poll in 1978 showed a considerable hardening of opinion against stag hunting; 74 per cent, compared with 65 per cent in 1966, approved of moves to abolish it.[1] There was little class, sex or rural/urban differences in these opinions, although those under 24 years of age were 16 per cent more in favour of abolition than those over 65 years of age. The major differences of opinion over stag hunting were products of political affiliation, for 87 per cent of Liberal, 71 per cent of Labour voters and 68 per cent of Conservatives favoured abolition.

Stag hunting is a relatively minor and frequently attacked sport which arouses fierce passions. Its supporters can draw some comfort from the fact that middle-aged Conservative voters and southern rural voters are less likely to demand its abolition than any other section of the voting community. These marginal differences do not, however, disguise the fact that stag hunting is generally unpopular. Even *The Times* in 1969, accepting that 'different societies have different standards at different times', concluded that deer hunting 'is not acceptable as a form of sport [and] is clearly an affront to British taste today'.[2]

Public attitudes towards fox hunting have hardened slowly since 1958 when 53 per cent stated that they would support moves to abolish it. Later polls in 1966, 1972 and 1978[3] all confirmed the general trend of opinion against the sport.

In 1966, rural voters, Conservatives and male voters were more favourable to the sport than other sections of society. There was a relative reluctance to call for the abolition of the sport by a number of people who nevertheless disapproved of it; 62 per cent disapproved of fox hunting while only 50 per cent wanted it abolished. The young were most antagonistic to fox hunting for 73 per cent of those between 21 and 24 favoured abolition compared with 55 per cent of those over 65. *The Times* was moved by this and other related evidence to say that, while the case against fox hunting was not conclusive, it 'would be hard to defend the custom with much conviction'.[4]

A poll in 1972 showed significant class differences in attitudes towards fox hunting: 32 per cent of classes AB approved of it (55 per cent against) while only 19 per cent of class DE approved (65 per cent against). There was also, in 1972, a political division over the activities of Princess Anne: 39 per cent of Conservatives and 59 per cent of Labour voters felt that she should not go hunting.

1 *Public Attitudes Towards Hunting with Hounds*, NOP/LACS, June 1978 (NOP Report 3440), Tables 10, 11 and 12.

2 *The Times*, 5 Nov. 1969, p. 9, leading article.

3 Conducted by NOP for the LACS.

4 *The Times*, 5 Nov. 1969.

These emerging political and class differences were put to the test in 1978 when a poll showed that in general 60 per cent of the electorate favoured a law to ban fox hunting while only 25 per cent demurred at this.[1] Class differences had narrowed since the 1972 poll, perhaps because no member of the Royal Family was involved, nevertheless the poll showed that the higher the individual's social class, the more against a bill to abolish fox hunting he was likely to be. Politically, Liberal and Labour voters were 68 per cent in favour of a bill whereas only 51 per cent of Conservative voters favoured moves to abolish the sport. Environment or place of residence emerged as a significant factor in this poll with 65 per cent of conurban dwellers, but only 53 per cent of rural dwellers, favouring a law against fox hunting.

In 1978, the largest sub-group differences on the fox-hunting question were between the urban, working-class, left-wing young females and the older middle-aged, upper-middle-class, Conservative rural men. The first are stalwarts of the anti-hunting community, and the latter provide the backbone of the hunting community. Environment, class and political affiliation are mutually reinforcing and establish the bases for those at the extremes who wish to become activists. In other words, while the majority tend to be against hunting but do nothing about it, there are two minorities at opposing ends of the spectrum whose beliefs are reinforced by their sub-culture and who therefore are motivated to defend or attack the sport of hunting.

By 1981 it was clear that antagonism to fox hunting had grown. The RSPCA survey in that year showed that 72 per cent of those sampled supported a ban on fox hunting. There was initially no difference on the basis of sex or class, differing ages and education did have an effect. Those under 24 were 18 per cent more likely to oppose fox hunting than those over 65. Those with tertiary education were slighly less against fox hunting than those who merely completed secondary school.

Coursing has like fox hunting been the subject of frequent polls. The first by NOP was taken in 1967 and later ones in 1975, 1976 and 1978 were taken to support parliamentary activity. In general they reinforced the finding of the 1967 poll. In 1967, 12 per cent of the population approved of coursing while 77 per cent disapproved, and 75 per cent of the electorate thought that the government should support Eric Heffer's bill to abolish it. There was little party political or urban/rural differences in these opinions.

1 See Table 9.3 for details.

2 RSPCA/Gallup 1982, Table IV, p. 18 and Table III, p. 14.

Table 9.3

1978 poll: Would you be in favour of or against a law to ban the hunting of foxes?

	Total	Sex		Class		Age			Voting			Environment	
		M.	F.	AB	DE	18–24	35–44	65+	Con	Lib	Lab	Con urb.	Rural
Strongly in favour	33	31	34	23)	(33	42	33	30	27	34	37	37	27
				)55	61(								
In favour	27	26	29	32)	(28	33	29	23	24	34	31	28	26
No opinion	17	16	19	13	21	10	18	20	16	12	17	17	18
Against	19	22	16	27)	(15	12	16	21	28	17	13	16	23
				)32	18(								
Strongly against	4	5	3	5)	(3	3	4	6	5	2	3	2	7

All figures are rounded percentages.

Source: NOP 3440 June 1978, Tables 4–6. Quoted with permission.

Table 9.4
Hare Coursing: are you in favour of or against the bill to ban live hare coursing?

	Jan. 1976	Sept. 1975
Strongly in favour	44	43
In favour	27	27
No opinion	24	21
Against	5	7
Strongly against	1	1

Source: NOP 8802 Sept. 1975, and NOP 9061 Feb. 1976.

The polls in 1975 and 1976 showed that 70 and 72 per cent respectively favoured moves to abolish coursing. The 1976 poll established that 12 per cent of the electorate, mainly working class and Labour voters, had never heard of the sport. However, when it was explained to them in neutral language, the majority then expressed disapproval of it. The polls also showed that higher social class groups and Conservatives were more likely than other groups to have no opinion. This suggests either that they are unfamiliar with coursing because it is essentially a working-class sport, or that it is a sport towards which they have no particular loyalty but about which they are reluctant, for political reasons, to express disapproval. Labour supporters, who tend to have a higher level of disapproval, have no political reasons for suppressing their true feelings.

The polls also showed a clear lessening of approval for the sport as the degree of urbanisation increased – 64 per cent of those in rural areas disapproved, while 75 per cent of those in conurbations disapproved. At the same time the numbers actually approving of coursing ranged from 9 per cent in rural areas to 4 per cent in conurbations.

Party political affiliation has had some affect on attitudes towards coursing. Attitudes underwent an apparent shift between 1975 when the gap between Labour and Conservatives was 1 per cent, and 1976 when the gap was increased to 8 per cent. The 1976 Bill was sponsored by the Labour government; this may have influenced Labour voters in its favour and alienated Conservative supporters.

The 1975 poll asked an additional question about the importance of the Bill in relation to other government bills. Of the 70 per cent who favoured the Bill, 67 per cent thought it either very or fairly important to press ahead with the Coursing Bill. There was, however, a party difference in this answer with 73 per cent of anti-coursing Labour

Table 9.5
Support for Hare Coursing Bill: How important is this Bill given that the Government cannot make all of its Bills now under discussion into law?

Support for Bill in general	% of all electors	Importance of Bill	% of all electors
Strongly against Against No opinion	2 7 21	Assumed not important, therefore not asked	30
In favour	27	Not at all important Not very important No opinion	3 18 2
Strongly in favour	43	Fairly important Very important	27) 47 20)

Source: NOP 8802, Sept. 1975, Tables 7–9.

voters thinking the Bill was important compared with 62 per cent of anti-coursing Conservatives. Of the total electorate 47 per cent felt that the Bill was, on balance, important.

Answers to the question (about the Bill's relative importance) showed significant differences between income groups and classes. The more urban and aged a person was, and the lower his income and ascribed social class, the more likely he, or especially she, was to consider the 1975 Bill very important. For example, only 17 per cent of those in classes AB felt the Bill was very important compared with 38 per cent in class DE, and 20 per cent of those with incomes over £3,500 felt the same compared with 42 per cent of those with incomes under £1,000.[1] The working-class rural poor appeared to have a fellow feeling for the coursed hare.

A further poll in 1978[2] showed a slight increase in public distaste for coursing, although the sub-group differences manifest in earlier polls narrowed – there being no significant class, age, sex or political party differences, probably because the poll was conducted at a time when coursing was not a political issue. However, suburban and mixed communities were more antagonistic than either conurban or rural dwellers, suggesting a tentative alignment of the middle classes against the mainly industrial working classes.

1 NOP 8802, Tables 7–8.

2 See Table 9.6.

Table 9.6
Live hare coursing – 1978 poll

Question 1 Do you approve of or disapprove of live hare coursing?

	Total	Sex		Class				Age group		Voting intentions			Environment	
		M.	F.	AB	C_1	C_2	DE	18–24	65+	Con	Lab	Lib	Conurb	Rural
Approve	6	7	4	5	6	6	4	7	7	7	5	1	6	6
Disapprove	77	75	79	77	74	79	77	79	73	77	78	85	77	75
No opinion	15	16	14	17	18	12	15	17	17	14	14	12	15	19
Don't know	2	2	3	1	2	4	2	2	3	2	2	1	3	2

Question 2 If a Bill banning this sport were introduced, would you be in favour of or against it?

	Total	Sex		Class				Age group		Voting intentions			Environment			
		M.	F.	AB	C_1	C_2	DE	18–24	65+	Con	Lab	Lib	Conurb	Urban	Mixed	Rural
Strongly in favour	41	42	40	35	41	45	38	42	40	39	44	39	42	43	41	35
In favour	35	32	37	41	34	32	36	36	35	36	33	44	31	36	39	37
No opinion/ don't know	18	19	18	18	19	16	21	16	18	17	17	15	19	17	14	22
Against	6	7	5	6	5	7	4	5	5	8	5	2	7	4	5	5
Strongly against	1	1	–	1	1	1	1	–	1	1	1	–	1	–	1	1

Source: NOP 3440, June 1978.

The 1978 poll, covering as it did all forms of hunting, made a significant discovery about the relative position of coursing. Fifty-seven per cent of those in favour of allowing people to hunt nevertheless disapproved of hare coursing and only 20 per cent of those who supported hunting also supported coursing.[1] This adds weight to the claim of many hunting people that coursing is an embarrassment to their cause and should be allowed to disappear.

The 1978 poll, which included a survey of attitudes to hare and otter hunting, showed quite clearly that the public divided hunted animals into two categories and offered them differing amounts of sympathy.

Table 9.7

Would you be in favour of or against a law to ban:

	The hunting of foxes %	The hunting of hare %	The hunting of deer %	The hunting of otters %	Hare coursing %
In favour of a law	60	62	74	72	75
Against a law	23	18	12	9	7
No opinion	17	20	14	20	18

Source: NOP Report 3440, June 1978.

Between 72 per cent and 75 per cent of the electorate wished to see coursing and deer and otter hunting abolished, but only 60 per cent and 62 per cent felt that fox and hare hunting should be banned. The 15 per cent difference between coursing and hare hunting showed how publicity had increasingly damaged coursing, whereas the relative public ignorance about hare hunting had worked to its advantage. Coursing and stag hunting, the objects of the greatest publicity, the least 'necessary' of all the field sports and the smallest in terms of active supporters, have captured the public displeasure and are therefore much more vulnerable to a concerted attack. Counter-publicity by the hunting community does not help, for keeping the sports in the public's consciousness would tend to increase general antipathy towards them. The 1981 RSPCA survey showed that antagonism to coursing had remained stable, with 77 per cent of the sample wishing to see it banned.[2]

1 NOP Report 3440, Table 20.

2 RSPCA/Gallup Poll, 1982, p. 14.

The 1978 poll, concerned with the political battles ahead, asked: 'If a political party promised in its election manifesto to bring in laws to stop hunting with hounds, would it make any difference to whether or not you voted for that party?' and, further, if it did make a difference, 'would you be more or less inclined to vote for that party?'.[1] To the surprise of the LACS leadership 9 per cent of the total said it would influence their vote in favour of the party in question and 1 per cent said it would influence them against. Fourteen per cent of younger voters, 18 to 24 years old, stated that it would influence the way they voted and 11 per cent of conurban voters thought it might influence them. However only 7 per cent of social classes AB expected to be influenced by the hunting issue.

These figures were substantially confirmed by the RSPCA poll in 1981 which showed that 4 per cent of the electorate would be very likely and 9 per cent fairly likely (total 13 per cent) to change their votes in favour of a party which showed greater concern for animal welfare. However, only 6 per cent of Conservatives would consider a change whereas 15 per cent of Labour voters and 17 per cent of SDP–Liberal Alliance voters stated a willingness to switch their vote on animal welfare issues.[2]

These figures were only of relative significance for they assumed that no other issues of greater importance would materialise in the manifestos or during the election campaign. Equally, since one and possibly two parties might make a commitment to abolish some forms of hunting, only the supporters of the third party would be tempted to switch their votes. Nevertheless the poll did show that a party which declared its intentions to abolish hunting would gain more votes than it would lose, and both polls in 1978 and 1981 had the effect of redoubling the efforts made by the LACS on behalf of GECCAP.

1 From NOP Reports, Tables 16–18.

2 RSPCA/Gallup Poll, p. 38.

10 Hunting and political parties

The Labour party

While the media and public opinion consolidated their opposition to hunting and coursing and while pressure groups were increasingly active, no political party government made a policy decision which acknowledged these facts. Of the two major political parties only Labour had a serious internal debate about its position in relation to animal welfare and field sports; even then, it was not until July 1978 that its position was formally made clear.[1]

One of the reasons for this delay was that the three constituent elements of the debate within the Labour party, the party membership, the backbench MPs and the party leadership, did not move together on the hunting issue. The upper class connotations of the sport undoubtedly made it a suitable target for the growing party. However, moves to abolish hunting during the Labour-controlled governments of the 1930s failed because other issues were felt to be more important, and it was not easy for the Labour party to convince its coalition allies that such legislation was desirable. Since then, the intellectual radicals have consistently opposed hunting and have led the movement both within and outside the Labour party to abolish it.

1 In *Living Without Cruelty: Labour's Charter for Animal Protection*, The Labour Party, London, 1978.

The party membership began the attempt to produce an official policy against hunting as early as 1928[1] when a motion against blood sports was moved at the Party Conference by Tom Williams, later Minister of Agriculture. The motion was nodded through but, like another animal welfare resolution at the 1934 Conference, was not debated. Following the Labour front bench refusal, led by Tom Williams, to vote for an abolitionist measure in 1949, another resolution was presented to the 1949 Conference but not debated. A further Conference motion in 1956 called for the abolition of fox and stag hunting and another in 1957 condemned blood sports in general. These motions were not discussed but were referred — that is, sent to a Committee of the party for discussion. In every case this procedure marked the end of the motion.

Labour backbenchers, meanwhile, attempted to promote anti-hunting or coursing bills, although it was necessary for them to gain the active support of their front bench, both in and out of office, for anti-hunting legislation to have any chance of success. It had been relatively easy for the abolitionists to get Labour backbench support before the war, so that when the MPs who served their apprenticeship in the 1930s became Ministers in the 1945–51 government, the abolitionists confidently predicted victory for their cause. However, the post-war Labour party leadership abandoned its generalised support for anti-hunting legislation in 1949 fearing for its relationship with the rural community. Tom Williams in 1949 agreed that he had supported an anti-hunting bill in 1925 but had changed his mind, stating: 'One should never be ashamed to own that sometimes one may have been wrong'.[2] Both he and Chuter Ede, the Home Secretary, had sponsored anti-hunting bills in the 1930s, but both voted against the Bill in 1949 when faced with the pressure of political realities.

The long period in opposition (1951–64) brought to maturity a new political generation within the Labour party, for whom the fear of losing rural votes was less important. There were Labour politicians such as Shirley Williams and Merlyn Rees who both intensely disliked hunting and coursing. Their presence undoubtedly hastened the eventual commitment of the Labour party to an anti-hunting policy and encouraged MPs to become anti-hunting activists. When Labour was returned to power in 1964, the general antipathy of Labour backbenchers to hunting and coursing was made apparent by Early Day Motions[3]

1 See *Hansard* (Commons), 1949, vol. 461, cols. 2249–50.

2 *Hansard* (Commons), 1949, vol. 461, col. 2227.

3 One Early Day Motion in 1966 was signed by 93 MPs and led *Horse and Hound* (19 Dec. 1966) to urge all field sportsmen to stick together since 'a threat to one is a threat to all'.

and by a spate of backbench inspired attempts to abolish coursing. The first of these bills was an attempt to abolish deer hunting in 1965, but more significant was Eric Heffer's attempt to abolish coursing in 1967, for it marked the beginning of a series of anti-coursing bills during which the Labour government moved from neutrality on the issue to active support for anti-coursing measures. Although the Labour government of this period would have preferred to leave animal welfare Bills to be brought forward by Private Members the success of the BFSS's tactics forced them to take sides and allow time for discussion. The Labour government ended its tradition of neutrality for as Merlyn Rees stated: 'that tradition depends upon a certain reasonableness in the handling of opportunities for parliamentary discussion, which has not been altogether evident in this case'.[1]

The anti-coursing initiatives were further aided by the Prime Minister, Harold Wilson, who thought that coursing was 'a barbarous anachronism' and believed that 'all civilised people are against hare coursing'.[2] In February 1970, Wilson was, according to Crossman, 'extremely anxious [in Cabinet] to give government time for, or indeed to take over as a government measure, the Deer Hunting and Hare Coursing Bill. He thinks this is an election winner'.[3] Wilson pushed the Cabinet into accepting his view that an anti-coursing bill should be encouraged. The Cabinet decided to break with the convention of government impartiality on such matters, and against the advice of Home Office officials made the ensuing Bill into a government one.[4] An *ad hoc* Committee consisting of the Lord President of the Council with junior Home Office and Agriculture Ministers was detailed by the Home Affairs Committee of the Cabinet to work out the best way of presenting the Bill. Even though the Cabinet knew that dissolution was imminent, it went ahead on a hare-coursing abolition bill and the Bill, which received second reading in May 1970, passed all stages before parliament was dissolved.

Wilson and the Cabinet in 1970 had assumed that adopting a Private Members' bill would be sufficient to get an anti-coursing measure on the statute books. However, it was soon apparent that the full weight of the hunting community and its friends was working, successfully, to stop these bills. Two things were clear to the Labour government: that even a simple anti-coursing bill was a very time-consuming matter, and

1 *Hansard* (Commons), 1970, vol. 801, col. 1525.

2 *Hansard* (Commons), 1969, vol. 792, col. 1291.

3 *The Crossman Diaries*, vol. III, Hamish Hamilton and J. Cape, London, 1977. Entry for 5 Feb. 1970.

4 Ibid. Entry for 12 Mar. 1970.

that to pass such a bill the Government would have to invoke the Parliament Acts of 1911 and 1949. Since the 1974–9 parliament was controlled by a minority Labour government, the likelihood that the 1949 Act would be invoked was slight, and anti-hunting MPs reluctantly accepted, after the BFSS's successful manoeuvres in 1976,[1] that coursing would not be abolished during the life of the 1974–9 parliament.

The Labour government of 1974–9 found it difficult to pass contentious legislation for technical reasons. Parliament was controlled by a minority government and therefore Standing Committees had equal numbers of Labour and Conservative members, plus one representative from the minor parties. The minor party representative during the Committee stage of the 1975 Anti-Coursing Bill was Clement Freud MP, a pro-coursing Liberal. His presence ensured that closure motions during the Committee stage were impractical and that a number of amendments to the Bill, which destroyed its essential purpose, were presented for third reading. This experience made the Labour leadership aware of the inordinate amount of time needed to push through a bill during periods of minority government. It was also made aware that any government, even one with a majority, needs to be able to point to a firm policy commitment before it can apply closure or guillotine motions to any contentious debate without creating massive amounts of ill will or a series of constitutional arguments.[2]

An alternative longer-term option existed for the abolitionists within the Labour party. It was realised, although not at an official level, that it might be possible to extract a commitment against coursing and hunting from the Labour party and to place this commitment in an election manifesto. In 1977, J. Holbrook[3] presented, through his local constituency party, an anti-hunting resolution for debate at the 1977 Party Conference. This resolution, like its predecessors, was remitted to the National Executive Committee (NEC) of the Labour party; however, unlike its predecessors, the resolution was remitted at a time when the inability to get a hare-coursing bill through parliament was causing frustration among concerned MPs, a number of whom were on the NEC.[4] The knowledge that the Labour party had never discussed or clarified its policies on animal welfare made the NEC more than willing to accept a further resolution by Norman Atkinson MP.

1 A Lords Select Committee persuaded the Lords to reject the Anti-Coursing Bill which the Commons had passed in 1975.

2 Since 1946 guillotine motions have been applicable to Standing Committees as long as the decision to apply it has been passed by the House itself.

3 He was rapidly co-opted on to the Executive Committee of the LACS.

4 E. Heffer, A. Benn, J. Maynard, among them.

The NEC decided to send the general animal welfare motion presented by Atkinson and the anti-hunting resolution submitted by Holbrook to the Agricultural Sub-Committee of the Home Policy Committee of the NEC. The discussions on the two motions were held together and occurred during the first six months of 1978. The Home Policy Committee of the NEC was chaired by Tony Benn MP, and included Eric Heffer among its members. The Agricultural Sub-Committee which actually discussed the motions was chaired by Joan Maynard MP. The Sub-Committee included representatives of farmers, farm workers, the Ministry of Agriculture and at least two MPs known to be concerned with animal welfare matters. Discussion papers were prepared by Transport House staff who solicited information from the LACS and other animal welfare organisations. The BFSS presented its views although these were submitted too late to have any effect on the early drafts of the papers and in any case fell victim to the personal prejudices of the Transport House researcher.

The discussion papers argued that the Labour party should promote measures to tighten controls on animal experiments, the transportation of live animals, factory farming, zoos and pets.[1] They also contained a section declaring that all forms of hunting and coursing should be banned.[2]

These policy recommendations were referred to and accepted by the Home Policy Committee of the NEC in June 1978. This produced a predictable flurry of activity in the media as every concerned organisation joined in the debate. *The Times* in an extraordinarily incoherent editorial condemned the move on a variety of grounds. It suggested that those with a 'progressive conscience' supported both abortion and the abolition of fox hunting and insinuated that this policy document was an attempt to put foxes before babies.[3]

The debate was premature, however, for the full NEC returned the draft policy document for revision since a number of leading figures, including Shirley Williams and the Prime Minister, James Callaghan, felt that an attack on fox hunting was politically ill-advised. Callaghan told the NEC during the debate on this motion that the party was in danger of 'scattering its shots too wide',[4] and should only include the more traditional targets of stag hunting and hare coursing since it was clear that most people were against them, whereas it was by no means clear what the public felt about fox hunting. The fear of losing votes in rural

1 *Living without Cruelty*, pp. 7–35.

2 Ibid., pp. 36–44.

3 *The Times*, 14 June 1978.

4 Quoted in the *Guardian*, 29 June 1978.

constituencies exercised the minds of a number of NEC members.[1] Older politicians could remember the immediate post-war period when rural seats such as Taunton and Bridgwater were either Labour or Independent.[2] However, the post-war mechanisation of agriculture has so reduced the number of farm labourers that the Labour vote in the majority of rural constituencies has dwindled into insignificance. Indeed in the 1974–9 parliament the Labour party held none of the 15 mainland seats where the numbers engaged in agriculture exceeded 20 per cent of the electorate.[3]

The Home Policy Committee ignored the Prime Minister's request to amend their stand on hunting despite his hint that a less contentious document, excluding fox hunting and beagling, would stand a better chance of getting in the Labour party manifesto.[4] On 10 July 1978, the Home Policy Committee, with Tony Benn in the chair, reaffirmed by eight votes to three their previous decision to oppose all forms of hunting.

On 16 July 1978, the full NEC met again and accepted, by a vote of nineteen to one, the Home Policy Committee's recommendation. Heffer assured the anti-hunting community that he intended to make sure that the new anti-blood sports policy of the party would go into the manifesto. Norman Atkinson, who moved one of the resolutions which led to this debate, told *Howl*: 'The current position is that a commitment will be given in favour of the banning of hare coursing and stag hunting, but fox hunting will probably be left to a "free vote" in the House of Commons'.[5] And Joan Maynard, who was Chairman of the Sub-Committee which discussed the paper, declared at the Party Conference in October 1978 that 'something will go in the manifesto' on animal welfare.[6]. She was right, for in April 1979 the Labour party manifesto included a promise to pass 'legislation to end cruelty to animals [which] will include the banning of hare coursing and stag and deer hunting'.[7] The Labour party was rewarded by a donation of £80,000 from the LACS.[8]

1 *Guardian*, 29 June 1978. The editorial.

2 Parts of Exmoor and the Quantocks, major hunting areas, are within these constituencies. North Devon has been either Conservative or Liberal since the war.

3 D. McKie, C. Cook and M. Phillips, *Election Guide*, Quartet, London, 1978, p. 209.

4 Barbara Castle led the group who attempted to find a compromise excluding fox hunting. *Guardian*, 11 July 1978.

5 *Howl*, 11, Autumn 1978, p. 1. This concurred with the opinion of A. Shaw MP, an anti-hunting activist.

6 Discussion with R. Course, LACS Committee member, Nov. 1978.

7 *Labour Party Manifesto 1979*, Labour Party, London, 1979, p. 31.

8 See LACS circular to members, Apr. 1979.

The leaders of the anti-hunting movement were aware that a Labour party manifesto commitment would make the House of Lords, with its built-in Conservative majority, reluctant to defeat a manifesto pledge, not least because such an action would provoke the Government into applying the Parliament Acts of 1911 and 1949. Since hare coursing is not of obvious constitutional significance, the abolitionists did not believe that the Lords would fight too hard against a manifesto-backed government bill to abolish hunting or coursing. It is for this reason that anti-hunting MPs accepted the lack of government activity after the Lords rejected the Anti-Coursing Bill in 1976. Since they were convinced that an election would be held in the autumn of 1978 they accepted a promise of future government action knowing that the Lords would use their delaying power to kill any contentious bill presented near the end of a period of minority government.[1] Labour backbenchers now felt that a future Labour government would be morally bound to keep its promises and push through an anti-hunting measure.

Labour governments responded only slowly to anti-hunting pressure from their backbenches; indeed they followed rather than led the campaigns against hunting. Traditionally governments left the arbitration of causes to Private Members' debates but during the 1970s the Labour governments decided that pressure group activity had so thwarted the popular will that governmental interference was needed. This change made hunting an overtly party political issue, and ensured that future decisions would involve governments as well as backbenchers.

Since this was 90 years after the foundation of the Fabian Society and over 60 years after the only significant piece of animal welfare legislation in the 20th century and since it was clear that public opinion and values were turning more and more against hunting this development in official Labour party thinking cannot be said to be precipitate or premature.

The Liberal and Social Democratic parties

Before the Labour party rose to prominence, the Liberal party contained the majority of anti-hunting parliamentarians and all anti-hunting measures in the early part of the century came from the radical wing of the party. Since 1945 the Liberal party at large has been relatively anti-hunting as the public opinion polls show, but their parliamentary representatives have been divided. Jeremy Thorpe, who represented North Devon from 1959–79 and whose constituency

1 Arnold Shaw MP and LACS Committee member stated that the next Labour government would introduce an anti-coursing bill and will, if necessary, invoke the 1911 and 1949 Parliament Acts. Interview 6 June 1978.

included most of Exmoor, has spoken against abolitionist bills, but his successor as leader of the Liberals, David Steel, has consistently voted for them. Five Liberals stayed up for the 2.44 a.m. vote for the third reading of the *Hare Coursing Bill* in 1975, three voted for the Bill and two voted against.[1] Because of this division the party has tended to avoid committing itself on the hunting issue.

The Liberals, under pressure from a spontaneous 'emergency' resolution engineered by GECCAP at their 1978 Party Conference, decided to discuss two animal welfare motions at their 25 November 1978 Party Council.[2] Both motions were based on GECCAP's resolutions but the detailed one made no mention of hunting or coursing. The resolutions were passed and the Liberal party committed itself to calling on Her Majesty's governments to establish a Standing Royal Commission on animal welfare.[3] It was not, however, committed to the abolition of hunting or coursing.

The November 1978 Council meeting decided to set up a working party, the Liberal Animal Welfare Group (LAWG), to investigate and debate Liberal policy towards animal welfare questions. Its Chairman was, and is in 1982, Richard Ryder, formerly chairman of the RSPCA. Its policy statement of 1983 spelt out official policy on a number of issues and lists other policy resolutions passed by the LAWG but not at that time adopted as official party policy. They included a statement that 'LAWG supports the outlawing of fox, stag and otter hunting and organised hare coursing'.[4] Pressure will be put upon the Liberal party to adopt these and other proposals and incorporate them into the party manifesto at the next election.

The Social Democratic Party, however, has no policy on hunting or any other contentious animal welfare issue. The Committee which will decide its policies towards hunting, probably the Ecology and Environment Committee, has not in late 1982 been officially formed, and no policy statement was expected until sometime in 1983. However, a spokesman said that while a number of SDP MPs were known to be anti-hunting, it was probably a matter which would be left to individual consciences.[5]

Despite or perhaps because of this vagueness some members of the SDP allied themselves with liberal activists and formed, with active encouragement from the League Against Cruel Sports, an organisation

1 *Hansard* (Commons), 1975, vol. 898, cols 1253–6.

2 For details, see *Liberal News*, 7 Nov. 1978, p. 8.

3 The commitment was included in the 1979 General Election Manifesto.

4 *Policies*, Liberal Animal Welfare Group, Jan.1982, p. 4.

5 SDP spokeswoman, Aug. 1982. An *ad hoc* committee was formed in March 1983.

called LASDAB or Liberals and Social Democrats Against Bloodsports. It circulated, through the League, a request that members of the Liberal and SDP parties write to their MP or candidate or to Roy Jenkins or David Steel urging them to ensure that a commitment against hunting was included in their respective party's manifesto. LASDAB has yet to have any impact on the debate but may, with further League backing, be an effective ginger group within the Centrist parties. If it can help to obtain from both parties a manifesto commitment against hunting and coursing it will have served its purpose.

The Conservative party

The Conservatives, like the Liberals, have strenuously avoided making any policy statements on hunting even when prompted to do so by GECCAP. The party is subject to a variety of pressures from groups of its supporters; the NFU, for example, is keen to ensure that the export of live animals is not stopped but is indifferent about animal experimentation; accordingly the party has attempted to deal with each animal welfare question on its own merits. On hunting and coursing the party is officially neutral and during the Conservative government of 1970–4 the Minister of State at the Home Office declared the party's 'strict neutrality'.[1]

The Conservatives' neutrality represents a shift, particularly since 1945, away from a position of active support. Before then, numerous Cabinet Ministers were hunting men. Lord Halifax remained an MFH until his appointment as Foreign Secretary in 1938, and Duff Cooper when Minister of War publicly declared his support 'for the great art of fox hunting'.[2] Lord Bayford was Minister of Agriculture in the 1920s before coming the first Chairman of the BFSS. R.A. Butler combined an interest in shooting with Cabinet posts for most of his career and James Ramsden remained a Master of Foxhounds during his period of office as Secretary of State for War (1963–4).

Since the 1939–45 war, however, support at Ministerial level has declined, and the Conservative party in parliament has contained fewer landowners and hunting members. For these reasons the parliamentary party has become less reliable in the eyes of the hunting community. Accordingly the hunting community has assiduously fostered good relations with the Conservative Whips' office and the leadership of the 1922 Committee. The Whips Office in both the Lords and the Commons has always contained major landowners. William Whitelaw, who

1 *Lords Debates*, 1972, vol. 330, col. 670.

2 Quoted in NSACS *Bulletin*, 26, 1936, p. 2.

was the Conservative Chief Whip in the Commons from 1964–70 gave 'active encouragement in our tactical battles and help in a major way.[1] In the Lords Earl Fortescue (Chief Whip 1945–58) and Lord Denham, the Conservative Chief Whip in 1982 (with over 20 years in the Whips' Office) have all been strong supporters of field sports. The leaders of the 1922 Committee have been equally reliable; three of the four Chairmen since 1955, including E. Du Cann the incumbent in 1982, have been actively pro-hunting.

In addition to the vital support of backbenchers there is, in the country at large, a network of leading Conservatives who support or lead the pro-hunting community and who are capable of ensuring that the party never makes an anti-hunting commitment. Since 20 per cent of MFHs are members or Chairmen of local Conservative party organisations, they with other Conservative hunting landowners are sufficiently influential in the rural Tory strongholds to ensure that anti-hunting sentiments do not prevail. Their task is made easier by the increasing number of professionals and army officers who have retired to the shires and have helped make rural England a preserve of the Tory party. The BFSS with its Conservative party connections is able to bring influence to bear if a Conservative candidate or MP appears to be against hunting.[2] In the House itself M. Kimball and his colleagues monitor the behaviour of the Conservative front bench to ensure that there will be no sudden changes in the traditional pro-hunting position of the Conservative party. They and their predecessors have hitherto been successful for no significant member of the anti-hunting community has ever been a Conservative member of either of the Houses of Parliament. The identification of the Conservative party with the hunting community has become so strong that even Conservative MPs who are unsympathetic to hunting and coursing feel unwilling to risk the odium of their fellow MPs by saying so.[3]

The Labour party's promotion of three bills to abolish coursing in the 1970s has made it easier for the BFSS to keep the Conservative party pro-hunting. Whereas ten and 12 Conservatives voted to support two anti-coursing bills in 1970, only five did so in 1975.[4] Indeed, the anti-bloodsports group in the 1974–9 parliament consisted entirely of Labour MPs. It is safe to assume that even fewer Conservative MPs will support anti-hunting bills if they become part of their opponent's official policy and are produced as government bills; however it is also probable that fewer Labour MPs will support Kimball and his associates

1 Letter from M. Kimball to H . Atkins, 12 Feb. 1975.

2 In April 1983 the selection of the Conservative candidate for SW Cambridge was not continued when it was discovered that his wife belonged to the LACS.

3 Confirmed during an interview with one of them.

4 *Hansard* (Commons), 1975, vol. 898, cols 1253–6.

in their defence of hunting. Undoubtedly these developments have made hunting more rather than less of a party issue and ensure that cross party compromises are less likely in the future.

The elevation of Mrs M. Thatcher to the leadership of the Tory party caused some dismay among hunting supporters for she had voted for the Labour government's bill to abolish coursing in 1970.[1] Indeed she argued with M. Kimball that the Conservative party should not struggle too hard to keep coursing within the law. This event caused Kimball to remind the Whips' office of the 'special relationship' between the BFSS and 'the Conservative party at constituency level, the House of Commons, and within your [the Whips] office'.[2] Kimball was moved to suggest politely that he might find it difficult to continue to obey the Conservative Whip if Mrs Thatcher in any way jeopardised the special relationship or attempted to undermine any tactical victories which the BFSS might achieve. To Kimball's relief Mrs Thatcher did not vote for the 1975 Bill to abolish coursing and in 1978 he declared that 'Margaret is much more sympathetic to our view now'.[3]

This enabled M. Kimball to continue as a loyal backbencher until he decided to leave parliament at the end of the 1979 parliament. In 1982, he was awarded a knighthood for services to the Conservative party and also for his ability 'to deliver the hunting vote'; a small but significant concern within parliament.[4]

Despite the apparent firmness of the Tory position, the activities of GECCAP may have produced some changes. The Conservative Central Office in 1978 received a 'considerable number of calls and letters' from Conservative ladies who threatened to vote Labour unless the party made a commitment to abolish hunting and coursing.[5] However, other letters and calls warned the Conservatives against changing their policy and, since hunting and coursing are not felt to be crucial political issues, the party has attempted as far as possible to 'leave the matter well alone'.[6]

It is unlikely that the position will remain stable. GECCAP attempted to capitalise on the fact that some Conservatives have consistently voted for anti-coursing bills and that a substantial group of MPs and delegates attended their meeting at the 1978 Conservative Party Con-

1 *Hansard* (Commons), 1970, vol. 801, col. 1602.

2 Letter to Chief Whip, Humphrey Atkins, dated 12 Feb. 1975.

3 Interview, May 1978.

4 Quote from a leading member of the hunting community.

5 Central Office spokesman, 10 Nov. 1978.

6 Ibid. Confirmed by spokesman, September 1982.

ference. GECCAP was also in direct contact with the Conservative Ecology group which has declared general support for animal welfare reforms. It hoped that this group would succeed in exacerbating the rift that exists between Tory middle-aged ladies and farmers on matters such as hunting and the export of live animals. The stereotype Tory lady is, after all, a fervent animal lover, and, as the 1978 poll showed, women are more likely than men to switch their votes on an animal welfare issue.[1] GECCAP hoped with the Ecology group's help to weaken the power of the pro-hunting farmers within the Conservative party and to influence party policy towards animals and against hunting.

These hopes were given a modest boost by a paper on animal welfare written by an Assistant Director of the Conservative Research Department who stated:

> As for hare coursing my personal view is that there is a strong case for banning it. Hare coursing has little or nothing to do with the control of hares. I hope that a further Private Members' bill to prohibit hare coursing will be introduced at an early date and that it will become law.[2]

However, the writer reiterated the Scott-Henderson view of 1951 that fox and deer hunting 'made a valuable contribution to the effective control of these animals and probably caused less cruelty than other methods of controlling them'. He went on:

> The Conservative party has always taken the view that the question of field sports is not one on which the party should have an official policy and, given the need for control and the fact that available evidence would seem to indicate that hunting is less cruel than other methods of control, this is clearly sensible.[3]

Until 1945 all party leaderships could avoid a commitment on hunting by declaring that it was a private matter but since then they have had to take a more active position. Labour leaders were at first cowed by the power of the rural establishment and their allies, the farmers, but subsequently took note of the élitist nature of hunting, the cruelty involved and the growing weight of public opinion. The result was a gradual change in the official position of the Labour movement to one which opposed hunting and coursing. This position was tempered only by a political rather than moral reluctance to attack fox hunting.

1 NOP 3440, June 1978, Tables 16–18.

2 Charles Bellairs 'Animal Welfare', *Politics Today*, no. 13, Sept. 1979, pp. 277–8.

3 Charles Bellairs 'Animal Welfare', *Politics Today*, p. 277.

The Conservative party and Conservative governments have had an easier task than Labour; they have been able to do nothing. But as the issue became more lively this lack of activity was clearly an overt acceptance of the pro-hunting position. The Conservative party relies heavily on the rural establishment for members and for grass-roots activists. It could not easily adopt a position against hunting, although coursing would not be stoutly defended. The Conservative leadership, therefore, has listened to its powerful rural supporters rather than to the opinion of the mass of the population. It would justify this by saying that it listens to those who understand and are concerned with hunting rather than to ill-informed urban outsiders. It has chosen, therefore, which sector of society it will listen to and which groups it will appease.

11 The parliamentary arena

The growth of animal welfare and anti-hunting legislation

The first animal welfare bill was presented to Parliament in 1800 by Sir William Pulteney.[1] It was an attempt to abolish bull-baiting, a sport that was losing its popularity; however it was narrowly defeated on third reading by 43 votes to 41. Among the supporters of the Bill were Richard Martin, a founder member of the RSPCA, and Richard Sheridan, the playwright. The leading opponents were George Windham, the Secretary of State for War, and George Canning, later Tory Prime Minister.

An attempt, in 1809, to curb cruelty to farm animals also failed since, by implication, it reduced a landowners rights over his property, which included absolute rights over the animals he owned.

In 1821 Richard Martin presented a Bill aimed at preventing the ill treatment of animals owned by someone else. This removed the property issue but despite this the Bill failed on its first attempt. It became law, however, in 1822, and was the first Act to offer any protection to any animal. The main beneficiaries were the larger farm animals: horses, cattle and sheep.

In 1835 Pease's *Protection of Animals Act* was passed, and extended the protection of Martin's 1822 Act to all farm and domestic animals.

1 *Cobbetts Parliamentary History*, vol. 36, 1801–3, col. 837.

It also prohibited all kinds of baiting whether of wild or domestic animals and made dog and cock fighting illegal. It was the first piece of legislation restricting the use of any animal for sport, and the first to infringe the property principle since by this Act a person could be prosecuted for being cruel to his own 'property'.

Although animals were beginning to receive protection in law no significant Bills followed. The *Prevention of Cruelty to Animals Act* of 1849 merely strengthened the 1835 Act; the baiting clauses were extended to include all wild or domestic land animals.[1] In 1854, the use of dogs in dog carts was made illegal, and in 1869 a number of designated sea birds were allowed a close season. This was the first bill affording protection to birds.

The first major piece of legislation after the Act of 1835 was one in 1876 restricting and, in theory, controlling animal experiments. The *Cruelty to Animals Act* made anaesthetics necessary in most experiments which would thenceforth only be undertaken by licensed individuals in licensed buildings. Prominent anti-vivisectionists felt that this was insufficient, and accordingly formed the *National Anti-Vivisection Society* which advocated a total ban on animal experimentation.[2]

In 1883 a Bill was introduced to extend the provisions of the 1849 Act and give some protection to all confined wild animals.[3] The promoter of the Bill, Mr Anderson, was primarily concerned with ending trap-pigeon shooting and improving the conditions of animals in menageries. However, the Bill failed largely because it was vaguely worded and included, by default, an attack on carted deer hunting and hare coursing. The following year the recast Bill failed to reach second reading; another Bill to prohibit rabbit coursing passed the Lords but lost its key clauses in the Commons.[4]

Thanks to the work of the RSPCA and the Humanitarian League a legal milestone was reached in 1911. The *Protection of Animals Act* was successfully piloted through parliament by Sir George Greenwood and his friends. It was, and still is, the major piece of animal welfare legislation.[5] It consolidated all existing legislations on the subject and added 'the commission or omission' of any act likely to cause unnecessary suffering and cruelty to the list of offences. This general provision

1 Fish and birds were therefore excluded.

2 Turner, *All Heaven*, p. 210. The 1876 Act is still, in 1983, the Act which controls animal experiments.

3 Cruelty to Animals Act (Amendment) Bill. See *Hansard* (Commons), 1883, vol. 276, col. 1692. It received a second reading.

4 A. Moss, *Valiant Crusade*, Cassell, London, 1971, p. 143.

5 1 and 2 Geo. 5, ch. 27 (Aug. 1911).

gave magistrates greater scope and enabled them to convict a greater proportion of transgressors. The Act protected any 'bird, beast, reptile or fish' and made it an offence to inflict mental as well as physical suffering. However, the drafters of the Bill, mindful of the impossibility of getting anti-hunting legislation through even a Liberal parliament, restricted the Act to 'captive and domestic animals' and excluded wild ones. They also specifically excluded the 'coursing or hunting of any captive animal unless such animal is liberated in an injured, mutilated or exhausted condition'.[1] Wild, hunted animals were therefore excluded from the Bill; so were carted stags and bagged foxes which became, once released, wild animals again. In 1921, an amendment was later added to restrict the abuse of this clause; it demanded a 'reasonable chance of escape' for coursed animals or wild animals released from captivity.[2]

The laws passed in the 19th century both reflected and influenced people's attitudes towards the relationship between parliament, animals and society. Principles which parliament and leaders of opinion had not been able to tolerate in 1800 gradually became acceptable during the century, and were consolidated in 1911 when the Acts of the previous century were subsumed into the *Protection of Animals Act*.

The first principle –that animals could be the subject of legislation – was established by Richard Martin's Bill in 1822. The second and third principles – that property and leisure were not sacrosanct – had been hesitantly established by Pease's Act of 1835. The abolition of baiting and cockfighting was not a triumph over the landed classes, for these sports had lost favour with them some time before and were popular only with the common people. The sports of the landed class were safe for as long as that class controlled parliament. The control of vivisection in 1876 established the additional principle that animals should not be allowed to suffer merely on the grounds that their suffering might produce medical benefits for mankind. In 1900 it was accepted that animals could suffer psychologically, when under the *Wild Animals in Captivity Protection Act* it was made an offence to 'tease' or to 'terrify' them.

Despite the wide acceptance of these developments, one important principle – that wild animals deserved the same protection as domestic animals of the same species – was not established. Accordingly the hunting community and its supporters in parliament have successfully managed to argue that wild, that is hunted, animals, are not eligible for

1 1 and 2 Geo. 5, ch. 27 (Aug. 1911), Clause 1, 3 (b).

2 11 and 12 Geo. 5, Cap. 14 S i.

any of the protection which tame and domestic animals receive.[1]

Since the 1880s, however, a variety of organisations and reformers have attempted to extend the existing laws and to abolish various forms of hunting. In almost every year between 1893 and 1912 bills with essentially the same purpose were presented in order to 'prohibit the hunting, coursing and shooting of animals kept in confinement'.[2] The bills were explicitly against carted stag hunting and against the coursing of captive hares and rabbits. These sports were obvious ones for the abolitionists to attack since, involving as they did the use of half-tame or captive wild animals, they offended against the sense of fairplay of an increasing number of people. However, only two of the bills, in 1893 and 1903, received a second reading. The first was drafted by H. Salt of the Humanitarian League and presented in parliament by MPs who belonged to the RSPCA; it, like the second, was debated but not voted on.

The 1911 Act was a major step forward for the animal welfare movement but it did nothing for confined animals, and it was not until 1921 that animals released for coursing were supposed to have 'a reasonable chance of escape'. This amendment signalled the end of enclosed coursing but made no difference to the majority of coursers.[3] Further bills to restrict the 'spurious sports' of coursing and carted stag hunting were introduced in the 1920s and in 1925 one of them received a short second reading.

The years 1929 to 1931 were important for the anti-hunting movement for these years marked a period of Labour government. In both 1930 and 1931 a Bill 'to prohibit the hunting of deer' was introduced. These Bills represented the first direct attack on wild deer hunting. Neither of them nor the Bills presented against coursing and carted stag hunting in the same year were properly debated;[4] nevertheless, they were significant. The anti-hunting community, led since 1924 by the LACS, was convinced that the Labour government would offer it support and the pro-hunting community, being similarly convinced, made a retaliatory decision to form the BFSS.

No major attempts to promote anti-hunting legislation were made from 1931 until the return of Private Members' time in 1948. Then two bills were presented, one of which, the *Prohibition of Hunting and Coursing Bill*, was given the fullest debate of any anti-hunting bill up to

1 This apparent anomaly is more severe with birds. Most wild and sea birds are protected as a result of legislation beginning in 1869, and especially the *Protection of Wild Birds Act* 1933, but tame hand-reared birds used for sport, i.e. pheasants, are not protected.

2 See Table 11.1 below.

3 Enclosed coursing virtually ceased in 1894. See Stable and Studdard, *Coursing*, p. 13.

4 They received no more than introduction or first reading under the 10-minute rule.

Table 11.1
Anti-hunting legislation

Date	Descriptive title	Comment
1893	Bill to Prohibit the Hunting, Coursing and Shooting of Animals Kept in Confinement	Received second reading
1894–96, 1898	Spurious Sports Bill, Sports Regulation Bill, etc.	Similar aim to 1893 Bill
1903–11	Spurious Sports Bill, etc.	Annual bills, essentially similar to 1893 Bill
Post 1911 bills		
1912	Cruelty to Animals Bill	See 1893 Bill
1921	Protection of Animals (Amendment) Act	Allowed coursed animals a reasonable chance of escape
1924–31) (annu- 1936–39) ally)	Protection of Animals Bill	Similar to 1893 Bill. Only 1925 Bill was debated
1930) 1931) 1939)	Protection of Animals (No. 2) Bill	'to prohibit the hunting of deer'
1948–49	Prohibition of Hunting and Coursing Bill	Mainly against stag hunting. Defeated on second reading after a full debate
1948–49	Prohibition of Foxhunting Bill 'to prohibit the hunting of foxes for the purpose of sport'	Withdrawn
1957–58) 1958–59) 1959–60)	Protection of Deer Bill	To abolish stag hunting; not debated except on first reading under 10-minute rule
1964–65	Protection of Deer Bill	No second reading
1966–67	Live Hare Coursing (Abolition) Bill	Talked out by supporters by mistake
1966–75	Annual anti-coursing bills (total of 13, including 3 government bills) were presented to parliament in this period. One in 1970 combined deer hunting with coursing	About half debated; none passed into law. Two started in Lords, one defeated (1972), one (1976) sent to a Select Committee which recommended rejection of the Bill
1967–68	Protection of Deer Bill	See 1957–60 Bill
1969	Protection of Otters Bill	No second reading
1972	Protection of Otters Bill	Brief first reading under 10-minute rule

N.B. None of these bills has been promoted by a Conservative MP, although a few Conservatives have supported them.

that time. Its defeat on second reading led to the promise of a Committee of Inquiry – the Scott Henderson Committee. For their part the abolitionists withdrew the second bill, the *Prohibition of Foxhunting Bill*, which, they perceived, presented even greater difficulties than the first, and optimistically awaited the Committee's findings.

Following the Scott Henderson Committee's Report, a disappointing one for the abolitionists, in 1951, no anti-hunting bills were presented until 1957 when, for three consecutive sessions, a Bill to abolish stag hunting was introduced, but not debated. The first important field sports debate after 1949 was on the *Live Hare Coursing (Abolition) Bill* presented by Eric Heffer in 1967. Because favourable publicity and a public opinion survey showed general antipathy to coursing, the sponsors of the Bill, including the LACS, had high hopes that it would succeed. However, neither it nor its numerous successors were destined to pass into law. Between 1966 and 1975 there were ten Private Members' bills which attempted to abolish coursing. One of these was introduced into the House of Lords by Alice Bacon. The government in this period promoted three other bills to abolish coursing, one passed all stages in the House of Commons but lapsed, since its success came at the very end of the Labour government of 1966–70; the second in 1975 passed all stages in spite of a filibuster and the third was introduced into the Lords in 1976, but lapsed when a House of Lords Select Committee decided that it should not proceed.[1]

Two attempts were also made in 1969 and 1972 to abolish otter hunting. The Bills made no progress but did draw attention to the plight of the otter, and speeded up the eventual demise of otter hunting which occurred when the otter became a protected mammal in January 1978.

The use of parliament by the pro- and anti-hunting communities

It was left to the Humanitarian League to draft and to its friends in parliament to present a series of bills between 1893 and 1911. The League assisted with the *Wild Animals in Captivity Protection Act* (1900) which made psychological cruelty an offence and tried to use this Bill to abolish the spurious sports of carted deer hunting and hare coursing on the grounds that these were captive animals.

The 1911 *Protection of Animals Act*, passed mainly because of the work of the Humanitarian League and the RSPCA ironically caused a significant division within the animal welfare fraternity. The RSPCA

1 *Hare Coursing Bill (H. of L.) Minutes of Evidence and Proceeding of the Select Committee on the Bill*, HMSO, London, May 1976. For further details see below.

leadership concentrated on applying and extending the provision of the Act to cover more fully the needs of captive and domestic animals. Others, however, including Sir George Greenwood, wanted to extend the provision of the Act to cover wild animals in order, first, to abolish the hunting and coursing of captive animals and, later, to abolish all forms of hunting and coursing. Henry Salt summed up the feelings of this group: 'We have to decide not whether the practice of fox hunting, for example, is more or less cruel than vivisection but whether all practices which inflict unnecessary pain on sentient beings are not incompatible with the higher instincts of humanity'.[1]

This question, central to the hunting debate, has divided both the animal welfare movement and society at large throughout the 20th century. It has ensured that parliament would become a significant arena for the conflict between the pro- and anti-hunting communities.

Parliament's role as a cockpit developed, as far as the hunting issue is concerned, in the late 1920s. The LACS in its early years published bills which attempted to abolish coursing and stag hunting and, in 1929, they published a Bill with the aim of abolishing deer hunting.[2] When this Bill was under consideration, the League organised a petition, and in seven months added 85,000 signatures to it which was then presented to the Home Secretary.[3]

In 1935, in an attempt to ascertain and influence the views of MPs, the League sent all of them a questionnaire with the statement that: 'If we do not hear from you, we shall feel justified in letting your constituents know that you have no objection to blood sports'. This was denounced as a gross breach of privilege by the House, but the League, although apologetic, felt that it had the right to ask MPs if they would support anti-hunting legislation. There was wide-spread public criticism of the League, and *The Observer*, on 19 May 1935, talked about 'traduced' MPs being 'pilloried' by this menace. However the *News Chronicle*, traditionally friendly to the League, felt: 'It is queer that, while so many MPs favour revoltingly cruel sports, they resist so strongly any attempt to get them to make a declaration as to where they stand'.[4]

The anti-hunting community could not indulge in politics during the war largely because of the suspension of Private Members' time. However, it believed that the post-war Labour government would be actively sympathetic to its views. Nevertheless, loss of nerve and in-

1 H. Salt, *Animals Rights*, G. Bell, London, 1892, p.v.

2 *Index to House of Commons Papers 1900–1949*, House of Commons, p. 40.

3 *Cruel Sports*, 1930, p. 42.

4 See *Cruel Sports*, 1935, p. 44, for a full discussion.

ternal quarrelling restricted the League's activity in the late 1940s. In 1947, before the restoration of Private Members' time, the League decided to concentrate on generating publicity and to accept its lack of skill in influencing parliament and government. Three Executive Committee members resigned because of this decision since they felt it was a mistake to forfeit the opportunity to develop contacts with MPs and government officials.

When Private Members' time was re-introduced in 1948 the League had lost the initiative to the NSACS. Anthony Greenwood, a leading member and later President of the NSACS, was the person who persuaded Mr Cocks (MP for Broxtowe) to present a bill drafted by the NSACS to abolish stag hunting and coursing when Cock's name appeared near the top of the ballot.[1]

During the campaign for this legislation the anti-hunting community concerned itself with letter-writing campaigns, arranging debates and meetings, publicising hunt misdemeanours and mounting poster demonstrations against a number of hunts. The League's focus throughout this period was on public opinion rather than on the corridors of power and this remained true even when the anti-hunting Bill was being debated. Its main political activity during this period was to circularise MPs with its literature. As a result the League, despite having a larger membership than the NSACS, played a relatively minor role while the NSACS briefly attempted to consolidate the influence it gained while the 1948–9 Bills were under consideration. Indeed during this period the BFSS felt that the NSACS was a more significant opponent than the League.[2]

Both the League and the NSACS made insignificant contributions to the Committee of Inquiry chaired by Mr Scott Henderson. Three of the League officers gave evidence and the NSACS made an 89 page submission which it supported with lengthy oral evidence, but they failed to make much impact on the Committee, who described the anti-hunting movement as 'small' and its representatives 'divided in their views'.[3]

Neither the League nor the NSACS took any important political initiatives until the mid 1960s, mainly because it was sure that the Conservative government of 1951–64 would not encourage anti-hunting legislation. This was confirmed when an anti-stag hunting Bill, published by the League in 1957, was presented at three consecutive parliamentary sessions but never debated.[4]

1 *Hansard* (Commons), 1949, vol. 461, col. 2168.

2 Letter from its Secretary, J. Fitzwilliams, in *The Times*, 21 Feb. 1949.

3 *Scott Henderson Report*, para. 130.

4 *Index to Parliamentary Papers*, 1950–9, House of Commons, p. 110.

In 1958, the *News Chronicle* sponsored a Gallup Poll on attitudes to hunting. The poll revealed that 65 per cent of the population would approve if parliament were to legislate against stag hunting,[1] and that just over 50 per cent would approve if fox hunting were abolished.

Encouraged by this evidence and later by the return of a Labour government in 1964, the League, once again the dominant anti-hunting society began to think more positively about parliamentary activity and to use opinion polls in support of its campaigns. The League decided that hare coursing was the weakest and least popular sport and, emboldened by the support of the Prime Minister, Harold Wilson, it launched a campaign against hare coursing in 1964. Things began well; in 1966 83 MPs signed a motion declaring that hare coursing was 'a disgrace to civilisation',[2] and in 1967 the League commissioned public opinion polls which showed that antagonism to fox and stag hunting had increased since 1958 and that feelings against coursing ran high.[3] This considerable shift in public opinion since 1958 almost certainly owed something to the publicity which the League had generated during that decade. However, the increased awareness of the public did not result in political successes.

In the 1966–7 session a bill prepared by the League was presented by Eric Heffer MP, and was debated on second reading in February 1967. However, it was talked out, as were a number of similar bills presented annually during the Labour governments of 1964—70. These bills were presented, as Private Members' bills, by a variety of Labour MPs, and all were similar to the bill drafted by the LACS. The League gave considerable publicity and support to these bills, and in 1969, when an anti-coursing and an anti-otter hunting Bill were presented, declared that it was: 'privileged and honoured in being able to play a major role in the promotion and preparation of these two important parliamentary Bills'.[4] MPs presenting these Bills in 1969 were told that the League's 'organisation [and funds] was entirely at their disposal'.[5]

The League had always felt that generating publicity and helping friendly MPs would be sufficient to begin the tide of anti-hunting legislation, but saw, after the failure of the 1975 Bill, that this was not adequate. From the late 1960s links with individuals at Westminster were fostered by Raymond Rowley and his allies. Eric Heffer became a Vice-

1 It was published on 21 Feb. 1958, the same day in which the Protection of Deer Bill was talked out.

2 *The Times*, 26 Nov. 1966.

3 See Chapter 9 for details.

4 LACS Annual Report, 1969, p. 13.

5 Ibid., p. 13.

President in 1970 and William Price joined the main Committee of the League in 1972. He remained for three years, during which time he and Heffer were leading members of a group of anti-hunting Labour MPs who met from time to time with officials of the League to develop a parliamentary strategy. The League stated that 'regular and highly satisfactory meetings have been held with an ever-growing number of MPs and never in the history of the League have we been so well connected with parliamentary affairs. Consequently we are now able to lodge complaints and make our presence felt in parliament with greater effect'.[1] The Annual Report of the following year, 1973, made essentially the same point.

When, however, Labour was returned to power in 1974, these links diminished, partly because some of the League's Labour supporters, such as Eric Heffer and William Price, became Ministers, and partly because the prospect of a government bill to end coursing reduced the need to plan strategy, since success was assumed to be inevitable. The failure of the Bills in 1975 led to a pause and no League-inspired anti-hunting or coursing bills were presented to parliament in the remaining years of the 1974–9 parliament. The reason was simple; the new leadership of the League under Lord Houghton were more concerned to get a Labour manifesto commitment to abolish some or all forms of hunting and coursing. They did this on the advice of their main parliamentary supporters, Heffer, Price and Shaw,[2] and in the light of the evidence from a further public opinion poll conducted in 1978.[3]

Some League members regretted the apparent concentration on politics at the expense of building-up sanctuaries and generating anti-hunting publicity; nevertheless, despite a heated debate, the membership at the 1978 AGM of the League gave overwhelming support to the political activities of its leaders. The central argument of the 1978–9 leadership was simple: only a government bill would succeed in passing all the parliamentary stages and only a manifesto commitment would be likely to get sufficient parliamentary time and attention to get the bill through the Lords. Hunting and coursing were felt by Lord Houghton, the Chairman, to be matters of public concern and, although non-party issues, they were nevertheless political issues because their abolition involved parliament and legislation.[4] Despite this belated

1 LACS, Annual Report, 1972, p. 12. The meetings included lunches, briefing sessions and the provision of 'literature'.

2 Arnold Shaw MP for Ilford (S) was in 1978, a member of the League's Committee. He introduced an unsuccessful Hare Coursing Bill in 1969.

3 The poll was widely advertised by the League in the press on 14 July 1978. See Chapter 10.

4 From notes taken at the LACS AGM, 8 July 1978.

recognition of the importance of legislation the League remained throughout the critical 1970s a relative novice in its approaches to parliament and lagged far behind the BFSS in both zeal and sophistication.

However the Conservative government of 1979 – while producing no debates on bills to abolish hunting or coursing did provide, in the Wildlife and Countryside Bill, a major opportunity for the LACS to develop its lobbying skills. Part I of the Bill, which became law in 1981, repealed, amended and re-enacted existing legislation on birds and animals. The animal welfare community led by the LACS was very active during the two years of consultation and debate; both the LACS and the BFSS made detailed suggestions, and most of the 2,300 amendments put forward were debated. When the Bill became law the BFSS declared that 'all members should be well satisfied with the outcome',[1] while the LACS said the Bill was 'regarded as thoroughly bad by most enlightened conservationists'.[2] The LACS view was undoubtedly coloured by the successful defence by BFSS supporters in both Houses of all attacks against hunting implied by a number of amendments. This was made possible by the support of the government which Michael Heseltine, Secretary of State for the Environment, made clear when he stated 'the government do not intend to allow this Bill to be used as a vehicle for attacking field sports'.[3]

Nevertheless the League was able to act on the political front with a sense of purpose for the first time in several years; it re-established its connections with a number of helpful MPs and produced what the BFSS admitted was a 'very gloomy and very professional'[4] briefing document containing twelve suggested amendments with the arguments and evidence to support them. Its lack of success was disappointing but convinced a number of waverers on the Committee that not only were animal welfare and hunting issues political but also that the passage of legislation depended on a friendly government.

The BFSS has always understood that the ultimate battleground is parliament and the Society has made sure that its links with both Houses have remained strong. Initially its tactics were simple: to stop any anti-hunting legislation. Following the October 1932 election, sympathetic Members of Parliament joined together and 'a strong and

1 BFSS Annual Report, 1981, p. 2.

2 LACS Annual Report, 1981, p. 6.

3 Quoted in LACS Annual Report, 1981.

4 BFSS Director, Aug. 1982.

augmented group was formed amongst members to assist the Society in its work'.[1] The support of a parliamentary agent was also enlisted to help this Committee and to keep a 'watching brief' on parliamentary developments.

During the 1930s the Parliamentary Committee became involved in debates on field sports and game laws. It was influential in stopping the abolition of gin traps and of carted stag hunting,[2] the latter being blocked 'through the good offices of our friends in parliament'.[3]

Before the war the majority of the BFSS's General Purposes Committee were members of the House of Lords so it was a simple matter for them to keep an eye on parliamentary developments and to feel confident that, if their allies in the Commons could not stop any legislation, they would be able to do so. After the war, however, it was apparent that the House of Commons was more important and it was there that the key post-war battle was fought in 1949. The leading hunting spokesmen within parliament during this period were J. Morrison MP, later Lord Margadale, Chairman of the BFSS from 1950 until 1967 and W. Clarke MP, Treasurer and Committee Member of the BFSS from the war until 1965. During the 1970s the Parliamentary Committee was led by M. Kimball MP, and included Sir Bernard Waley-Cohen (Treasurer) and the Director. Since 1946 the Committee has been assisted by its parliamentary agent, R. Hancock, an enthusiastic field sportsman and member of a well-known hunting family in West Somerset.[4]

The Parliamentary Committee's response to bills or awkward questions has remained essentially the same since 1949.[5] When alerted by rumour or by the order paper the Committee meets at short notice and decides its tactics. It used to be assumed that some action was desirable, but in the last few years it has been realised that bills under the 10-minute rule or bills presented near the end of a parliament's life are not worth speaking against on the floor of the House as this gives the bill publicity which it would not otherwise receive. If the bill is a Private Members' bill and is low on the ballot, cries of 'object' may successfully delay the bill and avoid the necessity of debating it.

1 Annual Report, 1932, p. 28.

2 Gin traps were discussed at length in 1934 and bills against carted stag hunting were briefly debated in parliament on 28 Apr. 1937; 25 Feb. 1948; and 26 Apr. 1939.

3 BFSS Annual Report, 1939, p. 42.

4 Hancock was still, in 1983, the BFSS's parliamentary agent.

5 The following account summarised the information given during interviews with two Directors of the BFSS, five of the MPs concerned and the parliamentary agent. It has been checked against the evidence from the 13 anti-hunting or coursing bills presented to parliament between 1967 and 1978.

If, however, the bill is near the top of the list for debate during one of the 20 Friday afternoons set aside for Private Members' time, then a different and more active set of tactics is applied. They concern the manipulation of parliamentary rules of procedure.[1] The basic tactic is simple: it involves talking at length on whatever bill precedes the anti-hunting Bill and, if necessary, continuing this tactic during the debate on the anti-hunting Bill itself. The BFSS's political office can and does supply at short notice five-hours' worth of information on any topic. This tactic is based on a desire not to 'embarrass friends' by talking at length about coursing or hunting itself, and it also has the desirable side-effect of annoying the opposition. The Bill's proposers may have realised that 'they have filibustered all day'[2] and that 'they were coming in and speaking for five or ten minutes one after the other to prolong the proceedings on the earlier business',[3] but can do little about it.

In 1967, 1970 and 1975, the government made time available for fuller debates on coursing bills and this made the task for the BFSS much harder. But the 1967 Bill was talked out by its own supporters by mistake,[4] and the 1970 Bill lapsed despite passing all stages in the Commons because it did not have time to proceed through the Lords before the 1970 election was held.

Despite the mounting evidence that most MPs were against coursing, the BFSS did not give up hope. Having successfully side-tracked a series of bills during the 1970–4 Conservative government, the BFSS and its supporters had to cope with a bill in 1975 which passed second reading and went to Committee. The BFSS commented smugly on its role during the Committee stage by stating: 'The task of using parliamentary tactics to the full in an effort to frustrate the passage of the Bill . . . was carried out with success. This is evident in the 310 columns of the report of the seven sittings (of the Committee) which were found necessary – a marathon and in many ways instructive performance, remarkable in relation to a Bill of only two short and apparently simple clauses'.[5] Nevertheless, the Bill proceeded to and passed third reading,[6] during which Marcus Kimball said: 'The words we have just heard . . . have

1 The useful tactic of counting out the House if fewer than 40 MPs were present on a Friday afternoon was abolished by R. Crossman in the 1970s.

2 *Hansard* (Commons), 1972, vol. 830, col. 916.

3 Ibid., col. 925.

4 *Hansard* (Commons), 1967, vol. 746, cols 5–48.

5 *Year Book*, 1976, p. 6.

6 The final vote was not taken until 2.44 a.m., nevertheless 265 MPs voted, 183 for the Bill and 82 against.

been the nightmare of the members of the Society of which I have the honour to be Chairman'.[1]

In 1975 there was no likelihood of an election and so the BFSS had to fight an action in the House of Lords. This was the second Lords' debate in three years but the first in which the feelings of the Commons and of the government were clear.[2] The BFSS quickly called for an Inquiry to investigate fully the coursing issue outside of the over-heated political arena in order to avoid a 'legacy of bitterness based on a sense of unfairness among sportsmen and well-wishers not only in the countryside but also in urban Britain'.[3] This cry for an Inquiry was echoed in the House of Lords by Lord Denham, Conservative Chief Whip and a member of the BFSS's Parliamentary Committee. He proposed a Select Committee of the Lords on the grounds that

> this Bill seeks to remove an ancient freedom . . . I do not believe that Members of any government should seek to remove such a freedom . . . without letting it be seen that they have taken every step and made every inquiry reasonably necessary to assure themselves that it is right to do so. And this Her Majesty's government have not done. A Select Committee of your Lordships' House, with the right to hear evidence, would go some way to repairing this omission.[4]

This cry to protect an ancient freedom was not spontaneous. Lord Denham, while Chief Conservative Whip, in the Lords, had in November 1974 written to Marcus Kimball outlining a strategy for ensuring that, even if the Bill passed Third Reading in the Commons, it would not pass through the House of Lords. His letter is worth quoting, virtually in full.

> Coursing (Abolition) Bill
>
> I know that you are extremely tied up at the moment with all the horrors threatened on this in the Commons, but I think we probably ought to give fairly early consideration to long-stop measures in the Lords.
>
> If, as may well happen, the Bill goes through the Commons, there is no reason why we should not throw it out at Second Reading here. Although it is to be a government Bill, it was not in

1 *Hansard* (Commons), 1975, vol. 898, col. 1221.

2 Baroness (Alice) Bacon introduced a debate on a Hare Coursing (Abolition) Bill to the Lords on 2 May 1972. It was defeated by 115 votes to 71. The government spokesman Viscount Colville declared during the debate (cols 664–9) that the (Conservative) government was neutral.

3 *Year Book*, 1975, p. 6.

4 *Lords Debates*, 1975, vol. 365, cols 1525–56. Denham remains both Chief Whip and a member of the BFSS Parliamentary Committee in 1983.

the Labour party manifesto, nor in the Queen's Speech. But for long term reasons, this may not be the wisest thing to do. Government peers would probably have a three-line-whip and I don't think any of them would vote against the Bill. The Liberals are very doubtful too. Going on previous form, our front bench would probably deplore this being introduced as a government Bill, but I do not think that they would take a definite line against the Bill itself. Although, with careful whipping, we could ensure that the Bill was thrown out, the government would almost certainly feel in honour bound to force it through under the Parliament Act.

There are two alternative courses of action. The first is to allow the Bill a second reading on the nod, but to debate at the same time, and vote on, a motion deploring the government's action. This too we could win, and probably with a small amount of Labour and Liberal support. But I don't think that this would be strong enough to kill the Bill in the end.

The remaining possibility, and the one which I think we should adopt, is again to allow the Bill a Second Reading on the nod, but to debate at the same time, and vote on, a motion to the effect that if the Bill gets a Second Reading it should be referred to a Select Committee of the House. I hope it would be possible to get front bench support for this motion, or even better for it to be moved from our front bench. The advantages of this course of action are as follows:

1. Such a select committee would have the power to hear evidence, and would be able to consider the relevant parts of the Scott Henderson and Stable reports.

2. It would take up quite a lot of time.

3. It would still be open to the House to throw out the Bill at Third Reading, and with very much more effect.

For tactical reasons, it would be very much better if this course of action was not known about by anyone until the Bill reaches this House, so I think it would be wiser not to discuss it in the Committee.[1]

Denham's letter proved prophetic; the government accepted his request for a Select Committee which held its Inquiry and reported that the Coursing Bill should not proceed. The report was accepted by the House and the Bill lapsed.

This victory for the supporters of the BFSS was aided by two further factors. Firstly, the idea of a Select Committee came, as it was intended to, as a complete surprise to the proponents of the Bill. Secondly, the Lords' Committee was constituted so that it was unlikely to want

1 Lord Denham to Marcus Kimball, Nov. 1974.

to 'remove an ancient freedom' unless the evidence was overwhelming. The Committee consisted of three life peers, three hereditary peers and one Bishop. Of the three life peers two were from the Labour benches, and they both with the Bishop voted against the final paragraph of the Report 'that the Bill should not proceed';[1] the four Conservative peers voted against. The Lords' Committee was advised by Lord Diplock, a law lord, that the Bill was impracticable and would be difficult to enforce. He did not inform the Committee that he had been a life-long supporter of field sports nor that he had, in the 1930s, written articles for the BFSS, nor that he was in close touch with the BFSS's tacticians in parliament. When the House of Lords' decision on the Bill was later debated, the Home Office, in the person of the Minister of State, rejected the arguments contained in Diplock's submission to the Committee.[2] It was felt by the Home Office that Diplock's enthusiasm for field sports had blunted his legal acuity.

Under the leadership of Kimball the BFSS has, in the last decade, increasingly applied itself to more positive parliamentary activity. It has written and promoted a variety of bills on areas of concern to field sportsmen. The *Deer Bill* 1963 is one of the most significant; it was drafted by their parliamentary agent, introduced by Jasper More – then on the BFSS General Purposes Committee,[3] and ultimately passed into law. It was essentially an anti-poaching law which attempted to effect a 'compromise between humane and sporting interests of farming and forestry'.[4]

This Bill and others like it enabled the BFSS and its members to be seen to be making a positive contribution to animal welfare and conservation and enabled them to defuse the charge that they were only concerned with protecting animals for sport.[5] In the *Rabies Bill* of 1974 they were able to help the government with advice on technical problems.

The positive approach allowed another set of tactics to be deployed. By supporting bills such as the *Sale of Salmon Bill* 1977,[6] which were not vital to the interests of the Society but obviously dear to individual Members of Parliament, the Society was able to build up tacit

1 Hare Coursing Bill, *Minutes of Evidence*, House of Lords, 6 May 1976, pp. 228–9.

2 *Lords Debates*, 1978, vol. 398, col. 942.

3 In 1978 J. More was Chairman of the BFSS Parliamentary Committee.

4 Annual Report, 1962–3, p. 18.

5 See also the Game Law (Amendment) Act introduced by Marcus Kimball in 1961. See *Baily's*, 1960–1, p. 296.

6 Introduced by C. Onslow MP.

alliances with relatively neutral MPs. Because of the help they had received from pro-hunting members, such MPs would be more reluctant to take a firm stand against hunting and coursing. In other cases the tactic is more calculated. Private Members' bills are discussed on Friday afternoons and many rural MPs, particularly those who have seats away from the Home Counties, do not wish to stay in London. Therefore only urban and London-based MPs are likely to find it easy to stay in the House. Accordingly the BFSS is assiduous in checking whether any *quid pro quo* can be arranged. By this device the support of Jewish MPs, many of whom sit for London constituencies, is sought simply by being seen not to attack causes which are dear to Jewish hearts. In the case of ritual slaughter the BFSS has decided that its Jewish friends are more important than its friends in the humane movement who object to the methods used by Kosher butchers.

The BFSS does not always manage its activities as well as it would wish. At its lowest point around 1960 it was declared 'moribund'[1] and even in 1977 it fell 'below its own high standards of parliamentary manoeuvre'.[2] On 25 January 1977, three bills concerning deer were introduced into the Commons and a bill with overlapping provisions was introduced into the Lords. All the bills were concerned with tightening up the provisions of the 1963 *Deer Act* and were essentially non-contentious. However, there was evidence of a lack of liaison between various BFSS Committees and a failure by the BFSS Head Office to get the approval of the NFU or to keep organisations such as the British Deer Society informed. This failure weakened the BFSS's claim to speak for all sporting groups and showed that its policy of 'circulating off-the-record bulletins of their parliamentary intentions, tactics and forecast'[3] was unreliable, particularly when, as in this case, the non-BFSS Bill was presented by a Labour peer. *The Field* was particularly saddened by the latter point since it seemed to it that the inability by the BFSS to liaise with a Labour peer tended to return the issue of field sports to party politics.[4] The BFSS's position was that a new Deer Bill would enable the LACS to attack stag hunting and that any tightening up of the law could be done by amending the 1963 *Deer Act*. The British Deer Society did not accept this, and produced a Bill which was blocked by the BFSS and the NFU. It was redrafted in such a way that it could not be used to attack hunting – but was then blocked by a spokesman for the LACS.

1 Brander, *Hunting and Shooting*, p. 123.

2 *The Field*, 17 Feb. 1977, p. 255.

3 *The Field*, 17 Feb. 1977, p. 255.

4 Ibid. The BFSS feels that *The Field* ignored its arguments and only accepted those of the BDS.

Nevertheless, whether the BFSS is trying to stop anti-hunting or anti-coursing legislation or is helping bills through parliament, its operations are generally characterised by two factors; care and dedication. The care is shown by attention to details; when difficult debates are looming it makes up a list of suitable speakers, provides them with information which does not overlap and 'programmes' their appearance. Most of its reliable supporters are Conservatives, and meetings of the 1922 backbenchers Committee are a good place to distribute information and call for supporters. Lord Margadale was Chairman of the 1922 Committee from 1955 to 1964, and he was followed in 1972 by E. Du Cann, a pro-hunting MP from West Somerset who is actively sympathetic to the BFSS and is one of its team of speakers.[1] The care shown by the BFSS also extends to the selection of parliamentary candidates, for it ensures that at their adoption meetings candidates are asked about their attitude to hunting.[2]

The dedication of the pro-hunting parliamentarian, particularly of Marcus Kimball, is the second ingredient of its success. He supports the thin end of the wedge argument, and, while not a courser himself, believes passionately that to abolish coursing for whatever reason would be a threat to democracy.[3]

Marcus Kimball has been described as a master tactician and 'a man who only appears in the House when animals are being debated',[4] and it is acknowledged by both sides that his commitment to the defence of all field sports and his knowledge of the rules is the main reason why coursing and possibly even hunting has continued to exist. On his retirement from the Chairmanship of the BFSS in 1982 he was compared by the BFSS Director General Sir Robin Brookbone with Field Marshal Montgomery for his ability 'to win battles that one is personally involved in'. The opponents of hunting accepted that 'we have no-one like him on our side'[5] and hope that Lord Houghton's attempts to bring animals into politics will provide a cadre of parliamentarians who will be able to apply themselves as steadfastly to pushing through the legislation which they desire. Kimball accepted that his enthusiasm for the cause gave him an advantage and believed that, if more of his

1 Du Cann made the key speech opposing the *Protection of Deer Bill* introduced by Sir F. Messer on 24 June 1959. *Hansard* (Commons), 1959, vol. 607, cols. 1206–14, and stayed up until 2.44 a.m. to oppose the *Hare Coursing Bill* on 27 Oct. 1975.

2 Interview with M. Kimball. The Conservative candidate for SW Cambridge in April 1983 was forced to withdraw only when it became known that his *wife* was a member of LACS. The wife of the President of the Constituency Association is (in 1983) a joint master of the Cambridgeshire Hunt.

3 More so than, for example, 'closed shop' legislation.

4 Comment by a fellow MP, during a private discussion in December 1977.

5 Interview with Executive Secretary of LACS.

opponents read the procedure book, life would be much harder for the BFSS.[1]

The very success of the BFSS's tactics in parliament has tended to interfere with its understanding of the wider issues. It protested in 1977: 'The Hunt Saboteurs Association and some individuals have shown during the year how fundamentally unacceptable in a country dedicated to the democratic process are those who think that the process is useful only when it suits them and that they can with justification and impunity follow an alternative course'.[2] They add: 'Right thinking and right action require acceptance of the democratic process without qualification or equivocation'.[3] This stirring rhetoric ignored the fact that only by luck and by skilful manipulation of the parliamentary procedures had BFSS supporters successfully stifled 13 anti-coursing bills in eleven years, three of which were government bills and one of which passed all stages in the Commons. It also ignored the fact in both 1966 and 1978 that 75 per cent of the population were in favour of a law banning coursing.[4] The success of the BFSS's tactics also influenced successive Labour governments to allow parliamentary time for attempts to abolish coursing. Numerous Labour MPs, and indeed the Labour government,[5] have expressed frustration at the delaying tactics and filibusters deployed by the Conservative hunting lobby. The BFSS's pride at being able to string out the Committee stage of the two-clause Hare Coursing Bill in 1975 was matched by the frustration of government Ministers, Labour backbenchers and civil servants who have had to endure the process.[6] They have become much less open to compromise and far more determined to use partisan antagonisms to push anti-coursing legislation through parliament. In this they were encouraged by Lord Houghton, the Chairman of GECCAP, for he saw a party political commitment to animal welfare as being more likely to produce results than carefully fostered cross-party initiatives which do not have a party machine behind them.

It has become clear to the LACS and the anti-hunting community in general that parliament is indeed the key to the success of their de-

1 He suggested that only Eric Heffer MP had done so.

2 *Year Book*, 1977, p. 9.

3 Ibid., p. 9.

4 NOP Surveys, published by the LACS.

5 *Hansard* (Commons), 1970, vol. 801, col. 1525.

6 See speeches during the 1975 debate by Dr S. Summerskill (Under-Secretary of State for the Home Department and responsible for the Bill). She referred to the string of 'Conservative amendments' and complained that points were being 'continually raised', *Hansard* (Commons), 1975, vol. 898, cols 976 and 1207. The defenders of coursing debated, amended, and forced votes at every stage of the 1975 Bill.

mands. As a result the LACS is less casual in its approach to legislation and has become more determined to seek the backing of people like Houghton and organisations such as GECCAP. The professionalism of the BFSS's operations has forced its opponents to improve theirs; a mirror image of the situation in 1929–30 when the BFSS was formed to counteract the apparently imminent success of the LACS.

The arguments deployed

Against hunting

Social changes over the last two hundred years have exposed hunting as a social anomaly, and have brought attacks on the sport from many quarters. The arguments against hunting sprang, as they still do, from two principal sources: the moral and the social. The major moral argument is that hunting is cruel to the animal hunted and degrading to the participants; the main social argument is that hunting is a divisive, class-based sport.

Since 1800, parliament has heard and Hansard has transcribed almost every conceivable argument against and in favour of hunting and the use of animals in sport. Despite the fact that these debates have extended over almost 200 years, the number of arguments adduced both in and outside parliament are relatively few, particularly when examination strips them of rhetorical embellishments. Some have remained in constant use since the debate began; some are developments of the same basic point. Many of the arguments presented are simple denials, by one side, of the case presented by their opponents. These factors enable the main arguments to be reduced to a manageable number and their changing importance to be more easily traced.

The quintessential argument against hunting is that it is cruel and inflicts unnecessary suffering. Cruelty is hard to define since it depends on what society finds acceptable at that time and is a relative rather than an absolute concept. Gratuitous cruelty, however, is easier to identify, and the infliction of pain for no other reason than to enhance the sport has been one of the bases of the attacks on hunting and coursing in the 19th and 20th centuries. In 1967, Heffer stated: 'I cannot think of anything worse than two dogs chasing a hare for pleasure. This in itself is unnecessary cruelty'.[1]

The basic argument of E.A. Freeman, later Professor of History at Oxford, presented in the *Fortnightly Review* in 1869, was that hunting was cruel and therefore immoral: 'The true question lies in a nutshell.

1 *Hansard* (Commons), 1969, vol. 746, col. 13.

Is it right to inflict, and to seek pleasure in inflicting, needless suffering on any creature whatever?'[1] Freeman did not deny man's rights to kill animals, nor that hunting produced certain social benefits by keeping gentlemen in the country and involved with the rural community, but he felt that these arguments were not relevant to an issue which centred on cruelty and morality. Avoiding cruelty, however, was not felt by everyone to be particularly important. Viscount Cranbourne, for instance, admitted that pheasant shooting was cruel and stated: 'If it were accepted that human beings should not inflict suffering on animals then let all such sports be stopped'.[2] He himself did not support that principle.

By the beginning of the 20th century it was generally accepted that cruelty was undesirable. Speakers who opposed reformist bills nevertheless were moved, with Sir F. Banbury, to declare that they 'yielded to no one in their desire to put down cruelty to animals'.[3] Following the *Protection of Animals Act*, 1911, when animal welfare legislation was clearly separated from anti-hunting legislation, the hunting community decided to declare its enthusiasm for the first and its opposition to the second. As the undesirability of cruelty was accepted by an increasing majority of the population, arguments concerning it became a central part of the anti-hunting debate. In 1949, Mr Cocks, who introduced the debate on the *Protection of Animals* (*Hunting and Coursing*) *Bill*, stated: 'Hatred of cruelty is common to every civilised, humane and adult mind'[4] and, 'This is a Bill to prevent cruelty';[5] no one argued with the first point but the pro-hunting community vigorously attacked the second. Merlyn Rees MP, who introduced the government's anti-coursing Bill in 1970, stated in his opening speech: 'So the basic issue is whether competitive hare coursing involves a measure of cruelty which today is no longer acceptable. The government have no doubt whatever that it does'.[6] The importance of cruelty in the debate was now understood to be a necessary part of the case against hunting and it was thought by some that proving the cruelty of hunting would be sufficient to win the debate and change the law.

The second moral argument against hunting and field sports is that they degrade the participants. Wilberforce felt that bull-baiting 'de-

1 Freeman,'The Morality of Field Sports', Oct. 1869, p. 378.

2 *Hansard* (Commons), 1894, vol. 22, cols 1091–2.

3 *Hansard* (Commons), 1903, vol. 122, col. 641.

4 *Hansard* (Commons), 1949, vol. 461, col. 2167.

5 Ibid., col. 2168.

6 *Hansard* (Commons), 1970, vol. 801, col. 1526.

graded human nature to the level of brutes',[1] and Sheridan that it encouraged 'idleness and drunkenness among the men and profligacy among the women'.[2] Other sports have been attacked for the effect that the commission of cruelty has had on the participants;[3] and this argument has been used frequently in the 20th century. In a brief debate on deer hunting in 1939, it was stated: 'Man's inhumanity to man is very often the reflex of his inhumanity to dumb creatures'.[4] And Lord Soper, for instance, stated with the utmost clarity in 1972 that coursing is 'a very ignoble and unworthy exercise'[5] and 'degrades those who take part in it'.[6]

The third argument against hunting is an extension of the second; it is that baiting, coursing, hunting and the infliction of any unnecessary suffering upon animals is anti-humanitarian, anti-Christian and, of itself, immoral. This point was a development of the emerging 18th century view that animals had some rights, a view only possible when the rights of people had been acknowledged. Sir Richard Hill, who introduced the 1802 debate against bull-baiting, felt it was the beginning of 'a system of humanity! a system of peace!'[7] for animals. Freeman agreed that 'the principle of humanity is now generally admitted', although 'real humanity, whether towards man or beast, is a very modern virtue'.[8] As acceptance of this virtue spread throughout society in the 19th and 20th centuries, pressure was put on governments to extend the rights of animals. In 1930, Isaac Foot stated the case fully:

> Interest in the protection of animals is the sign of a healthy social life and, whenever there has been a move forward in the relief of the burdens on men and women at the same time, the social conscience has been quickened as to its responsibility towards the animals under our care and attention. As interest was raised in the protection of animals in the early part of the last century so there was a movement to wipe out the penal laws which were at that time a scandal. It has been said that this House exists for the defence of the interests of the people and the whole community and,

1 *Cobbett's Parliamentary History*, 1801–3, vol. 36, col. 845.

2 Ibid., col. 850.

3 See *Hansard* (Commons), 1883, vol. 276, col. 1662. Trap pigeon shooting was described as 'a demoralising sport to all those who took part in it'.

4 *Hansard* (Commons), 1937, vol. 323, col. 348.

5 *Lords Debates*, 1972, vol. 330, col. 686.

6 Ibid., col. 689.

7 *Cobbett*, 1801–3, vol. 36, col. 830.

8 Freeman, *Morality of Field Sports*, p. 357.

> particularly, the most defenceless. The most defenceless things in our general community are the animals committed to our care, and their claims should receive attention.[1]

The ecology and animal rights movements have grown in importance in the last two decades. Many of the arguments produced, particularly by the anti-speciesists, have proved too extreme for most of those committed to a policy of gradual legislative reform; accordingly their views have not appeared in anti-hunting or anti-coursing debates. Nevertheless, they have taken the moral arguments several steps further and may yet shift the 'middle ground' of acceptable practices to a point where hunting becomes socially intolerable.

These philosophical developments are related to changes in public opinion which has in its turn influenced governments. When the Labour government promoted an anti-coursing bill in 1975 it did so on the grounds that coursing was cruel 'and is no longer acceptable to public opinion at large in this country'.[2] The hunting community chose to ignore the finding of public opinion polls and attempted to discredit them on the grounds of urban bias.[3] It was claimed also that the polls were 'inaccurate' and 'irrelevant'[4] to the major part of the hunting community's defence.

The argument that hunting is unnecessary has some logical value. The abolitionist maintains that there are substitutes both for the sport of hunting and for the control of foxes and deer. The LACS urges as a substitute sport 'the adoption of drag hunting. That is the using of a specially laid false trail instead of a live animal'.[5] The continuing existence of a number of bloodhound packs shows that this substitution is possible. Although alternative methods of control do not necessarily avoid cruelty, it was accepted by the Scott Henderson Committee that foxes could be effectively controlled by gassing.[6] Hare and deer are already controlled more by shooting than by hunting, and the abolition of coursing and stag hunting would make relatively little difference to their numbers.

The final important argument against hunting is that it is socially divisive, class-based sport. This is more a motivation than an argument

1 *Hansard* (Commons), 1930, vol. 236, col. 1668. Foot was the father of three post-war Labour government Ministers.

2 *Hansard* (Commons), 1975, vol. 893, col. 882.

3 *Hansard* (Commons), 1967, vol. 746, col. 27.

4 Interview with BFSS Director, 1978.

5 From LACS literature.

6 *Scott Henderson Report*, paras 167 and 419 (15). The inquiry did not feel, however, that the availability of an alternative means of control constituted a case against fox hunting.

for it rarely appears as a substantive point in hunting debates and is never introduced by those in favour of abolition. Frequently, however, the proponents of hunting attempt to show either that their antagonists are riddled with class hatred or that 'Hunting is the most democratic form of sport in the world'[1] and that there is 'no happier place for rich and poor than the hunting field'.[2] A clear statement that class differences produced different attitudes towards hunting was made in 1949. Professor Gruffydd, who favoured abolition, stated that the issue was 'not a party but a social matter', adding that those 'who have money and leisure tend to defend these blood sports' and that on this sort of issue it 'does not really depend so much upon what one thinks as upon the sort of person one is'.[3] Lord Masserene and Ferrard, from the other side, referred to the abolitionists as those who 'object to field sports, which they regard as the pastimes of the rich and privileged, or, if you like, on grounds of class. Those are unworthy motives and I will not discuss them further'.[4] Just as he felt that accusing the abolitionists of being against field sports for class reasons was sufficient to undermine their case, so many abolitionists are reluctant to make explicit the class nature of their activities. However, some are privately willing to admit that class antagonism fuels their enthusiasm.[5]

The issue of class division is used more by hunting people to condemn their opponents than by the anti-hunting community as an argument condemning hunting. Many MFHs feel that antagonism to field sports is 'almost entirely social' and comes from 'people who are against anything that smacks of the upper classes'.[6] Some Masters feel more strongly than this, one believing that 'the vast majority are motivated by class hatred and mistakenly think that hunting is a sport that only the rich can enjoy'.[7]

The class argument contains another element, that legislation tends to attack sports whose abolition would cause 'an abridgement of the amusements of the lower orders'.[8] Parliament was criticised for being willing to 'put down, one after another, the sports of the poor men –

1 *Hansard* (Commons), 1949, vol. 461, col. 2194. Speech by Sir J. Lucas.

2 *Hansard* (Commons), 1930, vol. 236, col. 447.

3 *Hansard* (Commons), 1949, vol. 461, cols 2215–16.

4 *Lords Debates*, 1972, vol. 330, col. 689.

5 Confirmed in interviews with members of the LACS and HSA.

6 MFH questionnaires.

7 From questionnaires. The same point was made by R. Paget, *Hansard* (Commons), 1970, vol. 801, col. 1575.

8 *Cobbett*, 1800–1, vol. 35, col. 211.

while they never touched the sports of the rich'.[1] Certainly the core sports of fox and stag hunting were not attacked until the late 19th century and all of those which have been attacked, including coursing in the 1960s, have tended to be fringe sports without much support from the élite. Indeed, coursing has been referred to by a supporter as 'a specialist sport, rather outside the social pale'.[2] The élite has been able to justify the continuance of its own sports; it was stated in 1883 that 'the upper classes conducted their sports with a minimum of cruelty because they had been educated up to the point; but unfortunately in the lower classes the cruelty still remained, and it must be repressed'.[3] This argument was repeated in 1949 by a speaker who stated: 'One must realise that the people who hunt are sportsmen. A sportsman is one who disdains to win on a foul'.[4] Such a man would not, therefore, behave as an ordinary countryman who, left to himself, would 'keep down the numbers . . . very cruelly and inefficiently'.[5]

However the opposite view has been put by Rev. J. Stratton who felt that the Royal Buckhounds was 'infinitely mischievous in its influence. The lower classes imitate the higher and, . . . seeing these barbarities, any of the lower orders who are disposed to be cruel feel justified in doing so'.[6] More recently an HSA spokesman stated 'many country people who follow hounds are just peasants. . . . The squire is the master of hounds and the man they doff their cap to'.[7]

These arguments were based on assumptions rather than on evidence, but they have had an effect on the leaders of anti-hunting groups who feel they must officially deny that class has anything to do with their case.[8] The argument that hunting is socially divisive could be a powerful one for the abolitionists, but, since it has already been used against them, it would be hard for them to deploy it effectively. The tactic of borrowing and subtly reshaping the opposition's arguments has been repeated by the hunting community in the last decade by its embrace of the conservationist argument. However, if the tactic is deployed carelessly, it may rebound. Windham, in 1800, argued for all field

1 *Hansard* (Commons), 1883, vol. 276, col. 1665.

2 Brander, *Hunting and Shooting*, p. 124.

3 *Hansard* (Commons), 1883, vol. 276, col. 1667.

4 *Hansard* (Commons), 1949, vol. 461, col. 2219.

5 Ibid., col. 2219.

6 Stratton, *Royal Sports*, pp. 12–13.

7 Quoted in the *Littlehampton Gazette*, 11 Feb. 1966.

8 From interviews and from the literature of the anti-hunting societies.

sports and said that, if bull-baiting was to be abolished, he would 'for the sake of consistency . . . bring in a bill to prohibit hunting, shooting, fishing and all the sports of the field practised by the higher orders'.[1] He felt, correctly at the time, that to attack all field sports was sufficiently ludicrous to ensure the defeat of a Bill against any one of them. However, the essence of Freeman's case in 1869 and of the entire anti-hunting movement since then has been that Windham's apparently extreme argument was sound. Abolitionists feel that 'cruelty and immorality are indivisible'[2] and that all blood sports should be stopped immediately. However, they have to try and get one bill through parliament at a time and are thus reduced to operating at the level of political expediency, only to find that their opponents are better at manipulating the political process than they are.

For hunting

The proponents of hunting have had an easier task than the abolitionists for they have had to defend only the status quo. Their task has been to keep both law and custom from changing rather than to refer to basic principles. Accordingly the majority of pro-hunting arguments are relative and comparative and must be so in order that they remain acceptable to changes in the contemporary political and social climate.

The pro-hunting arguments can be divided into defence and attack. The former tactic involves denying the essentially moral charges of the abolitionists and includes the occasional *ad hominem* attack on their motives, and the latter consists of putting forward arguments actively in favour of hunting.

The hunters' response to the charges that hunting is cruel, immoral and degrading is simple – they say that it is not. Few hunting people today maintain that the animals enjoy being hunted, although some suggest that they might do so.[3] In the past it has been usual to accept that hunting might involve some cruelty, but it was always emphasised that this was less than the cruelty to be found in nature.[4] It was accepted that cruelty might be an unfortunate and rare consequence of the hunt but never a necessary part of it. In almost every early debate against one form of hunting or another it was claimed that the sport

1 *Cobbett*, 1801–3, vol. 36, col. 841.

2 Interview with Lord Soper.

3 *Sheffield Telegraph*, 4 Nov. 1936. A correspondent claimed 'nine out of ten foxes actually enjoy being hunted'. In 1976, an MFH, while being interviewed, stated 'we do not know that the fox does not enjoy the hunt'.

4 See *inter alia Hansard* (Commons), 1967, vol. 746, col. 18, and *Hansard* (Commons), 1949, vol. 461, col. 2187.

under attack was less cruel than other sports and should therefore not be abolished.[1] This argument re-emerged in 1972 when Lord Templeman stated in defence of coursing that 'coursing is not more cruel than many other sports. In fact it is less so than some, including, in my opinion, shooting and fishing'.[2] It has also been asserted that 'killing by hunting is the least cruel method' of control.[3] The undoubted horrors of snaring, trapping, shooting and poisoning have been spelt out in debates and were fully investigated by the Scott Henderson Committee, which found little to say in favour of these methods of controlling wildlife.[4] The official and often-quoted view, formed by Scott Henderson, remains that hunting is not necessarily crueller than other forms of control.[5] None of these points prove that hunting is not cruel nor do they satisfy the anti-hunting community, nevertheless, they do give encouragement to the supporters of hunting.

The charge that coursing, hunting or baiting is degrading has been consistently denied. Canning felt 'the amusement (baiting) was a most excellent one; it inspired courage, and produced a nobleness of sentiment and elevation of mind'.[6] A speaker in the 1949 debate felt that 'it is surely very much less harmful that people should ride across open country or run across the country . . . than that they should be sitting in cinemas watching those films of lust, sadism, cruelty and murder which we show to our children'.[7] Coursing was recommended by Lord Diplock in 1972 as 'healthy open-air exercise', which enables one to get 'back to Nature from an artificial world'.[8]

Not surprisingly the hunting community rejected the claim that hunting was immoral and anti-humanitarian. Canning claimed that baiting was as innocent as boxing and dancing[9] and contributed to 'the genius and spirit of the age'.[10] In 1930, it was stated that stag hunting had 'played so valuable a part in the well-being and happiness of our

1 See *Hansard* (Commons), 1823, vol. 9, col. 443, and *Hansard* (Commons), 1883, vol. 276, col. 1687.

2 *Lords Debates*, 1972, vol. 330, col. 682.

3 *Hansard* (Commons), 1949, vol. 461, col. 2201.

4 *Scott Henderson Report*. See *passim* and 'Summary of Recommendations', pp. 107–9.

5 For example, see *Hansard* (Commons), 1967, vol. 745, cols 44–6.

6 *Cobbett*, 1800, vol. 35, col. 211.

7 *Hansard* (Commons), 1949, vol. 461, col. 2212.

8 *Lords Debates*, 1972, vol. 330, col. 674.

9 *Cobbett*, 1800, vol. 35, col. 211.

10 Ibid., col. 213.

race'.[1] Mr Cocks, in 1949, mocked the hunting community's traditional belief in the up-lifting qualities of field sports,[2] but even in 1976 Raymond Carr was willing to number himself with 'those British people for whom fox hunting remains a passion, a poetry and a mystique'.[3]

Few of these arguments disproved the allegations of the abolitionists and few confronted the charges head-on. However, the hunting community was not initially concerned to combat the moral charges against them, since these charges came from a morality that was neither widespread nor powerful in the 19th century. Indeed the motives of the abolitionists were frequently mocked, and Windham was moved to declare: 'Everything joyous was to be prohibited to prepare the people for the reception of their fanatical doctrines'.[4] To Windham these doctrines were the outcome of a Puritan, Jacobin and Methodist conspiracy; to Paget, 168 years later, the attempts to legislate against hunting came from 'the puritan joy of rebuking sin as long as it is somebody else's'.[5]

As the climate of opinion changed in the 20th century, hunting found itself a minority sport with vocal enemies. It became increasingly necessary, therefore, that hunting should produce arguments that were in keeping with the 'spirit of the age' and, if possible, should be substantive. The pro-hunting arguments which were developed can be divided into four categories: social, ecological, economic and political.

The main social arguments for hunting are that it is traditional, that it is manly, and that it is essentially a rural activity with which towns-people should not interfere. The feeling that hunting is 'characteristically English' and that parliament 'should not interfere with the traditional life of this country'[6] is deep-rooted in the hunting community. The argument appears in most hunting debates and even coursing has been praised as an 'ancient and rather esoteric pastime'.[7] The manliness of hunting has been expressed with considerable vigour. In 1883, one speaker roundly condemned 'the sickly philanthropists who would not be content until the youth of this country proceeded forth only on the bloodless bicycle and instead of training race horses, confined their attention to such innocent amusements as the cultivation of cucum-

1 *Hansard* (Commons), 1930, vol. 236, col. 447.

2 *Hansard* (Commons), 1949, vol. 461, col. 2169.

3 Carr, *Fox Hunting*, p. 250.

4 *Cobbett*, 1802, vol. 36, col. 833.

5 *Hansard* (Commons), 1970, vol. 801, col. 1575.

6 *Hansard* (Commons), 1949, vol. 461, col. 2214.

7 *Hansard* (Commons), 1967, vol. 746, col. 26.

bers'.[1] Earl Winterton, in 1969, supported coursing and hunting 'because they are outdoor sports requiring courage, endurance, and physical fitness, every one of which qualities is anathema to them'[2] – the opponents of hunting. Earl Winterton went further and suggested that some anti-hunters 'are slightly unbalanced mentally' and have had 'the misfortune in their lives of not succeeding in attracting the other sex'.[3] The more usual argument is that antis are 'wet'[4] or have a 'misplaced sentimentality'.[5]

The third social reason, that hunting is a rural sport which townsmen do not understand and should leave alone, has been in continuous use during the 20th century. It first appeared in 1883 when Lord Randolph Churchill attacked the ignorance of 'the counter jumpers of London'.[6] The argument was more prominent in 1949; one speaker felt the House should 'stop any interference with what we regard as rightful sport of the countryside',[7] and another felt it would be 'unjustifiable' if the House were to 'override the feelings of the minority who live in the country'.[8] The Minister of Agriculture accepted that the 1949 Bill was an 'interference with the liberties of the rural population',[9] and used this as one of the government's reasons for not supporting the abolition of hunting and coursing. In 1972, Earl Bathurst declared that the Bill involved sacrificing 'the interests of a large number of people in the country by a majority who live in the towns'.[10] The town against country argument is currently one of the most prominent in the anti-abolitionist's armoury. The countryman's suspicion of urban ways and fear of being swamped by urban values is genuine and deep-seated. Most MFHs put 'town dwellers', 'urban busybodies', etc., as their answer to

1 *Hansard* (Commons), 1883, vol. 276, cols 1660–61. See also Ibid., col. 1680.

2 *Hansard* (Commons), 1949, vol. 461, col. 2236.

3 Ibid., col. 2237.

4 Interview with a fox-hunting MP (R. Paget).

5 Questionnaire.

6 *Hansard* (Commons), 1883, vol. 276, col. 1686.

7 *Hansard* (Commons), 1949, vol. 461, col. 2206.

8 Ibid., col. 2206.

9 Ibid., col. 2233.

10 *Lords Debates*, 1972, vol. 330, cols 713–14. See also *Hansard* (Commons), 1975, vol. 898, col. 902.

the question 'what kind of people oppose hunting?',[1] and leading members of the hunting community cite as one of their main problems the lack of understanding by townspeople of the behaviour and values of countrymen.[2] Some claim that this is a major cause of the urban/rural cleavage and that the abolition of any field sport, even coursing, would 'increase the bitterness the countryman feels towards the town and tend to stiffen his back against all demands'.[3]

The ecological arguments in favour of hunting have become a more significant part of the case presented by the hunting community, particularly since the early 1960s. No longer is it maintained that the animals enjoy it, nor that hunting does not involve an element of cruelty, but it is claimed that hunting is an effective method of keeping a balance of nature. An early use of this argument occurred in 1883: 'Foxes would have long ceased to exist in this country had they not been used for the purpose of hunting and the race would have been exterminated instead of leading a short and merry life'.[4] The same point was couched in more acceptable language in 1930 by a hunting enthusiast who stated: 'Conservation and limitation is essential if the fauna of our country is to be preserved'.[5] From 1949 onwards it became a commonplace to remind the abolitionists that hunting on Exmoor ceased in the early 19th century and that 'during that period the wild deer were nearly exterminated'.[6] Since this was a period of rural poverty, enclosure and simmering class violence, the comparison between 1820 and 1950 was seductive but not altogether apt. In the last 150 years migration from Exmoor has reduced the local population and those who remained had a much higher standard of living. They were, therefore, much less likely to poach deer for food or to exterminate them out of vengeance than their 19th century predecessors. Indeed, when hunting was stopped during the 1939–45 war the deer population survived to be hunted after the war.

The traditional argument in favour of fox hunting is that it is the best method of finding and dispatching noxious vermin. In the Middle Ages the fox, like the wolf, had a price on its head but it quickly became scarce when fox hunting became an establishment sport. Never-

1 From questionnaire.

2 From interviews 1973–8.

3 *Hansard* (Commons), 1967, vol. 746, col. 30.

4 *Hansard* (Commons), 1883, vol. 276, col. 1659.

5 *Hansard* (Commons), 1930, vol. 236, col. 446.

6 *Hansard* (Commons), 1949, vol. 461, col. 2203. The point was emphasised during an interview with the Chairman of the D & SS.

theless, even the habit of importing 'bagmen' from Europe in order to restock the coverts rarely shook the hunting man's conviction that his sport was in the national interest.[1] Even today the belief that 'fox hunting is for the control of vermin' is central to hunting people.[2] This claim has always made them susceptible to the charge of 'fox preservers' by anti-hunting community's exposé of the existence of artificial earths and the continuation well into the 20th century of the practice of restocking earths with foxes from other parts of the country.[3]

One simple way around this problem has been to emphasise rather than deny the role of hunting in conservation. It has always been the concern of hunts to ensure that their quarry are sufficiently numerous to make hunting worthwhile, but not so numerous that farmers complain about damage to crops. Indeed, the hunt will arrange a 'shoot' in order to cull the local fox or stag population if the damage becomes excessive. This would be an embarrassment if hunting people remained concerned to promote the 'control' rather than 'conservation' argument. Now they claim to be able to maintain a balance of nature more successfully than any government agency which might be entrusted with the task – a task the government clearly does not want.[4]

Fox hunters also state, to further their conservationist case: 'It is the fit healthy fox that is not so likely to attack stock which has the best chance of escape from the hounds. The old, sick or injured fox, like the man-eating lion, goes for the easiest prey, is the one that causes the damage, and is also the one usually killed by the hunt. When caught it is always killed instantly – there is no wounding with hunting. It is a quick kill or a clean escape'. Ecologically, therefore, the hunt is the most natural method of control.[5] While this argument is simplistic – there is little chance of escape for any fox, however fit, surprised by 45 hounds in a piece of kale, when the entrances to the local earths have been blocked – it does represent a case for fox hunting. One reason why coursing is particularly vulnerable is that the ecological argument cannot apply, for coursing neither controls nor conserves hares.

The economic arguments in favour of hunting and coursing have always been prominent. It is claimed that hunting brings in tourists

1 Carr, *Fox Hunting*, p. 111.

2 Questionnaires.

3 A systematic attempt was made to show the errors and inconsistencies in the hunters' arguments in *Against Hunting*, (ed.) P. Moore. See especially ch. 2 and appendix A. See also the section on 'Fox Preservation' in *Foxhunting*, NSACS Pamphlet, 1965, pp. 15–25.

4 Confirmed by the Minister of Agriculture in *Hansard* (Commons), 1949, vol. 461, col. 2232. His statement has never been revised by government spokesmen.

5 BFSS Pamphlet, 'This is Foxhunting', 1977 edn.

from abroad and helps to keep army officers and leading showjumpers entertained. The contribution of hunting to tourism has been described as 'a smokescreen to hide the real issues'[1] and it is unlikely that the abilities of showjumpers and army officers would be seriously impaired if they were unable to gallop after foxes. It is also claimed that hunting contributes to the development of British bloodstock.[2] The hunting community and the HIS do undoubtedly make a major contribution to the quality of half and three-quarter bred horses and this has a direct and beneficial effect on racing and showjumping. However, in Germany the quality of showjumping is equally high, despite there being no hunting.

The central economic argument concerns employment and the sale of goods and services to the hunts by the local community. If over 300 hunts ceased operations immediately it would put over 1,000 people out of work and would be a blow to saddlers, tailors, taxidermists and hunt button makers.[3] However, it is probable that drag hounds would replace fox hounds in some areas and that game wardens, possibly drawn from hunt staff, would be needed, particularly in hilly areas, to control the deer, fox and hare populations. The net loss of jobs and income would, therefore, be less than the alarmists suggest. The abolition of coursing would, it is claimed, put 70 trainers out of work and would lead to the destruction of 2,000 dogs.[4] This assumes, however, that no alternative employment exists for greyhounds or their trainers.

A number of political arguments appear regularly in anti-hunting and coursing debates, although not all are concerned with the central issue. It has been pointed out many times since 1835 that the existing laws are quite sufficient to protect the animals from any incidental cruelty,[5] although this fails to mollify those for whom every aspect of hunting is intolerable. Similarly supporters of hunting have attempted to convince parliament that other problems are more pressing and that parliamentarians should concern themselves with social issues rather than the trivial question of coursing. W. Deedes MP stated: 'Those who espouse the cause of children, for example, feel bitterly about this kind of campaign'.[6]

1 *Living without Cruelty*, Labour Party, p. 53.

2 *Hansard* (Commons), 1949, vol. 461, col. 2206.

3 The economic argument was presented *inter alia* during the debate on the *Deer Bill* in 1930. See *Hansard* (Commons), 1930, vol. 236, cols 446–7.

4 *Hansard* (Commons), 1975, vol. 893, col. 868. M. Kimball during the same debate claimed that 180 people would lose their jobs. Ibid., col. 842.

5 See, for example, *Hansard* (Commons), 1949, vol. 461, col. 2186.

6 *Hansard* (Commons), 1970, vol. 801, cols 1537–8.

The hunting community is increasingly aware that values change and that yesterday's defence can become the basis of tomorrow's attack. Accordingly, it has tended to use the relative merits of the various field sports as a way of warning sportsmen that their sport may be next. This is known as the 'thin end of the wedge' argument and has been used for many years as a major defence for marginal sports such as coursing. Windham, in 1800, declared that the curtailment of bull-baiting would lead to the 'abolition of all rural sports';[1] a speaker in 1883 stated that the attempt to abolish tame pigeon shooting was 'a precursor of legislation under which fishermen would be imprisoned, butchers would be hung and we should all be ridden over by rampant vegetarians'.[2] The argument became more significant in the 20th century when attacks on the core sports of fox and stag hunting increased. In 1930, one hunting man questioned: 'How long will it be before we are asked to accept a Bill which will prevent sweet old ladies from keeping vicious cats to destroy the household mouse'.[3]

During the 1967–75 coursing debates the thin end of the wedge argument lost some of its power for it was, in a sense, introduced by both sides.[4] In earlier debates abolitionists frequently prefaced their remarks with the hope that the House would not allow the possibility of future legislation on other issues to cloud their judgement of the issue under debate. However, in 1970, A. Shaw MP accepted that the Anti-Coursing Bill was indeed the first of a list of anti-hunting bills,[5] and this point was repeated by W. Price MP in 1972.[6] This has had the effect of making coursing safer from Private Members' bills since the entire hunting community came to its defence, but it has the disadvantage of making other forms of hunting vulnerable in the event of a successful attempt to abolish coursing. For if one heavily-defended sport is abolished, the ammunition which might have been used to protect the others will have been squandered.

Another standard argument against the abolition of field sports is that field sports are a private matter and not suitable subjects for legislation. In 1800, Canning stated: 'If the legislature were to interfere to put a stop to every practice which might possibly be productive of mischief to any individual, the House must sit unremittingly, making

1 *Cobbett*, 1802, vol. 36, col. 834.

2 *Hansard* (Commons), 1883, vol. 276, cols 1675–6.

3 *Hansard* (Commons), 1930, vol. 236, col. 447.

4 *Hansard* (Commons), 1967, vol. 765, col. 20, for M. Kimball's defence of coursing. See also *Lords Debates*, 1972, vol. 330, col. 716.

5 *Hansard* (Commons), 1970, vol. 801, col. 1549.

6 *Hansard* (Commons), 1972, vol. 830, col. 915.

new laws, and many whimsical laws they would make'.[1] Peel in 1823 felt that the bill belonged to 'a class of subject which he did not think fit for legislation'.[2]

The argument appeared again in the 20th century, although, as governments spread their influence into wider areas, the argument was turned into one of political principle: that such legislation made another 'intrusion on the liberty of the subject'[3] and was another 'unnecessary interference with the way in which people amuse themselves and spend their leisure'.[4] This tactic was used against coursing legislation in the period 1967–75. The anti-coursing bills were described as an affront to liberty and democracy. R. Paget MP stated that the 1970 Bill introduced by the government was 'the very negation of democracy. Democracy is not merely the rule by a majority, it is the rule by a majority which recognises the rights of minorities and which recognises the duty to protect minorities and not merely to sacrifice minorities for its convenience'.[5] Eric Heffer MP felt that this argument was 'the most disgraceful of them all, but it has always been used. It was used against the abolition of child labour in the mines'.[6] Nevertheless, the hunting community has made this argument into a cornerstone of their defences and believes that in defending coursing they are defending the liberty of a rural minority and the sanctity of rural traditions.[7]

The range of arguments used by the hunting community to defend its sports against legislation have been bewildering in its variety. Some are trivial or involve *ad hominem* attacks on those who wish to see field sports curtailed or abolished. Others, however, are more substantial and the BFSS, its Sporting Sub-Committees and its Parliamentary Committee have refined their central arguments and produced an impressive case. The 'positive' points are that hunting is a pleasurable countryman's sport, conserves a balance of nature, improves the quality of horses, is accessible to the majority of the population, and provides work for a significant number of people. The 'negative' arguments in favour of hunting are that it is not particularly cruel, that the morality of hunting is for the individual to decide, and that the abolition of any of the sports would be a malicious interference by urban sentimentalists in the lives of rural people.

1 *Cobbett*, 1800, vol. 35, col. 211.

2 *Hansard* (Commons), 1823, vol. 9, col. 433.

3 *Hansard* (Commons), 1949, vol. 461, col. 2186.

4 Ibid., col. 2214.

5 *Hansard* (Commons), 1970, vol. 801, col. 1577. For a similar argument see Ibid., col. 1583.

6 *Hansard* (Commons), 1967, vol. 746, col. 15.

7 *Hansard* (Commons), 1975, vol. 893, col. 882.

The anti-hunting case is relatively simple and has remained unaltered for almost 200 years. It is that hunting causes cruelty, is unnecessary as a form of control, is degrading for the participants, and is, as a sport, unacceptably divisive in contemporary society. These principles do not always emerge clearly from the debate as the abolitionists spend a large proportion of their energies attempting to discredit the counter arguments of the supporters of hunting.

From 1800 to this day only declining sports have been attacked with any regularity. Bull-baiting and cock fighting were 'little attended except by the mob' when they were abolished in 1835;[1] carted stag hunting was attacked near the end of the last century when its popularity had waned; and coursing came in for severe attacks in the period 1967–75 only when it was shown that its following had sharply declined. This point was appreciated by R. Paget MP, who stated 'coursing is being hit, not because it is cruel but because it is weak'.[2]

The abolitionists have realised for a hundred years that their best chances of success lie with socially and numerically weak sports. However, despite the length and heat of the debate, the shift in public opinion and the developing skills of the anti-hunting pressure groups, no field sports have been abolished since bull-baiting and cock fighting were banned in 1835. More significantly the central sport of fox hunting has never been the focus of a debate in parliament.

1 Hansard. Quoted in Moss, *Valient Crusade*, p. 131.

2 *Hansard* (Commons), 1970, vol. 801, cols 1572–3.

PART IV

PRESSURE GROUP POLITICS

12 Groups, tactics and targets

Pressure groups compared

The groups involved in the hunting issue vary greatly. On one side is the pro-hunting movement led by the BFSS which acts as an umbrella organisation for the entire field sports lobby; on the other side is the anti-hunting movement represented by the NSACS, LACS and HSA, societies which, between them, cover the tactical spectrum. There have been other small groupings at both extremes. At one is the ALF which operates beyond the boundaries of social tolerance; at the other was GECCAP, an *ad hoc*, but expressly political conglomerate, which was concerned only with engineering changes in the political arena. The RSPCA has a separate role to play; it is working on behalf of all animals in a variety of fields. However, it did join GECCAP and the fact that many of its members belong to the HSA and the LACS ensures that it remains a significant, albeit passive, member of the anti-hunting lobby.

The effectiveness of a pressure group is dependent on three kinds of strength: organisational, social and political. Organisational strength results from the internal workings of the group, in particular with reference to its wealth, membership and leadership. Wealth is usually generated by membership subscriptions, legacies, or capital accumulated over the years. The RSPCA during its long history has acquired some capital but being accustomed to a high level of expenditure is very dependent on legacies which can and do fluctuate considerably as a source of income. Indeed, the early 1980s have been difficult for the RSPCA partly as a result of the disturbances within the Society during the 1970s.

Financial problems have affected most pro- and anti-hunting pressure groups at one time or another. All anti-hunting groups started as splinter groups from other organisations and have tended to benefit financially from the flurry of publicity produced by their establishment. The early years were difficult for the LACS and NSACS, but since the war the flow of income from investments and legacies has been entirely adequate for the level at which they have pitched their operations. This is less true of the BFSS which has always been expansionary in aim and activities and has therefore been constantly short of money. In the 1950s its activities were severely curtailed through lack of funds, although this situation eased in the 1960s when the threats to field sports produced, and has continued to produce, an increasing income.

Membership is important, not only with respect to members, but also with respect to its 'density', that is the proportion of the potential membership which actually belongs to the group. The extent to which the membership can hold together in difficult times, that is, its solidarity, is also significant but this is primarily a function of leadership style and ability.

None of the anti-hunting groups can claim a high density of membership. The total combined membership of the LACS, NSACS and the HSA in 1982, even ignoring membership overlap, was under 20,000 people and, since many of these already belonged to the RSPCA, this figure represents the total of those strongly motivated to act against hunting and coursing. It is a very low percentage of the popular majority who oppose hunting in principle, and compares unfavourably with the 62,000 members of the BFSS who represent a substantial percentage of those who actually hunt. These figures are not conclusive, for in the 1970s the BFSS was actively recruiting members to aid it in its struggle to defend field sports. The opponents of field sports, on the other hand, having noted both the hardening of public opinion against hunting and the attempts by Labour governments to abolish coursing, feel that there is no need to give a push to a well-financed bandwagon which is already moving inexorably forward. Nevertheless, the high proportion of potential members from the hunting community who actually belong to the BFSS gives it a genuine authority to speak on behalf of field sports and this in turn affects the way the BFSS is perceived by those in authority.

The quality of a group's leadership and the bureaucracy which it commands are vital factors, not just for the impression it gives to those to whom they seek access, but also to its membership. The way the leadership and bureaucracy of a group respond or fails to respond to pressures, and the ability of the group to mount speedy and effective recruitment and propaganda campaigns at times of crisis, will influence the degree of the group's success and will be a measure by which groups can be compared with other groups.

The extent of bureaucratisation within the groups varies considerably. The BFSS has only a small number of people at Headquarters but through its relationships with local hunting and sporting people, has developed a local network of official but unpaid helpers. From these people are drawn the experts who man BFSS Committees and interact with important official and unofficial bodies. The minor groups, the HSA and the NSACS, have almost no bureaucracy at all, but for different reasons. The HSA decided early in its existence to avoid a central organisation and to devolve decision-making to the locally active groups. The NSACS has never grown big enough to warrant more than a Secretary, but it has always required that local groups report to the centre. Relative to its size the LACS has been the least bureaucratised of all the groups. Most decisions have been made by the Chairman and the Secretary, who use part-time and voluntary help to carry out their decisions. The Committee has, in the past, only mattered when policy changes have been made or when the oligarchic leadership has failed to understand the mood of the Committee or of the membership. This extreme concentration of power taxes membership solidarity and accounts for the LACS's tradition of changing Chairmen and policies at sudden and unpredictable intervals. The Committee members of the BFSS may not be chosen any more democratically, but their system keeps disagreements internal and enables disputes to be solved quietly, with the result that, at least to external eyes, group solidarity is maintained.

The style of leadership and the nature of the groups' organisation are as much a product of group's view of itself as a reflection of which side it is on. Both major groups, the LACS and the BFSS (and indeed the RSPCA), have had at different moments unresponsive and oligarchic leadership. This has led to explosive confrontations and major changes at the top of the LACS and RSPCA. More gentlemanly values have prevailed within the BFSS which has solved its internal crises without excessive publicity. There are several reasons for this. The BFSS being an umbrella organisation has no rival and its oligarchic leadership is able to remove quietly any irritating personalities without changing the structures which hold the Society together. The cohesion of the Society is also a result of the overwhelmingly masculine leadership; only two out of 37 members of the BFSS Main Committee for 1981 were women, and this figure has remained constant for two decades. Clearly such a male-dominated leadership accords well with the Society's image of itself as an upholder of 'gentlemanly' behaviour and traditions, and it has predisposed the BFSS to accuse its opponents of 'suffering' from an overly feminine representation. In some cases this has been correct; the NSACS has been dominated by women throughout its existence. But although the proportion of women on the LACS Main Committee has always been high, eight out of eleven in 1965, a balance between the sexes was achieved by 1978 when the Society had seven women on its Committee of 15. As the Society became more determined by politics the number of women on the Committee decreased – to three out of eleven in 1981. The RSPCA has generally had a more equal ratio of men to women in its Council; there were for example ten out of 23 in 1978. However the number of women increased in 1980 to 14 out of 23 and in 1981 to 16 out of 23. Among the men to lose their places (or to resign) were Brian Seager, Richard Course and John Bryant, all leading members of the Radical Group. Their departure and the increase in the number of women undoubtedly produced a more conservative Council. The most 'unbalanced Society in terms of its representation of the sexes was the BFSS, but this has not prevented the BFSS from defining its opponents in terms of its own image of them – females 'who think more of their dogs than their children'.[1]

Social strength is largely a function of legitimacy. If a group and its leaders are felt by society to be the true representatives of a cause with which public sentiments are in general agreement, and if they express their feelings in an acceptable way, then the group will be considered legitimate. If there are competing groups, the ones which achieve most legitimacy will probably be favoured with the most access.

The cultural acceptability of a group and its demands will also have a major effect on its legitimacy. If a group finds that its major values and norms are socially unacceptable, there will be a tendency for 'strain' to manifest itself. This may mean that the group tends to short-circuit reality by claiming success when it has none, or that it restates its goals in unrealisable terms.[2] Strain may also encourage a group's norms to become more extreme when the typical attitudes of its (possibly silent) membership would suggest a moderate stance. Splits tend to occur when the mass membership ceases to be silent. This can happen when a group is denied access, or refuses to accept the fact that its case is hopeless. The notion of 'strain' helps to make clear why a group will seek unrealistic goals, why it will tell itself lies about its operations, and why its members may feel they have to resort to anomic and violent behaviour.[3] Attempts to cope with the 'strain'

1 From questionnaires.

2 Castles, *Pressure Groups and Political Culture*, ch. 7.

3 See also the discussion in Conclusion.

resulting from a lack of social and political acceptability have been a major cause of the upheavals within the anti-hunting movement.

The NSACS, the HSA, the Reform Group and the ALF in their very existence are manifestations of internal dissension (the other source of strain) in the anti-hunting movement. In the 1890s, the 1920s and the 1960s the RSPCA was a major cockpit of strife for anti-hunters and the reasons (which also explain the splits in the LACS and NSACS) were always the same. Differences existed between sub-groups within the RSPCA over hunting or attitudes towards the establishment, but unresponsive leadership was the norm. The leadership required faithful members who left legacies to the organisation; they did not require what they actually had in many of their members – ardent believers in a cause who wished to vocalise their enthusiasm. In its early years the RSPCA could comfortably contain dog-loving fox hunters and cat-loving anti-fox hunters, but, when the Humanitarian League and later the LACS tried to produce a commitment from the RSPCA to abolish hunting, a confrontation was inevitable. It was also inevitably public for, since the establishment of the Humanitarian League in 1891, there has always been another animal welfare organisation to publicise the 'failures' of the RSPCA or indeed of any animal welfare body with which it disagreed.

The BFSS on the other hand generally kept its internal crises out of the media, although this should not imply that there were no important disputes. The lack of sympathy between the hunting and shooting fraternities, the occasional ill-will between the aristocratic leadership and the ordinary, sometimes working-class, membership, and the entirely undemocratic procedures by which the Main Committee and the expert Sub-Committees were selected all produced strain within the Society. Internal divisions in the Society have mattered less since the mid-1960s for a regular stream of anti-hunting and anti-coursing bills have encouraged most members of the hunting community to close ranks in the face of a vastly more serious external threat. However, it is questionable whether this cohesion can survive in the face of diminishing public support for hunting.

Infighting does not help groups to improve legitimacy, nor does it help them to achieve access to political and governmental targets, although it can have a positive side. Firstly, it generates publicity which in the LACS's case helped it to survive the doldrum period of the 1950s when keeping in the public eye was more important than building legitimacy. Secondly, the emotionalism of the membership can only be channelled to the group's advantage if the group is achieving some success; if it is not, then a cathartic internal row is preferable to a general feeling of lassitude and a loss of membership. Thirdly, the turmoil which the LACS and the RSPCA endured in the 1970s had the effect of clearing the air and producing a more effective leadership which owed little to the past and which could concentrate on acting appropriately in the present. However, this cleansing effect was short-lived for the RSPCA which, in the early 1980s, embarked on another series of internecine battles about money, leadership and essential purpose.

The RSPCA's internal problems in the late 1960s were more destructive than they had been for the LACS because the Society already had a degree of legitimacy the loss of which could have hindered its operations in the non-hunting areas. However, anti-hunting RSPCA members could not accept that legitimacy was more desirable than intellectual honesty and maintained, after the crisis, that the RSPCA, by establishing its credentials for intellectual honesty, had actually increased its legitimacy. The argument also applied to the LACS and NSACS; the former accepted the implication of its more aggressive role in the 1930s and 1970s and emerged with strong and dynamic leadership. The NSACS could not face the emotional costs of a purgative debate and, except for a brief period in the late 1940s, was enfeebled as a consequence. Whether the experiences of the LACS and RSPCA will inculcate an acceptance of democratic processes and an open style of leadership is questionable, but the political culture in which the younger membership has grown up is less tolerant of heavy-handed oligarchies, particularly unsuccessful ones. Whether or not its membership has always appreciated legitimacy as a strength, the most legitimate of all animal welfare organisations has been the RSPCA which has had royal patronage, aristocratic support, a record of quiet but continuous success and over 150 years of history behind it. Most groups concerned with hunting have striven to match the RSPCA's level of legitimacy. It has been relatively easy for the BFSS since it could call on the traditional hunting aristocracy to support it. Its members are collectively wealthy, as the speedy collection of the £250,000 for the fighting fund suggests, and are drawn from leading members of the rural establishment who have individual prestige which is of obvious benefit to the Society. The BFSS has also found it relatively simple to show that its aims are culturally legitimate. It is, after all, defending traditional and well-supported sports. In response, the opposition has had to show that it commands mass rather than élite support.

In seeking legitimacy the LACS has had a more difficult task. It is attempting to change the law and to suppress ancient traditions. In the 1930s and 1940s it felt that it had public opinion and some of the media on its side, but knew that it did not have the support of the decision-makers or the media. In the 1980s it is aware that it has made inroads into the latter, but is uncertain about how to capitalise on its improved position.

The HSA, conscious of the fact that it could never achieve the same level of legitimacy of the BFSS or the LACS, has made no attempt to seek it. It was aware that working at the margins of social acceptability would earn no friends in high places but thought that its activities might have the effect of increasing the legitimacy of the LACS by making the LACS seem relatively moderate. Those HSA members who saw the value of impressing the public and the decision-makers have used the RSPCA and LACS as a channel for their socially more acceptable behaviour.

All groups concerned with hunting, except the HSA, have been keen to co-opt personalities or titled people as a means of acquiring additional social prestige and legitimacy. The BFSS has relied on the traditional aristocracy as a way of increasing its prestige but other groups have sought support from different sectors. The NSACS was backed by academic and literary patrons, while the LACS, which had originally preferred radical writers and churchmen, has grown to favour television performers, actors and writers. These connections confirm for each society that the outside world responds to its own image of itself; the BFSS is an upholder of tradition (and élitism), the NSACS values intellectual honesty and the LACS favours an appeal to a mass, but not necessarily discriminating, audience.

Political strength results from successfully balancing two opposing strategies, those of congruence and militancy,[1] in the search for access to decision-makers. Both leadership recruitment and organisational structure may (or may not) reflect a desire for congruence on behalf of a pressure group. Groups which believe in the value of congruence will tend to elect or recruit as leaders those who are of similar class or background to those to whom access is sought. Within these organisations a bureaucratic structure may develop, particularly in self-interested groups, which parallels the official bureaucracy with which the group will have to deal.

At first sight the BFSS, in its desire to maintain close links with governments, would seem to have consciously sought leadership congruence. In its attempt to resist change and to reassert the value of a traditional activity the BFSS has been automatically in league with the rural establishment which finds its natural home on the Conservative benches of both Houses of parliament. Since the top echelons of the legal profession and the civil service tend to be staffed by scions of affluent and frequently landed families, the connection between the

1 See H. Eckstein, *A Theory of Stable Democracy*, Princeton University Press, 1961. Congruence is a term from mathematics meaning 'having the same size and shape'. Hence, if pressure group leaders and government decision-makers have similar or congruent backgrounds, values and lifestyles, they will tend to be more acceptable to each other.

two, the BFSS and the establishment, seems very close.[1] However, it is equally valid to argue that many field sportsmen will have family or social contacts with the political and administrative élite and that, far from seeking out spokesmen or administrators who are equipped by background or training to talk with the élite, they find that members of the élite are already members of their organisation. Lord Margadale and M. Kimball were landowners and sportsmen before they were politicians, and the BFSS Director in 1982 was a keen sportsman whose early years were spent at Eton, Oxford and in the Lancers before he rose to become a General with experience of working in Whitehall. The BFSS has been assiduous in ensuring that any member of the social or political establishment who can be used to advantage is put on the relevant Committee in the belief that élite congruence will work to its advantage, although in certain circumstances, particularly during periods of Labour governments, these élitist connections could hinder the Society.

Nevertheless as Sampson pointed out in 1982, the Chairman of the BBC, the Editor of *The Times*, the Foreign Secretary, the heads of the Home and Foreign Civil Service as well as two of the four Chairmen of Britain's major banks were Old Etonians. This lends credence to the view that the establishment remains powerful, and the hunting community is sensible to encourage its connections with the élite.[2]

The LACS sought allies wherever it could find them; this was rarely in the establishment but even then it took the Society a long time to realise that the only significant support it obtained was from Labour parliamentarians. Under Rowley a political commitment was avoided but he was removed by a caucus of LACS members who wished to make clear their belief that hunting had long been a party political issue. In a sense the League's willingness to endorse Lord Houghton for its Chairman was explicitly an attempt to develop élite congruence, for he had been a Labour party insider for 30 years.[3] He was chosen, however, because he was willing and able to advance the cause and knew how to do it rather than merely who to do it with.

Attitudes towards militant behaviour and the desire of some to use all available weapons have been a source of contention both within and between pressure groups. Some groups have felt that militancy gener-

1 Nine out of ten judges in 1963 had attended public school and Oxford or Cambridge universities. See M. Zander, *Lawyers and the Public Interest*, Weidenfeld & Nicolson, London, 1968, p. 40.
Two out of three civil servants in the rank of assistant secretary or above in 1967 had attended fee-paying schools. See J. Westergaard & H. Resler, *Class in a Capitalist Society*, Penguin, Harmondsworth, 1976, p. 255.

2 See A. Sampson, *The Changing Anatomy of Britain*, Hodder & Stoughton, London, 1982.

3 Houghton was fourth in the ballot for shadow cabinet posts in 1970.

ates desirable publicity, and others that militancy would undermine their legitimacy. In its early years the LACS adopted a militant stance and attacked *inter alia* royalty, the BBC and the Church. In the 1960s, the LACS began to seek access through legitmacy. However, at this time members who believed that more benefit would accrue from militancy left the LACS and established the HSA. The NSACS avoided militancy, indeed split off from the LACS because of its aggressive tactics, but never grew sufficiently to achieve a lasting legitimacy. The increase in the political acceptability of the LACS in the 1960s, rather than being a reward for militancy, was a product of changes in public opinion, although militancy had had the effect of keeping the Society going until the state of public opinion became clear. By the 1960s, the League could no longer be entirely ignored by politicians and civil servants because it represented a majority view. Its increased acceptability gave it the access which its earlier militancy had indirectly helped to produce.

Neither the BFSS nor the RSPCA has a history of militancy, the former because its purpose is to maintain the status quo and only in moments of extreme crisis, such as the 1949 bills, has it arranged mass demonstrations or major petitions. The RSPCA has forsworn militancy because during its history it has managed to achieve and wishes to keep a high level of legitimacy. Militancy would jeopardise the inspectorate, animal hospitals and educational programmes which are seen as a long-term investment in the general welfare of animals. The RSPCA is not, unlike the LACS, seeking to end something, for while the areas in which it works will change, it perceives a continuous and continuing need for its services.

This is equally true for the BFSS, which has increased its contacts with parliament and the civil service, and provided a range of services for its members although these are for the benefit of the hunting community rather than in the interests of animals.

Nowadays an increasing reliance on expertise, efficient organisation and an ability to handle the media, make it unlikely that any organisation concerned to promote a cause or even to resist one would be greatly concerned with developing élite congruence or a parallel bureaucracy. Nor would militancy be a preferred *modus operandi* except in extreme cases. All techniques and tactics are for the purpose of developing legitimacy and improving access, in which case neither militancy nor congruence would be seen as significant. Even the influence of patrons cannot outweigh the impact of the prevailing political culture on the government of the day.

Non-political tactics and targets

Active pressure groups are forced by changing circumstances to vary their tactics and to seek access to different targets at different stages of their development. Direct, non-political activities may be at, or even beyond, the fringes of acceptability; they include demonstrations, slander, physical assault on opponents, the destruction of property and the sabotaging of hunts. Those group members who despair of the constitutional and legislative processes may believe that access to public opinion via the press is more important than the distant prospect of legislative change. They may seek to create newsworthy situations and therefore apparently anomic behaviour may be used by people who are in all other respects well integrated into society.[1]

Demonstration and disruption were initially the main policies of the LACS and had the desirable effect of ensuring it a growing membership and income. While understanding the value of a relationship with governments, the LACS has neither the technical skills, nor the expertise, nor weight of numbers to enable it to ingratiate itself with or to bargain with governments. Indeed, only in the 1960s did the LACS seriously begin to seek access to parliament and the executive branch government. During the 1948–9 period it forfeited the leadership of the anti-hunting movement to the NSACS whose quieter policies had, in the social climate of the period, given it more legitimacy and, for a brief period, more access. The NSACS failed to capitalise on its good fortune during this period and its reluctance to survive by publicity stunts during the long period of Conservative government (1951–64) signalled its decline and its eclipse by the more active LACS.

The HSA has continued with the direct tactics started by the LACS and has succeeded in annoying hunts and in generating valuable publicity. However, some of its supporters have joined the ALF in protest against the political system's refusal to act against hunting and they have resorted to violent and illegal behaviour. Their activities have been politically unacceptable and have probably harmed rather than assisted the anti-hunting cause.

The pro-hunting community has not, on balance, responded to the activities of hunt saboteurs or demonstrations with violence, partly because the BFSS has urged it not to but also because the publicity generated by incidents has not worked in its favour. However, in 1978–9, perhaps because the hunting community had become more fearful of its future, this changed. Indeed, violence on the property and persons of hunt saboteurs reached such a pitch that the HSA asked the BFSS for a meeting to discuss ways in which to defuse the issue.[2]

1 Marginal and illegal behaviour tends to be used by groups who are seeking to change cultural values and who, when unsuccessful, 'mobilise on the basis of a generalised belief'. See Castles, *Pressure Groups and Political Culture*, p. 88 and ch. 7. *passim*.
The Committee of 100 was this kind of group. See F. Myers, 'Civil Disobedience and Organisational Change: The British Committee of 100', *Political Science Quarterly*, LXXXVI, 1 Mar. 1971, pp. 92–112.

2 Interview with HSA Secretary and letter in *The Daily Telegraph*, 12 Dec. 1978.

Indirect non-political tactics concentrate on using the media to generate publicity for the cause. Holding meetings, writing letters to the press, and exposing the behaviour of the opposition all fall into this category. Other targets may receive attention because they can help to improve the legitimacy of the pressure group concerned and thus help to improve access. These targets include public opinion, because this can influence decision-makers, and the legal process, either because activity may help to interpret or change the law or, more simply, may be a way via court cases of generating publicity. Groups involved in the hunting issue spend a significant amount of energy squabbling among themselves to the extent that other groups, even friendly ones, become targets. The media are frequently used as channels for these interactions.

The media was a major focus of anti-hunting group activity in the 1930s. This was partly to rally the faithful and solicit funds, and partly to give the cause some publicity so that impending anti-hunting legislation would be influenced one way or the other. The media provided a direct route to public opinion and an indirect route to decision-makers. The groups involved realised that their shots would be widely scattered but this had the benefit, particularly for the LACS, of informing important but as yet unidentified people that the LACS was potentially a force to be reckoned with. It was only possible for the LACS and the BFSS to seek access to the most appropriate targets when the targets had been identified. Until then the indirect approach through the media was the sensible if not the ideal route.

As the groups developed the targets gradually changed, although the anti-hunting community has never forsaken its taste for publicity. The NSACS has tried to enhance its image as an educational organisation by printing booklets and pamphlets. Indeed the NSACS has worked on the assumption that a well written and well researched article was an end in itself. In its belief that the media was a target rather than a channel to other targets the NSACS has avoided activities which generate publicity and thereby provide access to potentially significant targets.

The HSA has concentrated on sabotage, its targets being the hunting community itself, but has welcomed the publicity which these activities produced. It has felt that demonstrations and even violence, whether inflicted on members or by them, generates publicity which will on balance harm the hunting community more than it hurts them. They eschew indirect non-political action such as letter writing and courting the media, which is the stock-in-trade of the NSACS.

The BFSS has, in recent years, treated the media with caution. It can no longer rely on favourable reporting of its activities and so its PROs look for ways of presenting its case to opinion leaders and decision-makers as well as to the general public. The BFSS has, for example, persuaded reluctant coursers to allow those parts of the media which seemed sympathetic to make films of coursing events. In February 1968, Lord Sefton, owner of the land on which the Waterloo Cup was held, was persuaded by Marcus Kimball and the BFSS to allow Fyffe Robertson of the BBC to film a coursing event. The resulting film was generally sympathetic to coursing and undoubtedly provided useful visual evidence where only conjecture and bias had existed before.[1]

The LACS has been virtually alone in deciding to further its cause by using the law. It has given free legal assistance to farmers and property holders who wished to sue hunts for trespass and damage and has regularly prosecuted hunts for trespassing on its Exmoor sanctuaries. This is done partly to annoy hunts but also to create publicity for the League.

The law has frequently been used against the HSA but it accepts the price which this involves in the belief that a legal case produces valuable publicity. In this it has carried on the radical tradition of the LACS. However, the case of Mrs Waters who was imprisoned under the *Justices of the Peace Act 1361* and the revisions to the *Criminal Trespass Act* in 1977 has curtailed the activities of HSA members who, although they may wish to annoy and obstruct hunting people, do not want to be imprisoned.[2] These developments have also fostered the belief among HSA members that local police and magistrates are either deferential to or of the same class as leaders of the hunting community so that when a confrontation occurs on the hunting field the authorities will, for class reasons, side with the hunting community.

While individual hunts may prosecute saboteurs or may fail to stop their supporters taking the law into their own hands, the BFSS has rarely used the law as a weapon because publicity, particularly about violent events, is felt to be counter-productive. However, it has encouraged hunts to prosecute saboteurs who inflict damage on hunt property in the belief that damage to property, for whatever reason, is viewed with distaste by the bulk of the British population.

Other pressure groups have been important subsidiary targets of non-political pressure group activity. This has sometimes been via the media, at other times surprisingly direct. It is natural for groups to attempt to undermine or discredit their opponents – and indeed the BFSS was set up explicitly to do that. The nature of this adversary-style of group interaction has ranged from HSA activists destroying hunt property and BFSS files, to BFSS hunt heavies horse-whipping saboteurs and damaging their vehicles. It has also involved the BFSS working to keep

1 It was shown to the House of Lords Select Committee in 1976 with the desired (for the BFSS) effect.

2 For details see section on the HSA in Chapter 5 below.

the RSPCA pro-hunting, and arranging for a supporter to work for the LACS as a 'spy'.[1]

These activities are part of the normal currency of cause group interaction; less usual has been the tireless capacity of the anti-hunting groups to indulge in fratricidal strife. There has, of course, been co-operation between groups, mainly with joint publicity campaigns and petitions, but rarely has co-operation extended over a long period. All the main anti-hunting groups were established because of rows with their 'parents' and independence has always been highly valued. Until the establishment of GECCAP no joint endeavours were ever tried and indeed, in 1978, the NSACS refused to meet with the HSA and LACS to discuss joint activities. Earlier they had removed HSA members from their Society and continue (in 1982) to exclude them. This strife, caused by personality clashes, disagreements over tactics and a sense that little progress was being made, inevitably produced strains within the anti-hunting groups. The NSACS and LACS had a series of internal upheavals and even the HSA suffered dissension within its ranks. However, since there was no oligarchic leadership against which to revolt those within the HSA who were most upset by continuing failure set up the Animal Activists and the Animal Liberation Front. The strain was not within the HSA but between individual activists and society. Nevertheless, this infighting served to reduce the legitimacy of the anti-hunting movement and made it easier for its opponents to label its supporters as trouble-makers. While the publicity might have increased membership of the fringe organisations it did nothing to improve the quality of access to decision-makers.

Political tactics and the importance of access to targets

The main political activities include lobbying individual MPs and civil servants, presenting deputations and hiring political agents as well as attempting to influence the political process by drafting legislation, or appearing before parliamentary Committees of Inquiry. Both sides have at one time or another used all of these tactics with various degrees of short term success.[2] Their significance has increased as hunting has become more of a political and less of a cultural issue.

The main political targets are parliament and the government. Activity against such targets is directed towards the legislative and administrative processes and structures as well as individual parliamentarians, civil servants and members of the government. Group leaders

1 *Labour Weekly*, 19 Jan. 1979, p. 5.

2 See Part IV for details.

'act on the basis of a "target structure", i.e. an appreciation of the most suitable part of the political system on which to exert influence or pressure'.[1] Pressure group leaders need to identify the right time to exert the appropriate pressure on the most significant target. However, this predicates access, not results.

In its early years the BFSS was content to counteract the activities of the opposition by supplying the media with alternative sources of information. But it was apparent as the legislative threats became more real that this was inadequate. Direct political tactics were tried during the 1948–9 period but success only brought complacency. Not until it latched on the conservation issue in the 1960s and combined this with a series of increasingly sophisticated ploys against anti-coursing legislation did the organisation change from an essentially defensive one to one which had an independent existence. Until the 1960s it depended on the anti-hunting lobby for its *raison d'être*, but in that decade it gradually became the spokesman group for field sportsmen and conservationists. It also became tactically more sophisticated; it put the expertise of its members to good use on the working parties studying Avian and Mammalian predators and it promoted a number of bills, among them the *Deer Bill*, 1963, which had the approval of conservationists. Through its friends in the BHS the BFSS even had a link with GECCAP. Its philosophy was that if access to civil servants and MPs was generated on non-hunting issues, the same people would be more sympathetic to the BFSS when the hunting issue was raised. Both the BFSS and the RSPCA were able to establish their credentials on a range of subjects. This was not a ploy which could be used by the HSA, the LACS or the NSACS.

This policy involved an element of luck for most civil servants have to respond to a variety of pressures and seek out information from a range of sources but manifestly if, as in the 1950s and 1960s, a time of relatively neutral governments, pro-hunting civil servants were befriended by leading members of the pro-hunting community, the task of the anti-hunting movement was made more difficult. The evidence suggests that disapproval by pro-hunting Home Office officials of the leadership and tactics of the LACS, combined with their friendship with the leadership of the BFSS, did have the effect of delaying Labour government action against coursing until 1970. The influence was not strong but was sufficient to delay the adoption by the Labour party and Labour government of a policy against coursing. Since the governments changed the successful delay in the short period before the 1970 election made the delay effective for the following period of Conservative government.

1 G.K. Roberts, *Political Parties and Pressure Groups in Britain*, Weidenfeld & Nicolson, London, 1970, p. 96.

Since the 1960s, the BFSS, in contrast to most of the anti-hunting groups, has been active on the political front. It has taken pains to ensure that all friendly MPs are kept briefed on new developments and has carefully assembled a team of MPs and Lords to speak or lobby on its behalf. This has paid off handsomely; Private Members' bills have been talked out in the Commons and the BFSS's long-standing relationship with Lord Denham and Lord Diplock contributed significantly to the demise of the Lords' Anti-Coursing Bill in 1976.

The LACS has intermittently engaged in political activities of both kinds. It has lobbied MPs and civil servants, and collected petitions. It has also appeared before parliamentary Committees and supplied MPs with questions to ask in parliament. These political activities increased when Lord Houghton became Chairman and are now thought by the Society to be a key to future success. Many of its political tactics, such as the decision, as a Society, to support and give money to the Labour party in the 1979 election,[1] were a product of the association with Lord Houghton. Whether this concentration on political initiatives can be sustained during a period of Conservative government is questionable, for there are many members who prefer the excitement of continuous publicity which non-political activities such as demonstrations against hunts, actions for trespass in sanctuaries and internal squabbles produce.

When legislative success seemed a possibility the LACS worked most energetically to achieve access to parliament and the executive. Unlike the BFSS which used its friends in parliament to do its lobbying for it, the LACS sought access on a broad and impersonal front. MPs were given dinners by the LACS and Eric Heffer was made a Vice-President. However, it was not until the 1970s that any MPs were encouraged to join the Committee and take an active and creative part in planning strategy. Although the League wished to generate all-party support in parliament almost all of its support came from Labour MPs. This was explicitly recognised by Lord Houghton who was quite willing to use his party political connections to advance the LACS's cause when he became its Chairman in 1977.

The LACS rarely attempted to gain access to the civil service. In its early years it considered that its goals were unlikely to be treated sympathetically and concentrated on influencing the administration indirectly by using the media to generate support for its cause. In the 1960s, when the League was closely involved with legislation, both Rowley and Hemingway felt that they were being snubbed by the civil service and this further reduced their desire to gain access to White-

1 Pre-election circular to members, Apr. 1979.

hall.[1] As the League grew more confident that public opinion was firmly on its side the value of treating the civil service as a target was reduced. The civil service view was inevitably affected by external changes in political and public opinion which, of course, the LACS and the NSACS could claim to have influenced by their publicity drives and educational programmes. Therefore the LACS used public opinion to influence politicians and tended to by-pass civil servants.

The League, chiefly because of the initiative shown by Houghton, has also taken the lead in treating political parties and trade unions as targets. Under the GECCAP umbrella, but led by an LACS Committee member, it dispensed information at the three major party conferences in 1978, and was instrumental in getting a statement, however vague, from the Liberal party. Houghton's connections with trade unionists (he was on the General Council of the TUC from 1952–60) enabled him to extract, in the year before the 1979 election, an anti-hunting commitment from a number of friendly trade unionists. This was nevertheless of limited importance; what mattered more was the decision by the Labour party to make a firm and continuing policy commitment against hunting and coursing and to include it in the 1979 election manifesto. This policy change was carried through by friends of the LACS such as Heffer, J.B. Boddy (of the National Union of Agricultural Workers) and sympathetic MPs and unionists on the relevant Labour party Sub-Committee. The League formally contributed to this important development by providing evidence to the researcher who prepared the discussion document on hunting and animal welfare.

Other members of the anti-hunting community, particularly those belonging to the HSA, have worked through their connections with either the LACS or the RSPCA. However, the NSACS, in keeping with its officially non-political stance, has kept out of the debate. Since the question is now an undeniably political one this has both rendered the NSACS even more irrelevant and has had the effect of making the LACS, which has accepted the political nature of the battle, the key anti-hunting organisation.

Access to the targets is not continuous; the major targets change and are not always approached directly. The LACS decided in its early years to seek access to decision-makers indirectly by creating publicity unfavourable to hunting. It felt quite reasonably that politicians and civil servants would be of little help. The NSACS has always believed that a sensible educational campaign was in the long run even more profitable for their cause than publicity. Since public opinion has increasingly accepted its case, it is impossible to say that it has been wrong.

The LACS has decreased its reliance on publicity since it was made

1 The civil service is reluctant in general to allow single cause groups access to Ministers, and Rowley in particular was personally disliked by one of the relevant Home Office officials in the early 1970s. From interviews in 1973 and 1978.

aware that public opinion was generally supportive of its views. It attempted to enlist the support of quasi-political agencies such as political parties and trade unions but gradually, from the 1960s, focused its energies more and more on the political process. The same general trend is true of the BFSS; it originally considered the media to be its prime target, indeed it was formed to counteract the League's apparent success in influencing the media but as it has built up legitimacy both with its potential membership and with the decision-makers, it too has responded to a variety of stimuli and sought access at different times to different targets. In general the political system has become the major arena of inter-group activity, since it is now clear to both sides that the battle for public opinion has been decided and that the battle for legislative change is now under way.

Just as targets change so also does the location of effective power to which access is sought. The words 'establishment' and 'decision-makers' are not absolutes, for the institutions which are the locus of power and the people and politicians who exercise it change rapidly over time. In the 19th century the landed aristocracy held power, made decisions, and controlled the legislative and administrative process. The position was much more complex in the 1960s and 1970s. The traditional élite had its power stripped from it but still retained a high degree of social influence which gave it authority on matters such as hunting. The administrative machine was still staffed by people who come from or aspire to the higher levels of the middle class so that only when a Labour party government controls the administration would a major clash of interests be likely between those bastions of the status quo, the civil service and the hunting community, and the socially radical Labour leadership. In times of a Conservative government, there is likely to be a high level of congruence, at least with respect to values, between the government, the administration and the leadership of the BFSS. In such cases the target structure of a pressure group will depend not on which target will grant most access but on which is most likely or competent to respond to the group's overtures. Here the apparent élite congruence of the BFSS is accidental, and the apparent failure of the LACS to apply pressure to the real holders of power is not a failure on their part but a realisation that the quality of access they could generate is likely to be insignificant. Whenever there is a Labour government some people in important and influential places, whether in trade unions, the backbenches – or in Cabinet posts, are likely to be known anti-hunters and can therefore be used by the League and its allies to influence policy making. It has become clear that without government help or an allocation, by the government, of parliamentary time, anti-hunting legislation is doomed. Some early LACS leaders perceived this and hoped to shame Labour governments into supporting them. Only

Houghton and those who have supported him have realised that they need to lobby strenuously for their cause since they do not expect moral arguments to sway many votes unless it is supplemented by pressure.

Most groups realise that the appropriate targets, for the pressure they wish to exercise, change over time. A target's appropriateness depends on the stage of development of the group, the state of public and political opinion and the views of the individuals who hold the power of decision-making. Eckstein's view that there will be a 'concentration of pressure group activity on the administrative departments'[1] is a gross oversimplification. This will tend to occur only when spokesman groups can afford to neglect the media or politicians and this will not happen when they are attempting either to stop or to promote further legislation. Cause groups, at whatever stage of their development, appear to spend relatively little time focusing their attention on the administration; rather they are forced to juggle with a range of changeable factors which will cause them to adjust their tactics and vary their targets in response to their own analysis of the situation. At certain times, particularly when the groups are being established they will concentrate on the media, and use publicity to influence public and political opinion.[1] At other times they will actively lobby parliamentarians in their attempts to encourage or halt a piece of legislation. Parliament is unlikely to respond to direct pressure from a group which, however sophisticated its tactics, has failed to generate public and political interest in the cause which it is promoting. Just as groups take time to develop so does public and political awareness and without a sympathetic political context in which the group can operate, access, however efficiently used, is not enough.

The politicisation of the issue

The last two decades have seen a series of crucial developments in the hunting debate. On the surface the pro-hunting community led by the BFSS has enjoyed a continuous run of tactical victories. Between 1967–77, 16 bills against hunting failed to reach the Statute Books. A number of these failures were directly attributable to the skills of Marcus Kimball and his Conservative pro-hunting colleagues; others were due to the vagaries of the procedures for Private Members' bills in the House of Commons. In the last two decades the BFSS has also succeeded in cementing alliances with important organisations, such as the BHS and the NFU, and has rapidly expanded its income and membership for the battles which it envisages ahead. It has improved its public relations, convinced wavering sporting bodies that they should

1 H. Eckstein, *Pressure Group Politics*, Allen & Unwin, London, 1960, p. 17.

ally themselves with the BFSS and embraced the popular cause of conservation and ecological balance. All in all the BFSS has become a well-known and efficient pressure group with a formidable record of success.

The anti-hunting community has been forced, as a result of its persistent failures, to reorganise its strategy in the 1970s. Following a series of *ad hoc* and essentially unrelated developments, a clearer pattern has emerged of the future problems and possibilities. The first and most vital development has been the growing certainty, reinforced by a series of public opinion polls, that the majority of the population is against hunting. This simple fact undermines a great deal of the rhetoric of the hunting community, who nevertheless continue to assert that they are safeguarding popular sports from petty-minded urban radicals.[1] The knowledge of public opinion's support has enabled the anti-hunting community to behave in a less strident manner and both its new maturity and the results of the polls themselves have had a major impact on the media.

The importance of political action has gradually been accepted by leaders of the anti-hunting movement, even if not all of them understand the constitutional implications. The RSPCA and the LACS were the keenest members of GECCAP, and the HSA, which had no formal connection, nevertheless sent an observer to all of GECCAP's 1978 Committee meetings. Even the NSACS offered funds to GECCAP, although it refused to allow this money to be used in direct support of any party or candidate.

The establishment of GECCAP in 1978 gave the anti-hunting movement a cohesion and sense of purpose which it had hitherto lacked and altered the balance of power in the hunting debate. It combined the resources and contacts of its constituent members who between them claimed a membership of over one million people. These resources gave it a legitimacy new to the anti-hunting community and enabled its politically acute leadership to achieve access when and where it sought it.

Within the present day civil service neutral members have replaced the former pro-hunting ones. The official civil service view now more closely parallels that of the Labour party, both organisations having been through similar processes of change in both membership and norms. Because of this, tension between the civil service and consecutive Labour governments has been avoided. However, if a future Conservative Minister attempted to persuade Home Office civil servants to produce arguments and data favourable to hunting, some strain would inevitably manifest itself, for the civil service machinery, after full deliberation, has deemed the evidence against all forms of hunting, with

1 *Baily's*, 1978–9, editorial, p. xxiii.

the partial exception of fox hunting, to be powerful enough for it to change its collective view.

The main significance of this shift, both personal and departmental, within the Home Office is that it is a reflection of other shifts of opinion. The civil service has noted that the RSPCA, the Labour party, the churches and the general public have become restive about the continuation of coursing and hunting. To these forces can be added those of the vegetarians and anti-speciesists, who have collectively helped to move the centre of accepted values and behaviour away from support for the hunting community and towards support for the opponents of field sports.

The issue is thus a political one, involving politicians, parliaments and governments. Political partiality is inevitable. A balanced detachment by political parties would if it existed probably cause anarchy since if pressure group strength and the degrees of access gained were to decide the issues there would be no constraint on group behaviour. On this question it cannot be decided objectively whether the hunting community consists of cruel countrymen opposed by right-thinking townspeople, or whether the anti-hunters are socialist conspirators attempting to destroy a basic freedom against the wishes of the democratic egalitarian hunting community. Only involved parliaments and governments can decide between the two sides. One side maintains that 'hunting should be a matter for private conscience, not state-imposed prejudice inspired by extremists who in many cases seem to be more motivated by political opportunism than a genuine concern for the welfare of animals involved in field sports'.[1] On the other side are many who believe that 'the human race should act as a trustee for the rest of the natural world and not its master'[2] and that since animal abuse and exploitation are reaching such high proportions the subject should not remain a private matter.

1 *Horse and Hound*, 27 Apr. 1979, p. 3.

2 *Liberal Party Resolution*, Nov. 1978. It reflects GECCAP's wording.

13 Conclusions

This book has investigated three major areas: (a) the social history of hunting, (b) the development and activities of the pro- and anti-hunting pressure groups and, (c) the public and political arenas in which the debate has taken place. So far, few conclusions have been drawn, since the primary purpose has been to uncover, examine and explain the processes which have occurred. However, it becomes necessary at the end of such a study to ask and comment on a number of questions, some concerning hunting, some pressure groups and some the political process. Six major questions will be discussed.

1. Can hunting, an activity deeply embedded into the upper class social fabric for a thousand years, survive the major social and political changes which have taken place in Britain during the 20th century? Is the social climate sufficiently antagonistic to hunting to generate the political will to abolish it?

The evidence in Chapters 1 to 3 shows clearly that for over a thousand years hunting has been central to the leisure pursuits of the ruling élite in British society. Until the 19th century hunting men protected their rights and privileges with the law, thereby making hunting by the mass of the population a crime punishable, in some circumstances, by death.

Certain social changes in the 19th and 20th centuries placed hunting in jeopardy. The rise of an egalitarian spirit fostered by utilitarianism and socialism produced governments explicitly concerned to improve the lot of the poor. A style of government gradually arose which took for granted its right to act in an increasing number of social spheres. The two world wars legitimised government interference in areas where it had previously been reluctant to tread, and, by the 1970s, legislation had appeared which controlled private as well as public morality.

In the 19th century Britain changed from being a rural to an urban society in which hunting became an anomaly. Given the resentments of earlier centuries and the class nature of the sport it became almost inevitable that the newly enfranchised urban majority would call for the abolition of those sports and activities which had in earlier years become a symbol of class oppression. There were two reasons why this did not happen immediately: first, the urban working class was not antagonised by the hunting community which inevitably remained rural and distant from urban existence; secondly, hunting became less élitist and modified itself as a sport sufficiently to defuse much of the resentment. In the late 19th and 20th centuries hunting became accessible to middle class professionals, farmers and foot supporters whose enthusiasm for the sport was encouraged rather than resented.

Hunting did, therefore, respond to changed conditions to a certain extent although it could not reorganise itself into an entirely democratic activity. Its natural context could only be the rural environment in which it operated, and the obvious conclusion to be drawn from the social and economic changes of the 19th and 20th centuries, the rise of the Labour party, and the antagonism to hunting of the majority of the population, is that hunting would quickly be abolished or would suffer a period of major retrenchment. This has been particularly likely in the 1900s, in the 1930s and in the 1960s when the anti-hunting movement has had allies in government. However, neither the public at large nor the anti-hunting movement in general have appreciated the extent to which pressure-group activity and the problems of gaining access to the decision-making process could delay the realisation of a 'popular' policy.

While it is recognised that in the early 1980s a clear majority of people are on the side of the anti-hunting community, it is doubtful whether pressure groups as political actors have had much direct influence on this process although their publicity-seeking activities have highlighted developments and illuminated the process whereby the feelings of the mass became clear. Pressure groups can claim to have accelerated the process of developing public opinion about hunting and they have provided a forum wherein the issue was debated. Pressure groups may have divined the state of political culture by conducting opinion polls or they may have decelerated the implementation of popular policies either by calling on powerful friends to help them or by manipulating the political process themselves; but they can neither make opinions nor force the passage of legislation because they are sub-groups in society seeking to promote a cause. They are not, in Finer's words,'themselves prepared to undertake the direct government of the country',[1] nor do they control the mechanisms which most influence the formation of opinion.

It therefore follows that legislation against hunting, and indeed on other issues where animals are involved, will come about primarily as a result of the interaction between the political process and the political culture and to a lesser extent as a direct result of pressure group activity.

It should also follow that the BFSS, now that it is working against popular opinion,will fail in its attempts to preserve hunting. However, it remains a possibility that the pendulum of opinion may swing back in its favour either because its opponents disgrace themselves in the public eye or because changes occur in other areas of the political culture which aid its cause.

Yet the political culture of the mid 20th century has given priority to the cluster of values surrounding environmental questions and there will inevitably, therefore, be clashes of opinion about the treatment of animals, about class, and about the maintenance of individual freedoms, and there will be clashes with respect to questions concerning sport, leisure and the environment. The ensuing debate can delay decision-making but not alter the fact that hunting is likely to remain under attack.

The response of the government, which is what counts in the long run, will depend on a number of factors. Governments sometimes form a policy incorporating their collective views for which they attempt to mobilise consent; at other times they respond to the pressures which are applied to them from the outside; or they may act because they feel they will gain popular support by taking a firm stand. It is possible that hunting will be abolished in the future not because major shifts have occurred in social attitudes or political behaviour but because all the relevant factors appear to be in alignment and because it is felt by parliament that the time for hunting to end has come.

The feeling that the time is ripe in the last quarter of the 20th century for the concluding round of the hunting debate is not entirely fanciful. Three separate forces are at work which point to this conclusion.

Firstly, an historical view shows that a 'movement' needs time to reach maturity; just as the trade unions took half a century to develop

1 *Anonymous Empire*, p. 3.

individually before combining to form the TUC in 1868 and took almost another half century before they managed to exercise much influence on the political process so the anti-hunting movement took 50 years to develop from the establishment of the LACS to the integration of anti-hunting groups into GECCAP in 1978. The tendency or groundswell of opinion was there but an organisation was not. It had to identify and integrate its supporters before it could seriously embark on political activity.[1]

Secondly, the political culture has not been ready to accept the ideas of the anti-hunting movement until the twentieth century. Concerned humanitarian members of society have felt that the conditions under which people lived and worked should be given priority. It has been inevitable that social welfare legislation should take precedence over animal welfare legislation, even though, to some extent, both movements spring from the same impulse, as Isaac Foot and Lord Soper among others have suggested.

Thirdly, the political system has not been able to cope with legislation of this kind until the mid 20th century. The squirearchy had first to lose its hold over parliament; then parliament and the public had to accept the right of governments to interfere in most areas of life. Both of these developments took place in the first half of the 20th century.

The recent politicisation of the hunting issue, the changes in Labour party policy, the emergence of GECCAP, and the increasing legitimacy of the anti-hunting cause, all combine to suggest that the world is falling in around the hunting community; it has lost the support of public opinion, and the Labour and Liberal parties are wholly or partially committed to ending its sports. Its tactical alliances, parliamentary manoeuvrings and carefully built-up relationships with civil servants and media people have served a valuable purpose, but *ceteris paribus* cannot prevail in the long run against the determination of one of the two major parties to put into effect a policy which is supported by two-thirds of the population.

This determination, which the Labour party had in the 1979–82 period may not survive a lengthy period in opposition or indeed a return to government since other factors, rising unemployment, the nuclear debate or a major world crisis, may reduce its significance and push the hunting question and even the ecology movement into the background. The pendulum may swing away from this kind of social concern, but it is nevertheless unlikely that it will swing away for ever.

2. The second question asks: who will actually initiate legislation against hunting and coursing? And if the evidence suggests that the

1 The same process over a similar time period occurred before laws affecting divorce and abortion were passed.

answer is pressure groups rather than governments, can the activities of these organisations which are by definition biased and partial in their aims be compatible with the 'public interest'?

The first part of the question is easy to answer. In the period leading up to 1970 all bills pertaining to hunting and coursing were presented to parliament by MPs who were closely involved with the anti-hunting movement. Governments were perfectly content with this arrangement because few issues concerning animals had been of a party political nature and no government had ever considered taking the lead on animal welfare matters. However, this changed with respect to coursing in 1970. Harold Wilson, believing that coursing had survived against the wishes of the majority, and conscious of potential votes for the Labour party gave instructions for a government bill to be presented for its abolition. Subsequently the Labour party, when in government, adopted an official stance against hunting and coursing because the repeated failure of Private Members' bills convinced the Labour party leadership that animal welfare issues could no longer be left to the individual.

This move was not dictated by moral considerations nor did the Labour party succumb reluctantly to the power of the anti-hunting forces. The policy was based on the realisation that public opinion concurred with the personal taste of most Cabinet Ministers.

Since governments both control access and also decide whether or not to give support to Private Members' bills it is unlikely that anti-hunting legislation will prosper during periods of Conservative government. The Conservative leadership will resist such legislation as much from personal taste as from the power of the pro-hunting lobby. What the pro-hunting lobby can do, and M. Kimball regularly did, is to remind Conservative leaders that a 'popular' policy would produce a major backlash from the important leaders of the shires. The BFSS by using its powerful friends in allied organisations is able to remind the Conservative leadership of the benefits to be derived from keeping the status quo.

Despite the significance of this pressure on the Conservative party it is likely that the changes in the political culture will place coursing, in particular, outside the pale. This will be primarily on the grounds of cruelty, although it is also true that coursing has been debased by betting to such an extent that its redeeming features as a sport are hard to find. It is probable, therefore, that a bill to abolish coursing will be passed sometime in the future. If there is a Labour government in power it may adopt a Private Members' bill; if there is a Conservative government it will make no attempt to defend the sport against a majority of MPs despite the pressure which the hunting community will undoubtedly bring to bear.

Whether coursing continues or is abolished the loss or gain will not be great; only a few hares would benefit from its abolition. Whether this gain would offset the ire of the coursing community and the economic losses of trainers and bookmakers is unanswerable. Nevertheless, there are philosophers who are prepared to claim that what is good for the hare is good for humanity on the grounds that, since coursing is cruel and cruelty is immoral, suppressing the sport makes a positive contribution to morality.[1] Politicians prefer arguments which dwell more on immediate social and economic benefits rather than on moral niceties of this kind. Any action politicians take while inevitably favouring one side or the other will be determined by their reading of the public mood and the extent to which they might derive some political advantage. They will be, in this case, responding to, but not controlled by, pressure groups.[2]

Pressure group studies inevitably raise the question: is the public interest being served by the activities of these groups?[3] The concept of public interest has been much debated by social scientists who seem unable to decide whether the notion concerns 'the conflict and accommodation of interests'[4] or whether it is 'an ethical standard for evaluating specific public policies and a goal which the political order should pursue'.[5] It can, in practice, be both a normative standard and a tool for analysing group strategies.

The first problem is to decide whose interests should be paramount for, in the hunting issue, there are a variety of publics whose interests are dear to them. The anti-hunters claim to speak both for animals and for human moral values. The pro-hunters claim to be conservationist and to be fighting for democracy and the freedom of choice. Since the interaction of their two 'publics' is a zero-sum game in which one side must lose, it is inevitable that the interests of the general public cannot be served. Power rests with governments who, using public interest criteria, must decide. But since the phrase 'public interest' has no *a priori* content governments will interpret it in terms of the prevailing political culture which is, in its turn, a dynamic concept. Public interest, along with the groups, individuals and governments with which it interacts, changes over time.

1 See Singer, *Animal Liberation, passim.*

2 For a discussion on the extent to which pressure groups earn their success and control of their destinies, see B. Pym, 'The Making of a Successful Pressure Group', *British Journal of Sociology*, Dec. 1973, p. 452. See also J.P. Nettl 'Consensus or Elite Domination; the Case of Business', *Political Studies*, 1965, pp. 22–44.

3 For a major survey of writings on the public interest see *Nomos V: The Public Interest*, (ed.) C. Friedrick, Atherton Press, New York 1962, and R.E. Flathman, *The Public Interest*, John Wiley, New York 1966.

4 C.E. Cochran, 'Political Science and the Public Interest', *The Journal of Politics*, 1974, p. 331.

5 Ibid., p. 330.

Since a consensus approach to this issue is not possible, governments are forced to ask: which is the larger good? It is important to the British political culture that the public interest is seen to be served for, although '[no one agrees] on what precisely constitutes the public interest, all agree it exists, must be respected and feel a sense of outrage when it is not'.[1] In this particular case the interpretation of the public interest depends on the judgement of parliaments and governments. They have to balance the opposing forces and hope to appease both sets of protagonists without offending the public at large. Given a non-economic issue of this complexity, they will prefer to follow rather than to lead.

3. To what extent is access a product of legitimacy and how important are both access and legitimacy to the eventual success of a pressure group?

While access is unquestionably a vital ingredient, its significance depends on both the state of political opinion and the nature of the targets to which access is sought. Access is improved by legitimacy, itself a function of status and congruence. Structural congruence, that is an organisational structure which mirrors the official bureaucracies with which they interact, has not been developed by the pressure groups in this issue primarily because the groups involved, with the partial exception of the BFSS, seek relatively little access to the administration. Social congruence enhances status and has proved its value to pressure groups involved with hunting. This is not so much a product of class conflict but rather a result of having support from people with an appropriate background; the leadership of the LACS has, for example, sought support from journalists to keep it before the public eye and from churchmen to give it righteousness, while the BFSS has used the 1922 Committee to influence the Conservative party leadership.

The extent to which pressure groups involved in the hunting issue can be described as successful is hard to assess. The BFSS has managed to stop a stream of anti-hunting and anti-coursing legislation, and has managed to make itself acceptable to many conservationists; the LACS has, by its land purchases, blighted the sport of several key West Country hunts and its activities have undoubtedly had some effect on public opinion and the views of leading members of the Labour party. In general, however, groups which seek major changes affecting social values are likely to be less effective, and therefore deemed less successful, than those which seek only marginal changes or wish to maintain the status quo. Groups which reflect or learn to use the existing structures and patterns of power will find their work easier than those who do not.

1 S.E. Finer, 'Interest Groups and the Political Process in Great Britain' in H. Ehrmann, *Interest Groups on Four Continents*, University of Pittsburg Press, 1958, p. 143.

The major task of the LACS and its allies has been to engineer changes in the political culture, and in order to do this they concentrated their early attentions with some success on public opinion and on the media. However, just as the media can only inform about but not dictate events so pressure groups can only tap sentiments which already exist, not create them.

In the more political arenas, particularly in relation to civil servants, political parties and parliament, the BFSS, with the task of preserving the status quo, was undoubtedly more effective than its opponents until the 1970s. However, once it was apparent that it had lost the sympathy of public opinion its position became less secure. Equally, the value of its close relationship with the Conservative party was diminished in the 1970s as the anti-hunting movement successfully colonised the Labour party, giving both sides nearly equal access to parliament and the legislative process.

Finer predicted parliamentary success for a pressure group which, when lobbying, could 'squeeze the Minister between the official opposition and his own backbenchers', that is engineer a backbench revolt.[1] However, this tactic is only relevant when the front bench is taking a lead. In the hunting issue pressure groups have been articulating demands for 50 years, and parliament has been the cockpit for frequent debates. The front bench has rarely played a significant role. Nevertheless, as the 1948–9 and subsequent debates have clearly shown, without front bench or cross bench support hunting legislation is doomed. The BFSS has managed to ensure that the Conservative front bench has remained relatively pro-hunting and that the Labour front bench has avoided, until the mid 1970s, giving support to calls for parliamentary time from its own backbenchers. However, the increasing sophistication of the anti-hunting side and the change in official Labour party attitudes means that in the 1980s hunting and its supporters will be much more on the defensive.

The disparities in both access and results enjoyed by the pro- and anti-hunting groups have made it obvious that the anti-hunting groups, despite the support of public opinion, have had a much harder task than their opponents. The lack of legitimacy of the anti-hunting pressure groups restricted access and therefore initially worked to their disadvantage. It was difficult for them to develop legitimacy and at the same time increase membership by publicity-seeking activities. Only when it was clear that public opinion supported its cause did the legitimacy of the LACS, the leading anti-hunting group, increase significantly. It was only then able to focus on political targets at the expense of public ones. Its apparent political naïvety can be justified on the grounds that it needed a firm basis of support on which to build.

1 Finer, *Anonymous Empire*, p. 75.

The pro-hunting community began with more social acceptability and with the support of the politically powerful rural establishment and therefore they found it easy to get access to powerful élite-dominated targets.

Developing into an effective group requires more than legitimacy. Groups have to overcome a series of structural handicaps before they are adequately prepared for the battles ahead. They need to acquire sufficient income and membership to operate independently and they need a leadership which has clear goals and is willing to take initiatives. Not all groups are capable of changing to meet new situations and,when groups are competing with each other, some will not survive the competition. With respect to an issue such as hunting, a strong group on one side tends to create its own opposition. An action produces a reaction so that influence never operates in a vacuum. The LACS was soon countered by the BFSS, and within the RSPCA the work of the pro-hunting members produced a backlash in the form of the Reform Group.

It is sometimes useful to regard pressure groups as a process rather than an entity. Some groups like the HSA develop and mature, others such as the NSACS, fossilise; some are stable and unified for a decade and then succumb, like the RSPCA, to an internal upheaval. Others, the best example being the LACS, prosper when out of tune with society and find it hard to alter its style and tactics when society is in accord with it. 'Protective' groups like the BFSS find it hard, particularly when achieving their short-term aims, to avoid becoming smug and complacent thus jeopardising their long-term goals. In learning to cope with governments, the media and each other, pressure groups' reactions have depended as much on their own stage of development as on the state of public or parliamentary opinion. Judgements about their success have to take into account their state of internal development and the coincidence of that with changes in public or parliamentary opinion, rather than dealing with their short-term tactical abilities in isolation.

4. The fourth question follows the previous one: will cause groups with their volatile memberships be able to cope with the strain of delay or with failure to achieve their aims?

If a pressure group has the general support of public opinion its goals will appear legitimate and the right to pursue these goals will be recognised by decision-makers, the media and the group's membership. There will be no incentive, therefore, to use anti-social methods.

However, if a group is unsure whether its goals are legitimate in the eyes of public opinion or the decision-makers, it will more readily use questionable tactics. These tactics will attract unfavourable publicity which will in turn decrease the group's legitimacy, alienate public opinion, and frustrate its members. Groups must be sensitive to the impact they make on their members and on the people they are trying to influence, and be ready to change their approach if they have caused offence.

The history of the RSPCA, LACS and BFSS suggests that in all these cases the iron law of oligarchy prevails so that the leadership tends both to control and to ignore its membership. This means that only internal violence will effect changes, although the violence itself will do nothing to remove the oligarchic structure. The changes in the LACS and RSPCA in the 1970s were achieved by reference to almost forgotten rules, but whether the new leaderships, particularly of the RSPCA, will continue to remember the democratic processes which enabled them to overthrow the old guard is a matter for conjecture.

If groups, particularly relatively small cause groups led by tightly-knit cabals, are incapable of devising structures or developing patterns of behaviour which enable them to remain open and flexible then they are likely to be vulnerable to outside manipulation. However, in practice plots to undermine the enemy have been less prevalent than power struggles between groups on the same side. The LACS publicised the shortcomings of the RSPCA; the NSACS removed members who also belonged to the HSA; two members of the RSPCA Council became involved in a £20,000 libel case with each other in the late 1960s; and Rowley and Course of the LACS spent more time fighting than working together. The BFSS was delighted to be able to draw attention to this internecine warfare but it refrained from interfering. Such interference might be thought unfair by those whom the BFSS wanted to impress. Rather than lose legitimacy by this process the BFSS concentrated less on attacking its enemies and more on securing a firm hold over the ground where the future major battles would be fought. This relative willingness to adapt and the lack, until the 1970s, of serious threats to its position discouraged individual members from indulging in anomic behaviour and enabled the BFSS to become an effective aggregator and articulator of pro-hunting opinion.

The position of its opponents was considerably more difficult. Being culturally out-of-step for the first 50 years of the 20th century and a long way from their goals since then has created a great deal of strain both within anti-hunting organisations and between members of the organisations and society. Indeed this unenviable position has produced the popular but essentially false idea that many of the activists are Marxists and revolutionaries. The Reform Group of the RSPCA and the anti-Rowley group within the LACS have both been labelled in this way not because of any political statements but because of their passionate involvement in and continued frustration with the progress of the anti-hunting movement. While the enthusiasm of many was informed by a socialist view of the world it is clear that there is no necessary connection between social radicalism and a political commitment to revolution.

As long as the social system can cope with change most of the radicals will attempt to operate the system. The behaviour of Ryder, Seager and Bryant after the success of the Reform Group of the RSPCA bears this out and the so-called 'revolutionaries' within the LACS have been among Houghton's most ardent supporters. Even the ALF were quiet during the late 1970s when it seemed likely that the Labour party was committed to take action on behalf of animals. There is no guarantee that this will be a permanent state, however, for the cleavage between the values of the strongly anti- and the strongly pro-hunting communities is such that competitive colonising of political parties could result in outbursts of anti-social behaviour from both sides. Anti-hunters could become violent when Conservative governments or Conservative groups in the Lords thwart anti-hunting bills and less likely but not impossible is the prospect of violence from hunt heavies when anti-hunting legislation looks like succeeding.

Britain is essentially a semi-pluralist state in which pressure groups are accepted as a necessary but not altogether praiseworthy part of the system.[1] In certain sectors of society a type of corporatism prevails where major groups such as the NFU negotiate with the government and produce a collective view without consulting the mass of opinion.[2] This enclosed functional representation is not appropriate when 'causes' are being disputed, for British political culture does not generally attempt to impose a collectivist framework where social issues are concerned. There is, in practice, a modified pluralism at work in 20th century Britain which provides a context for the hunting debate. It legitimises pressure group activities and expects groups to be granted access to their chosen targets while putting their respective cases to a relatively neutral state. However, the state is only neutral in this case because the issue has not been judged particularly significant. If the issue gained in significance, perhaps because of its relationship to ecological and conservationist questions, violence could become a possibility and state action a necessity.

5. In the literature on pressure groups the role of the individual is minimised. However, with respect to the hunting issue it would appear that the individual's role is highly significant.

Bentley and Truman tended to play down the effect of the individual despite Truman's assertion: 'We do not, in fact, find individuals otherwise than in groups' and ' "The individual" and "the group" are at most

1 See S.H. Beer, *Modern British Politics*, Faber, London 1968, *passim*, and Wootton, *Pressure Groups in Britain*, ch. 3 and pp. 99–111.

2 Self & Storing, *The State and the Farmer, passim*.
See also A. Cawson, 'Pluralism, Corporatism and the Role of the State', *Government and Opposition*, Spring 1978, pp. 178–98.

convenient ways of classifying behaviour, two ways of approaching the same phenomena'.[1] Truman's approach dispenses with individuals and concentrates on their collective acts in groups; the locus of power is within groups and politics to Truman concerns the interaction of groups with the political process. Even Millett writing on 'the role of a lone spokesman of an organised interest group'[2] in parliament focuses on the clash of roles and concludes that the key to success lies in group cohesion and the support of public opinion.[3] In Pym's study of cause groups the individual is secondary to the organisation. Pym explicitly reifies the group at the expense of the individual since 'what is done by group members is thought by them to be done in the name of the "whole group"'.[4] She accepts that individual MPs were of significance but that for 'these men the parliamentary role was the primary identification and that it is therefore misleading to call their efforts, efforts in the name of the group'.[5] However, in the hunting issue at least one MP, Kimball, accepts that his primary identification is with the hunting cause, and was prepared to risk his position within the parliamentary Conservative party in order to protect hunting.

This study shows that individualism survives in spite of the nature of pressure groups and in spite of the government's desire to negotiate with groups rather than with individuals. Groups concerned with the hunting issue reflect the character and behaviour of individuals rather than the other way around. The LACS was strident in the 1950s and 1960s because of the influence of its Chairmen, Hemingway and Rowley; the HSA remained non-bureaucratic and tolerant of a wide range of views because that reflected the character of David Whetton, the Secretary, and some of his colleagues; the BFSS has always reflected the gentlemanly and traditional values of people such as Fitzwilliam, Morrison and Kimball. The genteel intelligence of the NSACS is exactly that of its leading members. These groups have not moulded their members; the leaders have stamped their personalities on each group.

Individuals make a major difference to the direction that societies take; indeed in difficult times the very survival of certain societies has depended on the determination of individuals. Rev. Broome kept the RSPCA going in the 1830s and but for Mrs Chapman and Mr Sharp the NSACS and LACS respectively would not have survived the Second World War.

1 Truman, *Governmental Process*, p. 48.

2 'The Role of an Interest Group Leader in the House of Commons', *Western Political Quarterly*, 1956, p. 915.

3 Ibid., pp. 925–6.

4 'The making of a successful pressure group', *British Journal of Sociology*, Dec. 1973, p. 450.

5. Ibid., p. 450.

Individuals are also to be found behind sharp changes in tactics. Kimball's chairmanship of the BFSS coincided with the beginning of a new outward looking set of politics, and Houghton's arrival at the LACS led to an immediate concentration on the political process. When Houghton retired, Richard Course had to struggle to keep the LACS from turning away from politics.

It is possible to argue that the group will produce the individual, that if Kimball and Houghton had not existed, someone else would have appeared to play exactly the same part. This is false on two counts; firstly, it is *ex post facto* reasoning – someone did emerge and therefore the reasoning goes, someone was bound to. Secondly, there is no way of knowing whether the 'right' person has emerged. It is the individual who takes the lead not a policy which seeks a standard bearer. Those who believe that the cause will find the man have to answer the questions, where was the LACS's leader in 1948–9, and where is the person to halt the NSACS's 20-year long slide into well-funded oblivion?

Individuals matter at another level – they negotiate with other individuals. Houghton used his knowledge of the Labour leadership to work out which approach was most likely to succeed and which people would be the most influential. As chairman of GECCAP in 1978–9 he arranged for R. Ryder of the RSPCA rather than himself to approach the Chairman of the Conservative party because 'Ryder gets on with Thornycroft'.[1]

The strife within groups, particularly cause groups, is also a product of individual temperaments. The inability of one dedicated but obstinate man to negotiate with another has on countless occasions worked to the disadvantage of the groups. Personality clashes rather than arguments over tactics have been at the root of the majority of intra-group problems.

The keys to group success, legitimacy and access, also depend to some extent on individuals. Legitimacy can be enhanced by having socially acceptable people as group leaders and can be destroyed by 'unacceptable' behaviour. Access is an opportunity not a state of affairs and thus dynamic individuals are needed to take advantage of the opportunity.

These points are particularly relevant to cause groups which tend not to become large bureaucratic aggregations but they also apply to a considerable extent to the workings of two groups which are partially spokesman groups, the RSPCA and BFSS. In both of these organisations the bureaucratic process and the day-to-day operations have (generally) continued to work smoothly; nevertheless the development of new policies and the promotion and protection of the main aims of

1 GECCAP meeting, 1978.

the Society have depended on highly involved individuals not on officialdom or on the mass membership. Ryder, Kimball and Houghton with Course have used the RSPCA, the BFSS and the LACS respectively to support goals in which they had an emotional investment; they as leaders were never mere mouthpieces for their Society's views.

6. The final question is a more general one: why has hunting survived, and given the changes and developments detailed in this book can it continue to do so?

The survival of hunting in modern British society is in many ways a mystery. While hunting as a sport in the 19th century was buttressed by the dominance of the class which most enjoyed it, social change in England since then has shifted the middle ground of respectability, leaving hunting as an obvious target for attack at the edges of social and moral acceptability. Yet there is a sense in which the mystique of the countryside, the claims of tradition and the upper class values of hunting people do provide a genuine case for hunting which is recognised by the political and administration élite who themselves remain surprisingly upper class in origin. The BFSS therefore is able to make statements about political extremism, class consciousness and the foolishness of sentimental women because it feels itself to be comfortably placed in the main stream of British social values. Hunting people and their supporters respect the tough amateurism of hunting and feel that since hunting has not become obsessed with money (like cricket and football) or with betting (like racing and coursing) it has a right to continue unmolested.

The hunting community longs for the apparently simple values of the past and out of this has grown a mythology about the social benefits of hunting every bit as profound as the deeply ingrained mythology of the sport itself. The 'golden age' of foxhunting, when Masters were powerful, horses plentiful, women knew their place and the minority who actively disapproved of hunting could be dismissed as cranks, was in the 19th century. However, the mythology remains, and political opinion has been influenced by it; no legislation seriously affecting hunting has been added to the statute books since 1912 and no attempts to abolish major field sports have ever succeeded.

Part of the credit for this must go to the BFSS and to hunting supporters themselves. The hunting field is more democratic than it was and welcomes new members who pass the test of acceptability on the grounds of land, money or social status. In addition, hunting was and is controlled by Masters of Hounds, who are still recruited from the rural élite, and are sufficiently similar in background and attitudes to their middle-aged and middle-class peers that they do not generally stir up resentments among the non-hunting rural élite, nor among the leaders of opinion in Westminster and Whitehall.

But although field sports in the past may have been able to adjust to or to counteract developments in the social and political environment, it is doubtful whether this process can continue *ad infinitum*. Even if cruelty can be avoided by chasing a drag, and élitism neutralised by supporters following hounds on bicycles while wearing overalls and a cloth cap, whatever 'sport' emerges will not be hunting.

Moreover, the long-term survival of hunting depends to a considerable degree on the membership of the hunting community. Today, not only are the younger farmers who would, in the future, provide the backbone of hunting no longer politically dominant but they are also, as a group, less interested in hunting. Intensive farming methods, greater access to consumer goods and alternative recreational activities which do not rely on a ready supply of horses, all reduce the strength of the historical links between farmers and hunting. Institutional landlords obviously are not concerned to encourage farmers to assist the local hunt, and modern middle-class farmers who are owner-occupiers cannot be forced by hunting squires to allow hunting across their land. If the children of today's farmers are expected to provide the future backbone of the hunting community the evidence suggests that there are insufficient numbers of farmers' sons interested in the sport for them to do so.

The girls (who hunt much more than boys) who wish to continue hunting will either have to marry a farmer or someone who keeps horses or remain single and hence have the freedom to spend their leisure time hunting. In each case the following generation will find that hunting will be a much less 'normal' part of everyday rural life.

Ultimately the future of hunting and coursing depends on a balance of forces. If the moralists gain converts then some field sports will disappear, and if the opponents of speciesism increase their influence other activities which inflict mass cruelty such as factory farming and shooting will come under heavy attack. Coursing is particularly offensive to moralists for while it involves fewer animals and thereby inflicts less cruelty it is considered to be more degrading to the participants. Some people are persuaded against coursing by the argument that it is the most unnecessary of all field sports, for even shooting (although not tame bird shooting) can be defended on the grounds that it helps to control the balance of nature.

It is inevitable that field sports will continue to be attacked and to be extremely vulnerable in the social climate of the 1980s. The first sports to be abolished will be those which lack élite support and a mass following. Coursing lacks both; stag hunting has élite support but no mass following except on Exmoor; beagling, although more widespread, has followers but no significant amount of élite support. Coursing will therefore be abolished first and will be followed by stag hunting rather than beagling because stag hunting has suffered most from the adverse publicity generated by the LACS. Of all field sports stag hunting is also the least necessary for control purposes. Undoubtedly fox hunting will be the last form of hunting to be abolished for it has numbers, tradition and the rural establishment on its side.

When the process of abolishing hunting will begin is impossible to say. Such action undoubtedly depends on a strong Labour or left of centre Alliance government whose period in office is not entirely dominated by violent economic or political crises. In the meantime the pressure groups concerned will continue to be active. The pro-hunting community will claim that they are protecting popular rural sports, accuse their opponents of malicious envy caused by out-moded notions of class hostility, and attempt to show that defending hunting is defending liberty. The anti-hunting community will focus its attention on questions of cruelty, morality and conservation. As long as Lord Houghton or a person with a similar political background is available, the anti-hunting community will continue to work with GECCAP or its successors and try to keep its self-destructive tendencies under control for as long as political success remains reasonably close at hand.

The more hunting becomes a party political issue the more difficult it will be for pressure groups to maintain a high degree of access to all branches of government. A group cannot focus its attention on the administrative departments, because 'political' decisions are not made there. It would be counter-productive for group leaders to show deference to the norms of the political system or to attempt to colonise administrative departments for that would not bring hunting to the attention of the media whose significance increases as that of the administration decreases. Pressure groups must nevertheless expect incremental change, but not merely because this is preferred by civil servants who 'have a horror of "portmanteau" legislation'.[1] Incremental change is probable on the grounds that the opposition will fight each step and therefore sensible anti-hunting groups will begin at the 'thin end of the wedge' as a matter of policy as well as expediency.

While the opponents of hunting establish their priorities society has to assess the claims made by the hunting community that hunting makes a positive contribution to society and that for outsiders to interfere in a minority rural pastime is anti-democratic. There is no simple way of deciding whether the abolition of cruelty or the defence of liberty is more important since neither value can be subjected to a cost-

1 A phrase used by a senior civil servant during an interview in 1978.

benefit analysis. It is therefore most probable that future developments will be conditioned by public opinion, political expediency and the willingness of the hunting community to cut their losses. Compromise rather than principle will govern the future activities of the groups concerned with hunting and political advantage their relationship with governments.

Pressure groups have become a 'fifth estate, the means by which many individuals contribute to politics'.[1] This legitimises the pressure which cause groups attempt to apply, and encourages the groups' membership to accept incremental changes worked out in conjunction with governments. During the 1970s groups involved with hunting found that their legitimacy in the eyes of the decision-makers increased, and so to a minor degree did the access they were granted.

Mackintosh, in 1977, believed that the 'biggest single change' in British political life was a 'move towards a sharing of power between government and pressure groups'.[2] The BFSS perceived this and tried to make itself acceptable to decision-makers as a spokesman group. The abolitionists, however, concentrated on mobilising public opinion and delayed the breakthrough which for them only came when they accepted the party political nature of their aims, and encouraged the Labour party to 'adopt' their cause. Their failure to do this until the late 1970s and the reluctance of the Labour party to risk losing rural votes has been one of the major reasons why the anti-hunting movement has not achieved any of its major goals to date.

Mackintosh felt that a 'government [had] to be careful to choose its ground and to have public opinion on its side', and that if it did so public and political interests would be adequately served.[3] He was referring mainly to the spokesman groups which command a significant amount of power, particularly trade unions and employers' organisations such as the CBI. However, as the big groups develop their muscles other minor groups should benefit, for if governments expect to negotiate with spokesman groups on economic issues they should find it a simple matter to negotiate with cause groups on social issues.

Certainly the solution to the hunting question lies less and less in the hunting field and more and more in the media and in parliament. Hunting has become involved with the increasingly political questions of class, ecology and cruelty and can never again be treated as a simple non-political issue. Nor will the problem fade away for it has entered

1 J.D. Stewart, *British Pressure Groups*, Oxford University Press, London, 1958, p. 244.

2 J.P. Mackintosh, *The Government and Politics of Britain*, Hutchinson, London, 1970 and 1977, p. 9.

3 Mackintosh, *Government and Politics of Britain*, p. 90.

into the consciousness of many people who, on one side, believe that they have a right and even a duty to fight for justice for other powerless and voiceless groups, and who, on the other side, believe they have a right to fight for freedom of action for themselves.

This interplay between the political culture, the political process and concerned pressure groups and individuals displaying the widest range of arguments on both sides of the issue allows the public interest to be served as well as can be expected in a complex society. Only the animals will not be consulted.

Abbreviations used in the text

ALF	Animal Liberation Front
BFSS	British Field Sports Society
BHS	British Horse Society
BUAV	British Union for the Abolition of Vivisection
CLA	Country Landowners Association
CRAE	Committee for the Reform of Animal Experimentation
D and SS	Devon and Somerset Staghounds
EEC	European Economic Community
GECCAP	General Election Co-ordinating Committee for Animal Protection
HIS	Hunter Improvement Society
HSA	Hunt Saboteurs Association
LACS	League Against Cruel Sports
LPCS	League for the Prohibition of Cruel Sports (later LACS)
MDHA	Master of Deerhounds Association
MFH	Master of Foxhounds
MFHA	Master of Foxhounds Association
NAVS	National Anti-Vivisection Society
NCC	National Coursing Club
NEC	National Executive Committee (of the Labour Party)
NFU	National Farmers Union
NOP	National Opinion Polls
NSACS	National Society for the Abolition of Cruel Sports
RSPCA	Royal Society for the Prevention of Cruelty to Animals

A bibliography of major sources

Part I: History, society and politics

A Books

Almond, G.A. and Powell, G.B., *Comparative Politics: a Developmental Approach*, Little Brown, Boston, 1966.

Almond, G.A. and Verba, S., *The Civic Culture*, Little Brown, Boston, 1965.

Ashley, M., *England in the Seventeenth Century*, Penguin, Harmondsworth, 1952 (rev. 1973).

Bagley, J. and Rowley, P., *A Documentary History of England*, vol. I. Penguin, Harmondsworth, 1966.

Beer, S.H., *Modern British Politics*, Faber, London, 1965.

Blondel, J., *Voters, Parties and Leaders*, Penguin, Harmondsworth, 1963.

Bottomore, T.B., *Classes in Modern Society*, Allen & Unwin, London, 1965.

Bovill, E.W., *English Country Life 1780–1830*, OUP, London, 1962.

Bowle, J., *The English Experience*, Weidenfeld & Nicolson, London, 1971.

Britain, HMSO, London, annually.

Burnett, J., *Plenty & Want: a Social History of Diet*, Penguin, Harmondsworth, 1966.

Butler, D.E. and Stokes, D., *Political Change in Britain*, Penguin, Harmondsworth, 1969.

Butler, D.E. and Freeman, J., *British Political Facts, 1900–60*, Macmillan, London, 1963.
Castles, F.G., *Pressure Groups and Political Culture*, Routledge & Kegan Paul, London, 1967.
Chambers, J.D. and Mingay, G.E., *The Agricultural Revolution 1750–1880*, Batsford, London, 1966.
Crossman, R.H.S., *Diaries of a Cabinet Minister*, Hamish Hamilton and Jonathan Cape, London, 1975–7.
Eckstein, H., *Pressure Group Politics*, Allen & Unwin, London, 1960.
Erhmann, W.H., *Interest Groups on Four Continents*, Pittsburg University Press, 1958.
English Historical Documents, vols I–XII, Eyre & Spottiswoode, London, 1953–77.
Eysenck, H.J., *The Psychology of Politics*, Routledge, London, 1954.
Finer, S.E., *Anonymous Empire*, Pall Mall, London, 1965.
Gregg, P., *A Social and Economic History of Britain, 1860–1972*, Harrap, London, 1973.
Hoskins, W.G., *The Making of the English Landscape*, Penguin, Harmondsworth, 1955.
Hill, C., *Reformation to Industrial Revolution*, Penguin, Harmondsworth, 1969.
Hobsbawm, E., *Industry and Empire*, Penguin, Harmondsworth, 1969.
Johns, E.A., *The Social Structure of Modern Britain*, Pergamon, London, 1972 (rev. edn).
Kerridge, E, *The Agricultural Revolution*, Allen & Unwin, London, 1967.
Kimber, R. and Richardson, J.J., *Pressure Groups in Britain: a Reader*, Dent, London, 1973.
Mackintosh, J.P., *The Government and Politics of Britain*, Hutchinson, London, 1977 (4th edn).
Mathias, P., *The First Industrial Nation*, Methuen, London, 1969.
Moodie, G.C. and Studdert-Kennedy, G., *Publics, Opinions and Pressure Groups*, Allen & Unwin, London, 1970.
Moser, C.A. and Calton, G., *Survey Methods in Social Investigation*, Heinemann, London, 1971.
Myers, A., *England in the late Middle Ages*, Penguin, Harmondsworth, 1963.
Newby, H., *The Deferential Worker*, Allen Lane, London, 1977.
Plumb, J., *England in the 18th Century*, Penguin, Harmondsworth, 1950 (rev. 1963).
Postan, M., *The Medieval Economy and Society*, Penguin, Harmondsworth, 1975.
Potter, A., *Organised Groups in British Politics*, Faber, London, 1961.
Punnett, R.M., *British Government and Politics*, Heinemann, London, 1968 and 1976.

Roberts, G.K., *Political Parties and Pressure Groups in Britain*, Weidenfeld & Nicolson, London, 1970.

Roebuck, J., *The Making of Modern English Society from 1850*, Routledge, London, 1973.

Rose, R., *Politics in England*, Faber, London, 1965.

Rose, R. (ed.), *Studies in British Politics*, Macmillan, London, 1966 and 1969.

Ryan, A., *The Philosophy of the Social Sciences*, Macmillan, London, 1970.

Sampson, A., *The New Anatomy of Britain*, Hodder & Stoughton, London, 1971.

Self, P. and Storing, H., *The State and the Farmer*, Allen & Unwin, London, 1962.

Stenton, D., *English Society in the Early Middle Ages*, Penguin, Harmondsworth, 1951.

Stewart, J.D., *British Pressure Groups*, OUP, London, 1958.

Thompson, E.P., *Whigs and Hunters; the Origin of the Black Act*, Allen Lane, London, 1976.

Thompson, F.M.L., *English Landed Society in the Nineteenth Century*, Routledge, London, 1963.

Thomson, D., *England in the Nineteenth Century*, Penguin, Harmondsworth, 1950.

Thomson, D., *England in the Twentieth Century*, Penguin, Harmondsworth, 1965.

Truman, D.B., *The Governmental Process*, A.A. Knopf, New York, 1964.

Westergaard, J. and Resler, H., *Class in a Capitalist Society*, Penguin, Harmondsworth, 1976.

Wilson, H.H., *Pressure Group*, Secker & Warburg, London, 1961.

Wootton, G., *The Politics of Influence*, Routledge, London, 1966.

Wootton, G., *Pressure Groups in Britain 1720–1970*, Allen Lane, London, 1975.

B Articles

Almond, G.A., 'A Comparative Study of Interest Groups and the Political Process', *American Political Science Review*, 1958, pp. 270–82.

Beer, S.H., 'Pressure Groups and Parties in Britain', *American Political Science Review*, 1956, pp. 1–23.

Castles, F.G., 'Towards a Theoretical Analysis of Pressure Politics', *Political Studies*, 1966, pp. 339–48.

Christoph, J.B., 'Capital Punishment and British Party Responsibility', *Political Science Quarterly*, 1962, pp. 19–35.

Eysenck, H.J., 'Social Attitudes and Social Class', *British Journal of*

Social and Clinical Psychology, 10, 1971, pp. 201–12.
Harrison, B., 'Animals and the State in Nineteenth Century England', *English Historical Review*, Oct. 1973, pp. 786–820.
Hindell, K. and Sims, M., 'How the Abortion Lobby Worked', *Political Quarterly*, 1966, pp. 269–82.
Macridis, R., 'Interest Groups in Comparative Analysis', *Journal of Politics*, 23, Feb. 1961, pp. 25–45.
Millett, J.H., 'The Role of an Interest Group Leader in the House of Commons', *Western Political Quarterly*, 1956, pp. 915–26.
Mackenzie, W.J.M., 'Pressure Groups: the Conceptual Framework', *Political Studies*, 1955, pp. 247–55.
Mackenzie, W.J.M., 'Pressure Groups in British Government', *British Journal of Sociology*, 1955, pp. 247–55.
McKenzie, R.T., 'Parties, Pressure Groups and the British Political Process', *Political Quarterly*, 1958, pp. 5–16.
Nettl, J.P., 'Consensus or Elite Domination: the Case of Business', *Political Studies*, 1965, pp. 22–44.
Peterson, P.E., 'British Interest Group Theory Re-examined', *Comparative Politics*, 1971, pp. 381–402.
Potter, A.M., 'Attitude Groups', *Political Quarterly*, 1958, pp. 72–82.
Pym, B.A., 'Pressure Groups on Moral Issues', *Political Quarterly*, 1972, pp. 317–27.

Part II: Hunting and animal welfare

A Books

Baily's Hunting Directory, J. Allen, London, annually.
Beckford, P., *Thoughts on Hunting*, London, 1781.
Brancer, M., *The Hunting Instinct*, Oliver & Boyd, London, 1964.
Carr, R., *English Fox Hunting*, Weidenfeld & Nicolson, London, 1976.
Clark, S., *The Moral Status of Animals*, OUP, 1977.
Chalmers, P., *The History of Hunting*, Seeley Service, London, n.d. (1936?).
Fairholm, E. and Pain, W., *A Century of Work for Animals*, J. Murray, London, 1924.
Godlovitch, S. and R. and Harris, J. (eds), *Animals, Men and Morals*, Gollancz, London, 1971.
Hutchings, M.M. and Caver, M., *Man's Dominion: our Violation of the Animal World*, Hart-Davis, London, 1970.
Itzkowitz, D.C., *Peculiar Privilege*, Harvester Press, Brighton, 1977.
Longrigg, R., *The History of Foxhunting*, Macmillan, London, 1975.
Moore, P. (ed), *Against Hunting*, Gollancz, London, 1965.
Moss, A.W., *Valiant Crusade: the History of the RSPCA*, Cassell,

London, 1961.
Page, R., *The Hunter and the Hunted*, Davis-Poynter, London, 1977.
Paterson, D. and Ryder, R., *Animals Rights – a Symposium*, Centuar Press, Sussex, 1979.
Pine, L., *After Their Blood*, W. Kimber, London, 1966.
Pine, L., *The History of Hunting*, LACS, London, 1973.
Richardson, C., *The Complete Foxhunter*, Methuen, London, 1908.
Ryder, R., *Victims of Science: the Use of Animals in Research*, Davis-Poynter, London, 1975.
Sabretache (pseud), *The Monarchy and the Chase*, Eyre & Spottiswoode, London, 1948.
Singer, P., *Animal Liberation*, Jonathan Cape, London, 1976.
Sperlinger, D. (ed.), *Animals in Research*, John Wiley, London, 1981.
Stable, O. and Studdard, R.M., *A Review of Coursing*, BFSS, London, 1971.
Strutt, S., *The Sports and Pastimes of the People of England*, Methuen, London, 1801 and 1903.
Surtees, R.S., *Handley Cross or Mr Jorrock's Hunt*, Edward Arnold, London, 1845.
Turner, E.S., *All Heaven in a Rage*, Michael Joseph, London, 1964.

B Articles

Freeman, E.A., 'The Morality of Field Sports', *Fortnightly Review*, XII, 1 Oct. 1869, pp. 353–85.
Freeman, E.A., 'The Controversy on Field Sports', *Fortnightly Review*, XIV, 1 Dec. 1870, pp. 674–91.
Trench, C.C., 'Nineteenth Century Hunting', *History Today*, 23, Aug. 1973, pp. 572–80.
Thiebaux, M., 'The Medieval Chase', *Speculum*, 43, 1967, pp. 260–74.

Part III: Miscellaneous sources

A Official publications

Cobbett's Parliamentary History 1801–3, London.
Hare Coursing Bill (House of Lords): Minutes of Evidence and Proceedings of the Select Committee on the Bill, HMSO, London, May 1976.
House of Commons Official Report: Parliamentary Debates (Hansard), HMSO, London, 1809–
House of Lords Official Report, HMSO, London.
Report of the Committee on Cruelty to Wild Animals, Chairman J. Scott Henderson QC, HMSO, London, 1951, Cmnd 8266.

B Unofficial publications

BFSS	*Yearbook* and Annual Report	1932–
HSA	*Newsletter*	1971–3
	Howl	1973–
LACS	*Cruel Sports*	1927–
	League Doings	1940–58
Labour Party	*Living without Cruelty: Labour's Charter for Animal Protection*	1978
NSACS	*Bulletin*	1932–
	Annual Report	1933–
	Miscellaneous Publications	1932–
RSPCA	Annual Reports	
	Today	1970–
	Report on the Affairs of the Royal Society for the Prevention of Cruelty to Animals, C. Sparrow QC, et al.	1974

C Magazines

Horse and Hound
The Field
New Statesmen

D Newspapers

The Times
Daily Telegraph
Guardian
Daily Mirror
West Somerset Free Press

Index

Organisations are referred to in the subheadings by their abbreviations, a list of which will be found on page 289.